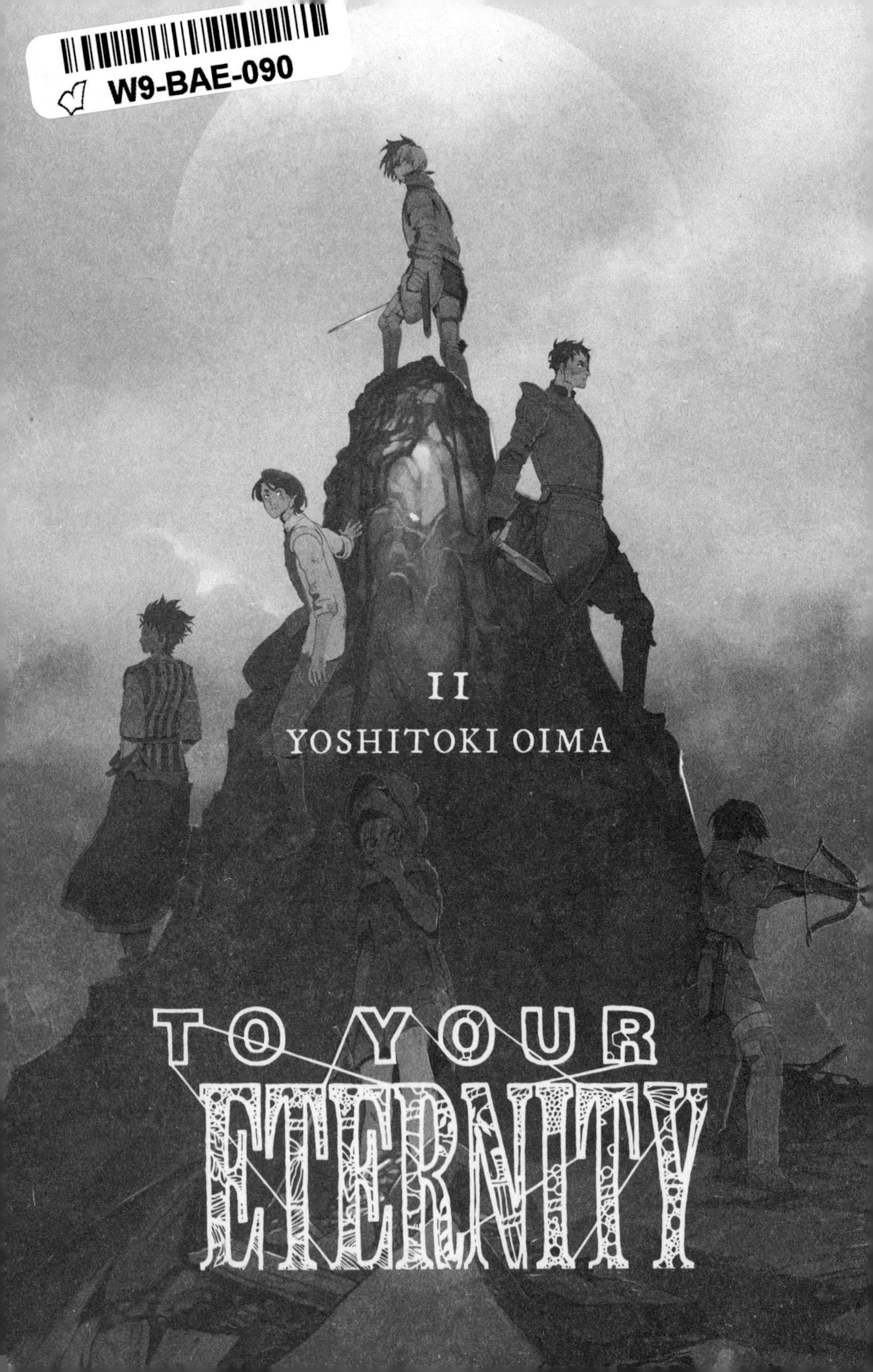
II
YOSHITOKI OIMA
TO YOUR
ETERNITY

CONTENTS

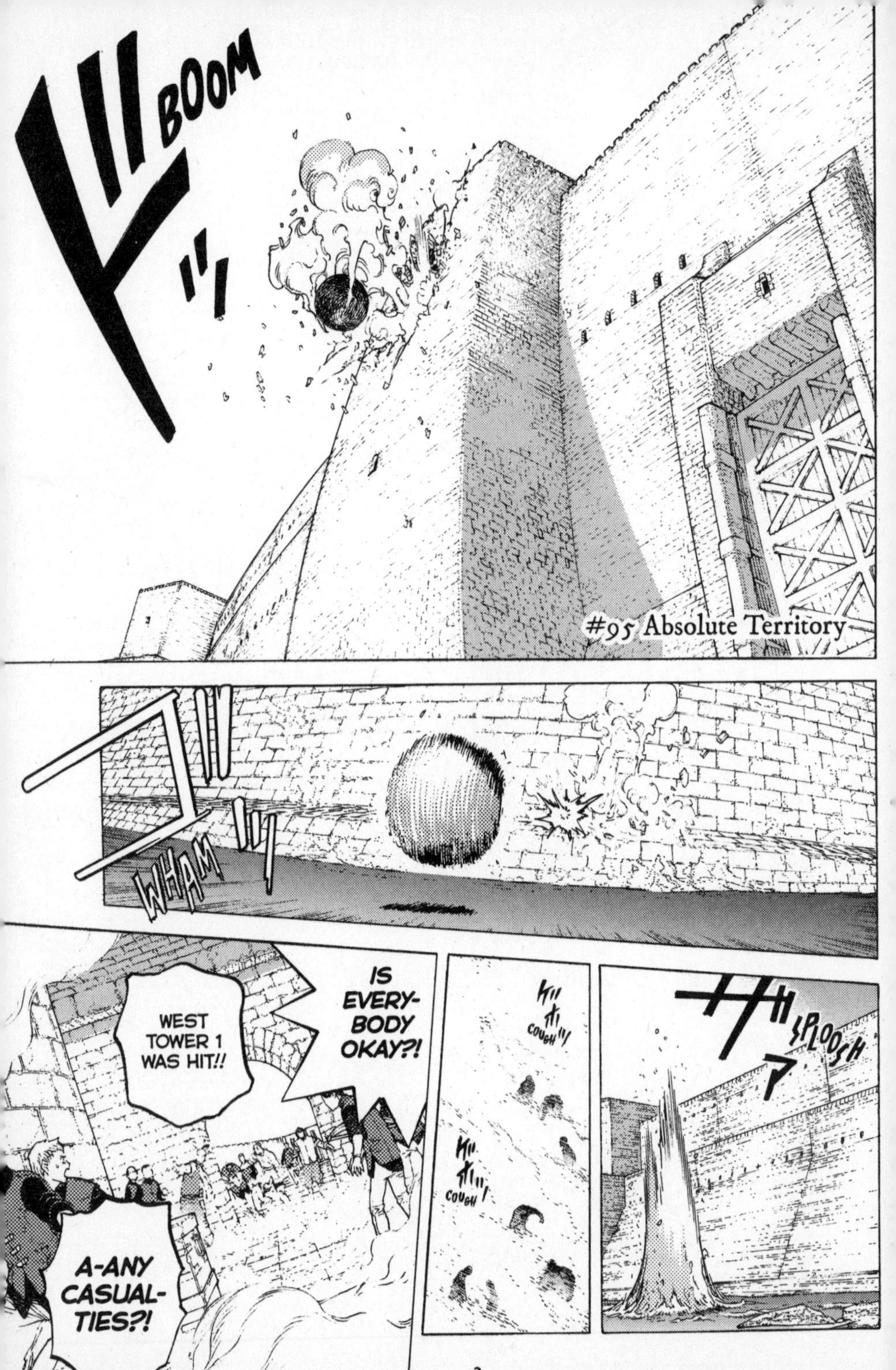
BOOM
#95 Absolute Territory
WHAM
SPLOOSH
COUGH
COUGH
IS EVERY-BODY OKAY?!
WEST TOWER 1 WAS HIT!!
A-ANY CASUAL-TIES?!

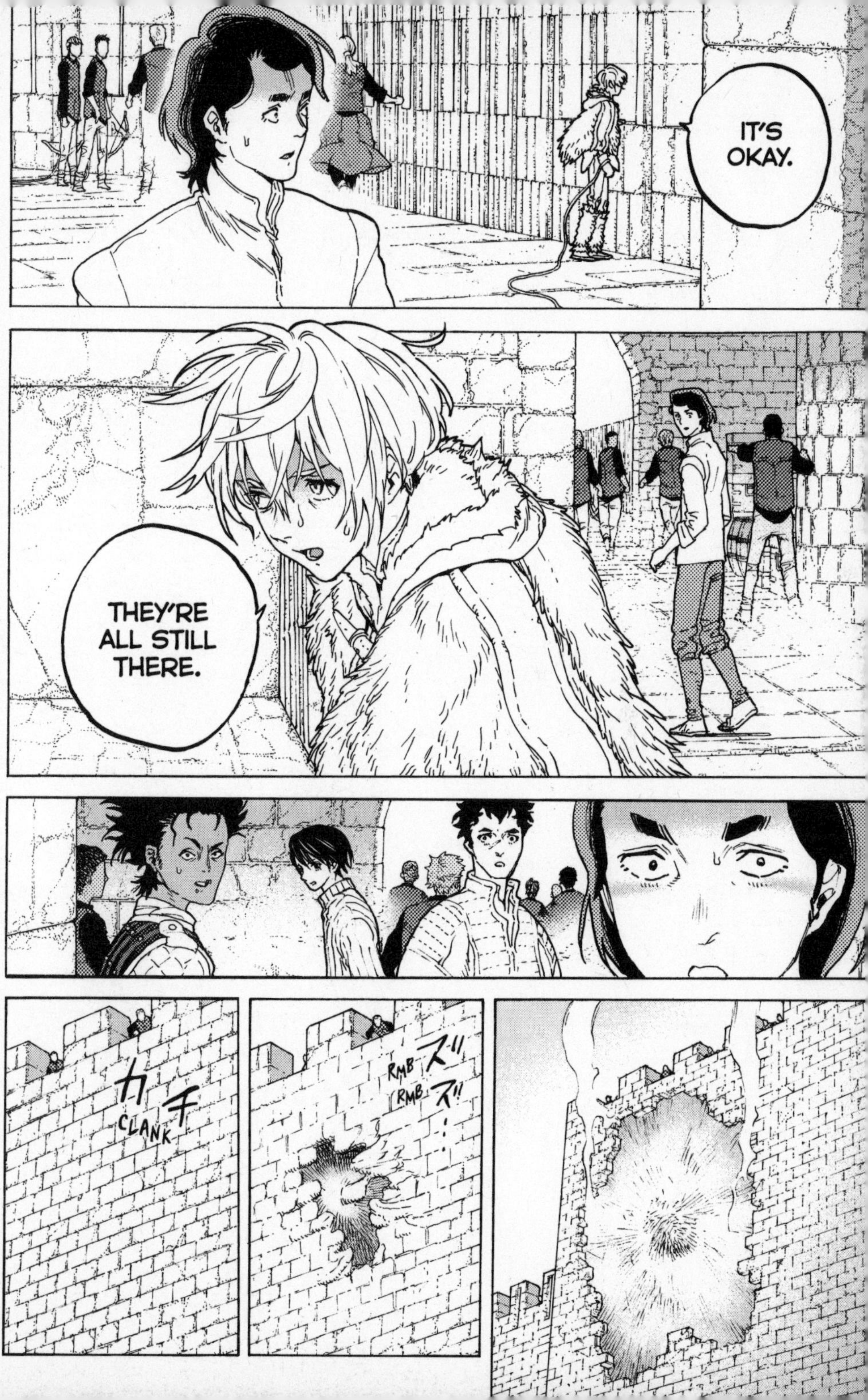
IT'S OKAY.
THEY'RE ALL STILL THERE.
RMB RMB
ズ‼ ズ‼
カチ
CLANK

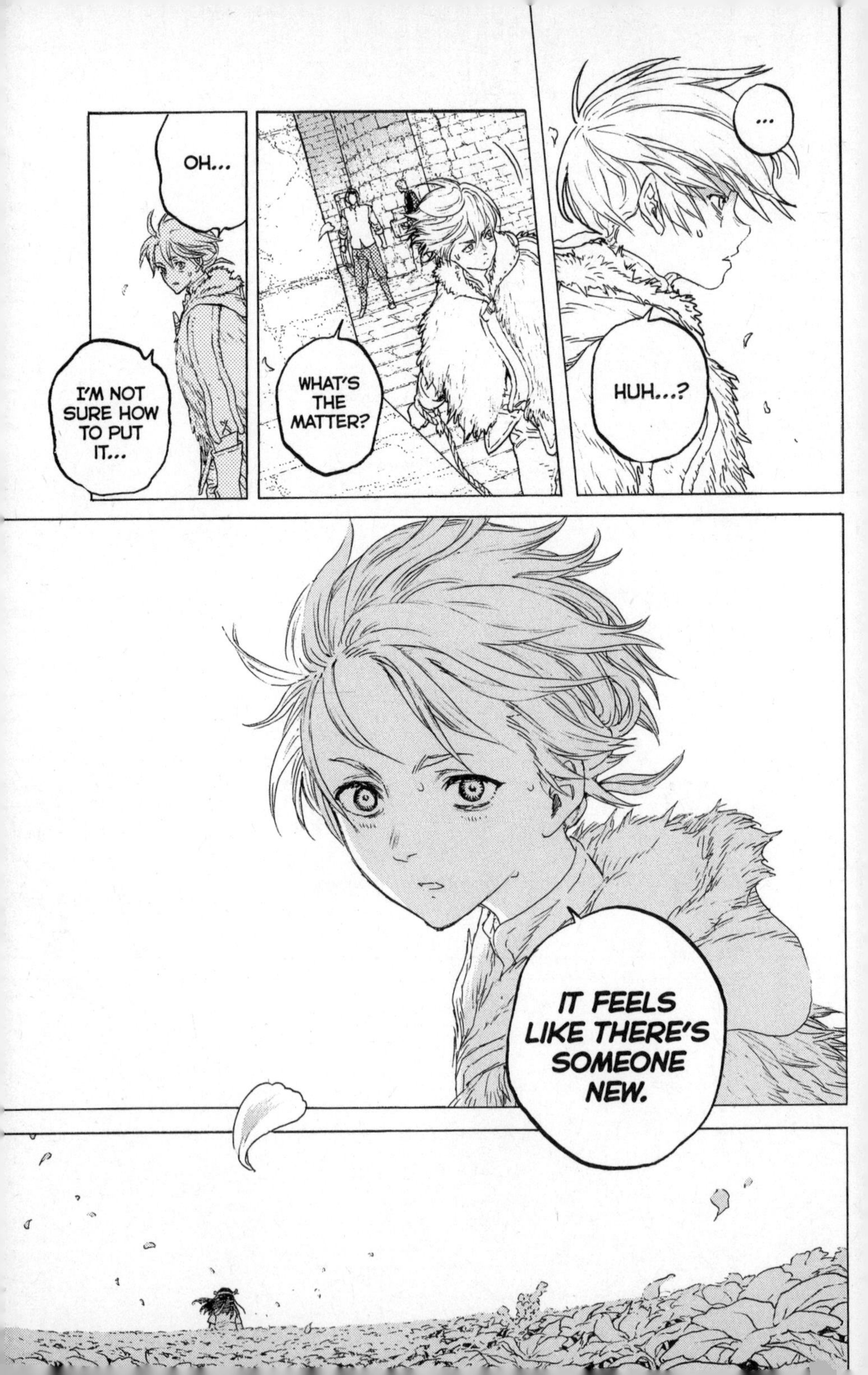
...
HUH...?
WHAT'S THE MATTER?
OH...
I'M NOT SURE HOW TO PUT IT...
IT FEELS LIKE THERE'S SOMEONE NEW.

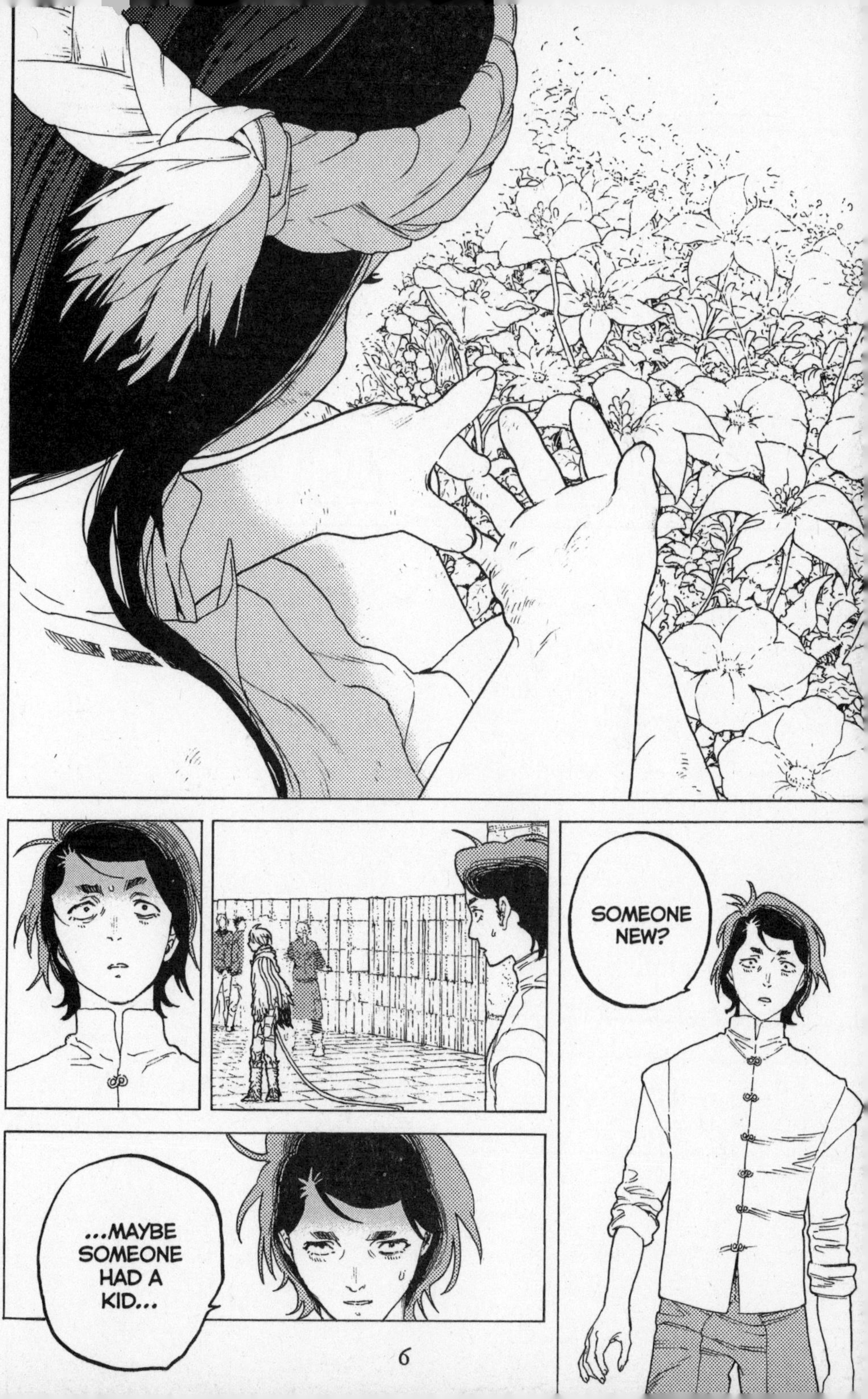
SOMEONE NEW?
...MAYBE SOMEONE HAD A KID...

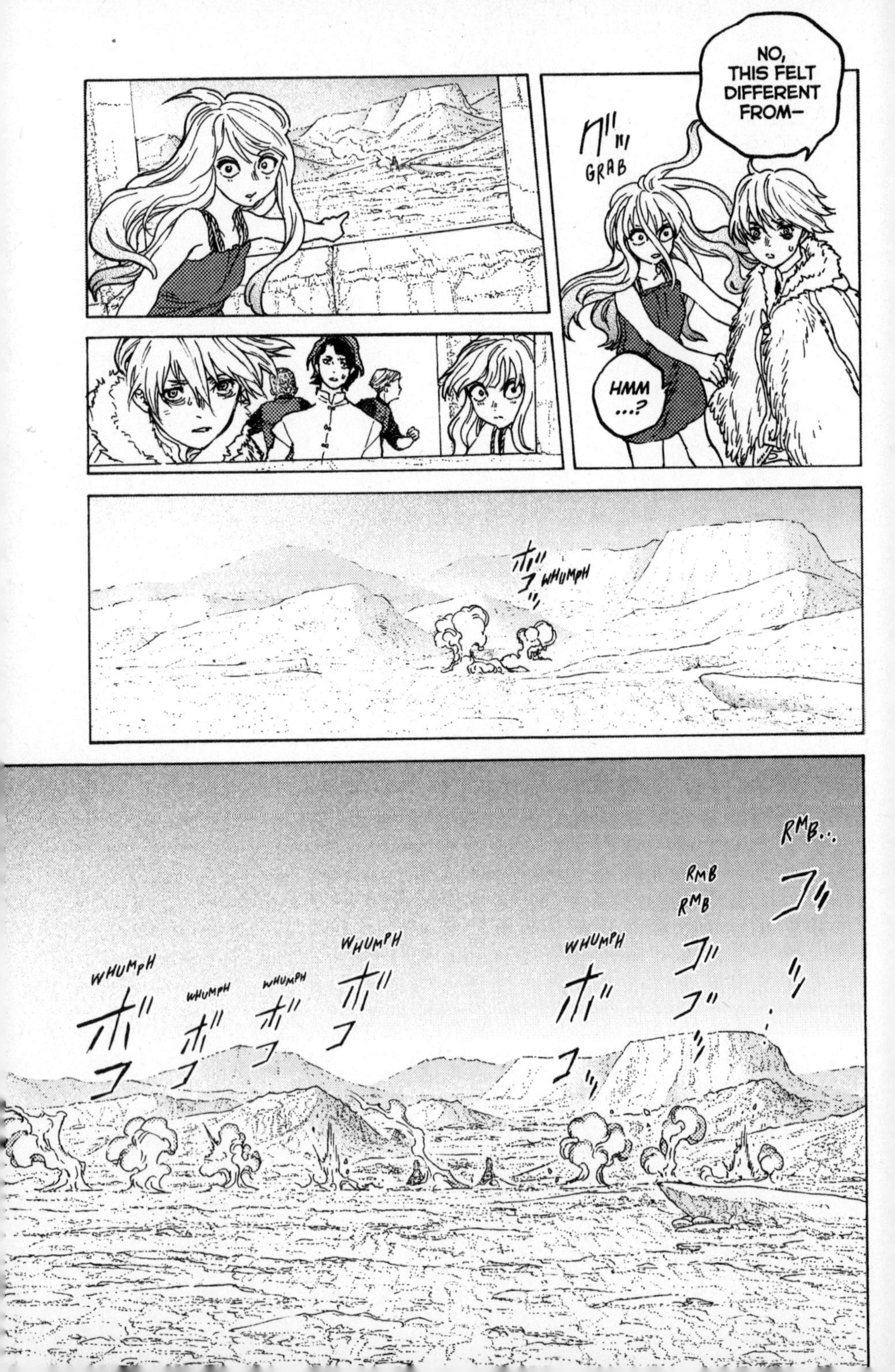
NO, THIS FELT DIFFERENT FROM—
GRAB
HMM ...?
WHUMPH
RMB...
RMB
RMB
WHUMPH
WHUMPH
WHUMPH
WHUMPH
WHUMPH

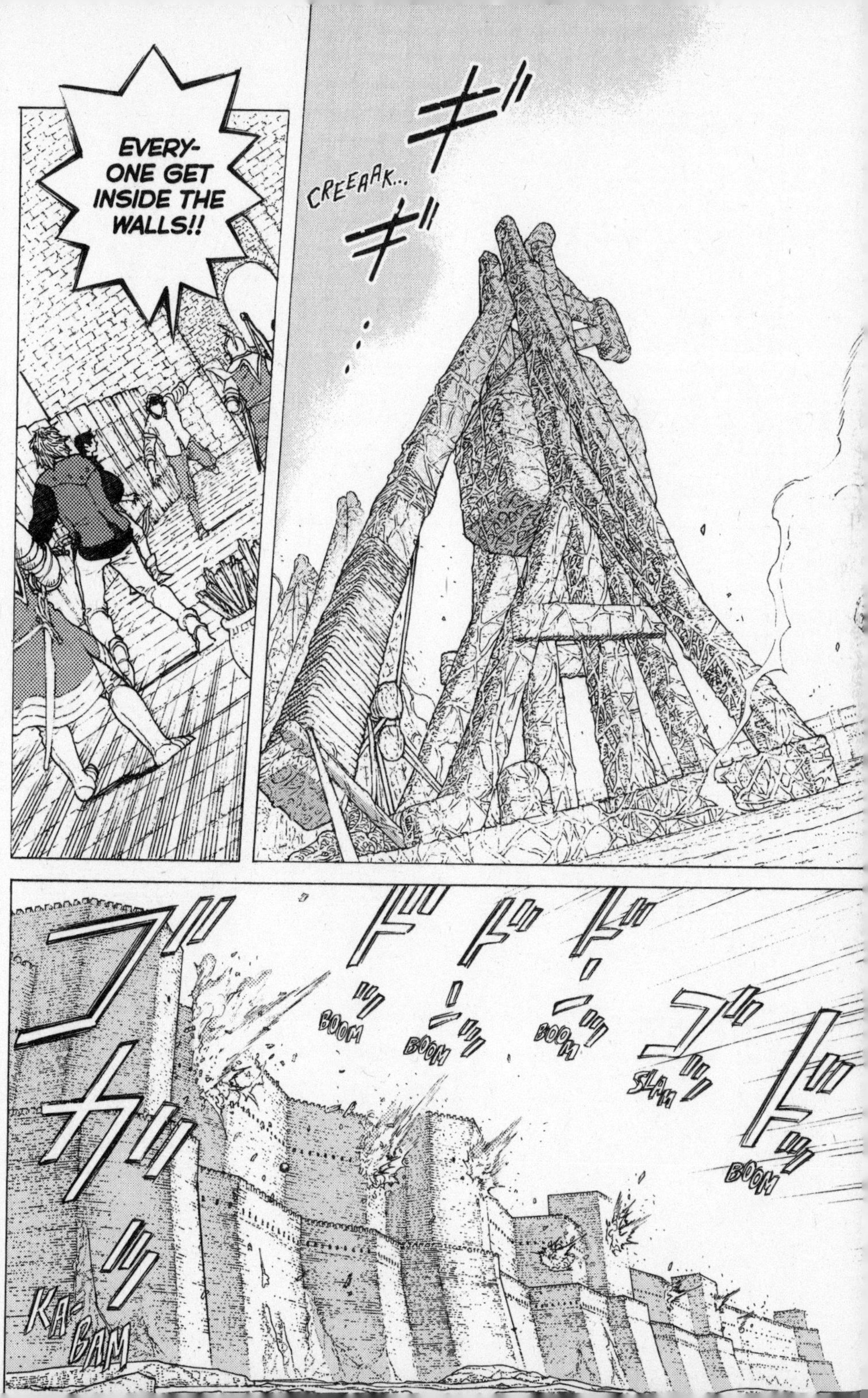
CREEAAK...
EVERY-ONE GET INSIDE THE WALLS!!
BOOM
SLAM
BOOM
BOOM
BOOM
KA-BAM

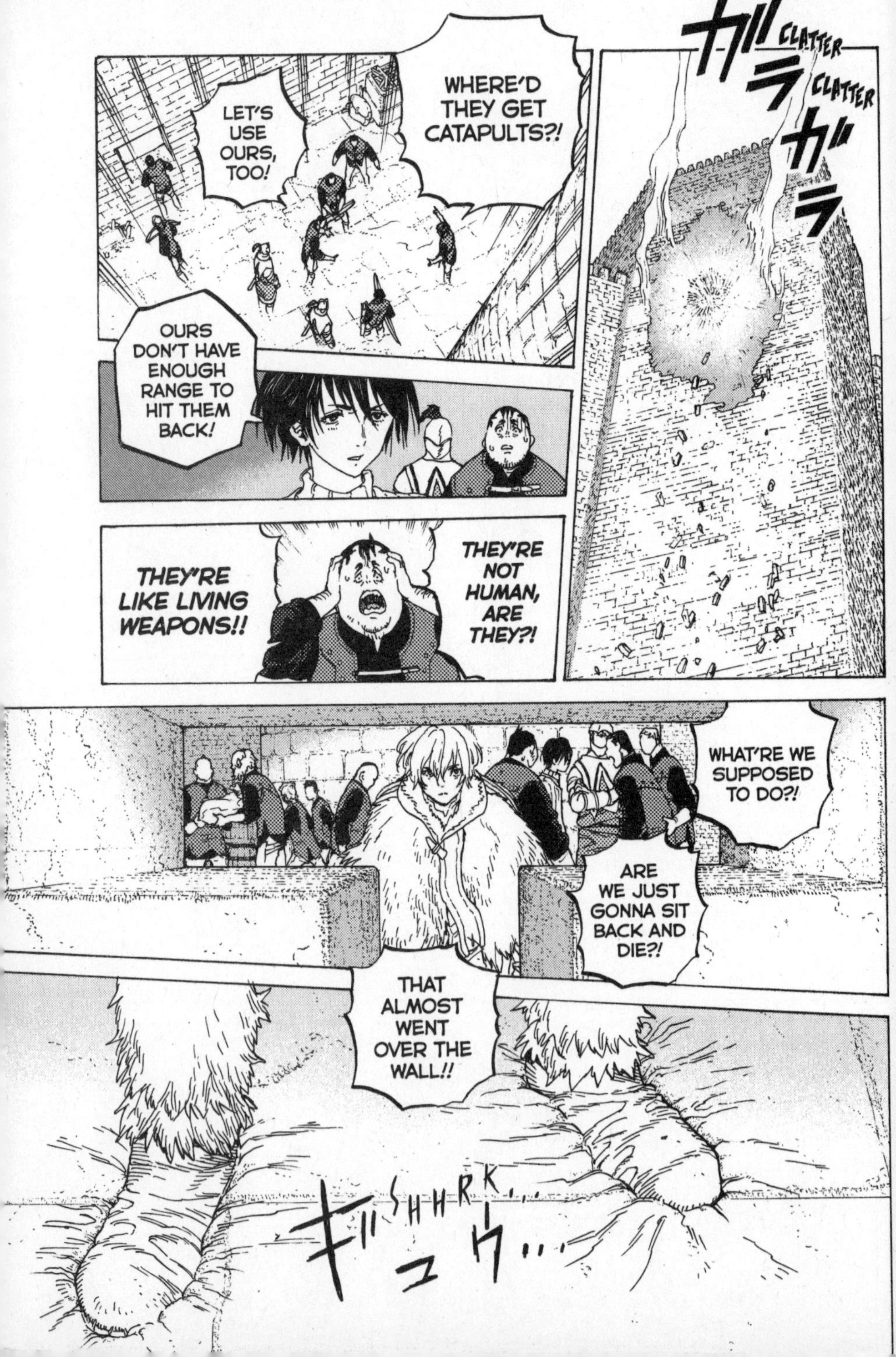
CLATTER
CLATTER
WHERE'D THEY GET CATAPULTS?!
LET'S USE OURS, TOO!
OURS DON'T HAVE ENOUGH RANGE TO HIT THEM BACK!
THEY'RE NOT HUMAN, ARE THEY?!
THEY'RE LIKE LIVING WEAPONS!!
WHAT'RE WE SUPPOSED TO DO?!
ARE WE JUST GONNA SIT BACK AND DIE?!
THAT ALMOST WENT OVER THE WALL!!
SHHRK...

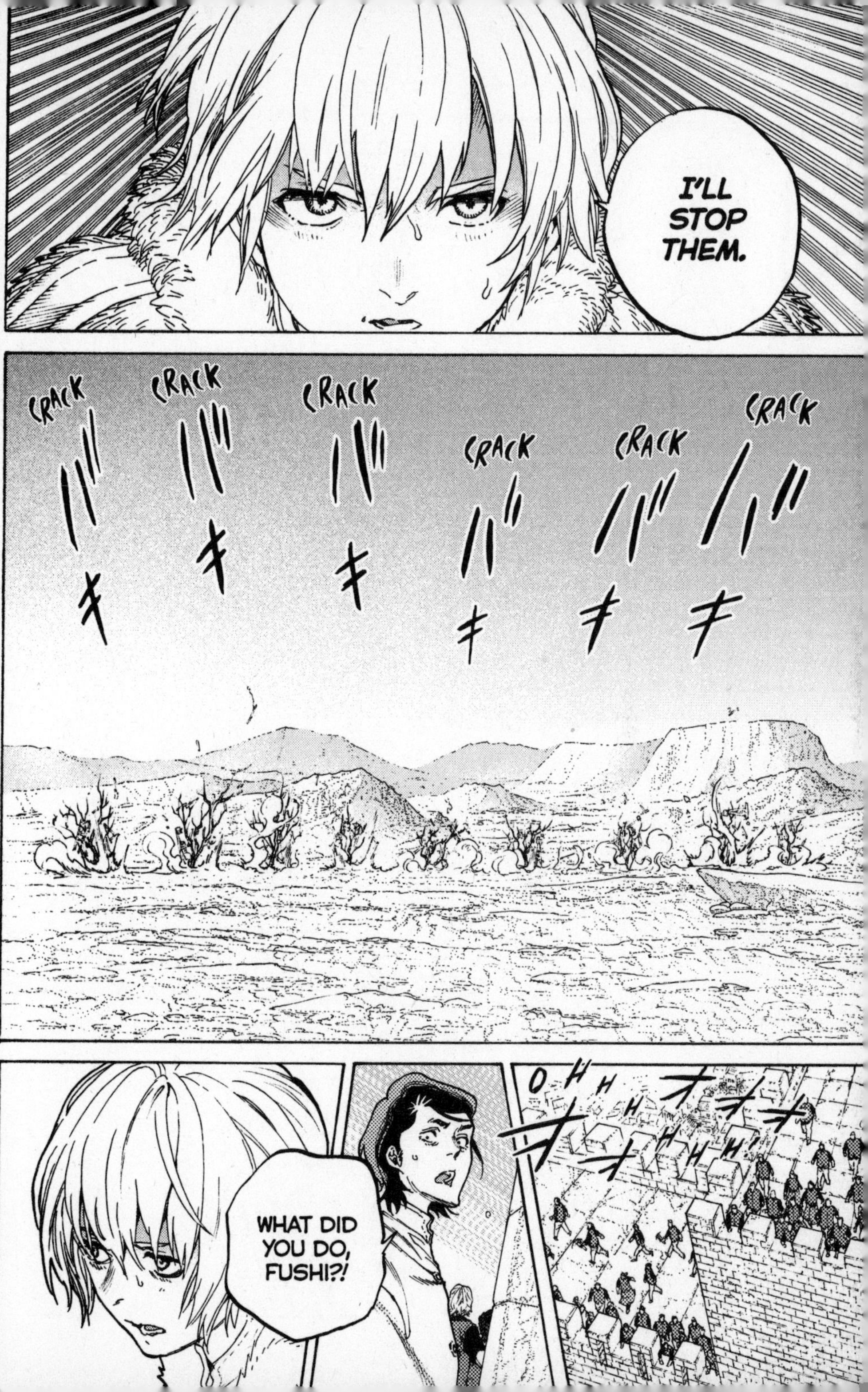
I'LL STOP THEM.
CRACK
CRACK
CRACK
CRACK
CRACK
CRACK
OHHHHHHH!
WHAT DID YOU DO, FUSHI?!

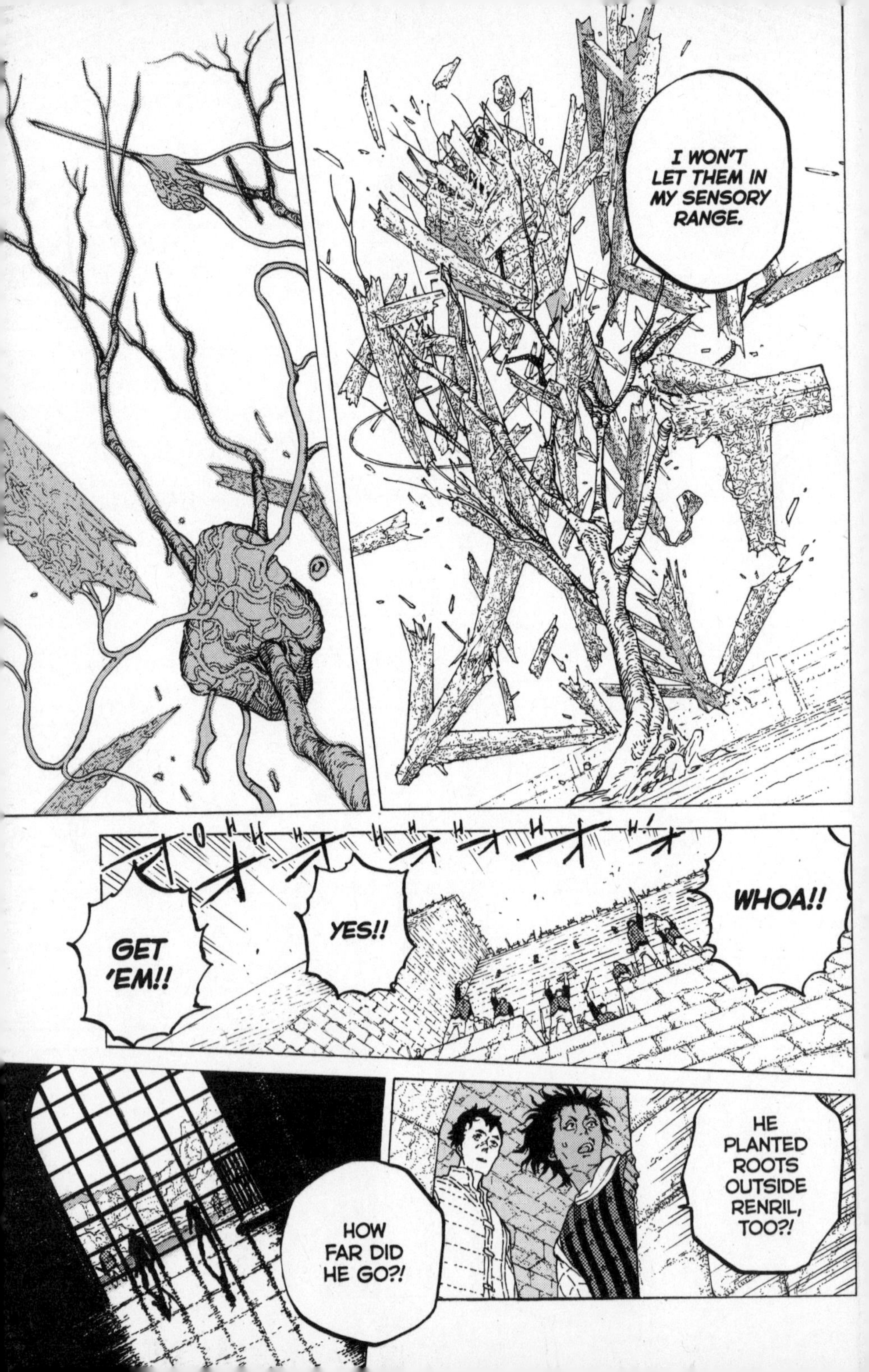
I WON'T LET THEM IN MY SENSORY RANGE.
WHOA!!
YES!!
GET 'EM!!
HE PLANTED ROOTS OUTSIDE RENRIL, TOO?!
HOW FAR DID HE GO?!

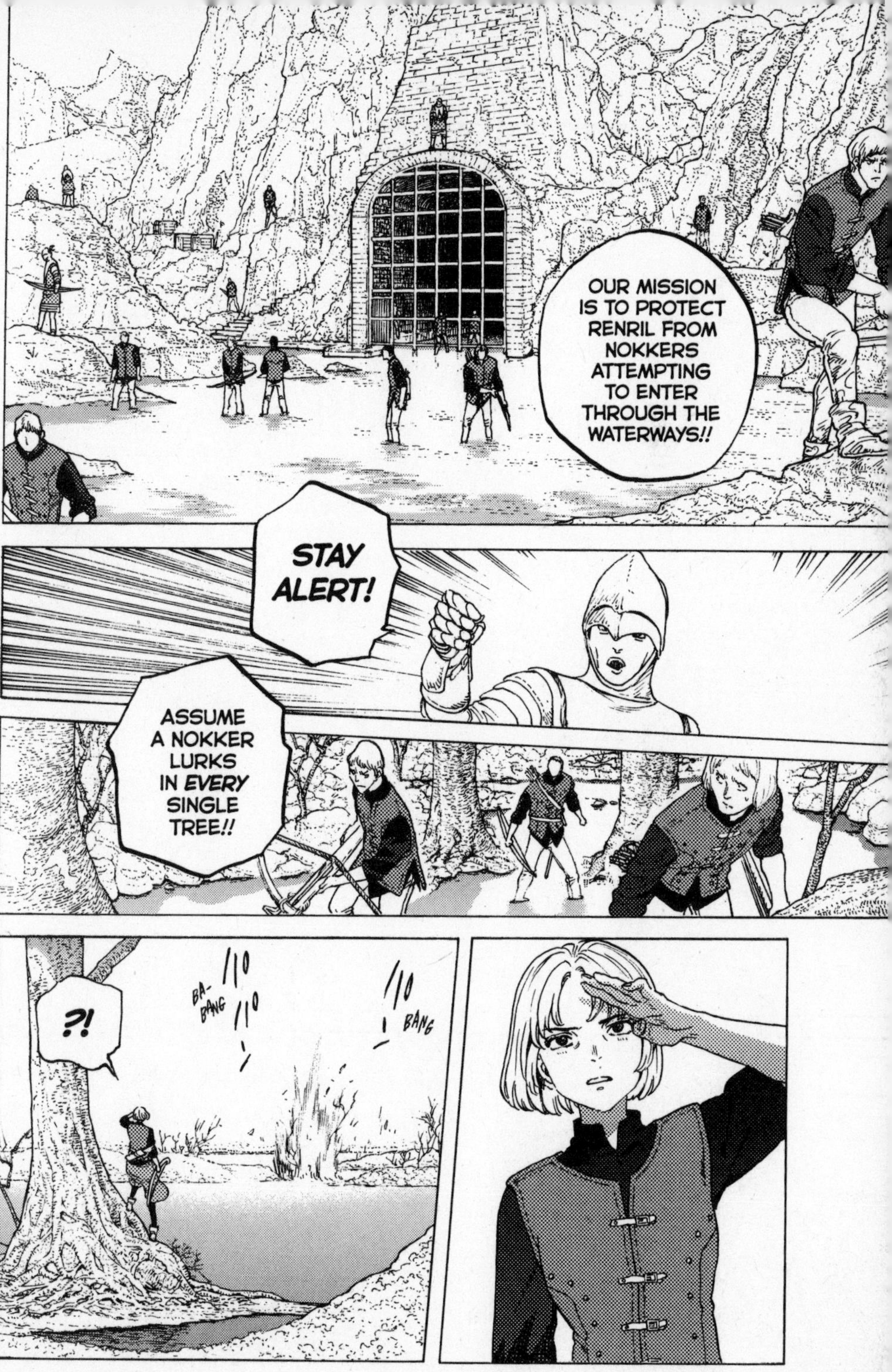
OUR MISSION IS TO PROTECT RENRIL FROM NOKKERS ATTEMPTING TO ENTER THROUGH THE WATERWAYS!!
STAY ALERT!
ASSUME A NOKKER LURKS IN *EVERY* SINGLE TREE!!
BANG
BA-BANG
?!

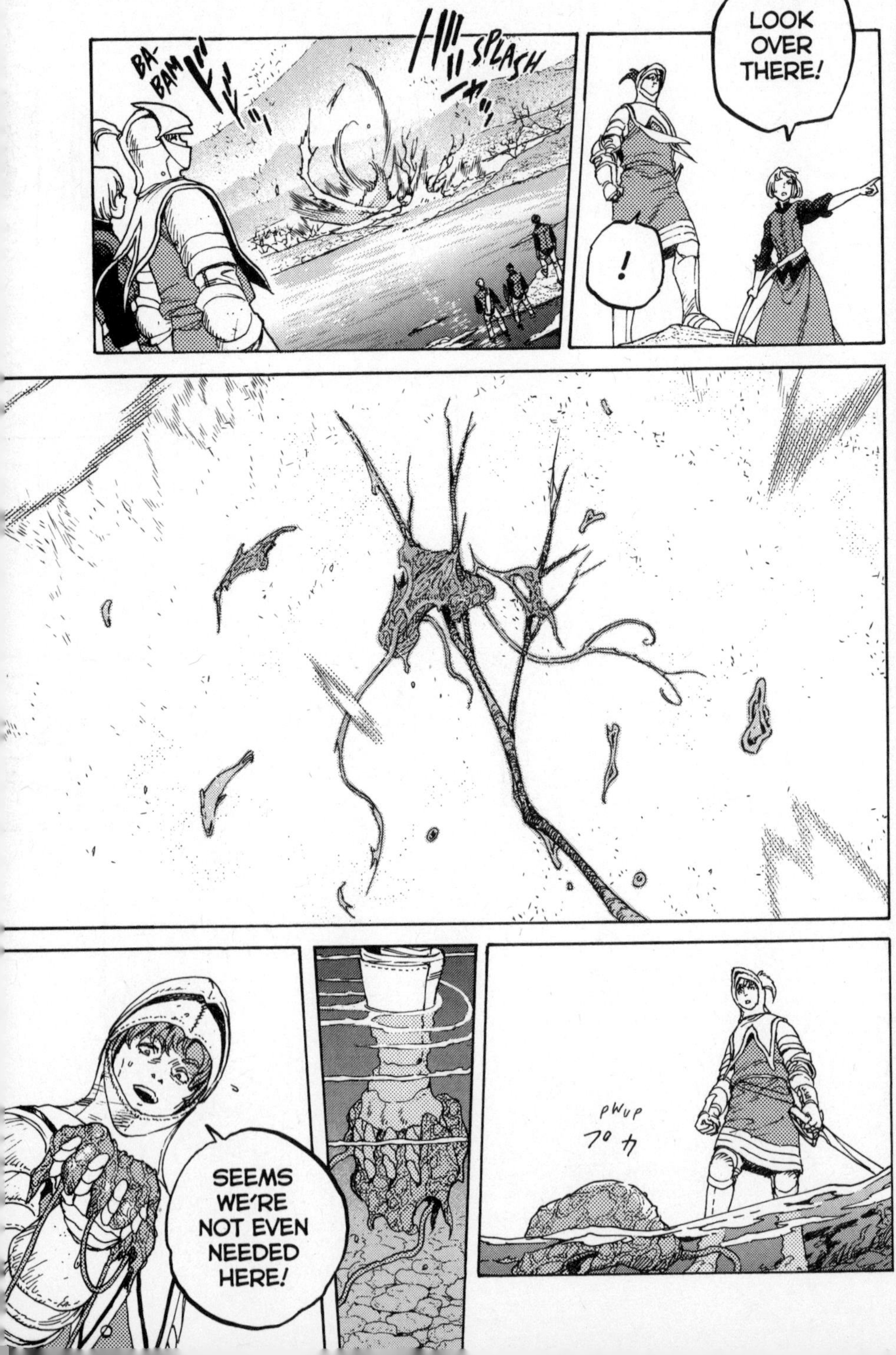
LOOK OVER THERE!
!
BA-BAM
SPLASH
PWUP
SEEMS WE'RE NOT EVEN NEEDED HERE!

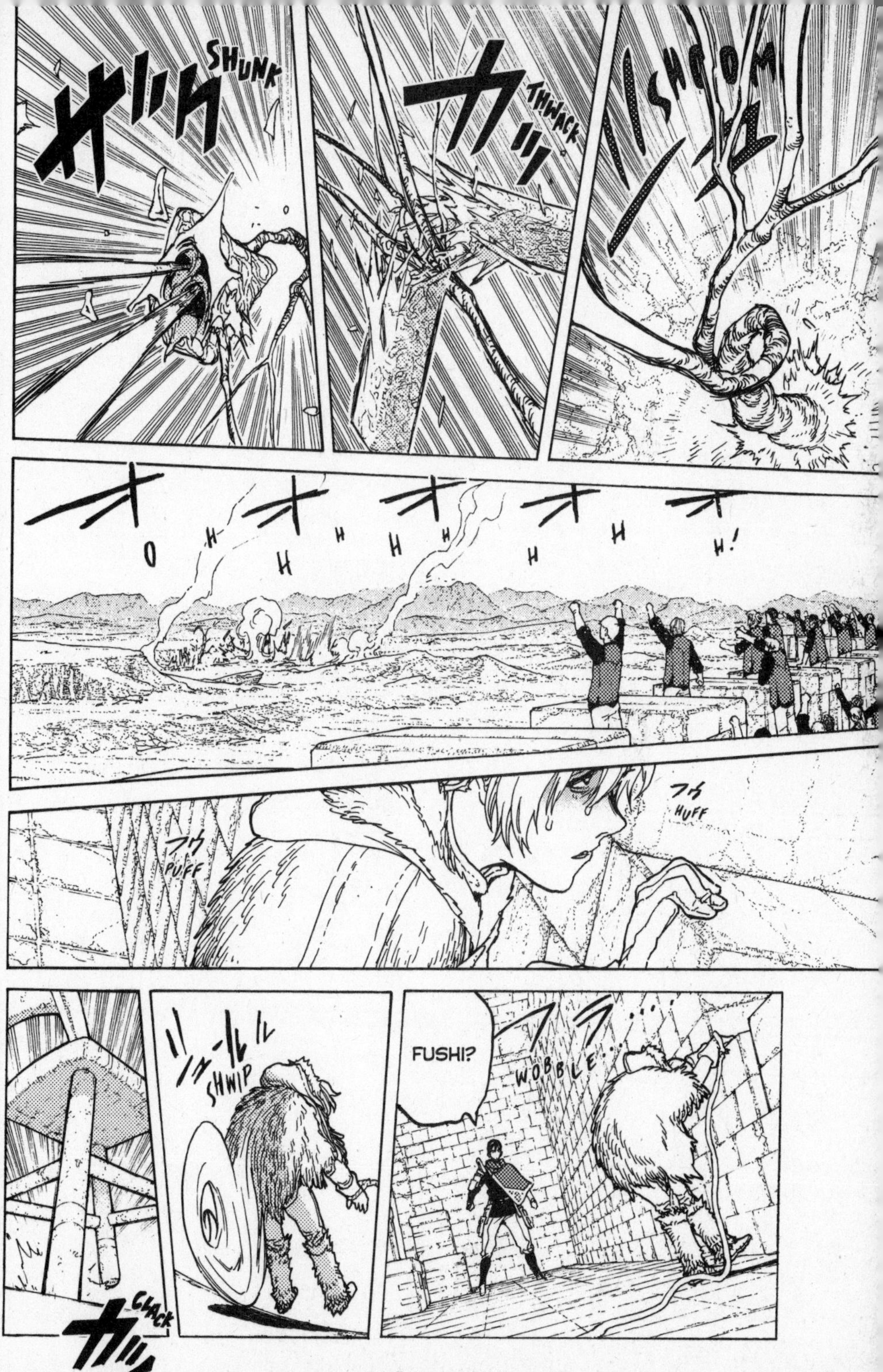
SHOOM
THWACK
SHUNK
OHHHHHHH!
HUFF
PUFF
FUSHI?
WOBBLE...
SHWIP
CLACK

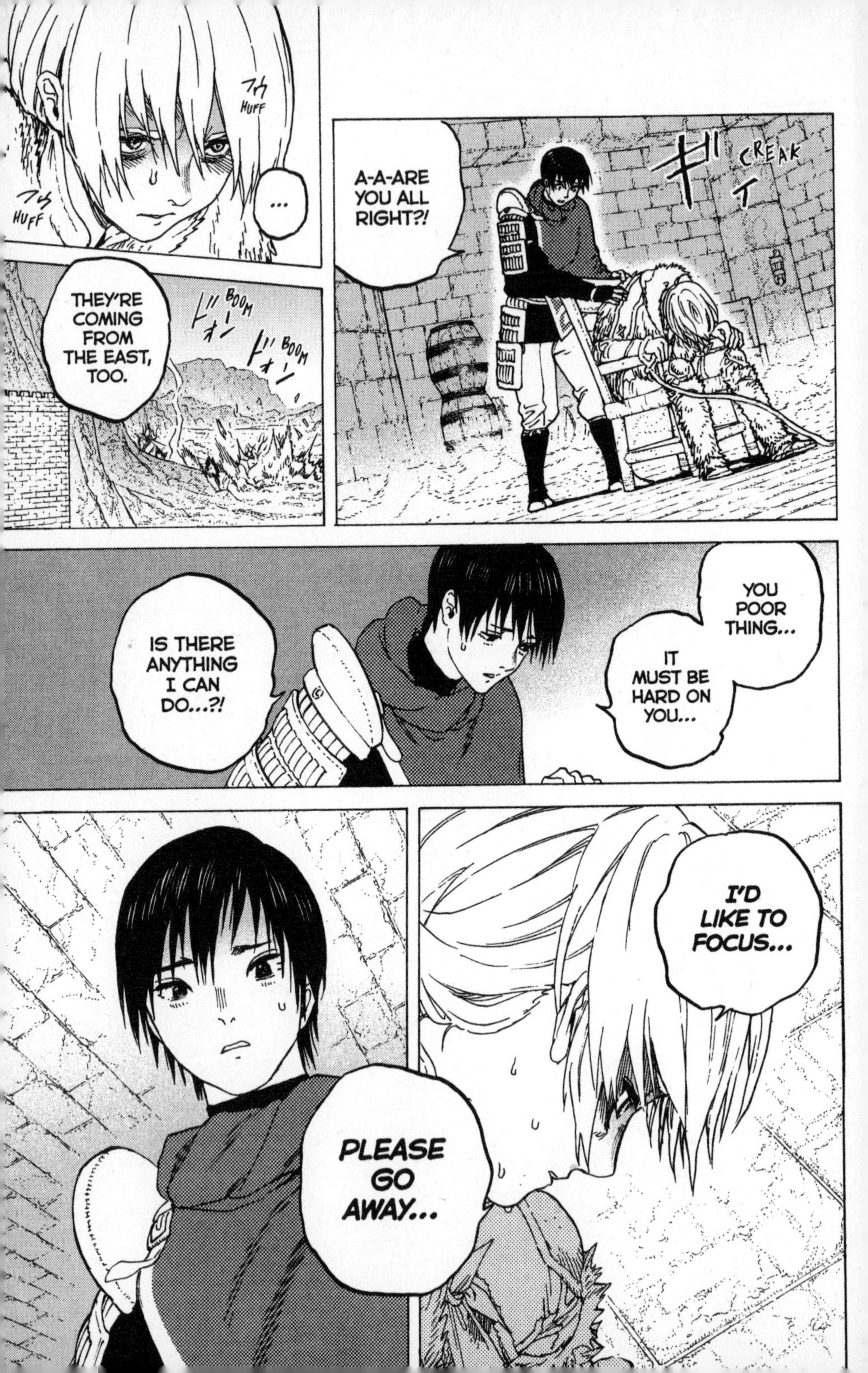
ギイ
CREAK
A-A-ARE YOU ALL RIGHT?!
フゥ
HUFF
フゥ
HUFF
...
ドォン
BOOM
ドォン
BOOM
THEY'RE COMING FROM THE EAST, TOO.
YOU POOR THING...
IT MUST BE HARD ON YOU...
IS THERE ANYTHING I CAN DO...?!
I'D LIKE TO FOCUS...
PLEASE GO AWAY...

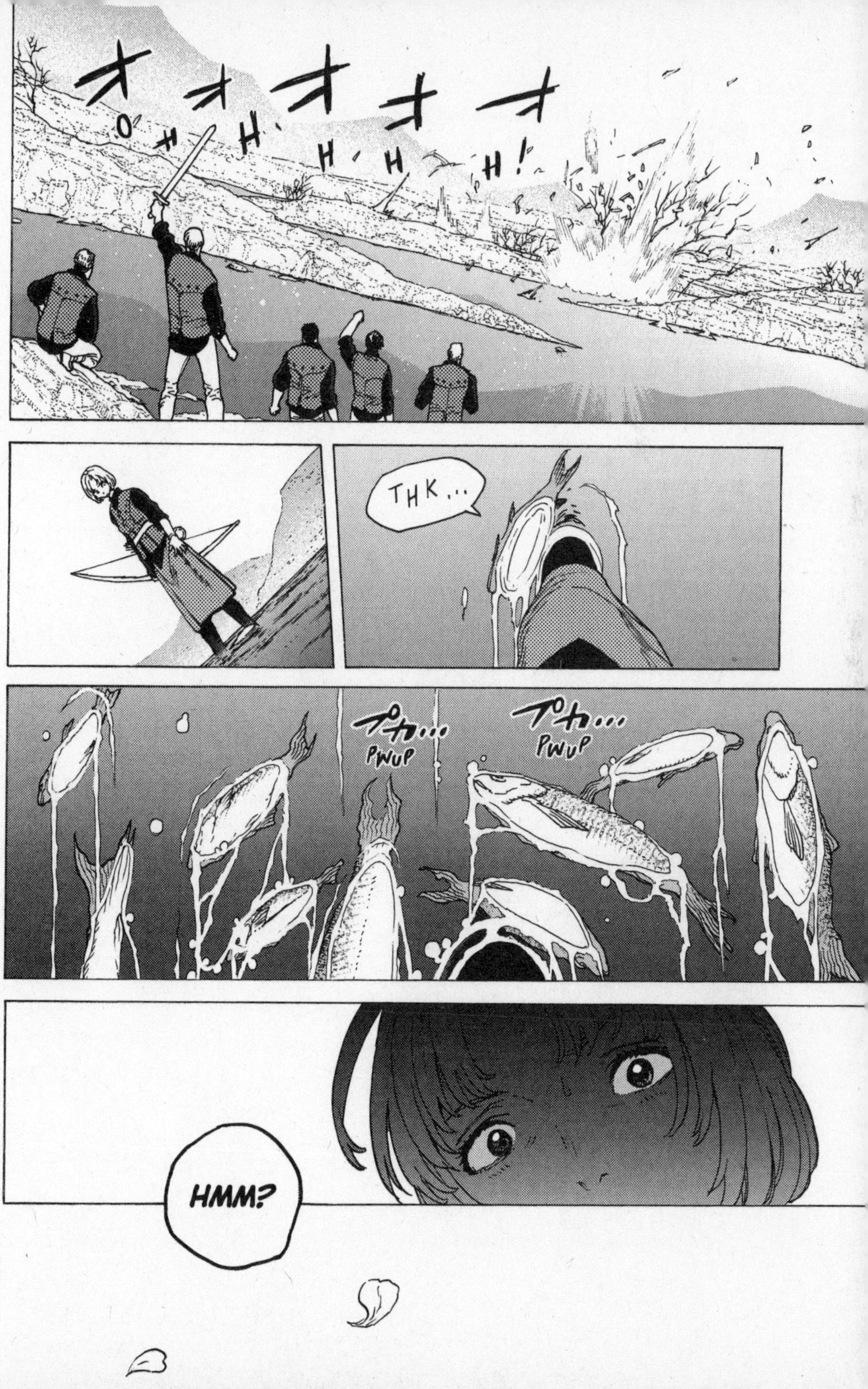

オオオオオ
OHHHHH!
THK...
プカ...
PWUP
プカ...
PWUP
HMM?

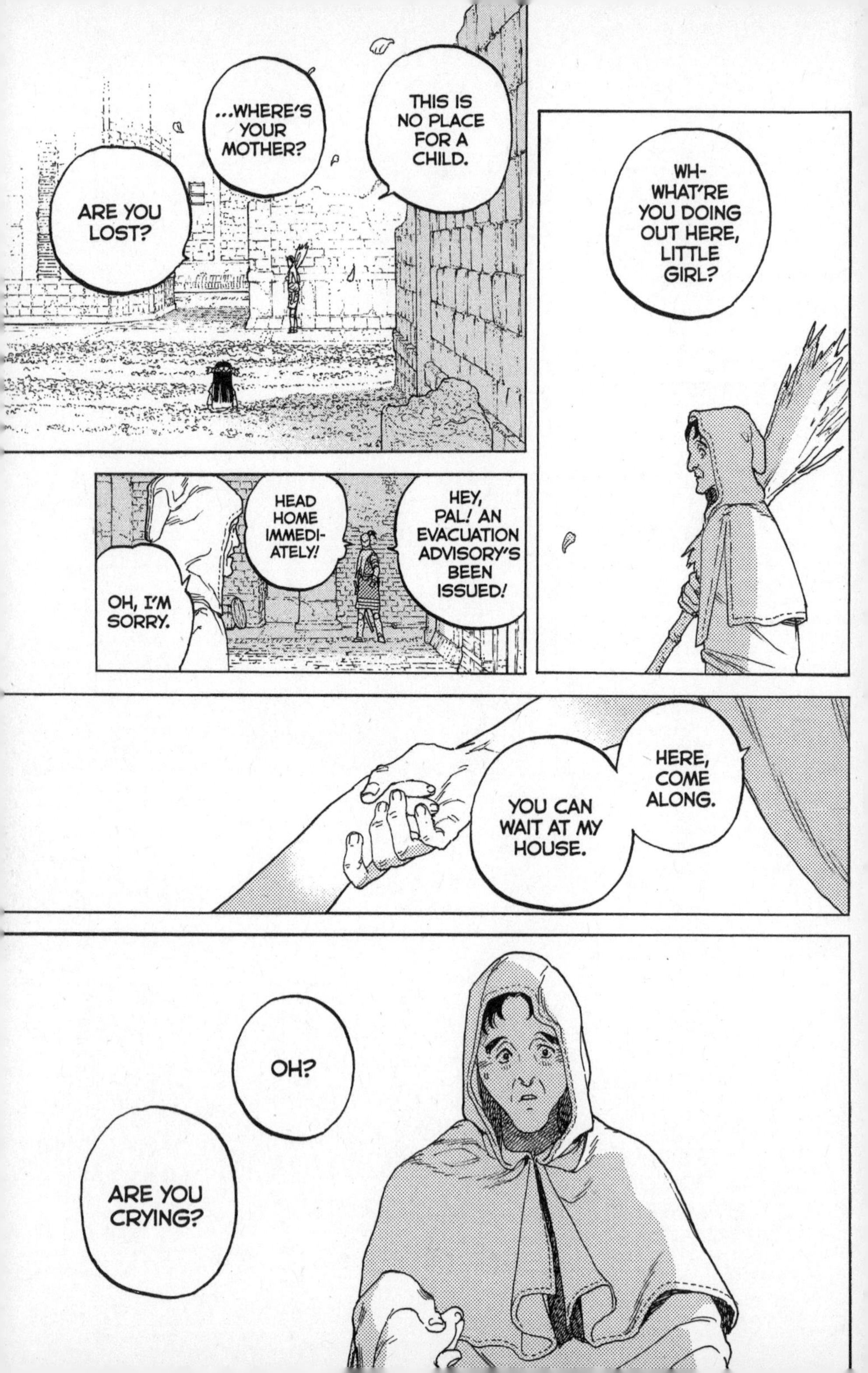
WH- WHAT'RE YOU DOING OUT HERE, LITTLE GIRL?
THIS IS NO PLACE FOR A CHILD.
...WHERE'S YOUR MOTHER?
ARE YOU LOST?
HEY, PAL! AN EVACUATION ADVISORY'S BEEN ISSUED!
HEAD HOME IMMEDI-ATELY!
OH, I'M SORRY.
HERE, COME ALONG.
YOU CAN WAIT AT MY HOUSE.
OH?
ARE YOU CRYING?

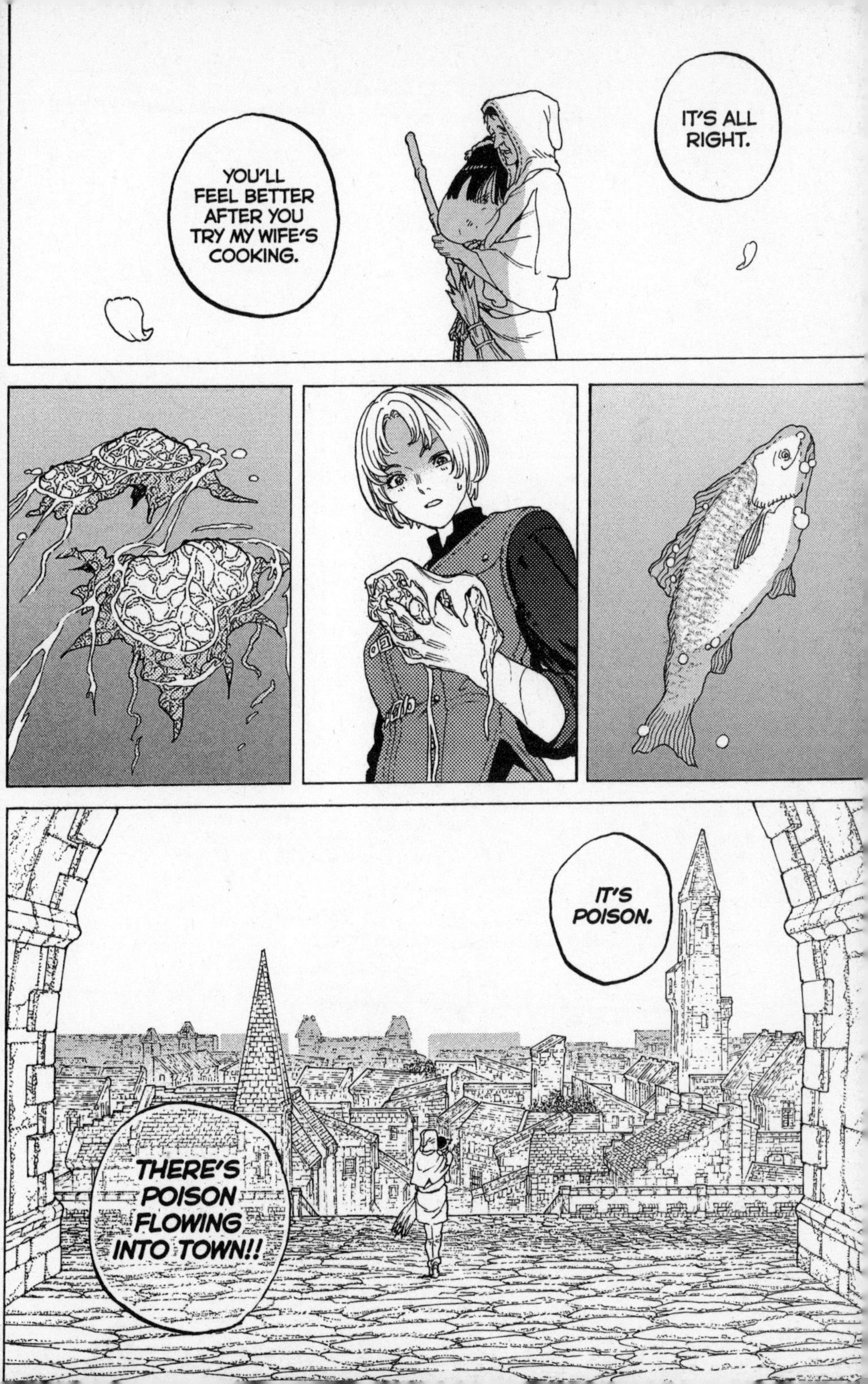
IT'S ALL RIGHT.
YOU'LL FEEL BETTER AFTER YOU TRY MY WIFE'S COOKING.
IT'S POISON.
THERE'S POISON FLOWING INTO TOWN!!

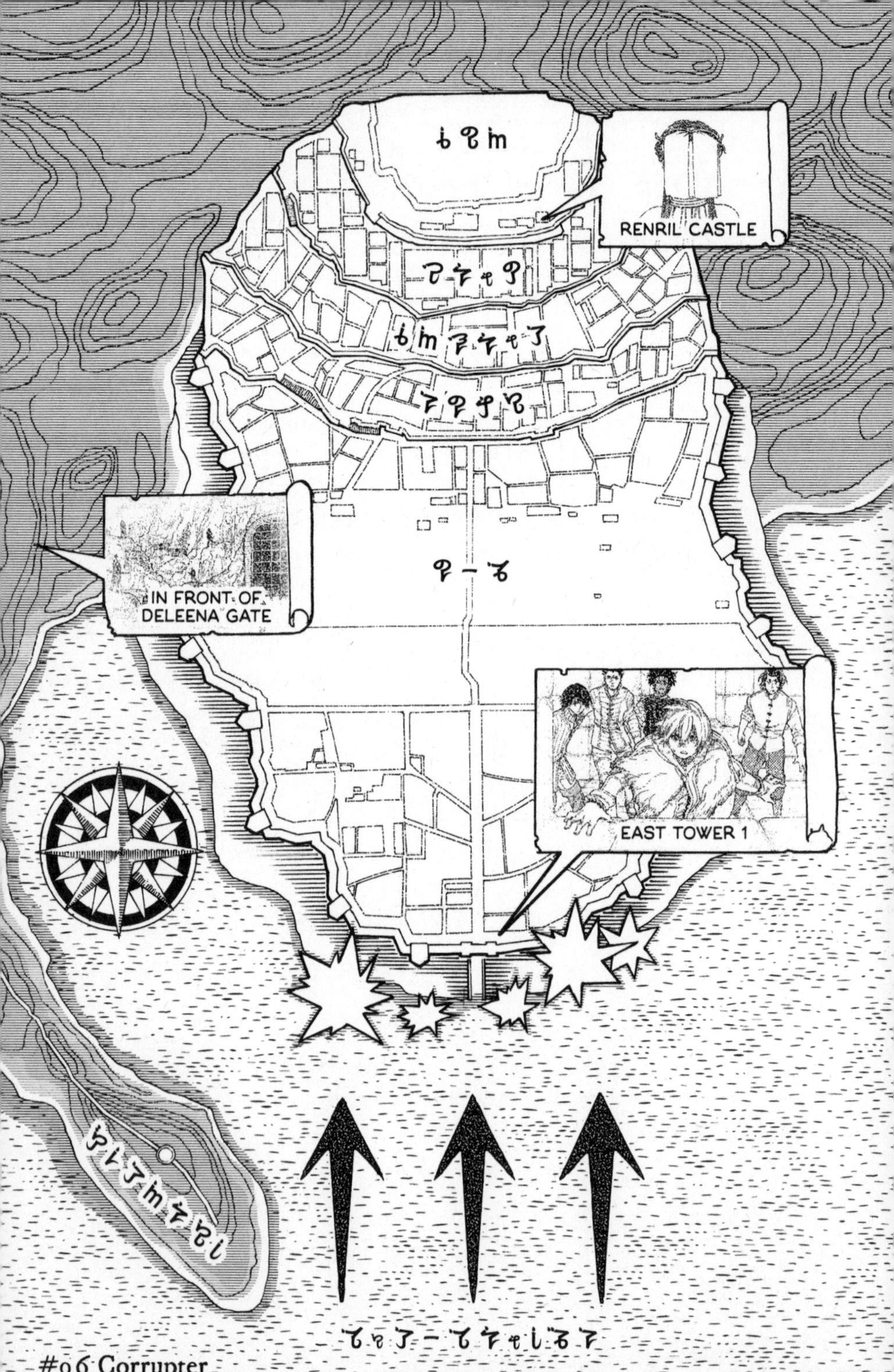
RENRIL CASTLE
IN FRONT OF DELEENA GATE
EAST TOWER 1

#96 Corrupter

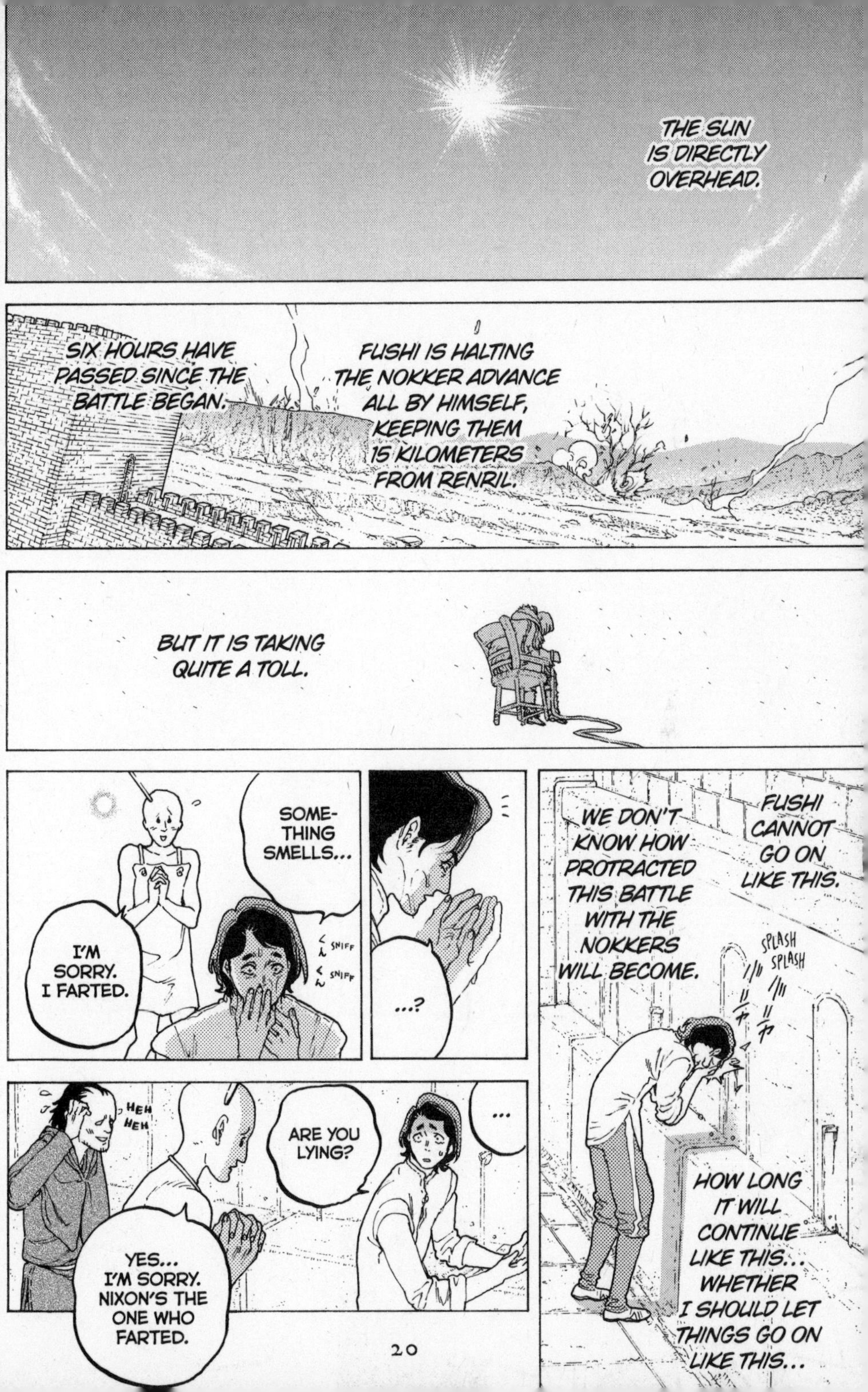
THE SUN IS DIRECTLY OVERHEAD.
SIX HOURS HAVE PASSED SINCE THE BATTLE BEGAN.
FUSHI IS HALTING THE NOKKER ADVANCE ALL BY HIMSELF, KEEPING THEM 15 KILOMETERS FROM RENRIL.
BUT IT IS TAKING QUITE A TOLL.
FUSHI CANNOT GO ON LIKE THIS.
WE DON'T KNOW HOW PROTRACTED THIS BATTLE WITH THE NOKKERS WILL BECOME.
SPLASH SPLASH
HOW LONG IT WILL CONTINUE LIKE THIS... WHETHER I SHOULD LET THINGS GO ON LIKE THIS...
...?
SOME-THING SMELLS...
SNIFF SNIFF
I'M SORRY. I FARTED.
...
ARE YOU LYING?
HEH HEH
YES... I'M SORRY. NIXON'S THE ONE WHO FARTED.

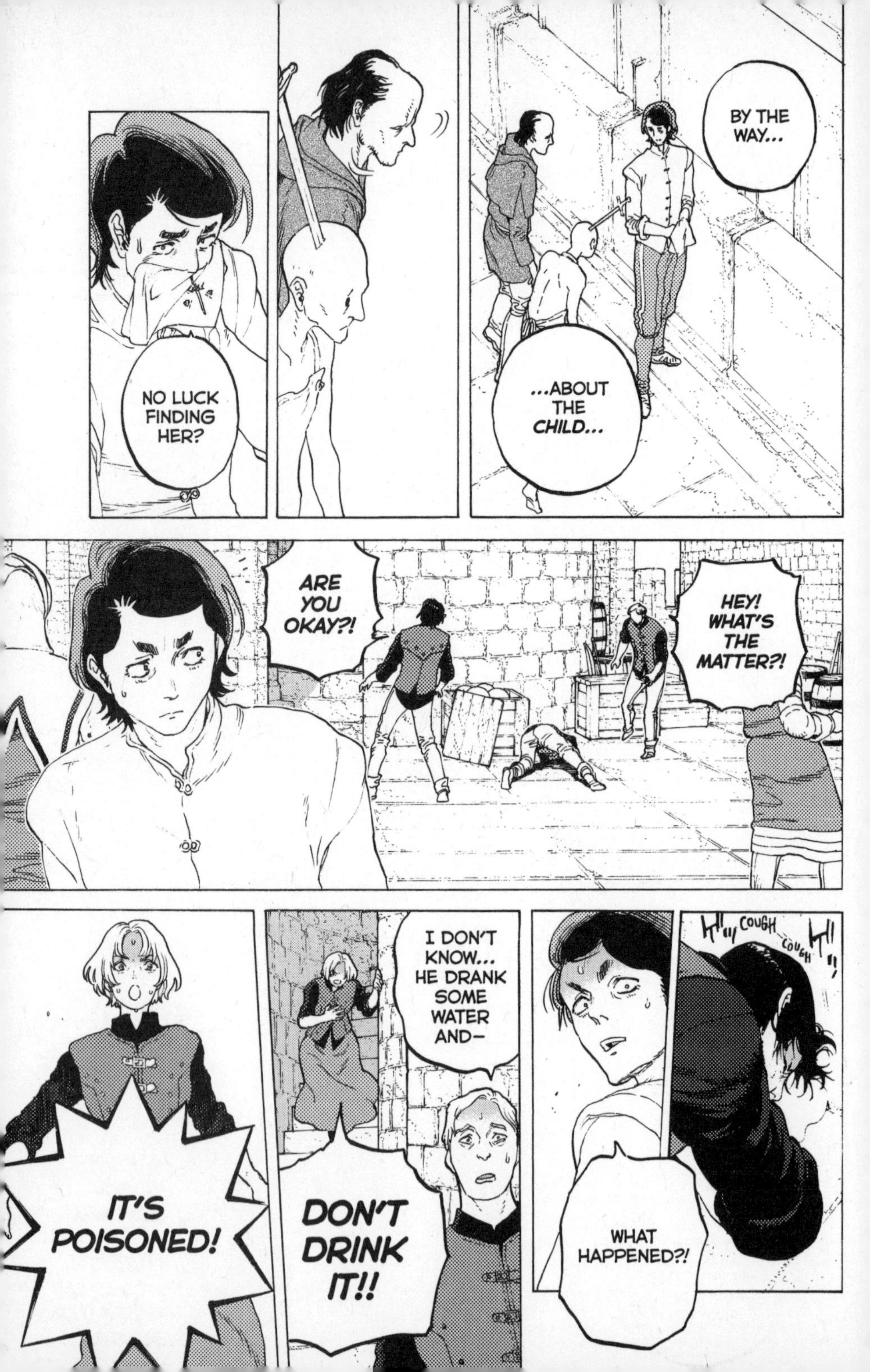
BY THE WAY...
...ABOUT THE CHILD...
NO LUCK FINDING HER?
HEY! WHAT'S THE MATTER?!
ARE YOU OKAY?!
COUGH COUGH
WHAT HAPPENED?!
I DON'T KNOW... HE DRANK SOME WATER AND—
DON'T DRINK IT!!
IT'S POISONED!

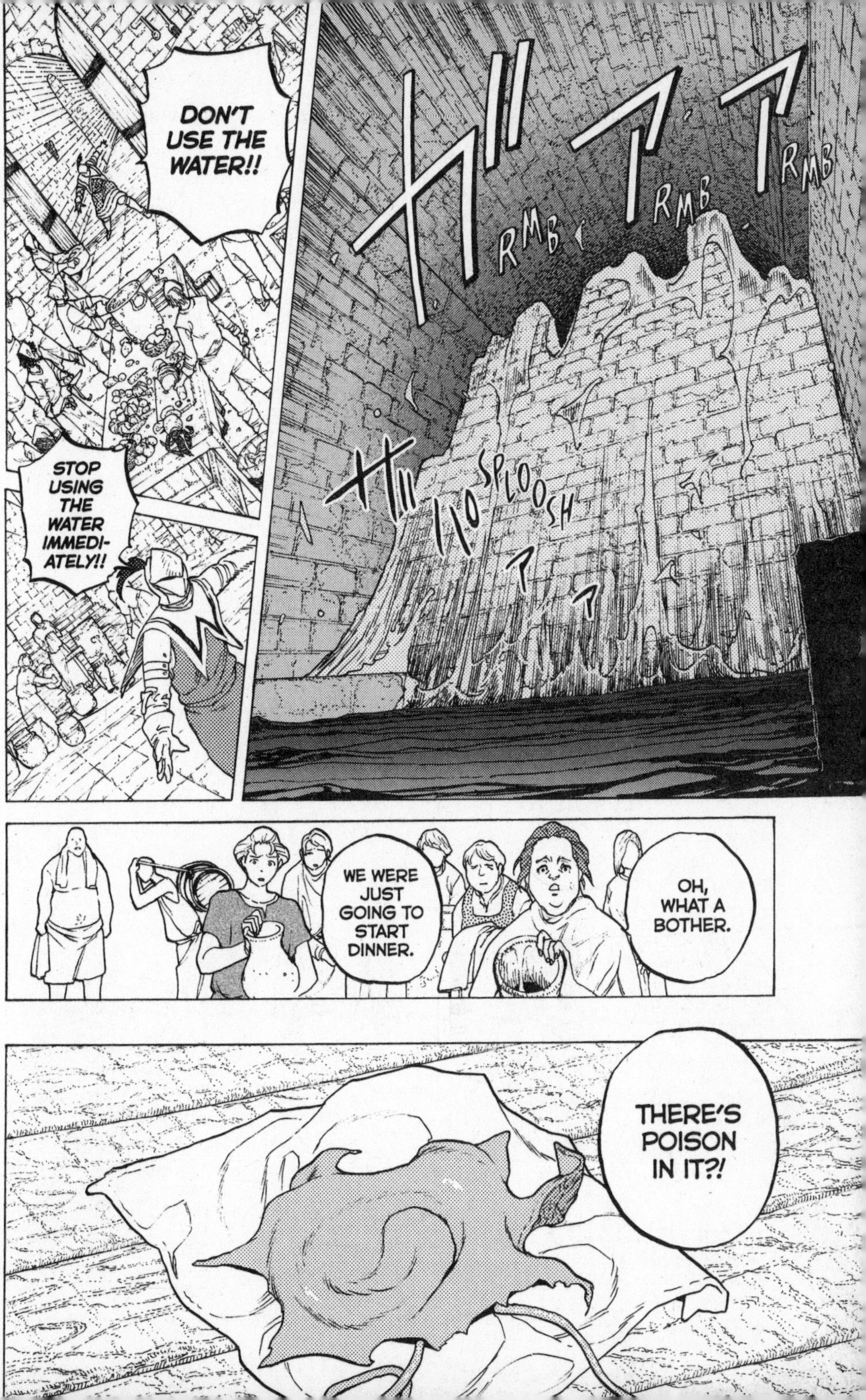
RMB
RMB
RMB
SPLOOSH
DON'T USE THE WATER!!
STOP USING THE WATER IMMEDIATELY!!
OH, WHAT A BOTHER.
WE WERE JUST GOING TO START DINNER.
THERE'S POISON IN IT?!

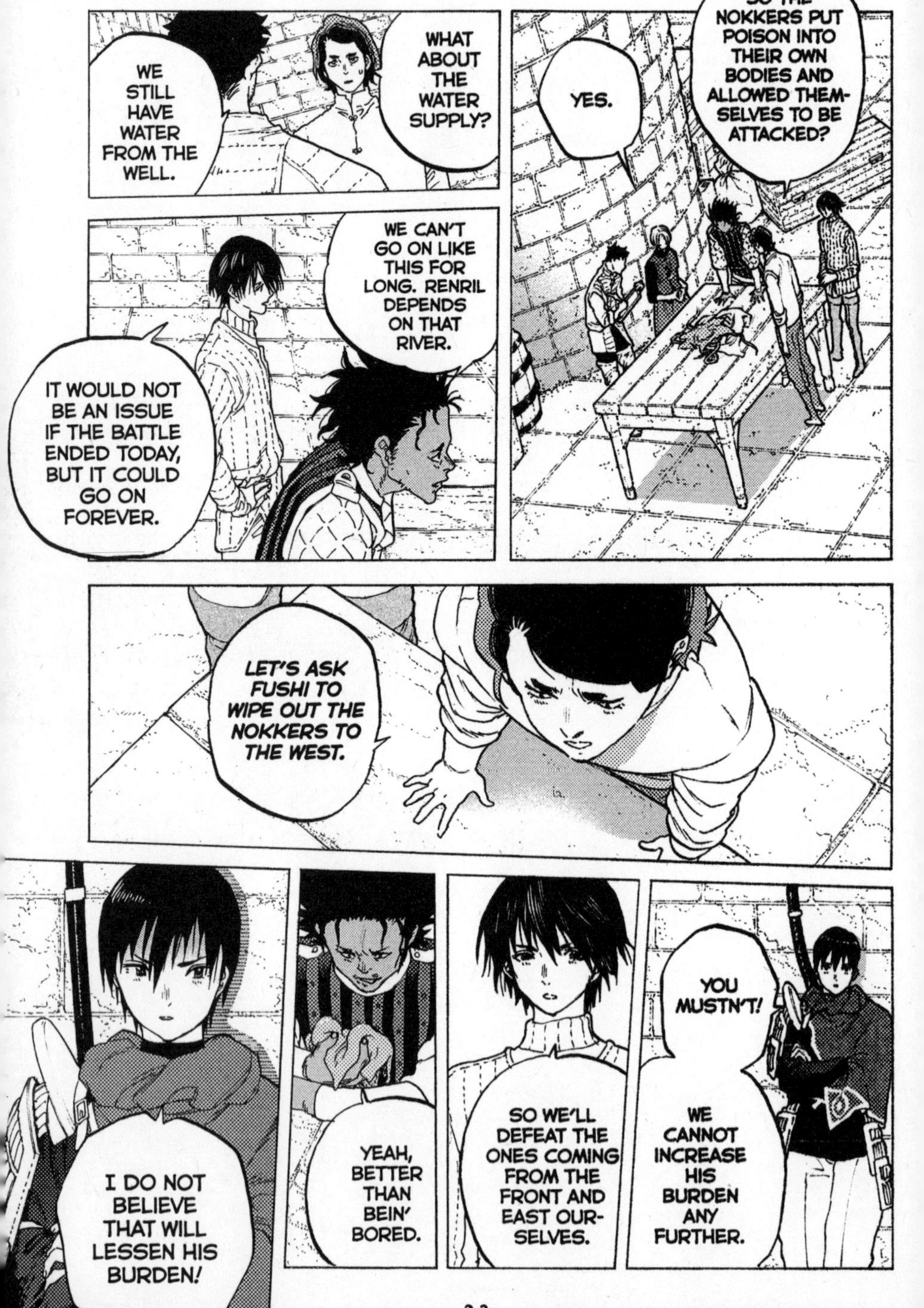
SO THE NOKKERS PUT POISON INTO THEIR OWN BODIES AND ALLOWED THEMSELVES TO BE ATTACKED?
YES.
WHAT ABOUT THE WATER SUPPLY?
WE STILL HAVE WATER FROM THE WELL.
WE CAN'T GO ON LIKE THIS FOR LONG. RENRIL DEPENDS ON THAT RIVER.
IT WOULD NOT BE AN ISSUE IF THE BATTLE ENDED TODAY, BUT IT COULD GO ON FOREVER.
LET'S ASK FUSHI TO WIPE OUT THE NOKKERS TO THE WEST.
YOU MUSTN'T!
WE CANNOT INCREASE HIS BURDEN ANY FURTHER.
SO WE'LL DEFEAT THE ONES COMING FROM THE FRONT AND EAST OURSELVES.
YEAH, BETTER THAN BEIN' BORED.
I DO NOT BELIEVE THAT WILL LESSEN HIS BURDEN!

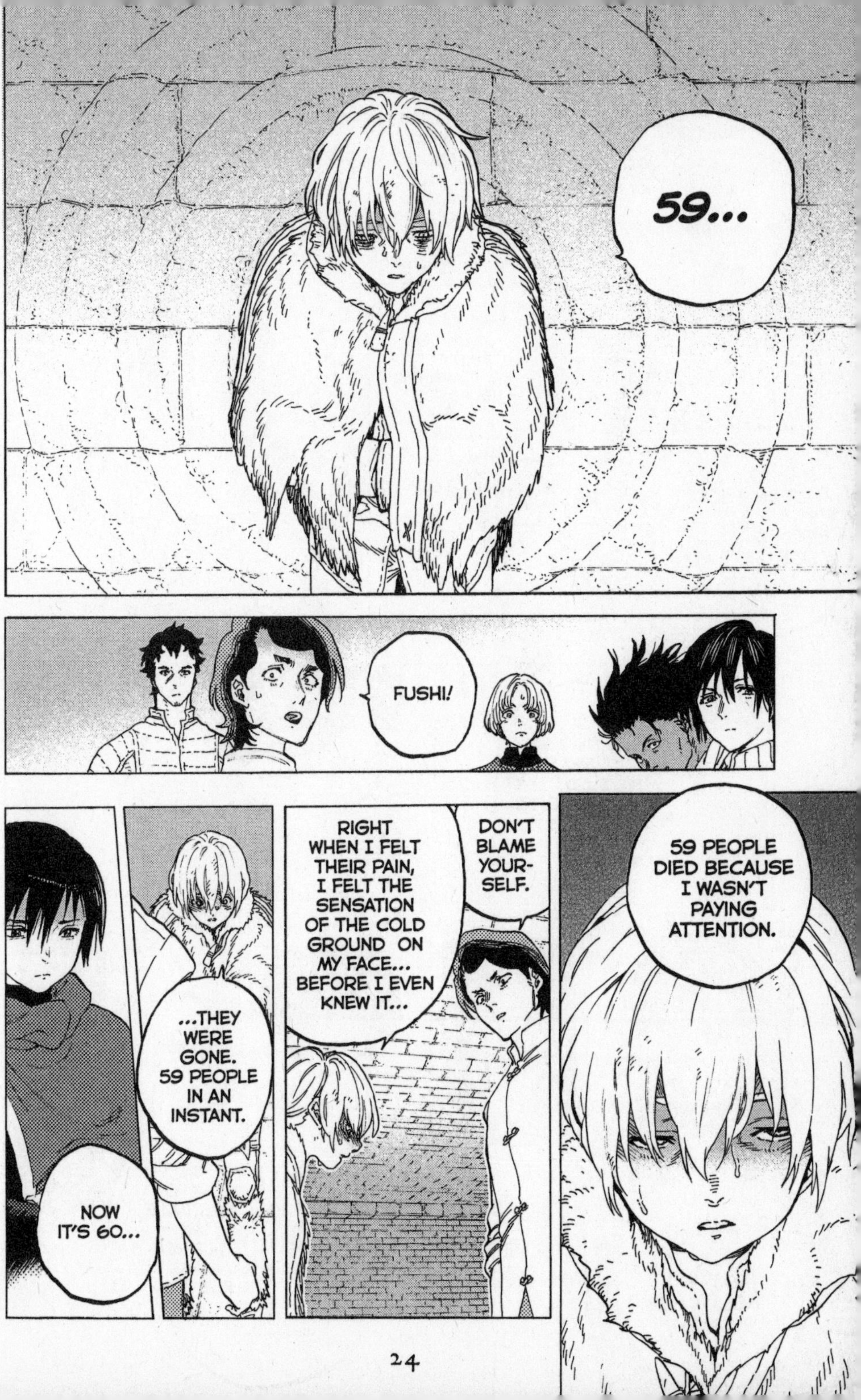
59...
FUSHI!
59 PEOPLE DIED BECAUSE I WASN'T PAYING ATTENTION.
DON'T BLAME YOUR-SELF.
RIGHT WHEN I FELT THEIR PAIN, I FELT THE SENSATION OF THE COLD GROUND ON MY FACE... BEFORE I EVEN KNEW IT...
...THEY WERE GONE. 59 PEOPLE IN AN INSTANT.
NOW IT'S 60...

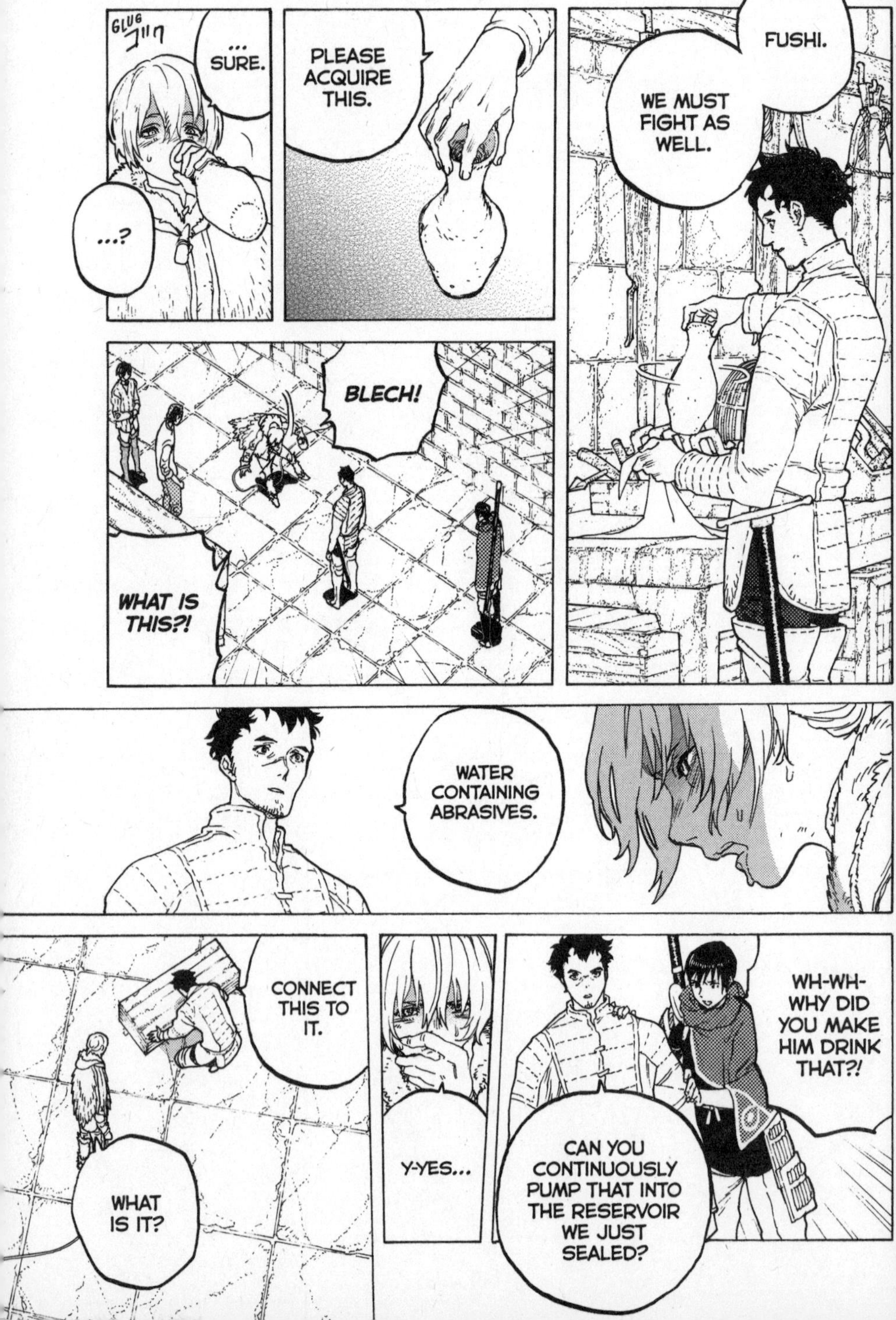
FUSHI.
WE MUST FIGHT AS WELL.
PLEASE ACQUIRE THIS.
GLUG
... SURE.
...?
BLECH!
WHAT IS THIS?!
WATER CONTAINING ABRASIVES.
WH-WH-WHY DID YOU MAKE HIM DRINK THAT?!
CAN YOU CONTINUOUSLY PUMP THAT INTO THE RESERVOIR WE JUST SEALED?
Y-YES...
CONNECT THIS TO IT.
WHAT IS IT?

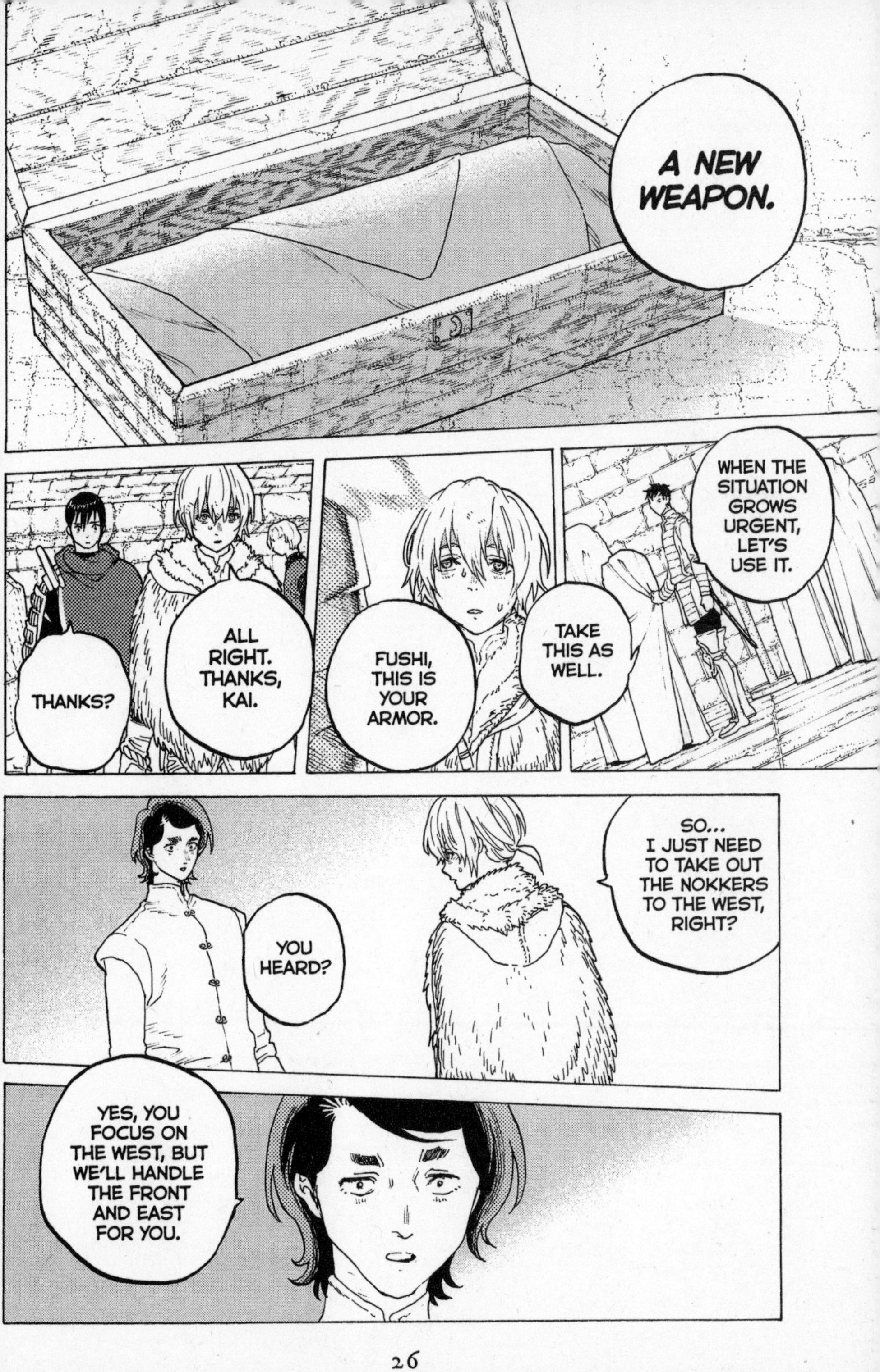
A NEW WEAPON.
WHEN THE SITUATION GROWS URGENT, LET'S USE IT.
TAKE THIS AS WELL.
FUSHI, THIS IS YOUR ARMOR.
ALL RIGHT. THANKS, KAI.
THANKS?
SO... I JUST NEED TO TAKE OUT THE NOKKERS TO THE WEST, RIGHT?
YOU HEARD?
YES, YOU FOCUS ON THE WEST, BUT WE'LL HANDLE THE FRONT AND EAST FOR YOU.

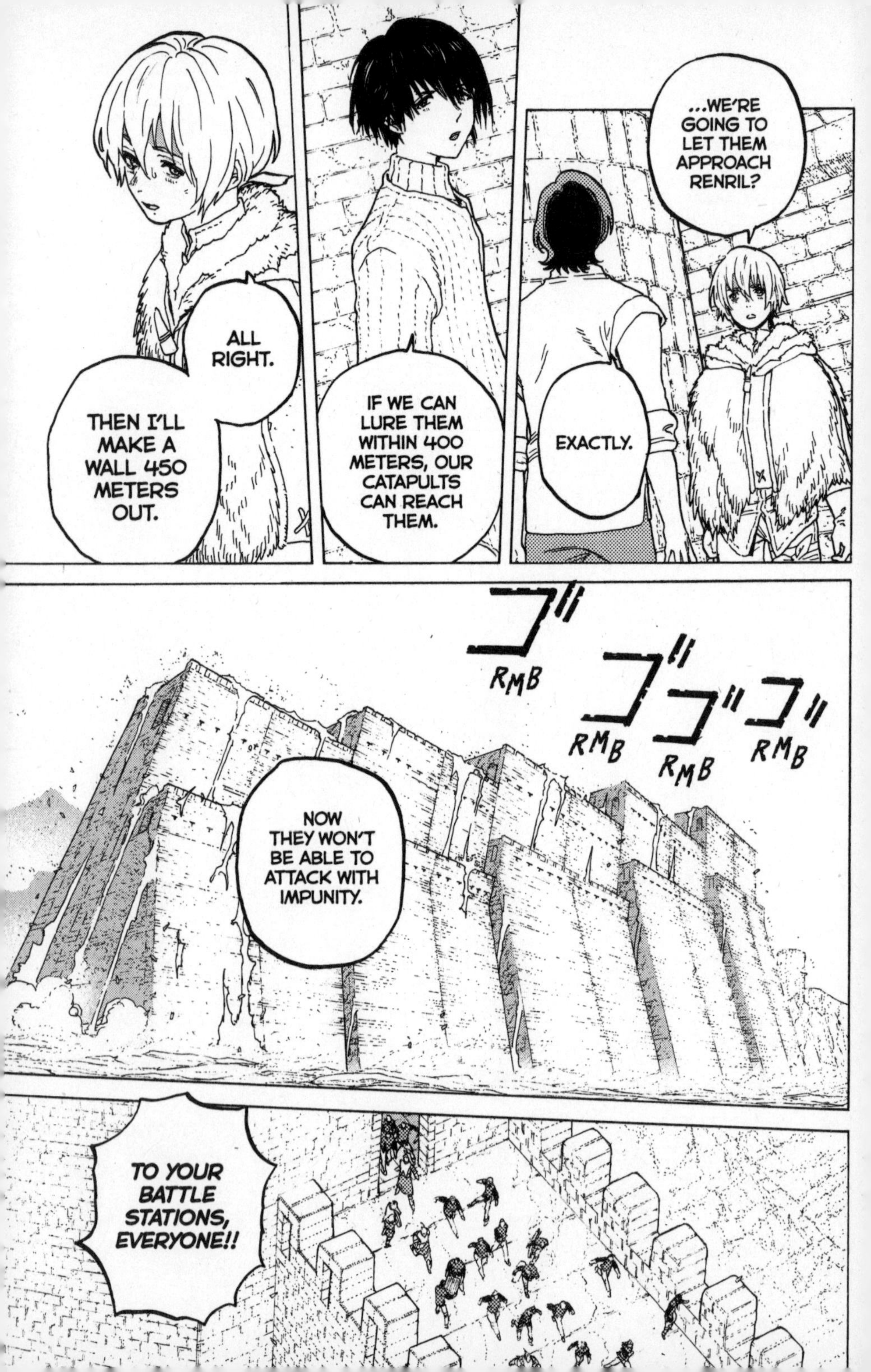
...WE'RE GOING TO LET THEM APPROACH RENRIL?
EXACTLY.
IF WE CAN LURE THEM WITHIN 400 METERS, OUR CATAPULTS CAN REACH THEM.
ALL RIGHT.
THEN I'LL MAKE A WALL 450 METERS OUT.
ゴ
RMB
ゴ
RMB
ゴ
RMB
ゴ
RMB
NOW THEY WON'T BE ABLE TO ATTACK WITH IMPUNITY.
TO YOUR BATTLE STATIONS, EVERYONE!!

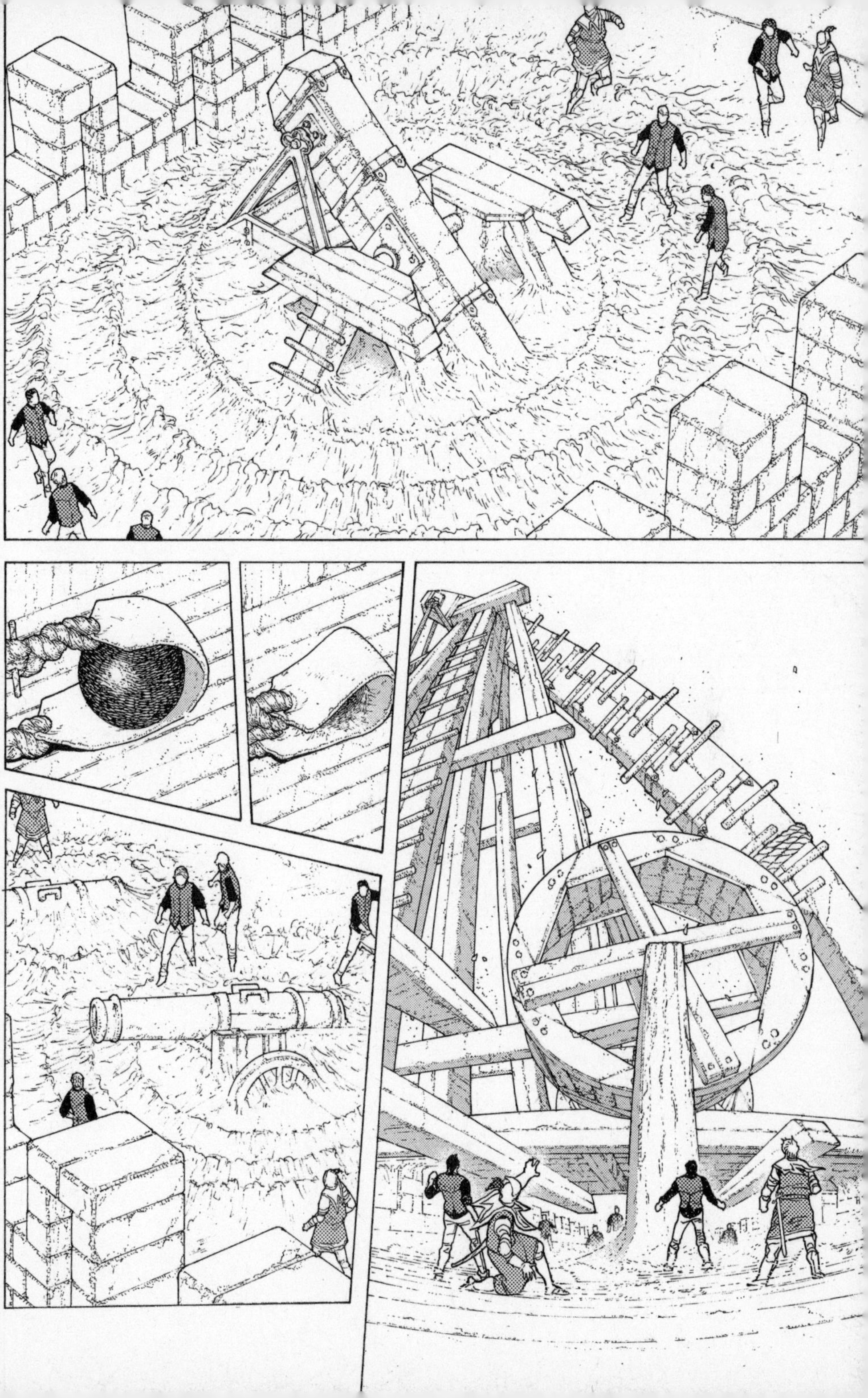

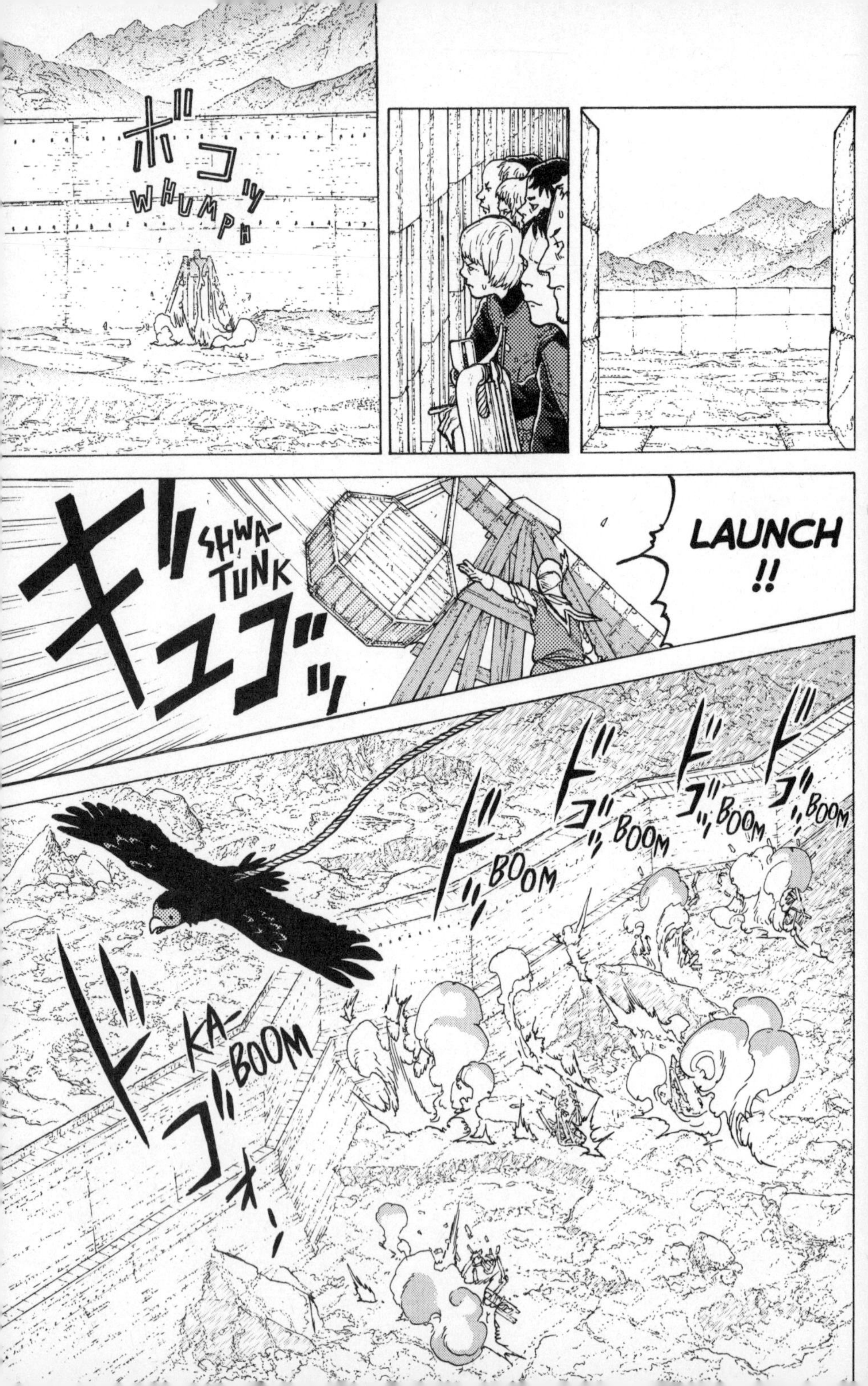
ボゴッ
WHUMPH
LAUNCH!!
キュゴッ
SHWA-TUNK
ドゴッ BOOM
ドゴッ BOOM
ドゴッ BOOM
ドゴッ BOOM
ドゴォ…
KA-BOOM

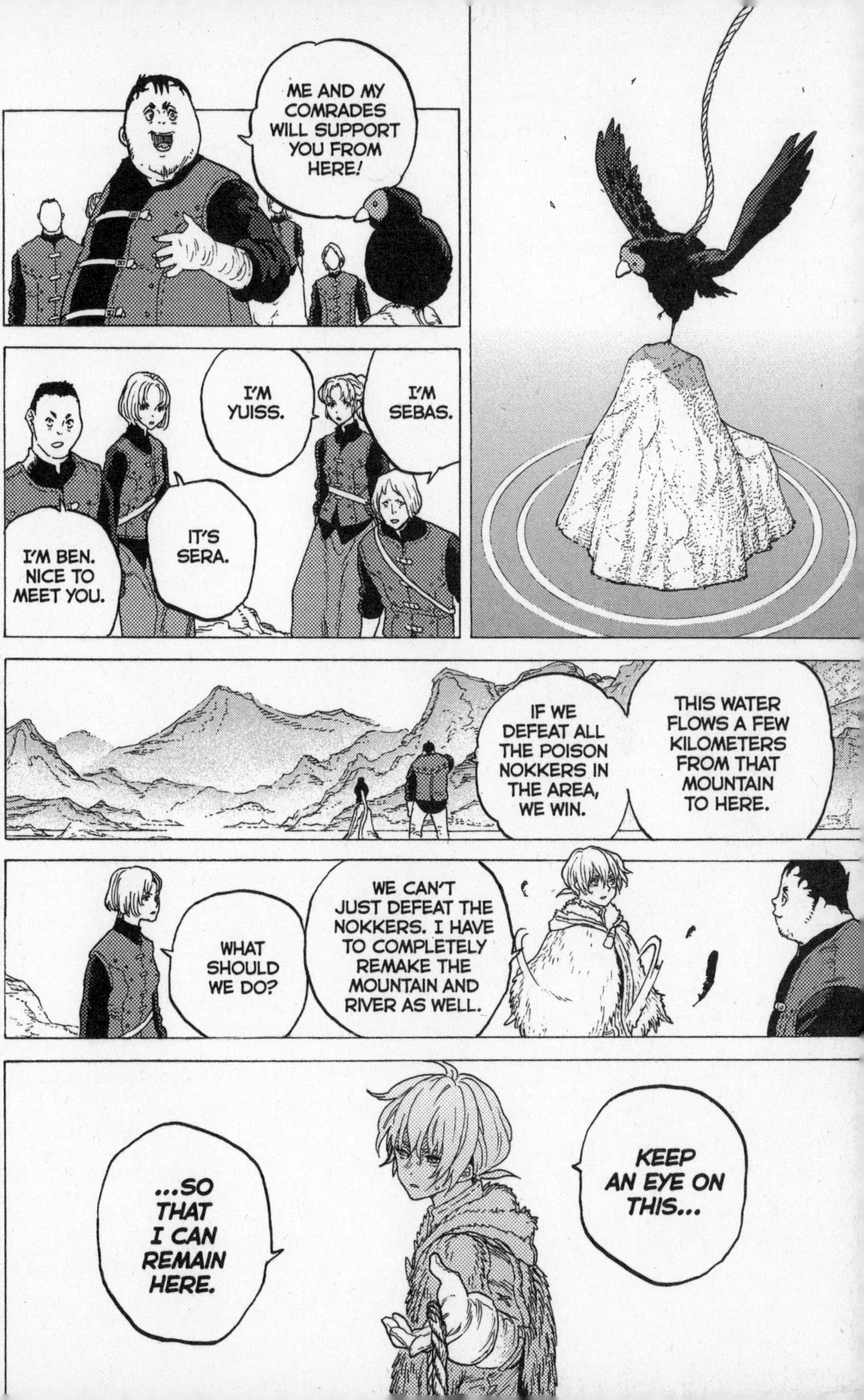
ME AND MY COMRADES WILL SUPPORT YOU FROM HERE!
I'M SEBAS.
I'M YUISS.
IT'S SERA.
I'M BEN. NICE TO MEET YOU.
THIS WATER FLOWS A FEW KILOMETERS FROM THAT MOUNTAIN TO HERE.
IF WE DEFEAT ALL THE POISON NOKKERS IN THE AREA, WE WIN.
WE CAN'T JUST DEFEAT THE NOKKERS. I HAVE TO COMPLETELY REMAKE THE MOUNTAIN AND RIVER AS WELL.
WHAT SHOULD WE DO?
KEEP AN EYE ON THIS...
...SO THAT I CAN REMAIN HERE.

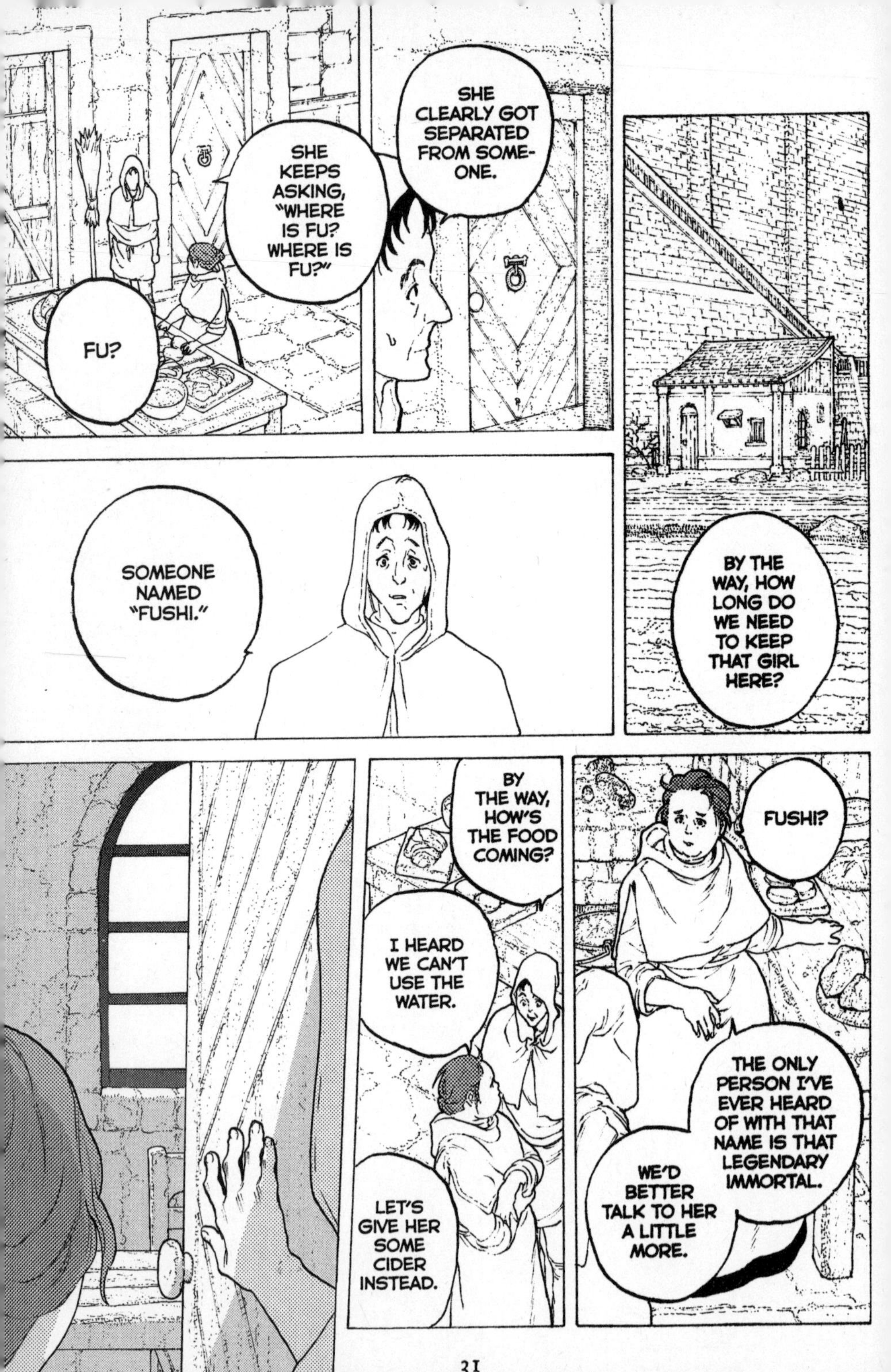
BY THE WAY, HOW LONG DO WE NEED TO KEEP THAT GIRL HERE?
SHE CLEARLY GOT SEPARATED FROM SOME-ONE.
SHE KEEPS ASKING, "WHERE IS FU? WHERE IS FU?"
FU?
SOMEONE NAMED "FUSHI."
FUSHI?
THE ONLY PERSON I'VE EVER HEARD OF WITH THAT NAME IS THAT LEGENDARY IMMORTAL.
WE'D BETTER TALK TO HER A LITTLE MORE.
BY THE WAY, HOW'S THE FOOD COMING?
I HEARD WE CAN'T USE THE WATER.
LET'S GIVE HER SOME CIDER INSTEAD.

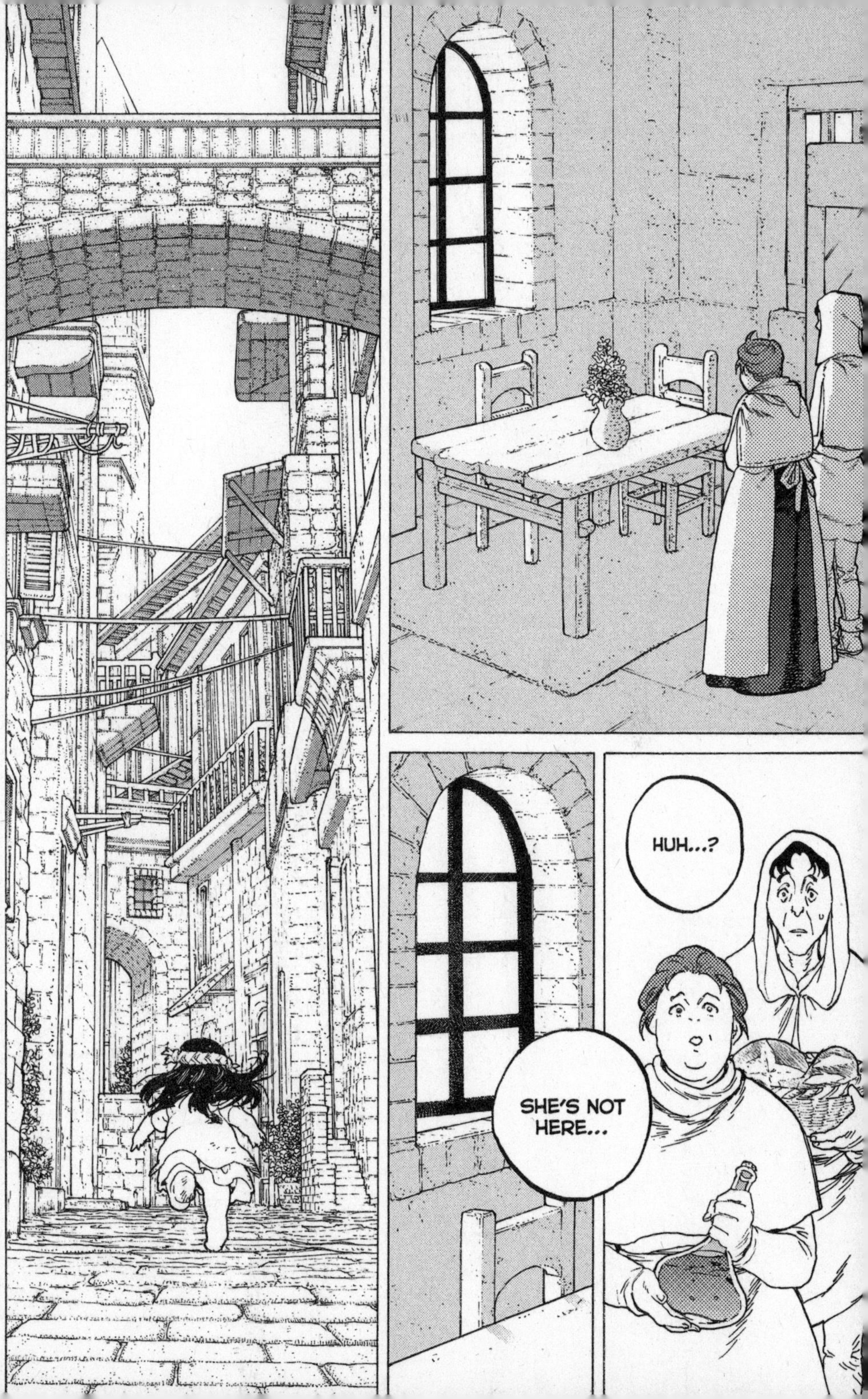
HUH...?
SHE'S NOT HERE...

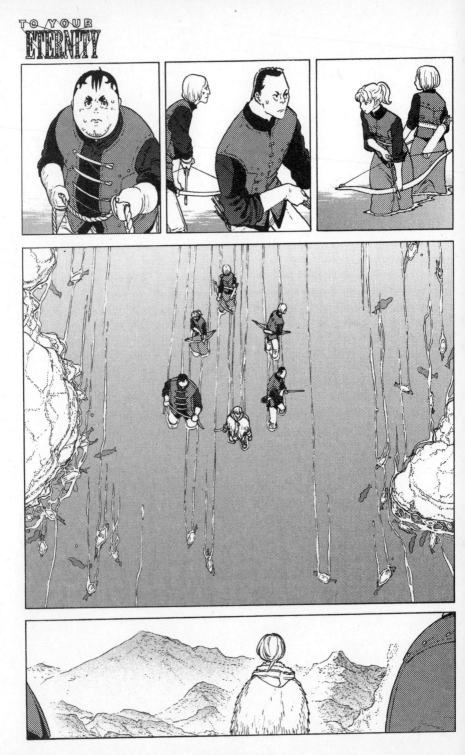

#97 Eroding Self

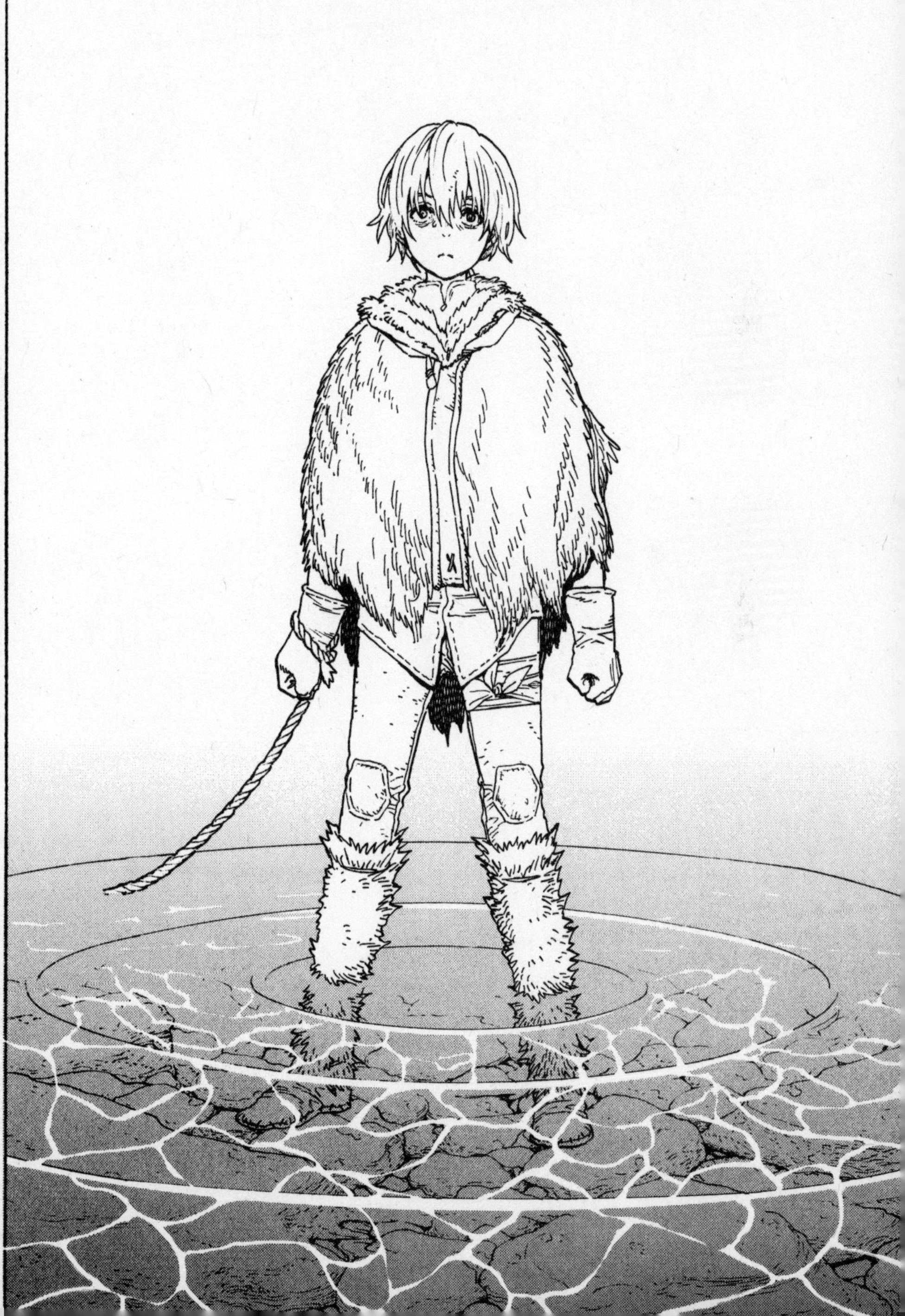

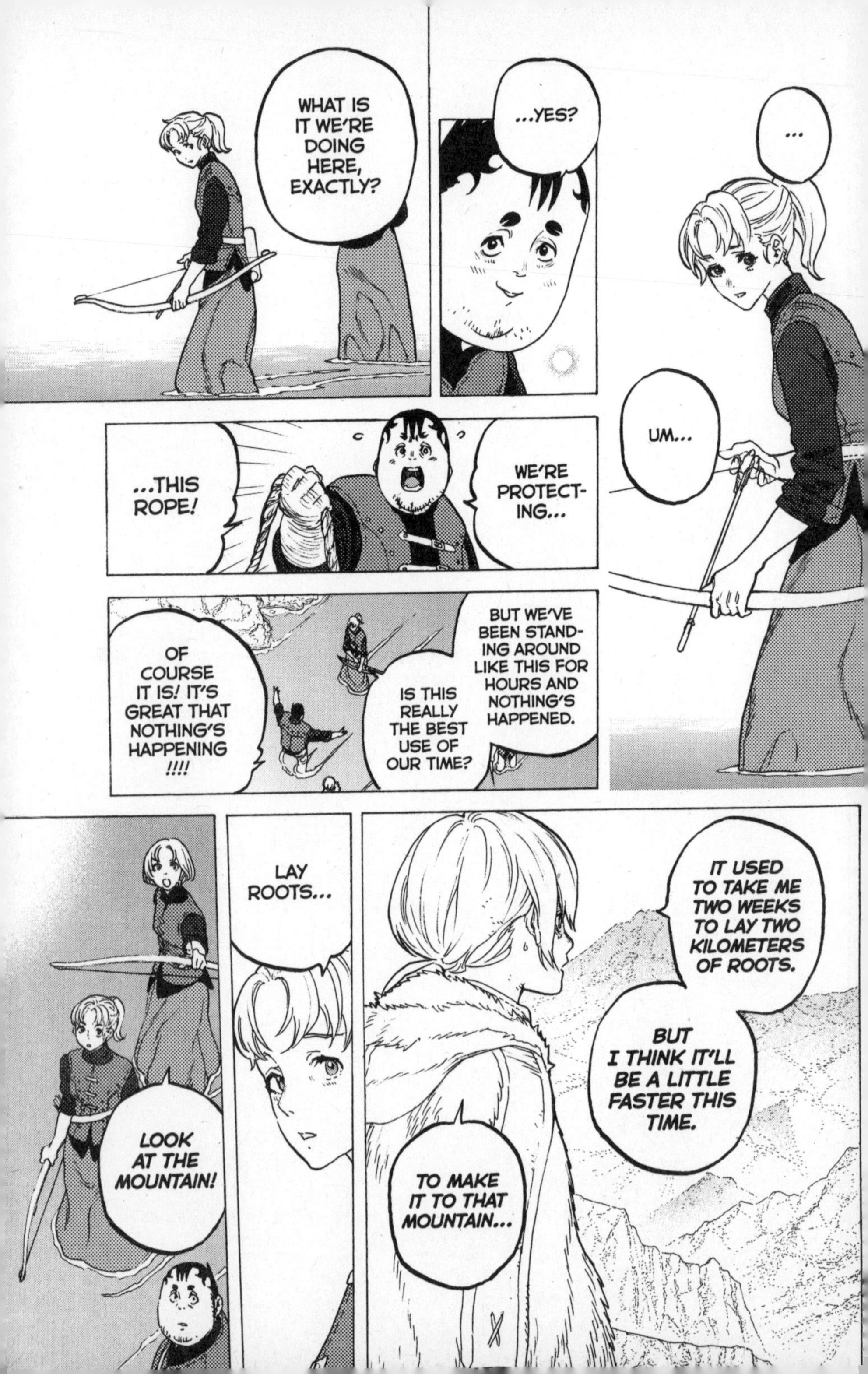
...
UM...
...YES?
WHAT IS IT WE'RE DOING HERE, EXACTLY?
WE'RE PROTECTING...
...THIS ROPE!
BUT WE'VE BEEN STANDING AROUND LIKE THIS FOR HOURS AND NOTHING'S HAPPENED.
IS THIS REALLY THE BEST USE OF OUR TIME?
OF COURSE IT IS! IT'S GREAT THAT NOTHING'S HAPPENING!!!!
IT USED TO TAKE ME TWO WEEKS TO LAY TWO KILOMETERS OF ROOTS.
BUT I THINK IT'LL BE A LITTLE FASTER THIS TIME.
TO MAKE IT TO THAT MOUNTAIN...
LAY ROOTS...
LOOK AT THE MOUNTAIN!

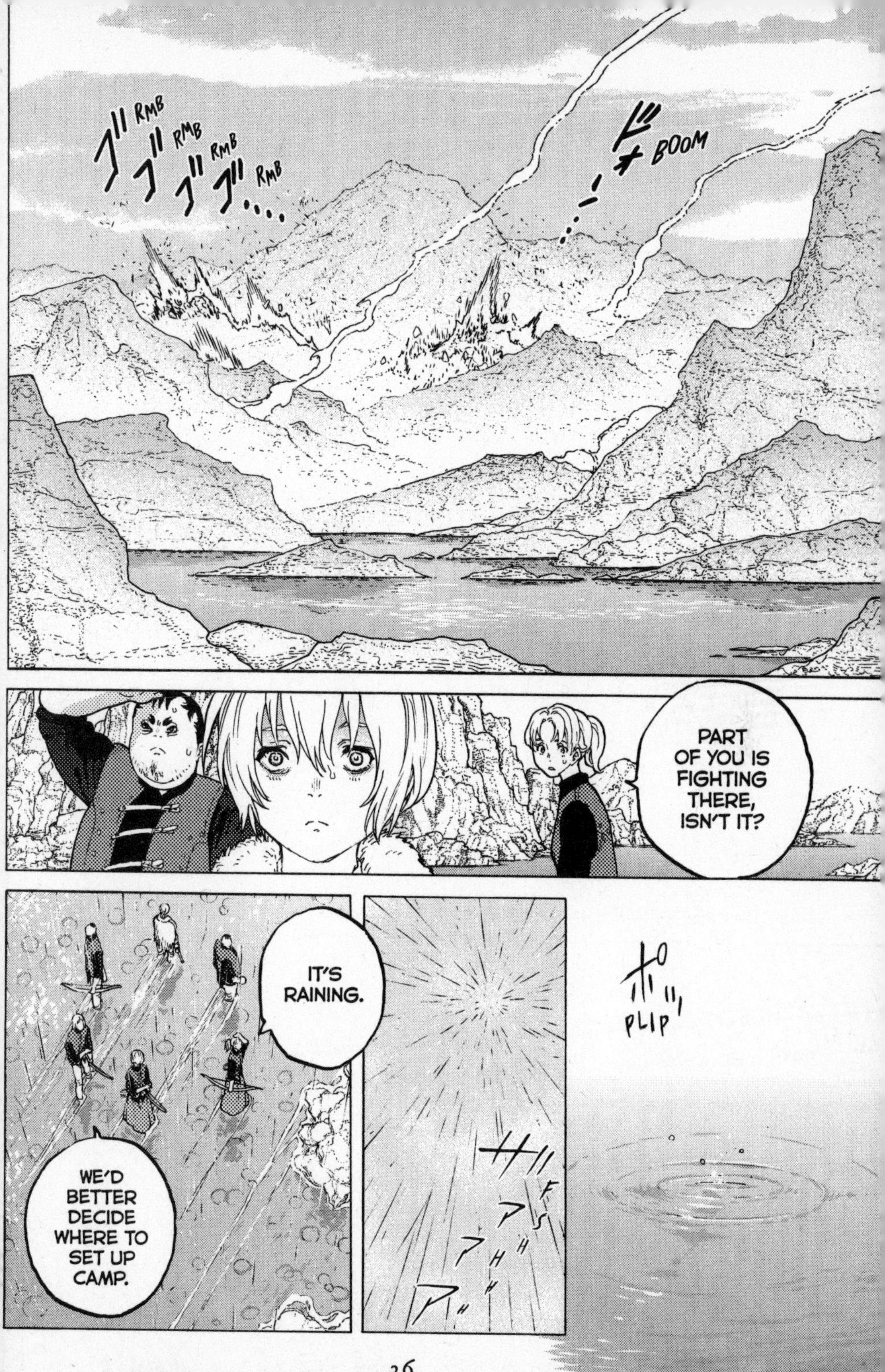
BOOM
RMB
RMB
RMB
RMB
PART OF YOU IS FIGHTING THERE, ISN'T IT?
PLIP
FSHHHH
IT'S RAINING.
WE'D BETTER DECIDE WHERE TO SET UP CAMP.

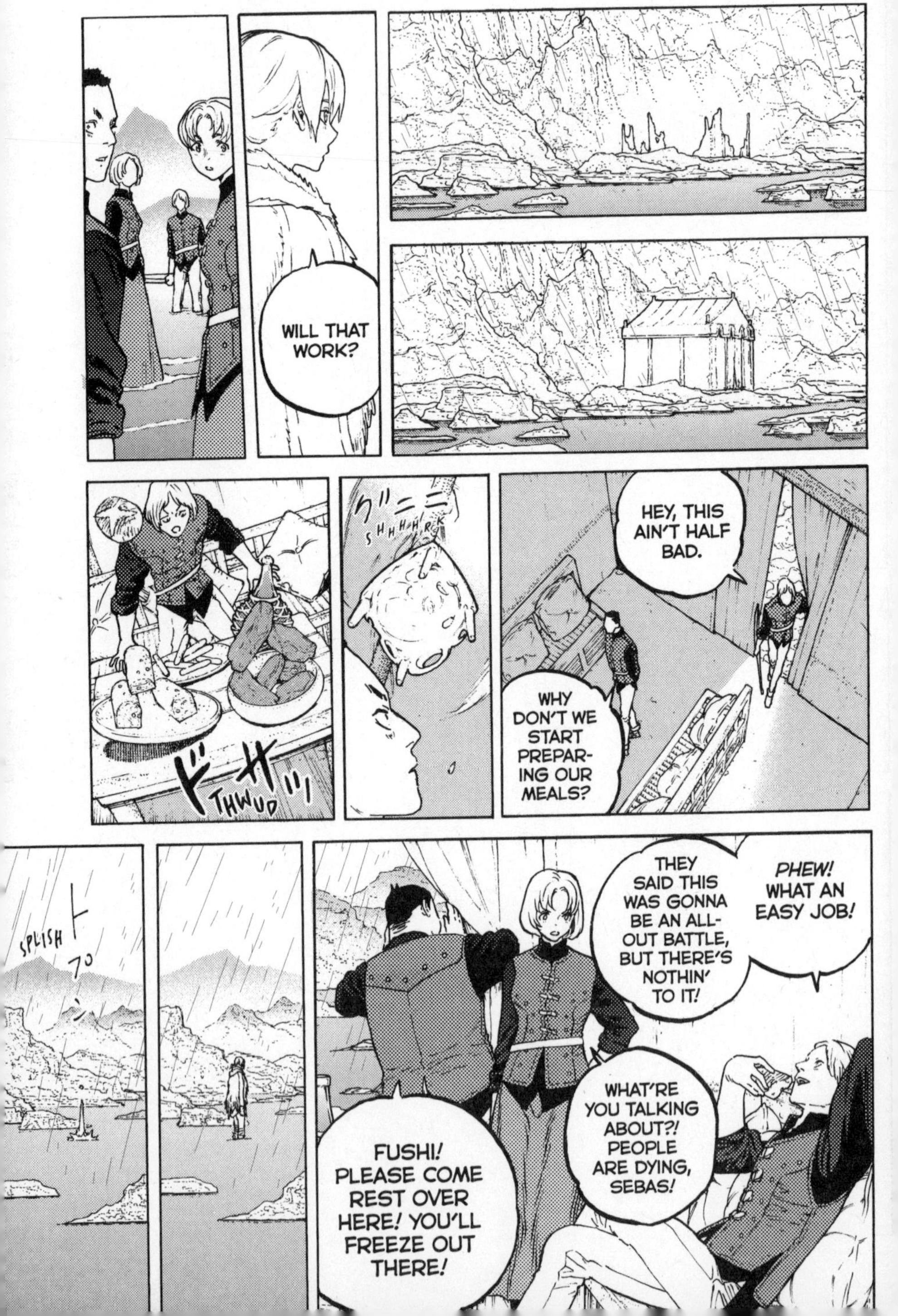
WILL THAT WORK?
HEY, THIS AIN'T HALF BAD.
WHY DON'T WE START PREPARING OUR MEALS?
SHHHHRK
THWUD
PHEW! WHAT AN EASY JOB!
THEY SAID THIS WAS GONNA BE AN ALL-OUT BATTLE, BUT THERE'S NOTHIN' TO IT!
WHAT'RE YOU TALKING ABOUT?! PEOPLE ARE DYING, SEBAS!
FUSHI! PLEASE COME REST OVER HERE! YOU'LL FREEZE OUT THERE!
SPLISH

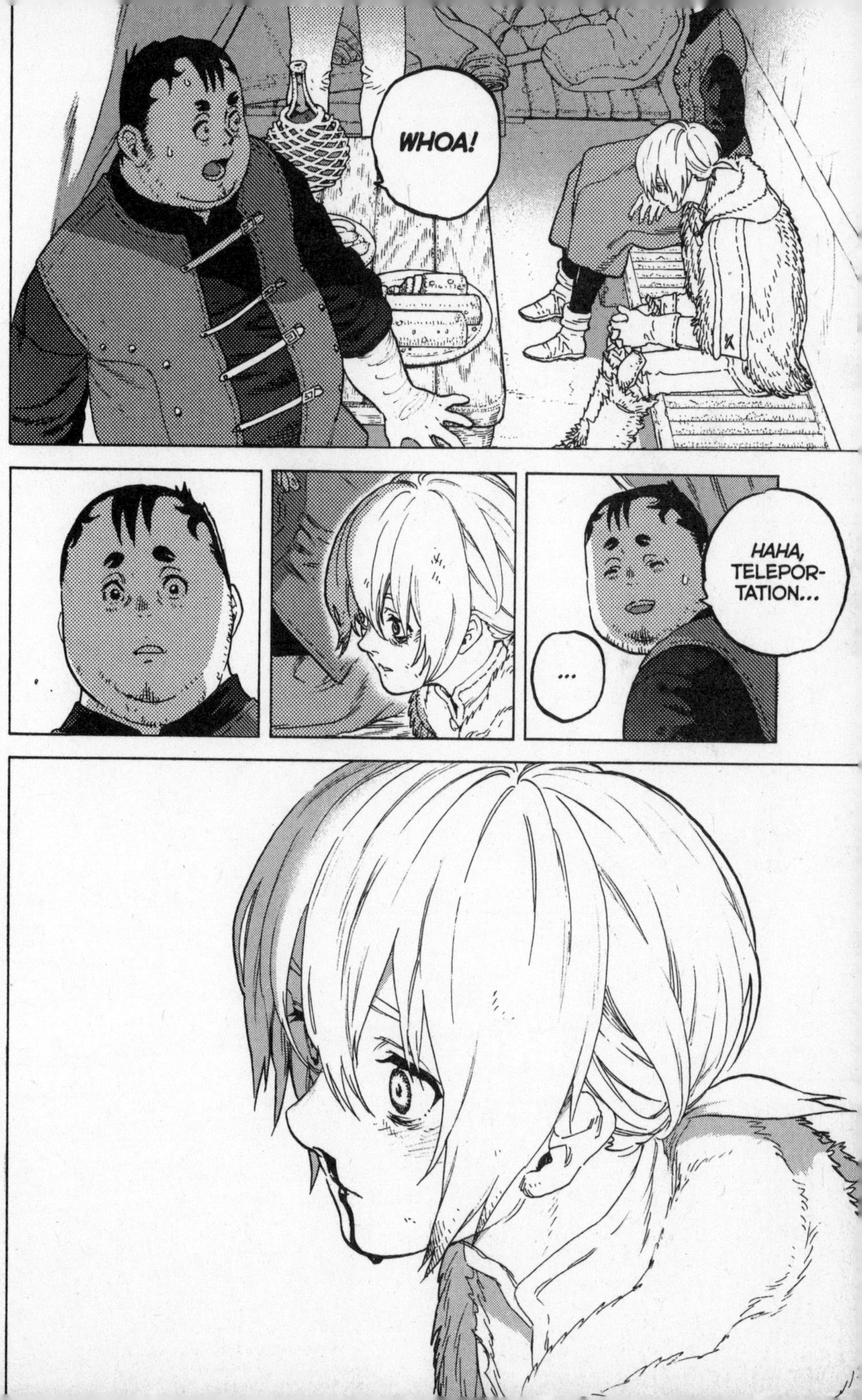
WHOA!
HAHA, TELEPOR-TATION...
...

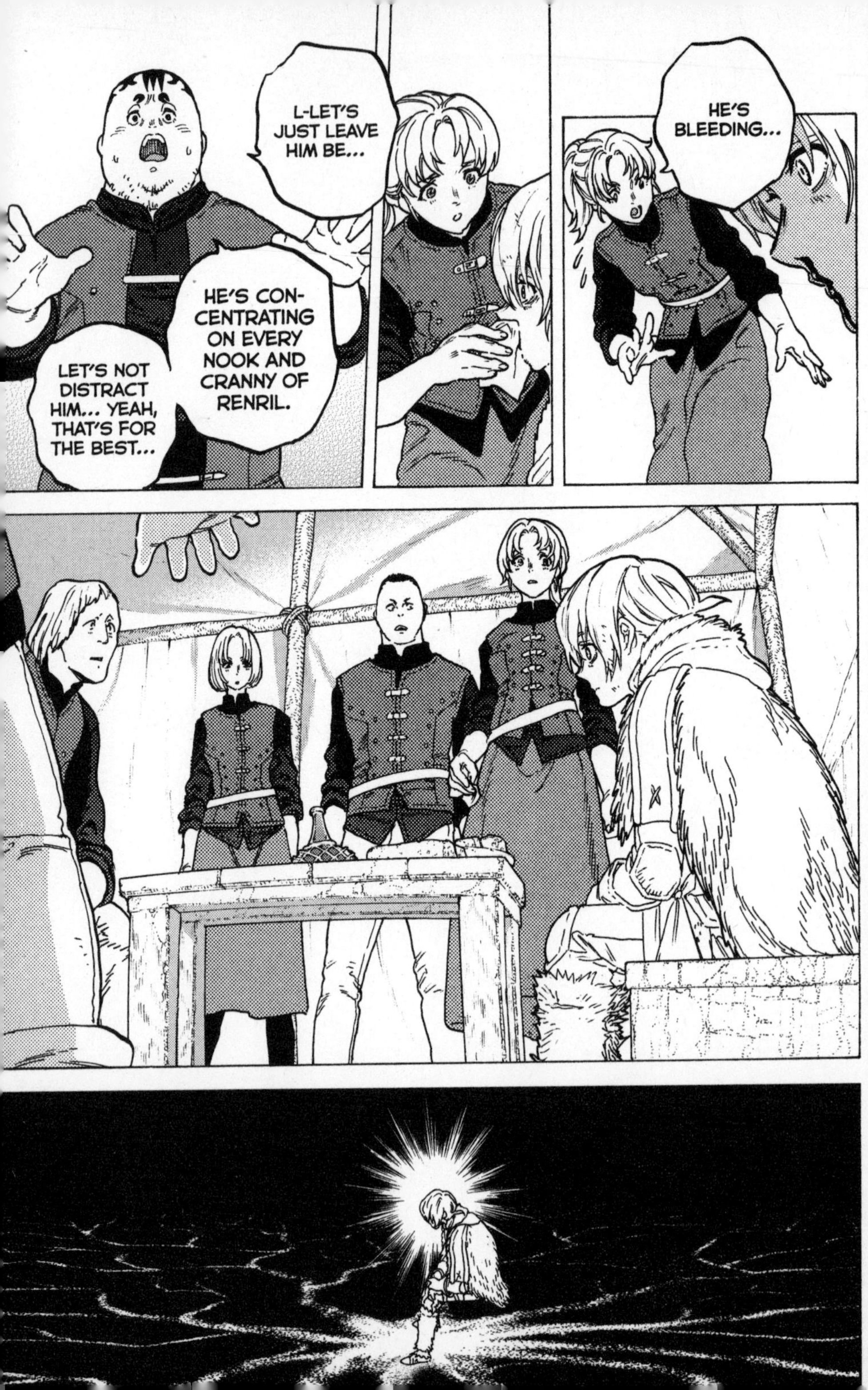
HE'S BLEEDING...
L-LET'S JUST LEAVE HIM BE...
HE'S CON-CENTRATING ON EVERY NOOK AND CRANNY OF RENRIL.
LET'S NOT DISTRACT HIM... YEAH, THAT'S FOR THE BEST...

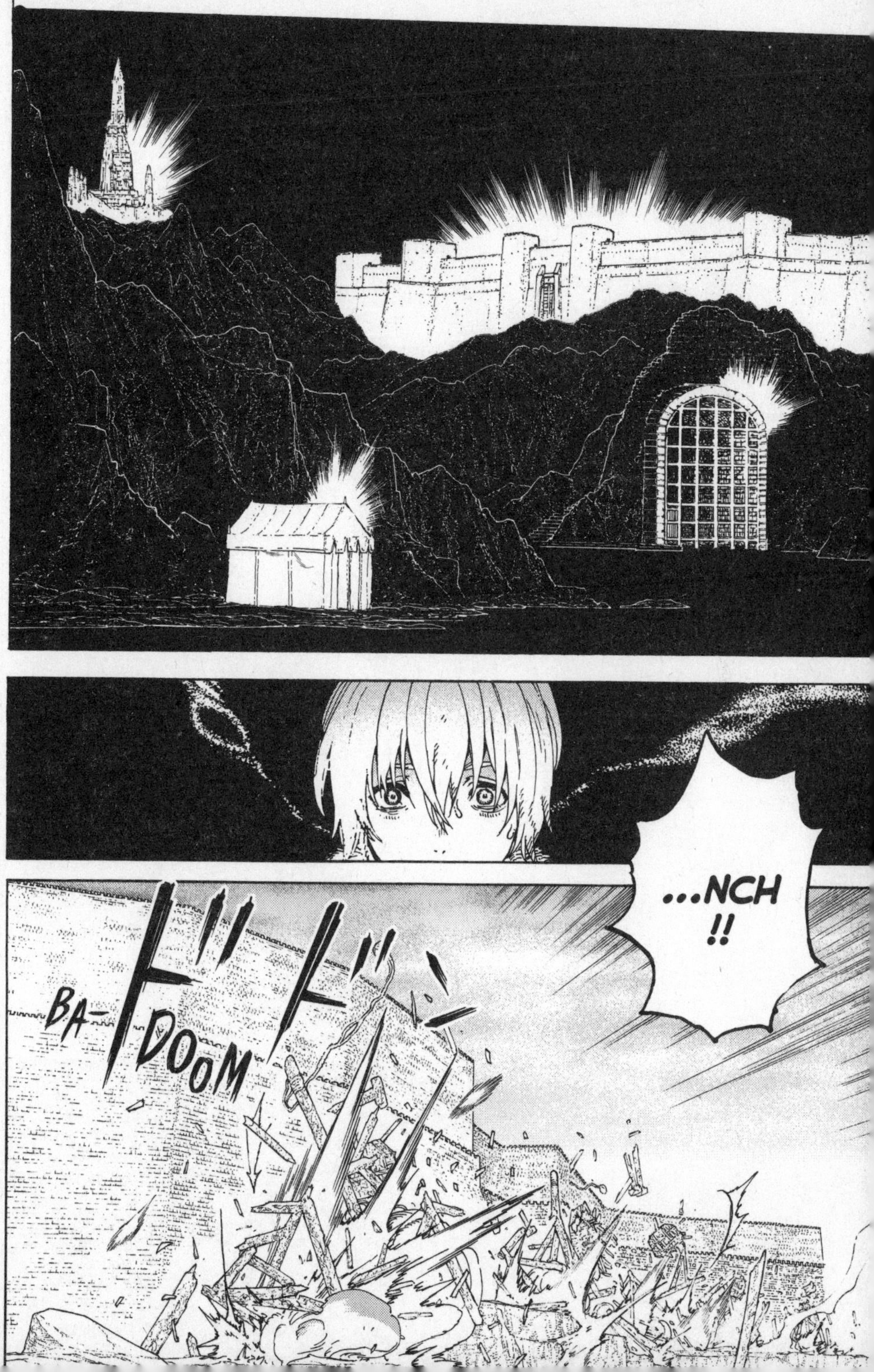
...NCH !!
BA-DOOM

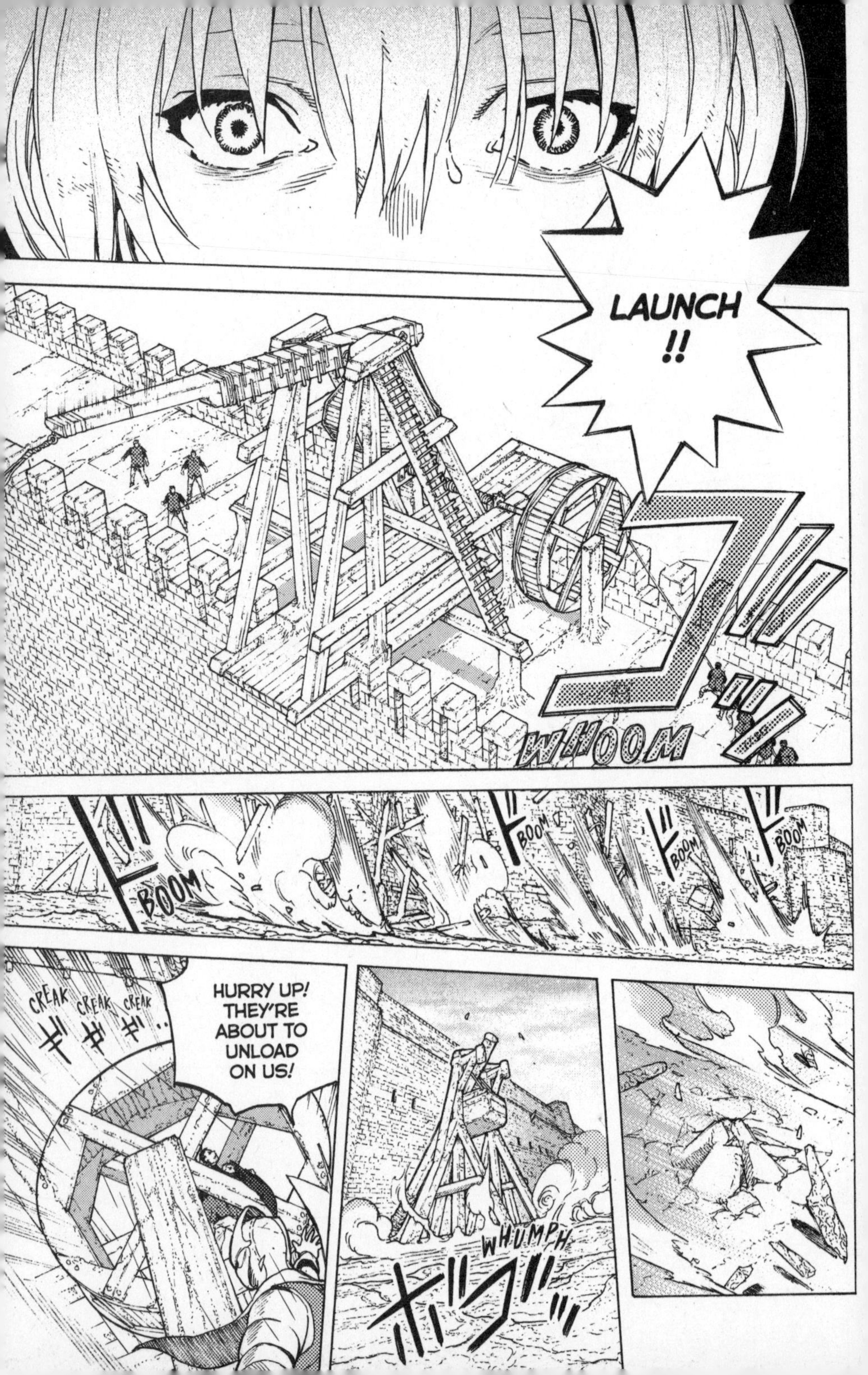
LAUNCH!!
WHOOM
BOOM
BOOM
BOOM
BOOM
WHUMPH
CREAK CREAK CREAK
HURRY UP! THEY'RE ABOUT TO UNLOAD ON US!

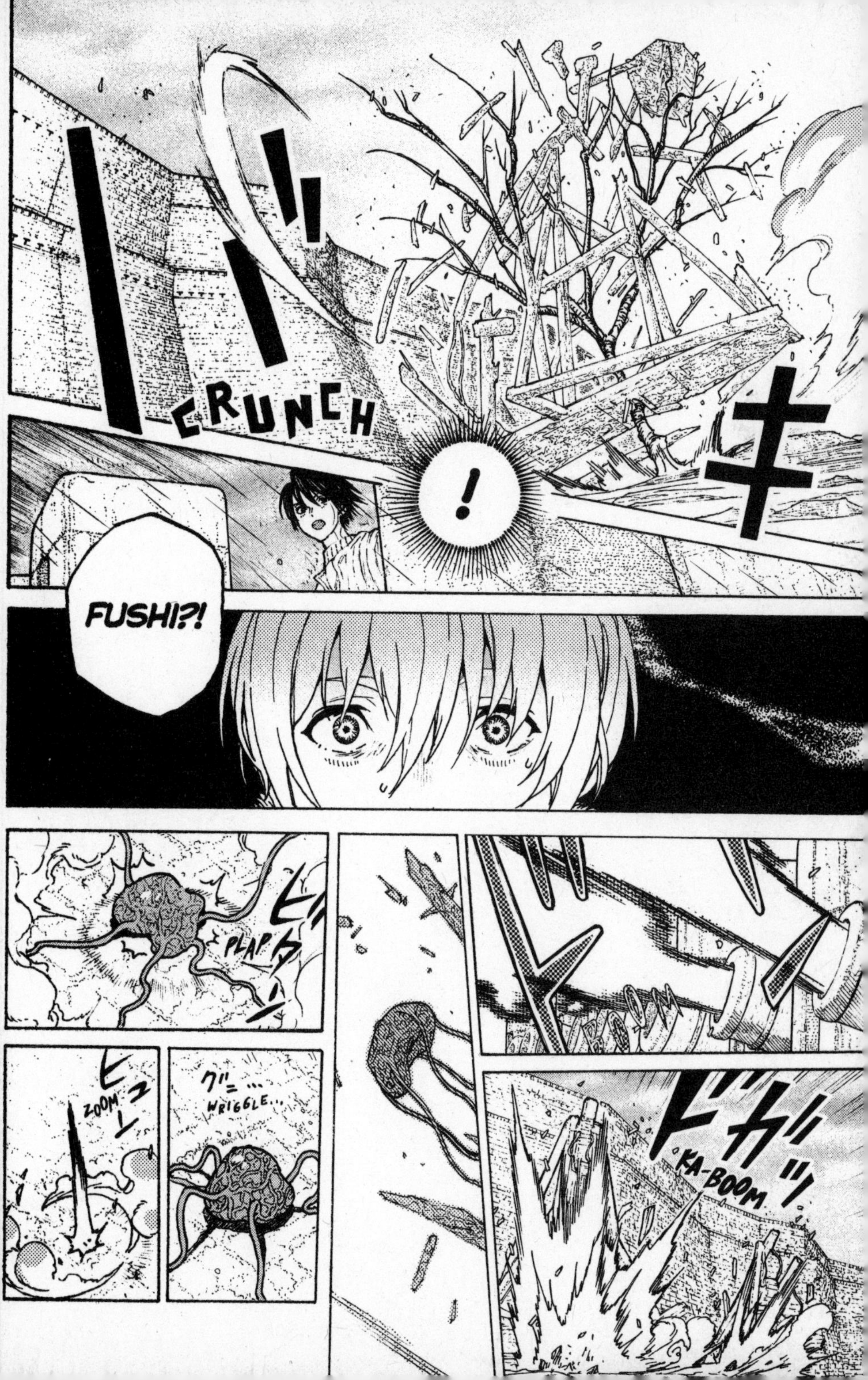
CRUNCH
!
FUSHI?!
KA-BOOM
PLAP
WRIGGLE...
ZOOM

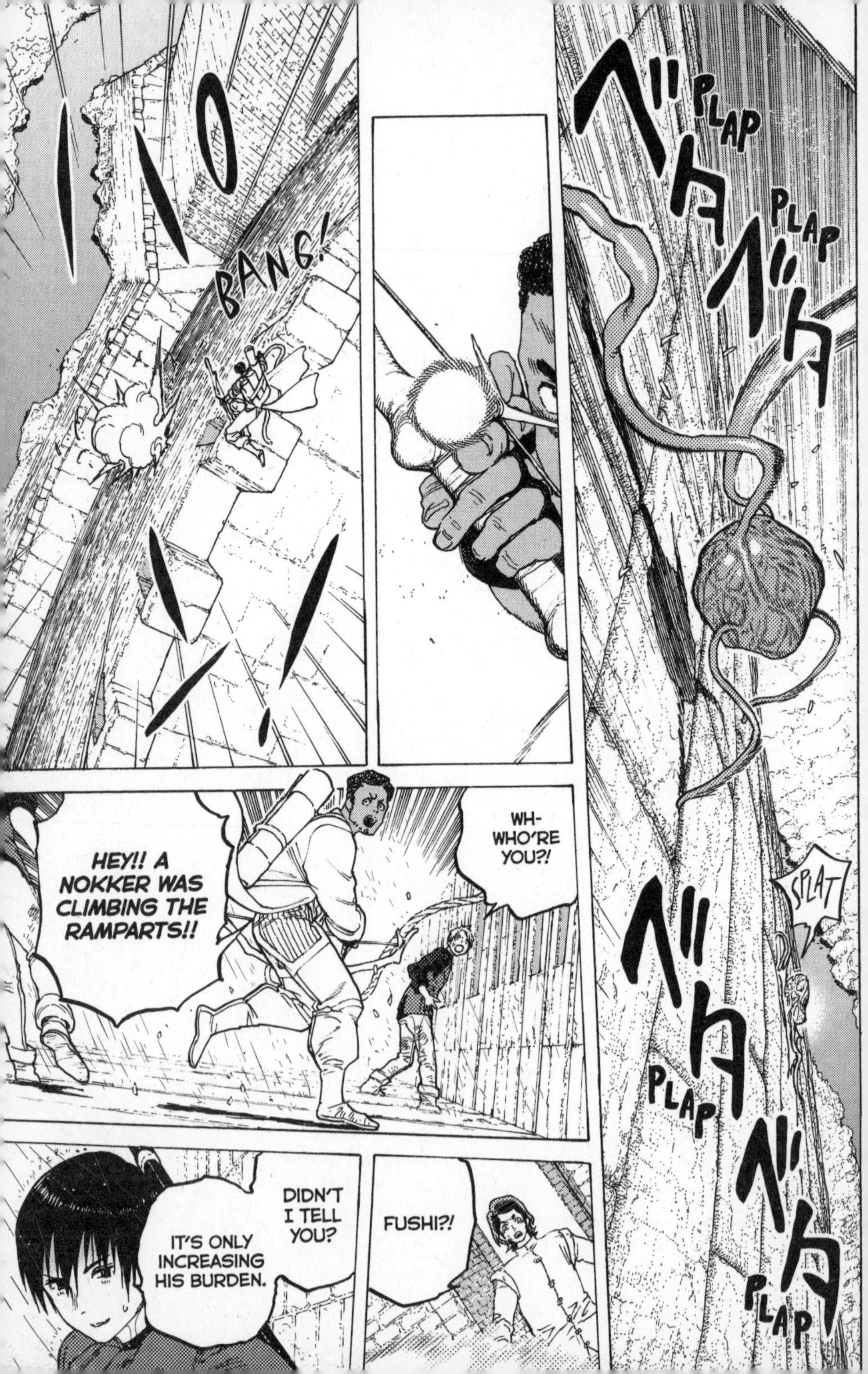
PLAP PLAP
SPLAT
PLAP PLAP
BANG!
WH-WHO'RE YOU?!
HEY!! A NOKKER WAS CLIMBING THE RAMPARTS!!
FUSHI?!
DIDN'T I TELL YOU?
IT'S ONLY INCREASING HIS BURDEN.

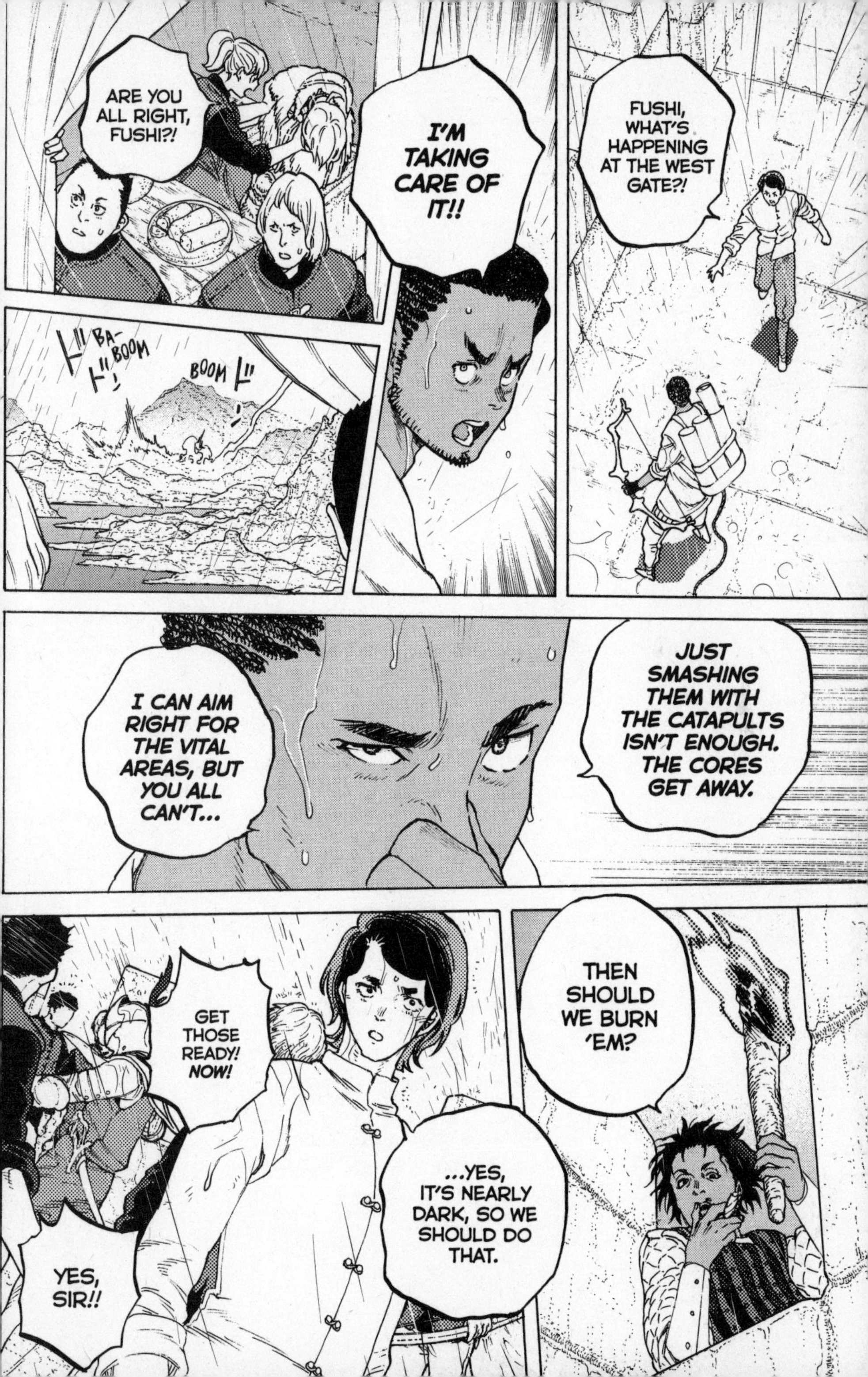
FUSHI, WHAT'S HAPPENING AT THE WEST GATE?!
I'M TAKING CARE OF IT!!
ARE YOU ALL RIGHT, FUSHI?!
BA-BOOM
BOOM
JUST SMASHING THEM WITH THE CATAPULTS ISN'T ENOUGH. THE CORES GET AWAY.
I CAN AIM RIGHT FOR THE VITAL AREAS, BUT YOU ALL CAN'T...
THEN SHOULD WE BURN 'EM?
...YES, IT'S NEARLY DARK, SO WE SHOULD DO THAT.
GET THOSE READY! NOW!
YES, SIR!!

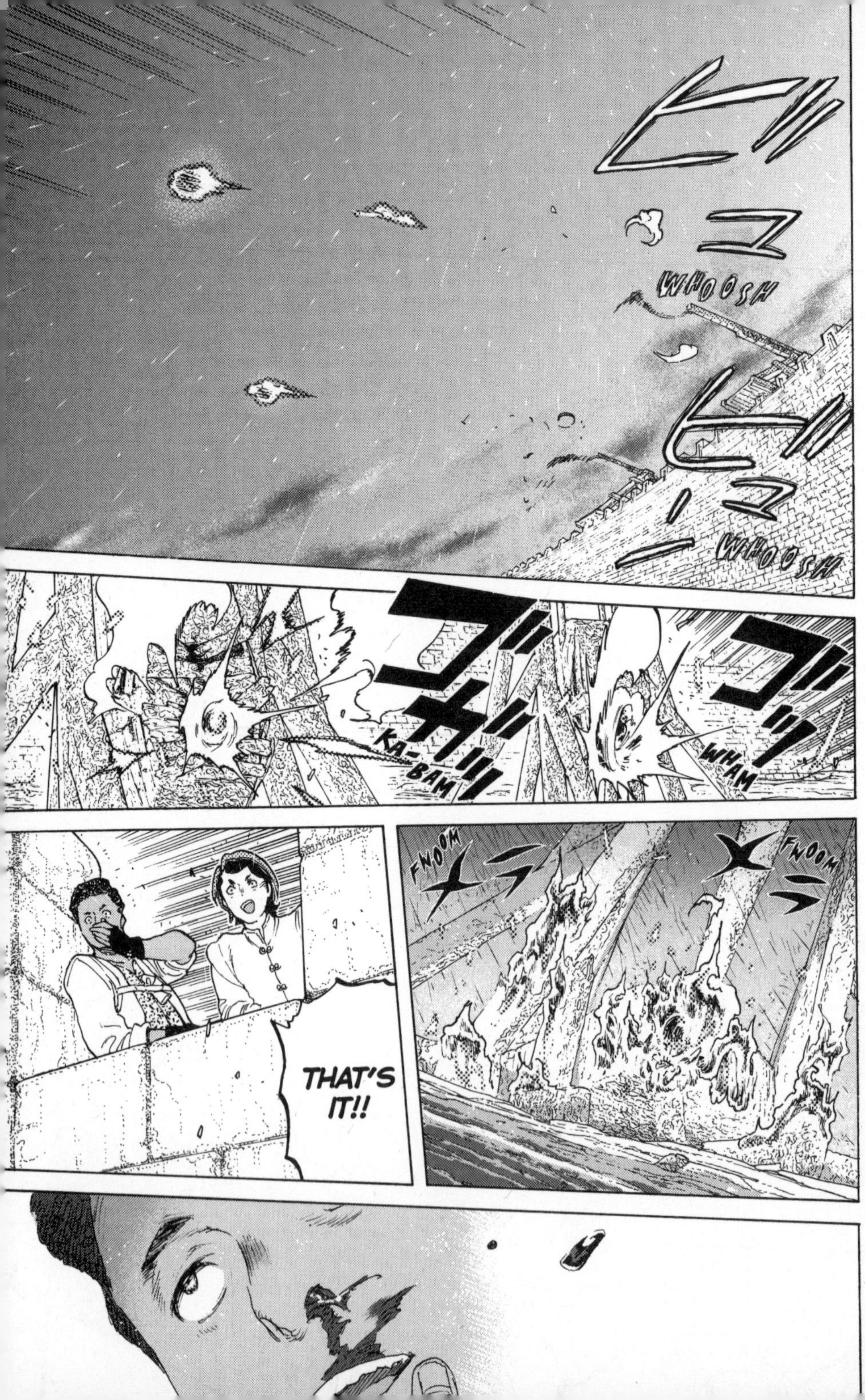
WHOOSH
WHOOSH
WHAM
KA-BAM
FWOOM
FWOOM
THAT'S IT!!

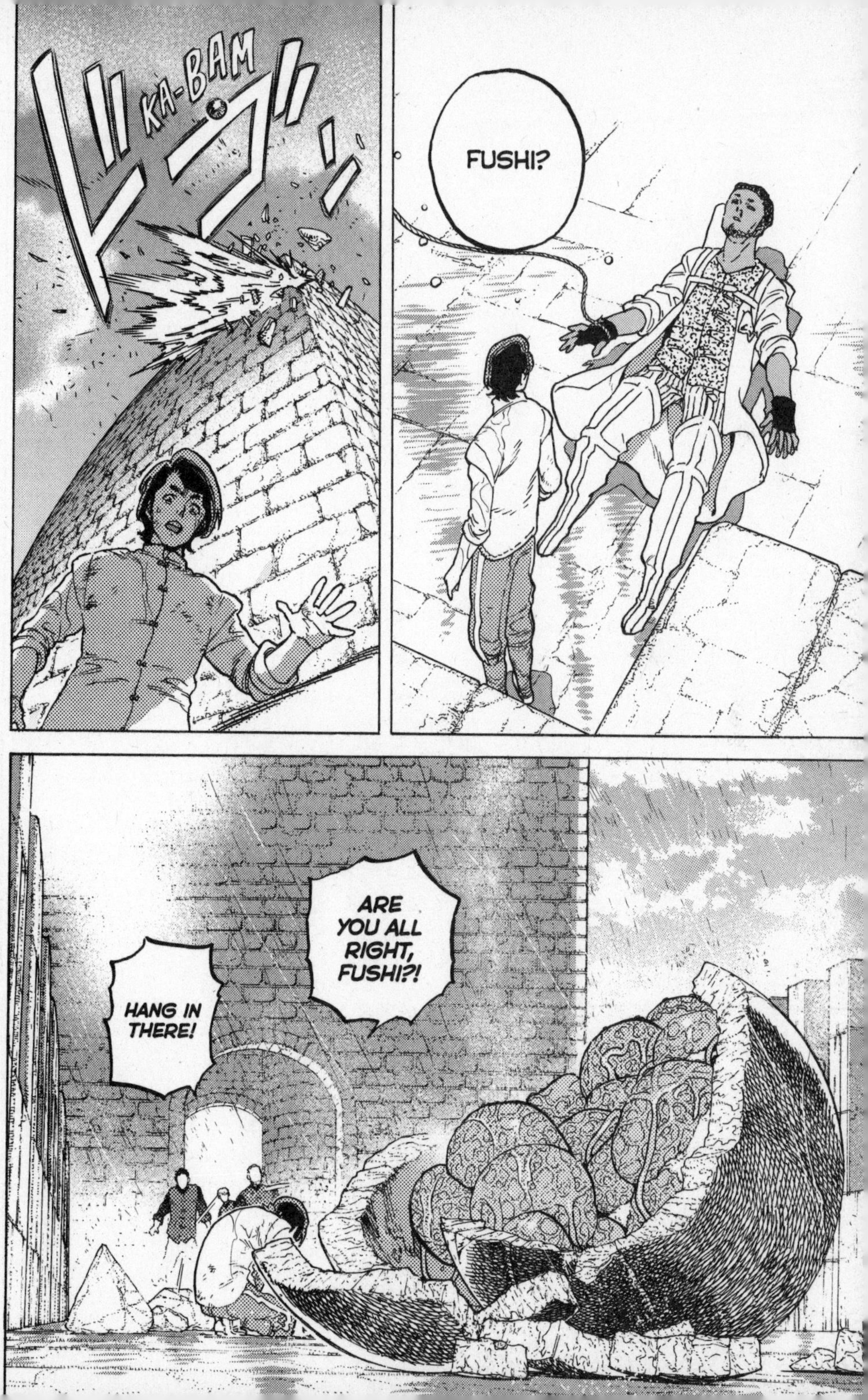
FUSHI?
KA-BAM
ARE YOU ALL RIGHT, FUSHI?!
HANG IN THERE!

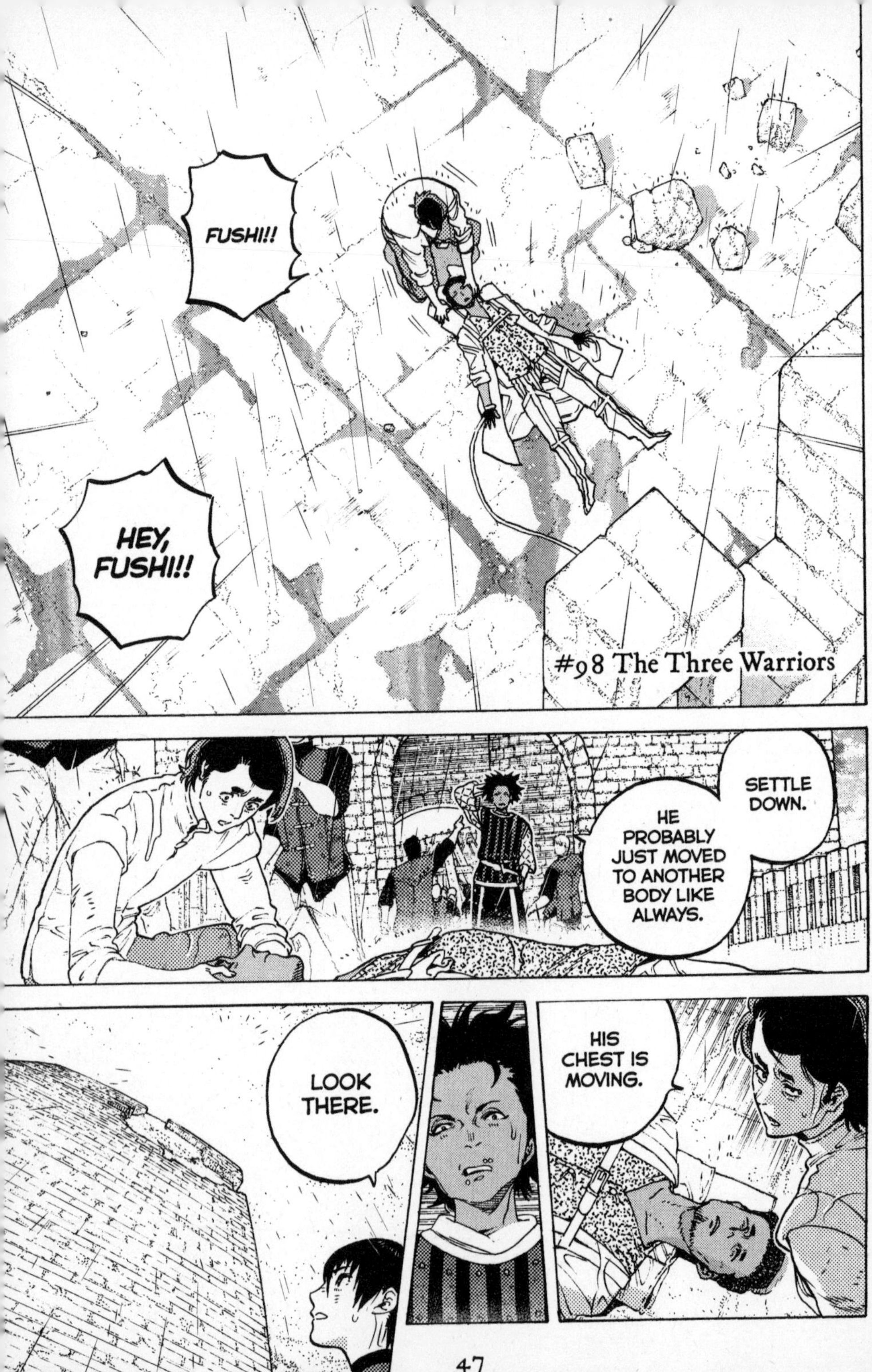
FUSHI!!
HEY, FUSHI!!
#98 The Three Warriors
SETTLE DOWN.
HE PROBABLY JUST MOVED TO ANOTHER BODY LIKE ALWAYS.
HIS CHEST IS MOVING.
LOOK THERE.

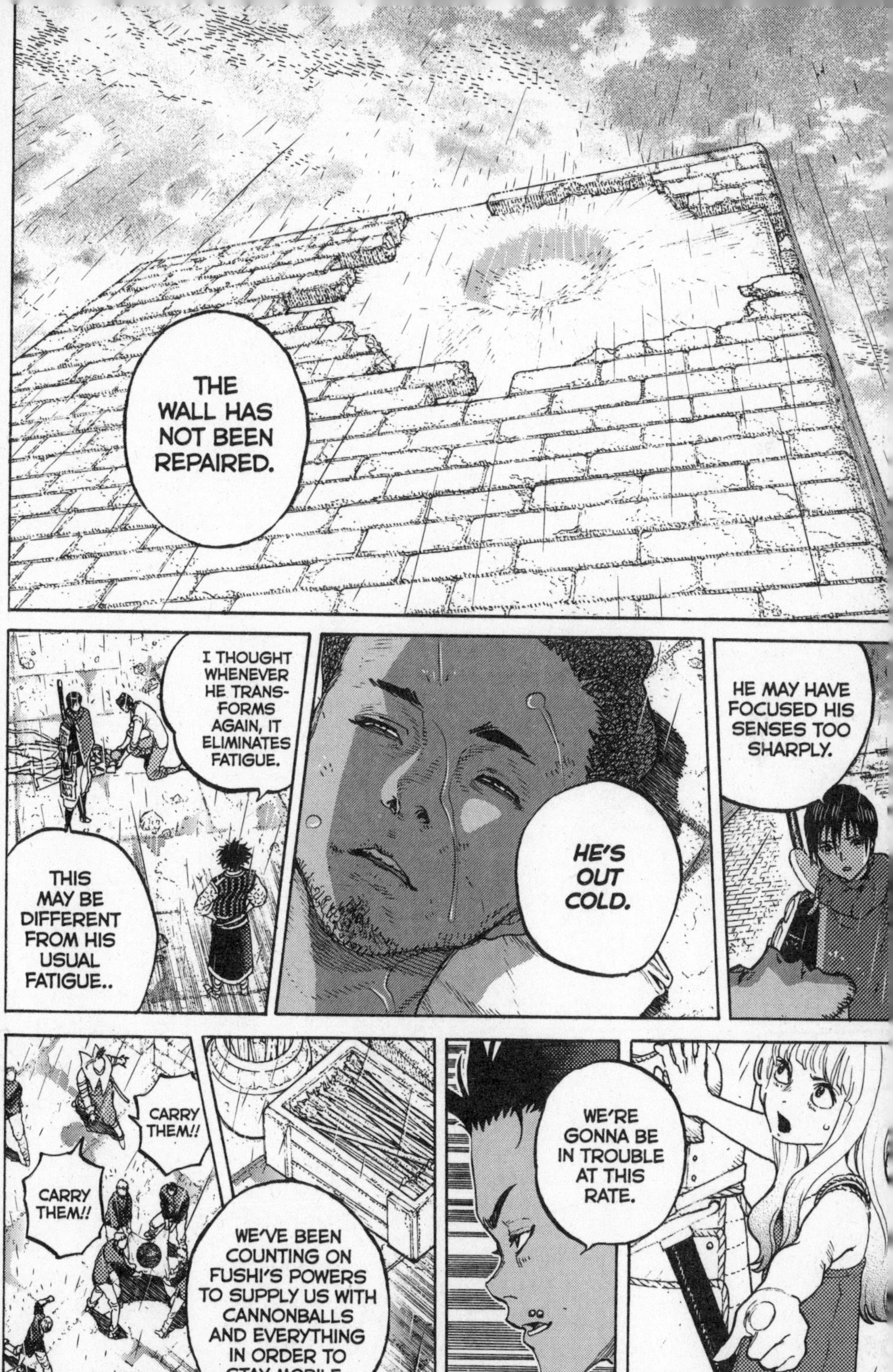
THE WALL HAS NOT BEEN REPAIRED.
HE MAY HAVE FOCUSED HIS SENSES TOO SHARPLY.
HE'S OUT COLD.
I THOUGHT WHENEVER HE TRANS-FORMS AGAIN, IT ELIMINATES FATIGUE.
THIS MAY BE DIFFERENT FROM HIS USUAL FATIGUE..
WE'RE GONNA BE IN TROUBLE AT THIS RATE.
WE'VE BEEN COUNTING ON FUSHI'S POWERS TO SUPPLY US WITH CANNONBALLS AND EVERYTHING IN ORDER TO STAY MOBILE.
CARRY THEM!!
CARRY THEM!!

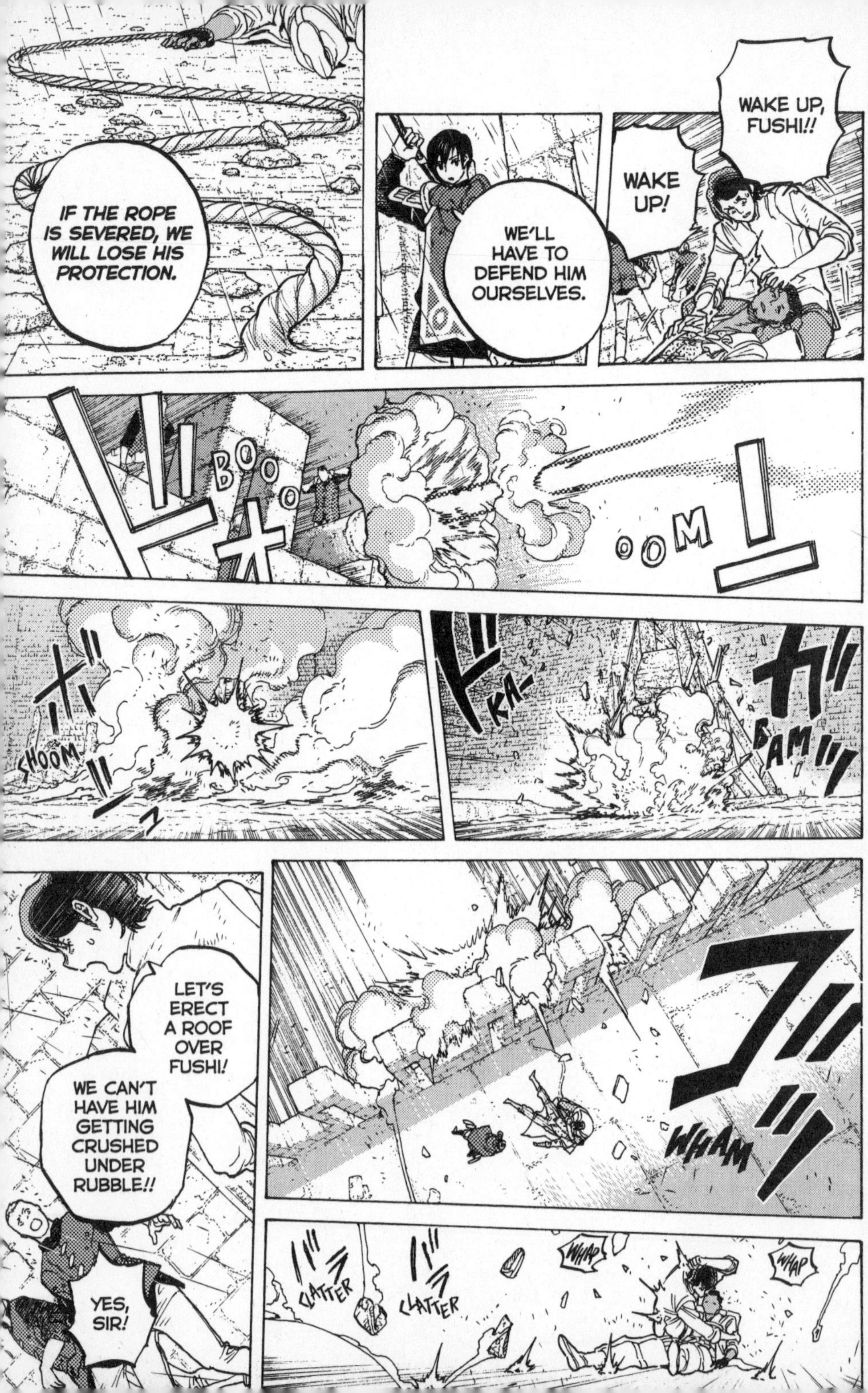
WAKE UP, FUSHI!!
WAKE UP!
WE'LL HAVE TO DEFEND HIM OURSELVES.
IF THE ROPE IS SEVERED, WE WILL LOSE HIS PROTECTION.
BOOOOOM!
KA-BAM!!
SHOOM
WHAM
WHAP
WHAP
CLATTER
CLATTER
LET'S ERECT A ROOF OVER FUSHI!
WE CAN'T HAVE HIM GETTING CRUSHED UNDER RUBBLE!!
YES, SIR!

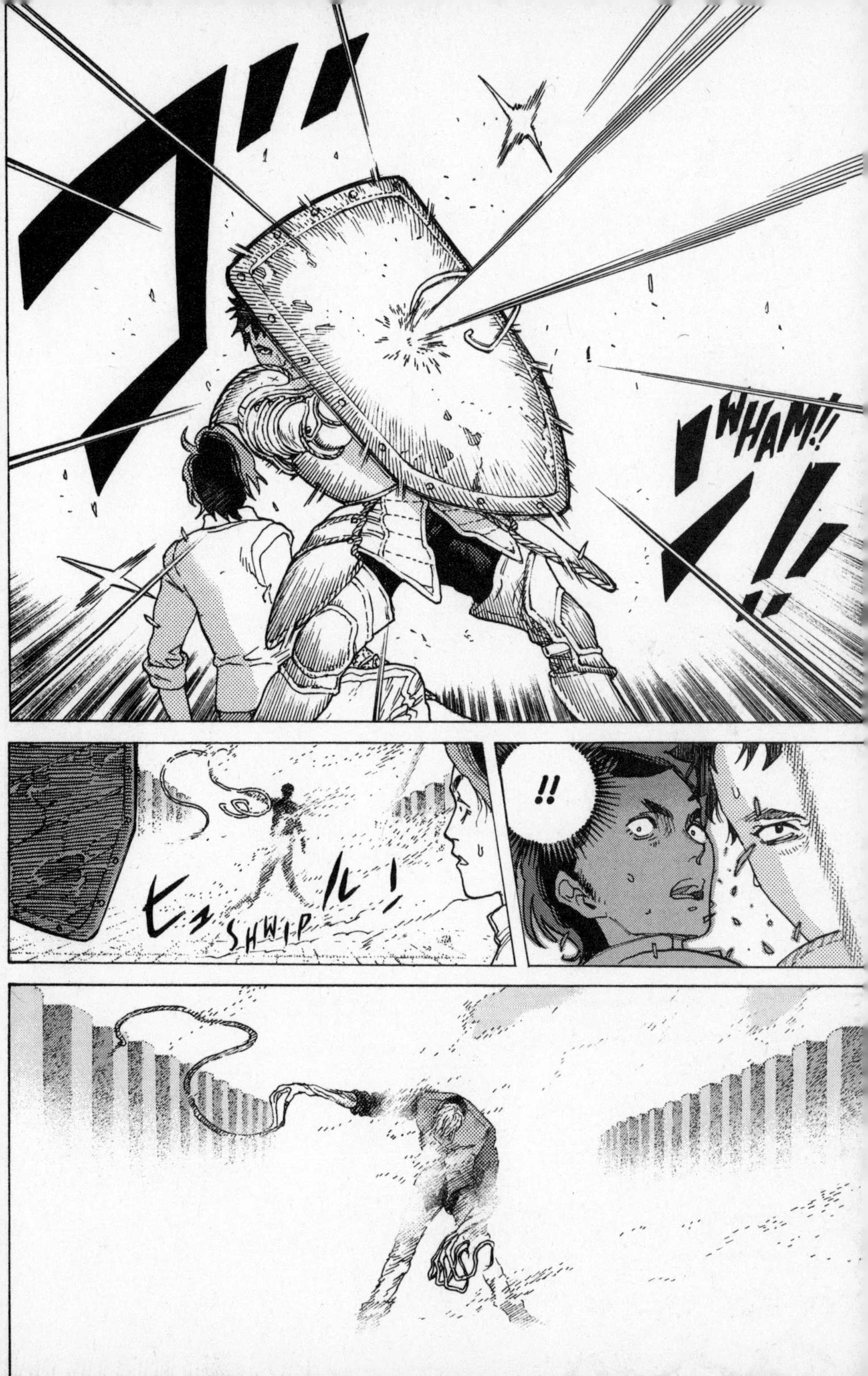
WHAM!!
!!
SHWIP

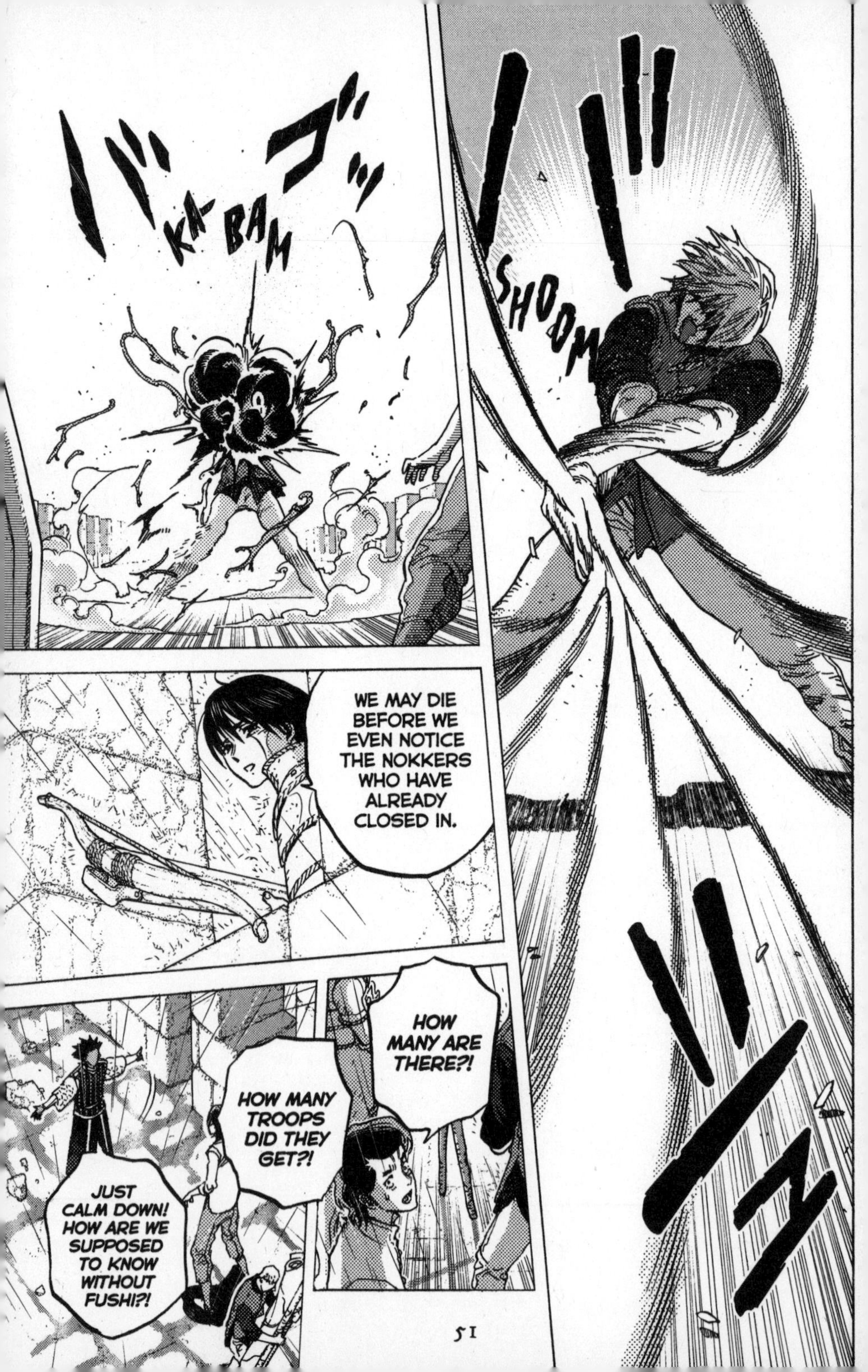
SHOOM
KA-BAM
WE MAY DIE BEFORE WE EVEN NOTICE THE NOKKERS WHO HAVE ALREADY CLOSED IN.
HOW MANY ARE THERE?!
HOW MANY TROOPS DID THEY GET?!
JUST CALM DOWN! HOW ARE WE SUPPOSED TO KNOW WITHOUT FUSHI?!

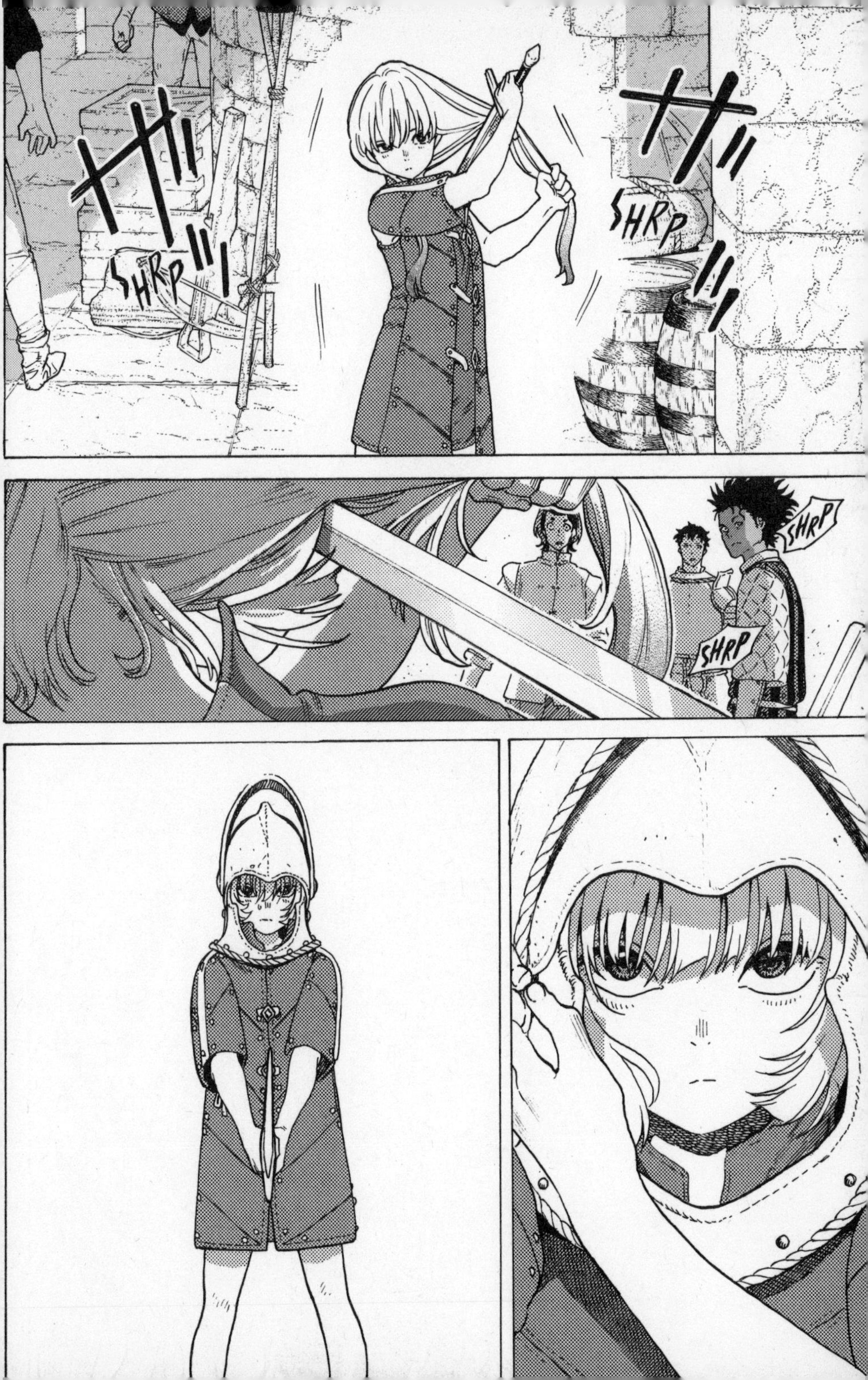
SHRP
SHRP
SHRP
SHRP

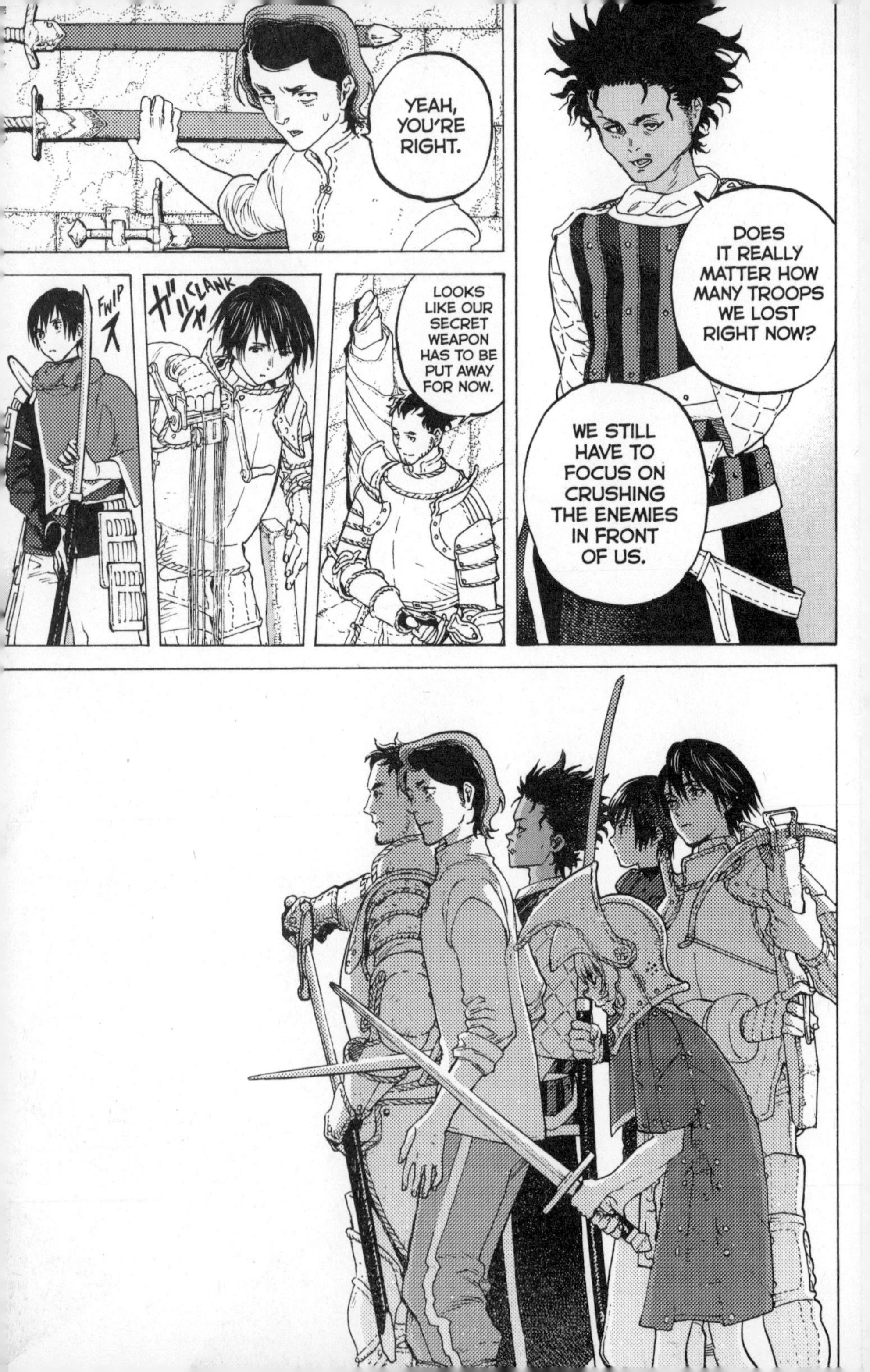
DOES IT REALLY MATTER HOW MANY TROOPS WE LOST RIGHT NOW?
WE STILL HAVE TO FOCUS ON CRUSHING THE ENEMIES IN FRONT OF US.
YEAH, YOU'RE RIGHT.
LOOKS LIKE OUR SECRET WEAPON HAS TO BE PUT AWAY FOR NOW.
CLANK
FWIP

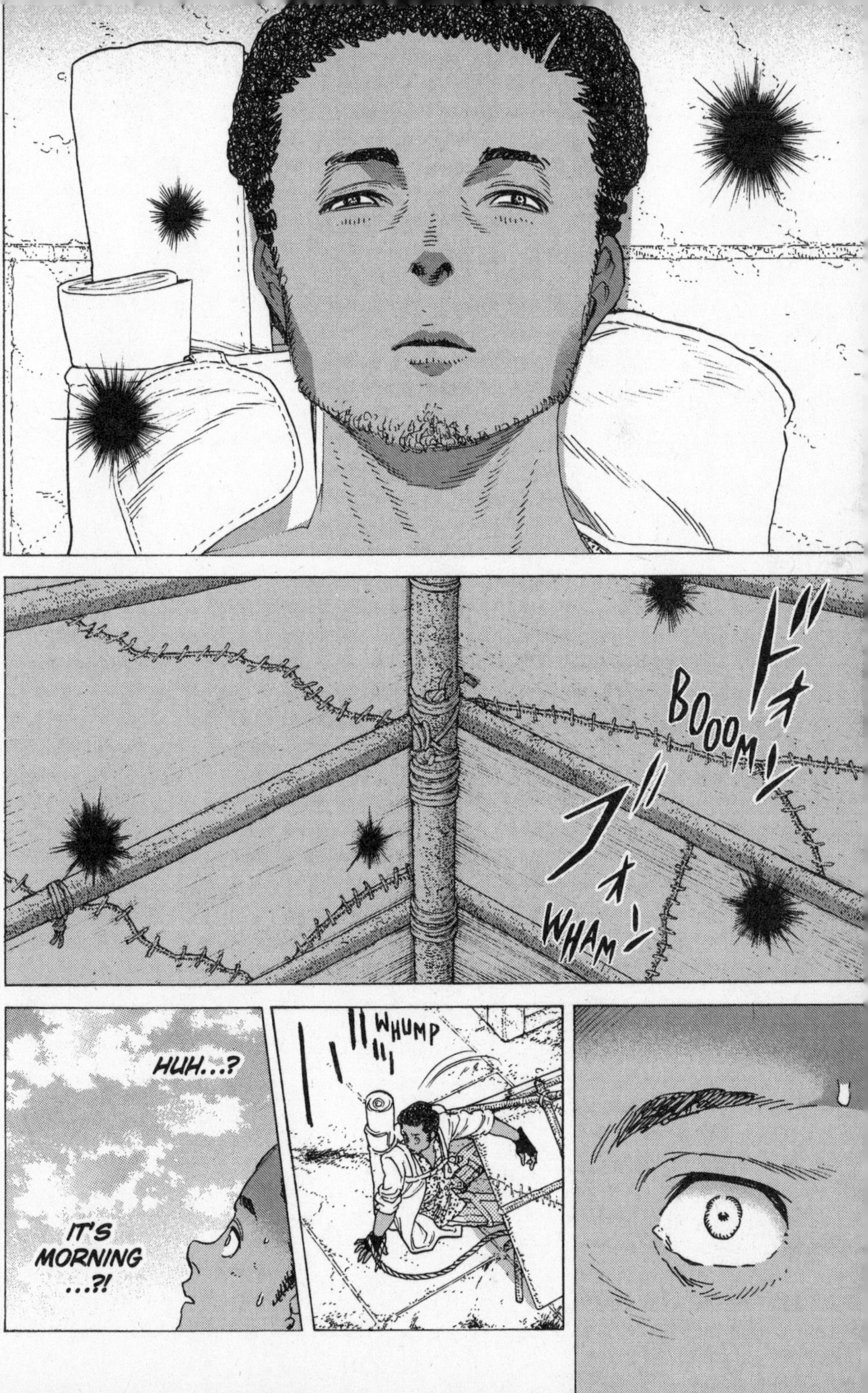
ドォン
BOOOM
ブォン
WHAM
WHUMP
HUH...?
IT'S MORNING ...?!

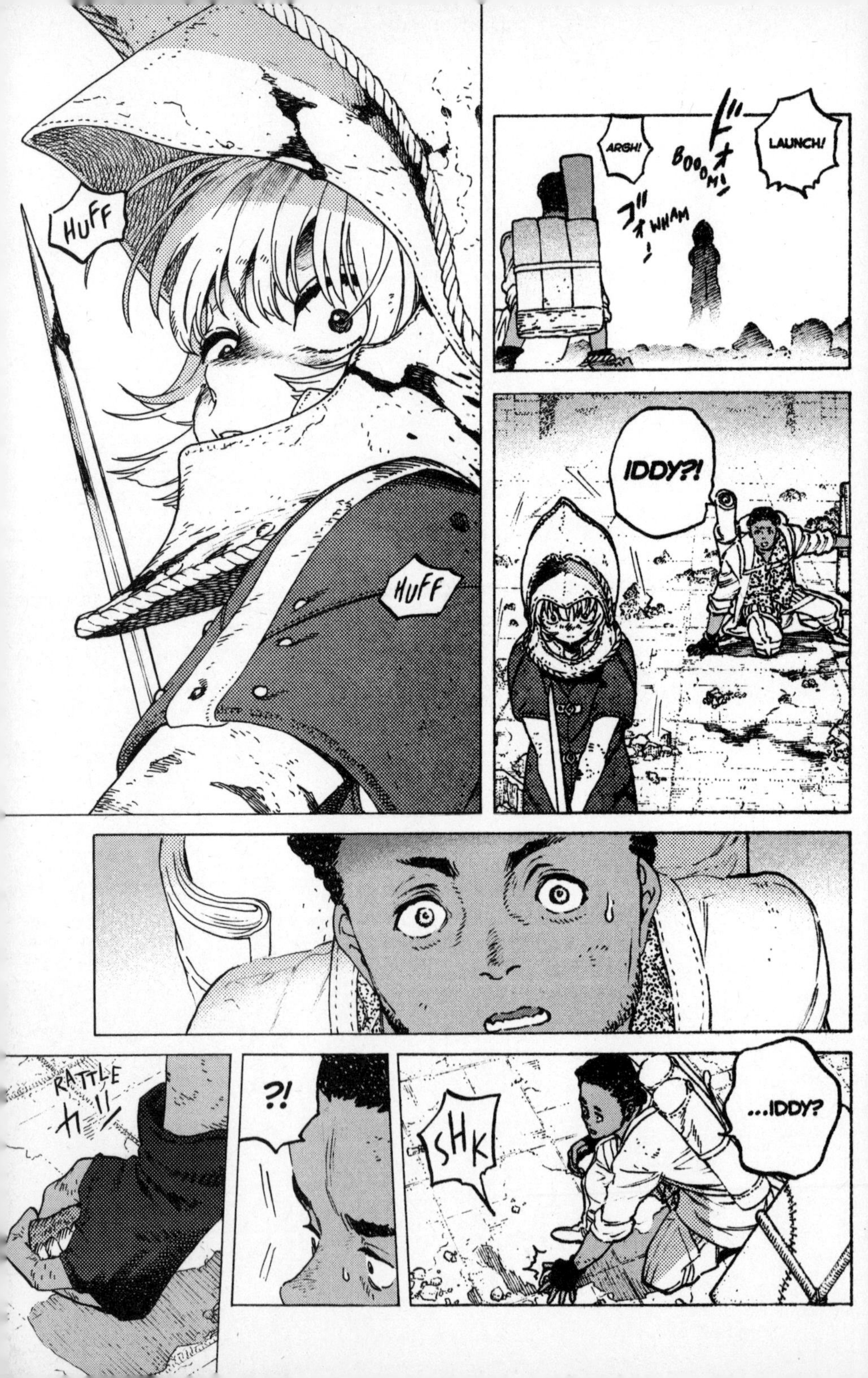
LAUNCH!
BOOOM!
ARGH!
WHAM
IDDY?!
HUFF
HUFF
...IDDY?
SHK
?!
RATTLE

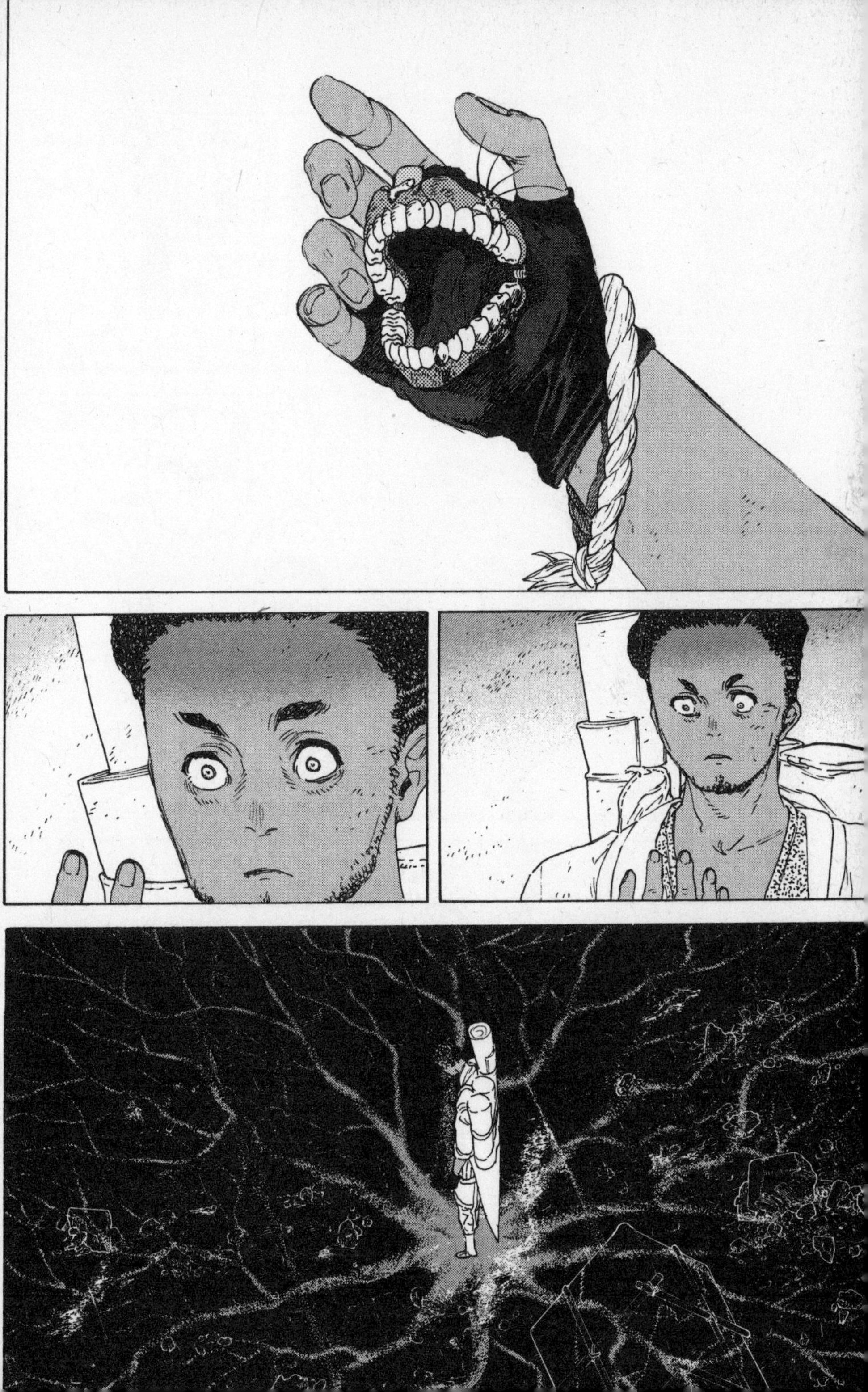

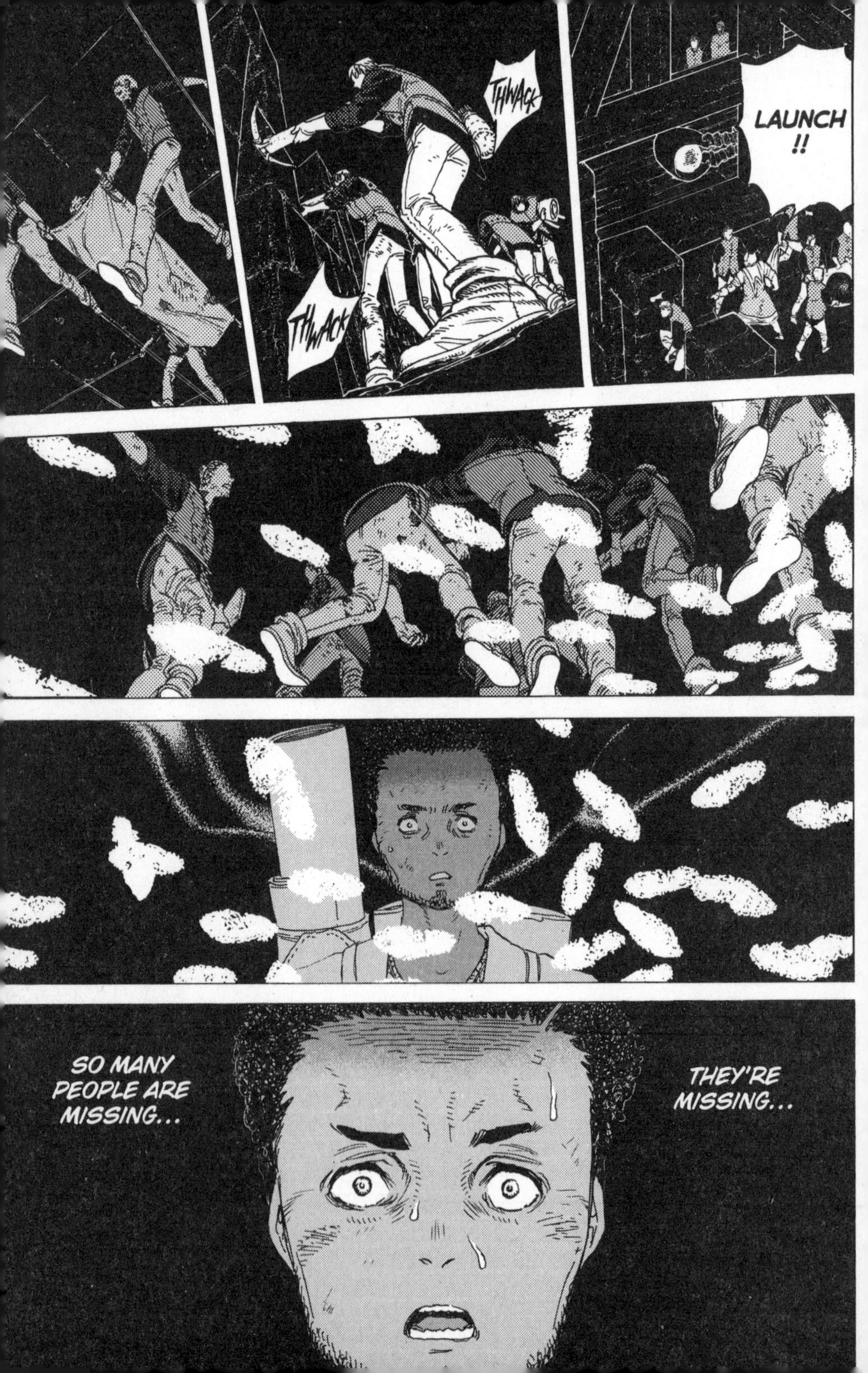
LAUNCH !!
THWACK
THWACK
THEY'RE MISSING...
SO MANY PEOPLE ARE MISSING...

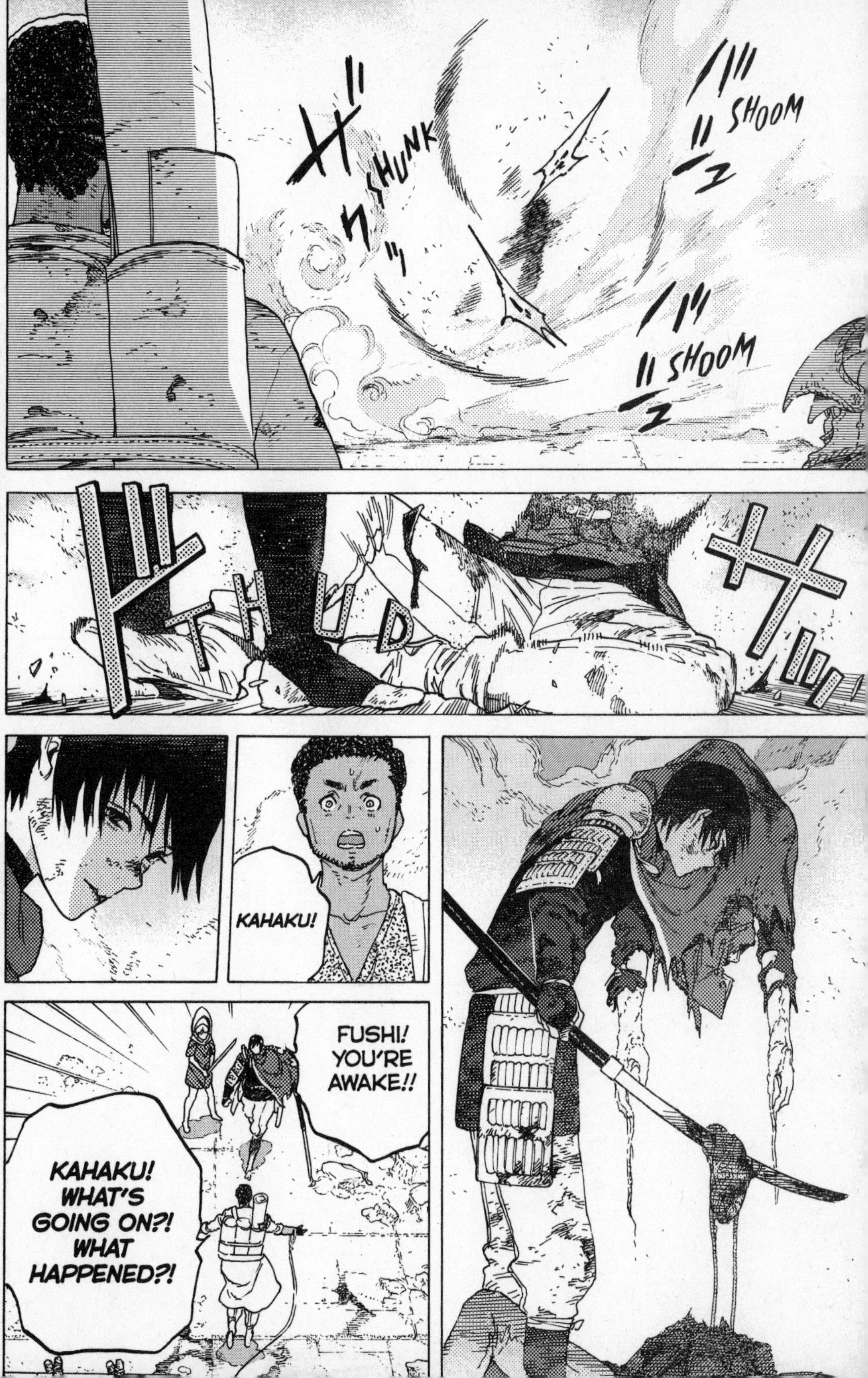
SHOOM
SHUNK
SHOOM
THUD
KAHAKU!
FUSHI! YOU'RE AWAKE!!
KAHAKU! WHAT'S GOING ON?! WHAT HAPPENED?!

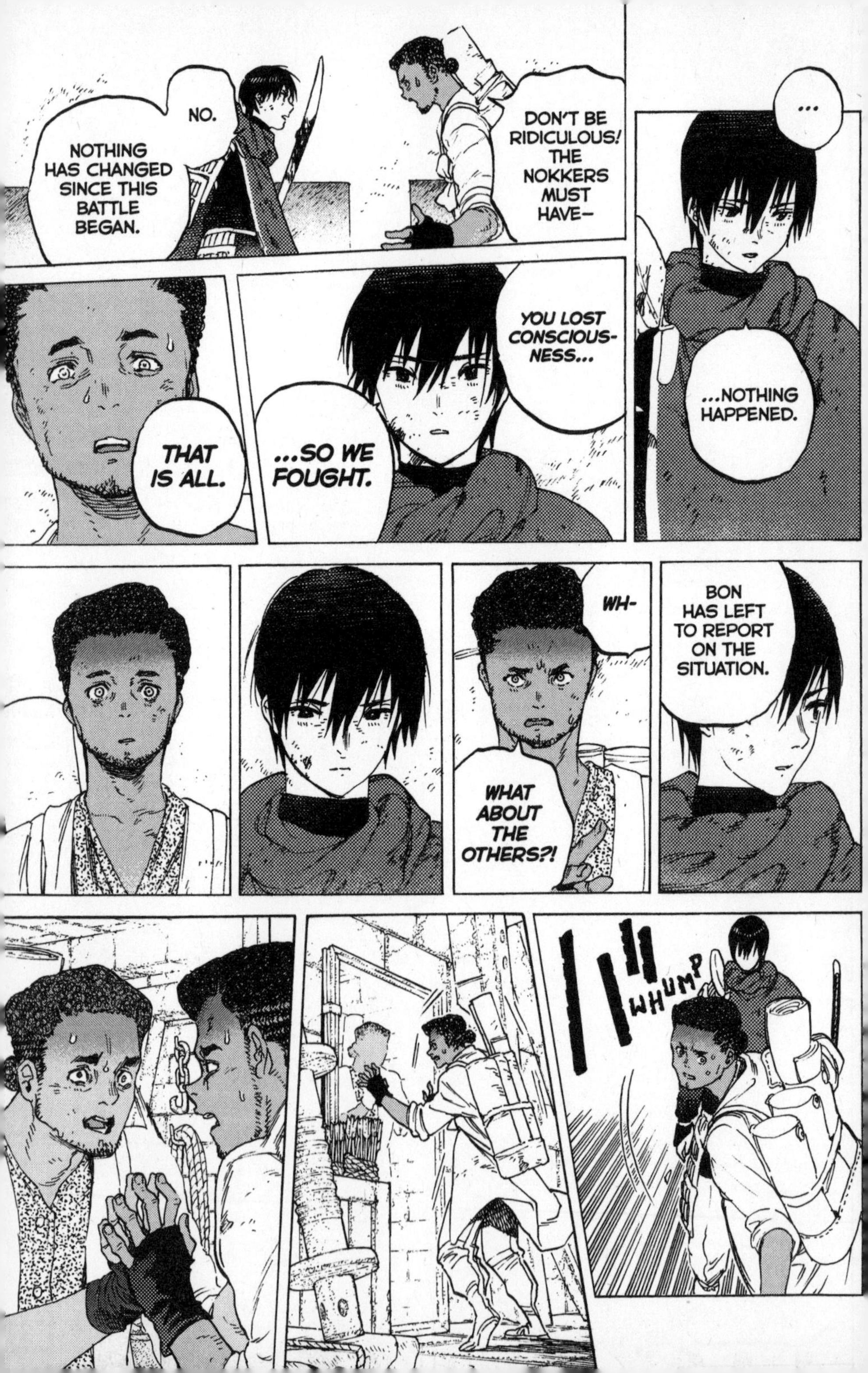
...
...NOTHING HAPPENED.
DON'T BE RIDICULOUS! THE NOKKERS MUST HAVE—
NO.
NOTHING HAS CHANGED SINCE THIS BATTLE BEGAN.
YOU LOST CONSCIOUSNESS...
...SO WE FOUGHT.
THAT IS ALL.
BON HAS LEFT TO REPORT ON THE SITUATION.
WH-
WHAT ABOUT THE OTHERS?!
WHUMP

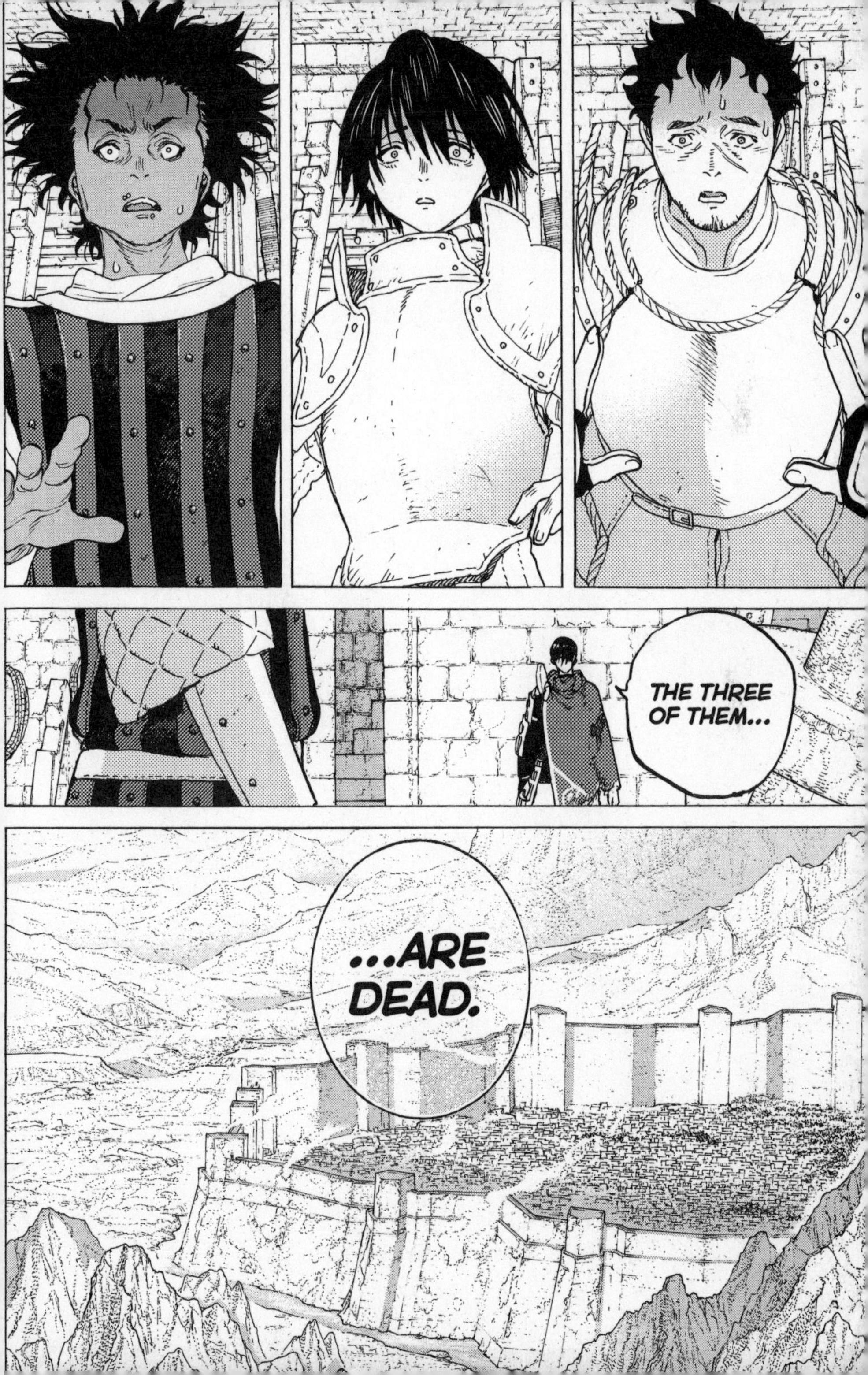
THE THREE OF THEM...
...ARE DEAD.

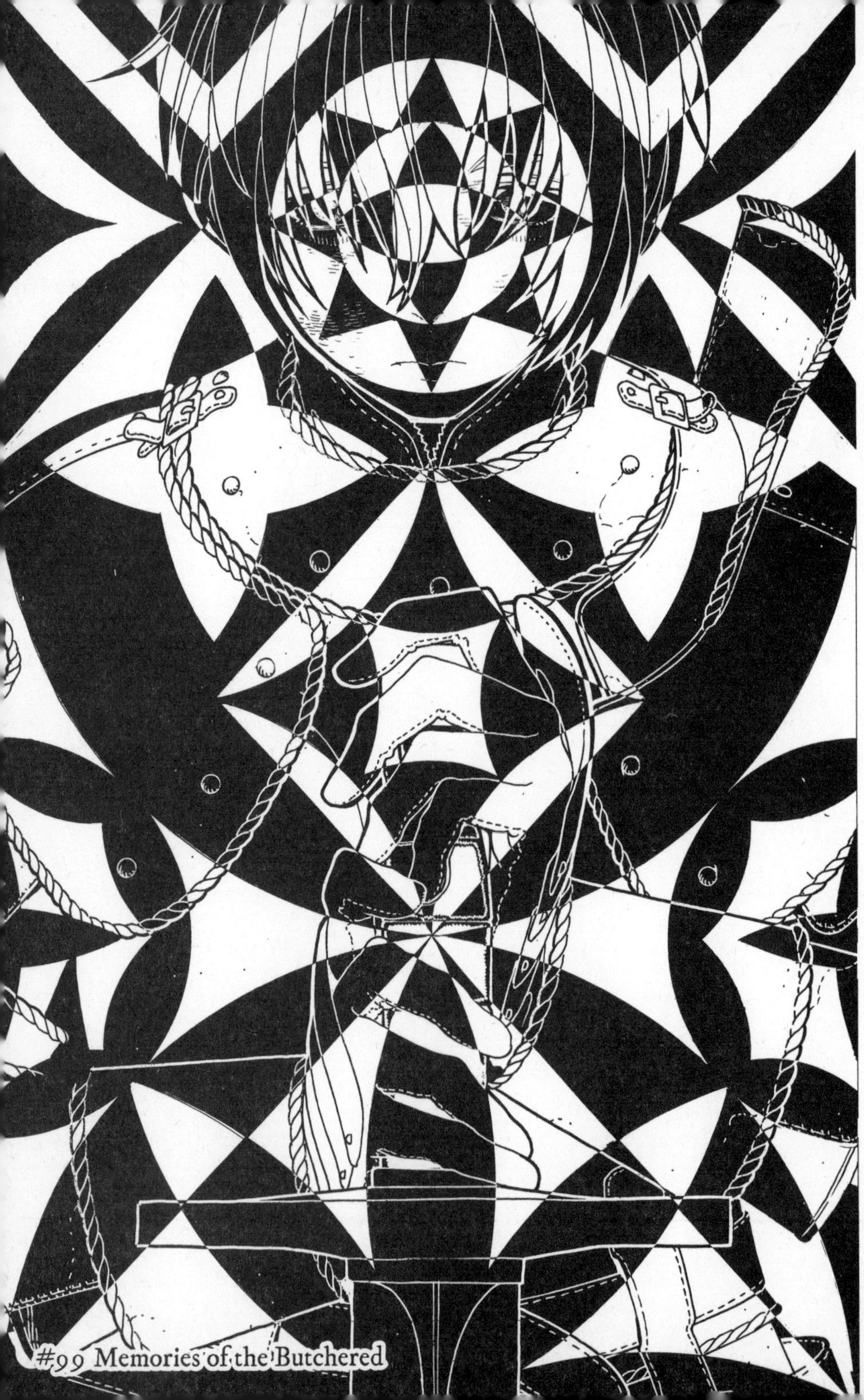

#99 Memories of the Butchered

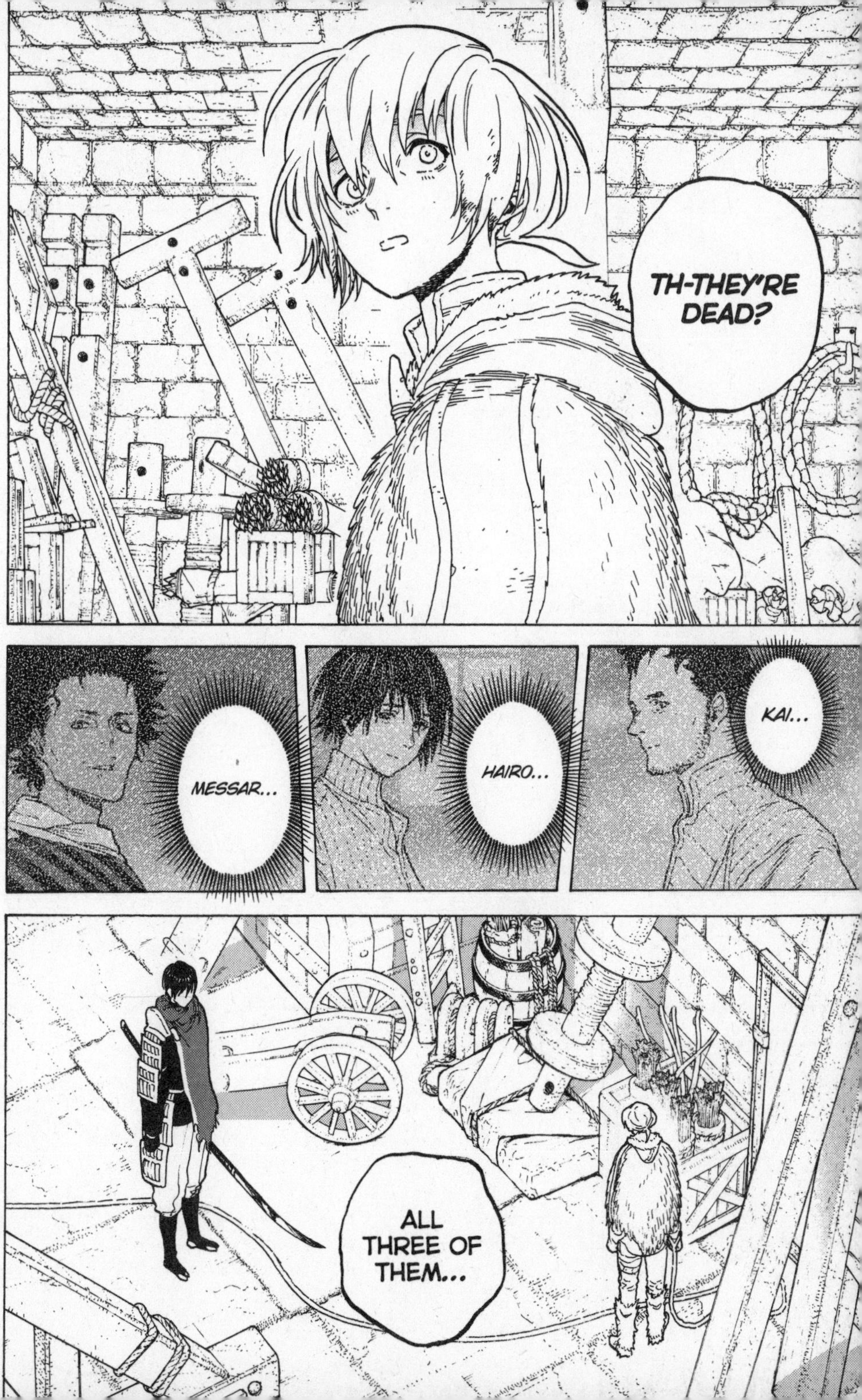
TH-THEY'RE DEAD?
KAI...
HAIRO...
MESSAR...
ALL THREE OF THEM...

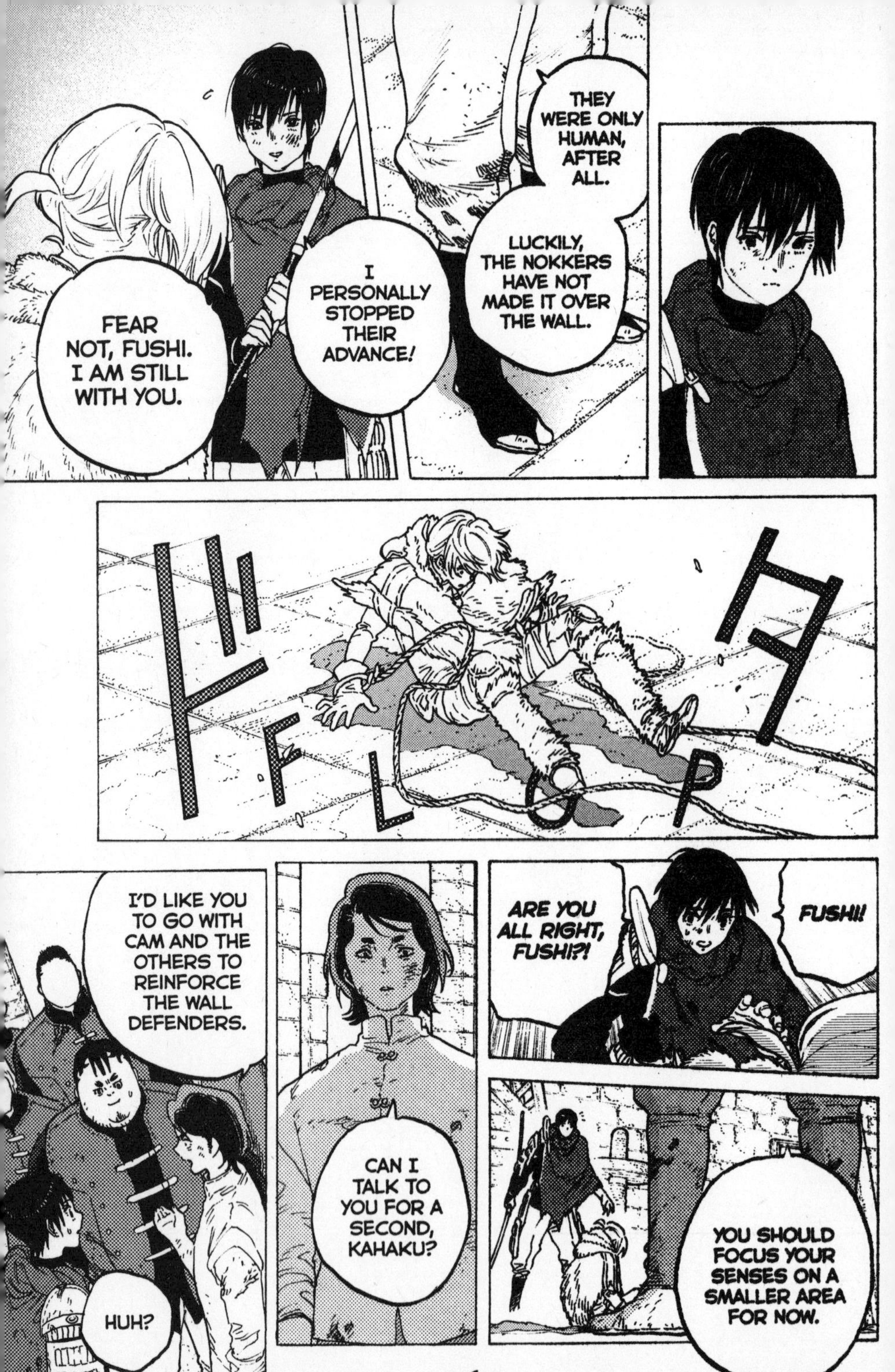

THEY WERE ONLY HUMAN, AFTER ALL.
LUCKILY, THE NOKKERS HAVE NOT MADE IT OVER THE WALL.
I PERSONALLY STOPPED THEIR ADVANCE!
FEAR NOT, FUSHI. I AM STILL WITH YOU.
ドタ
FLOP
FUSHI!!
ARE YOU ALL RIGHT, FUSHI!?!
YOU SHOULD FOCUS YOUR SENSES ON A SMALLER AREA FOR NOW.
CAN I TALK TO YOU FOR A SECOND, KAHAKU?
I'D LIKE YOU TO GO WITH CAM AND THE OTHERS TO REINFORCE THE WALL DEFENDERS.
HUH?

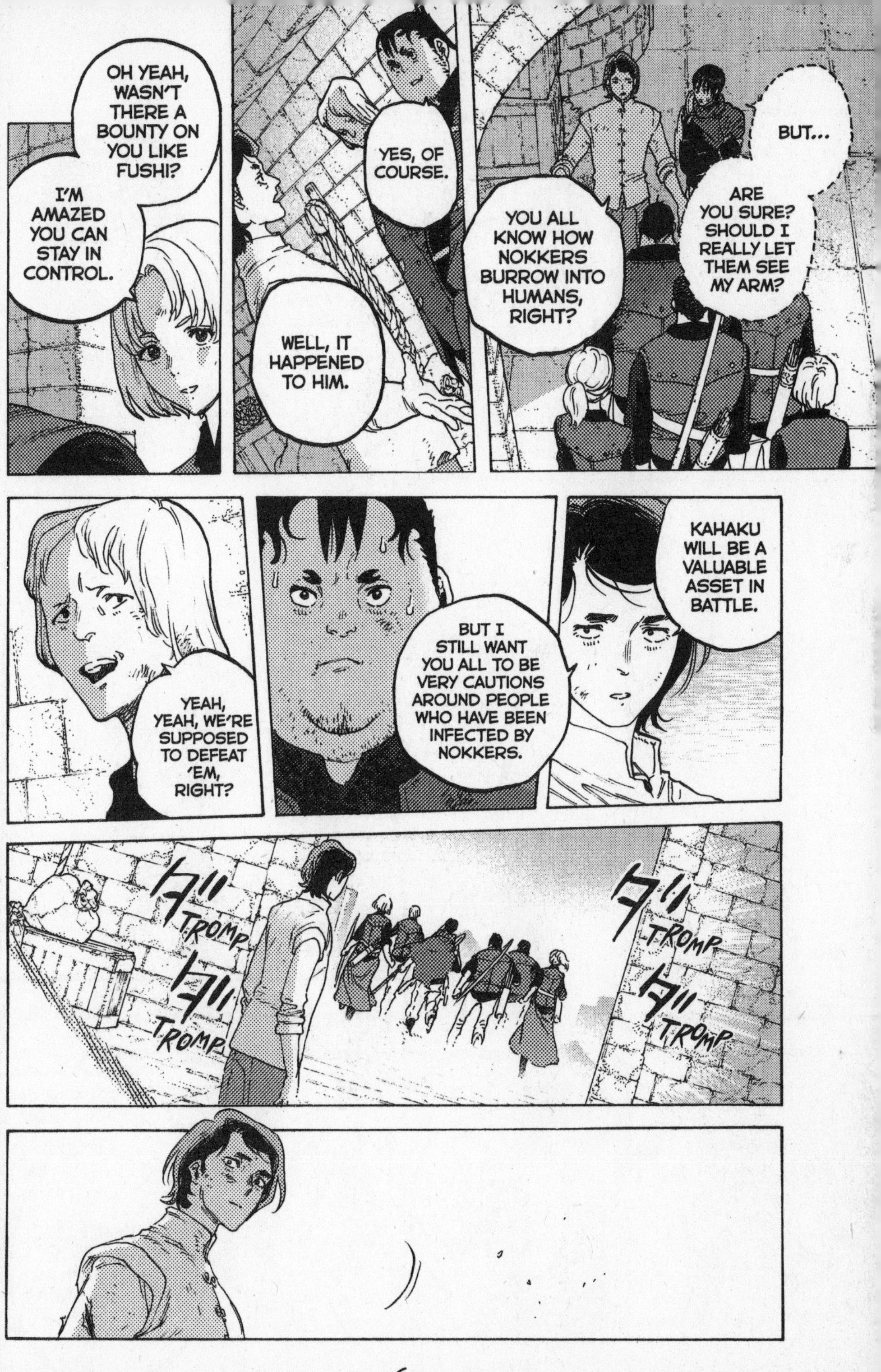
BUT...
ARE YOU SURE? SHOULD I REALLY LET THEM SEE MY ARM?
YOU ALL KNOW HOW NOKKERS BURROW INTO HUMANS, RIGHT?
YES, OF COURSE.
WELL, IT HAPPENED TO HIM.
OH YEAH, WASN'T THERE A BOUNTY ON YOU LIKE FUSHI?
I'M AMAZED YOU CAN STAY IN CONTROL.
KAHAKU WILL BE A VALUABLE ASSET IN BATTLE.
BUT I STILL WANT YOU ALL TO BE VERY CAUTIONS AROUND PEOPLE WHO HAVE BEEN INFECTED BY NOKKERS.
YEAH, YEAH, WE'RE SUPPOSED TO DEFEAT 'EM, RIGHT?
TROMP
TROMP
TROMP
TROMP

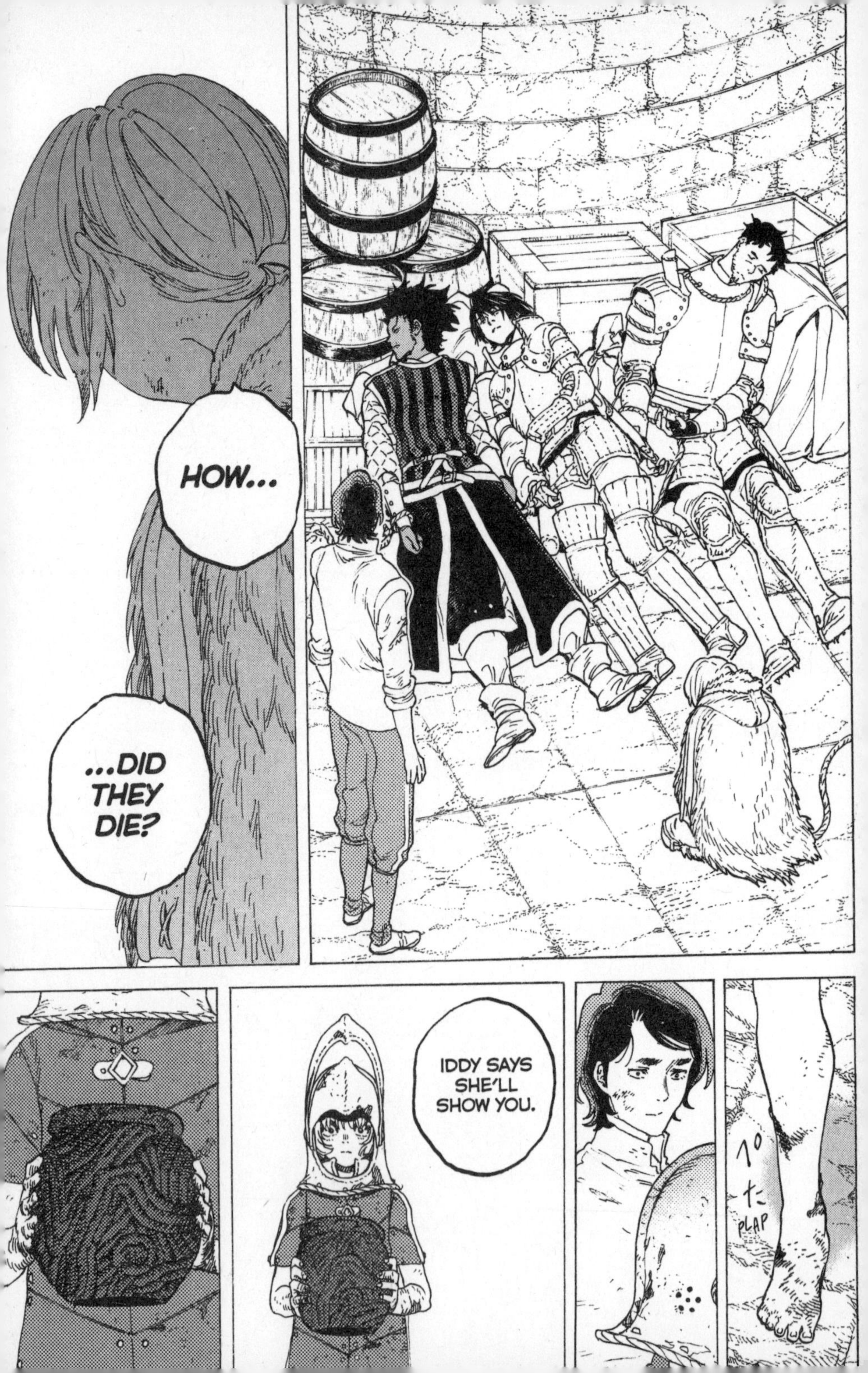
HOW...
...DID THEY DIE?
PLAP
IDDY SAYS SHE'LL SHOW YOU.

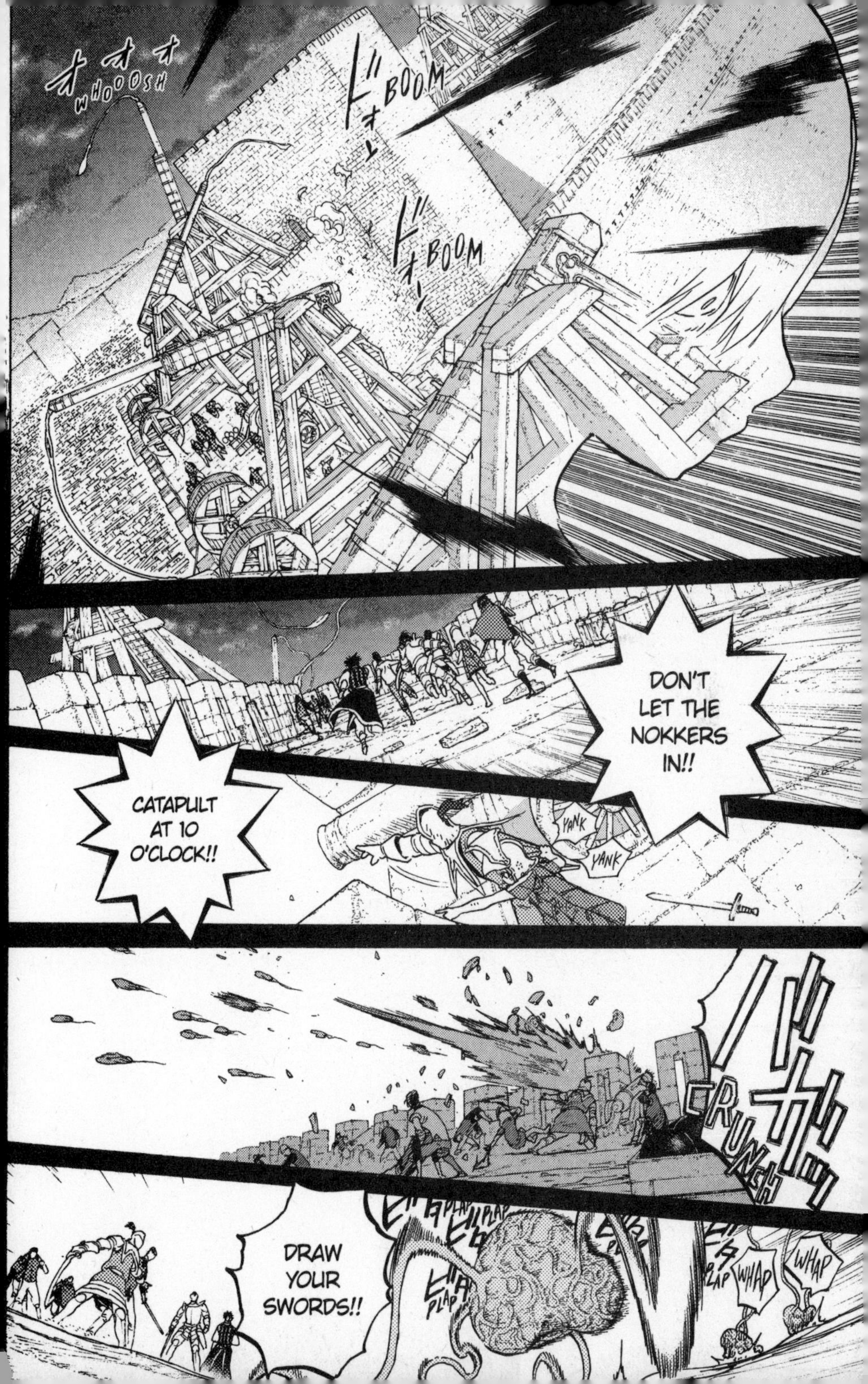
BOOM
BOOM
WHOOOSH
DON'T LET THE NOKKERS IN!!
YANK
YANK
CATAPULT AT 10 O'CLOCK!!
CRUNCH
WHAP
WHAP
PLAP
PLAP
PLAP
PLAP
DRAW YOUR SWORDS!!

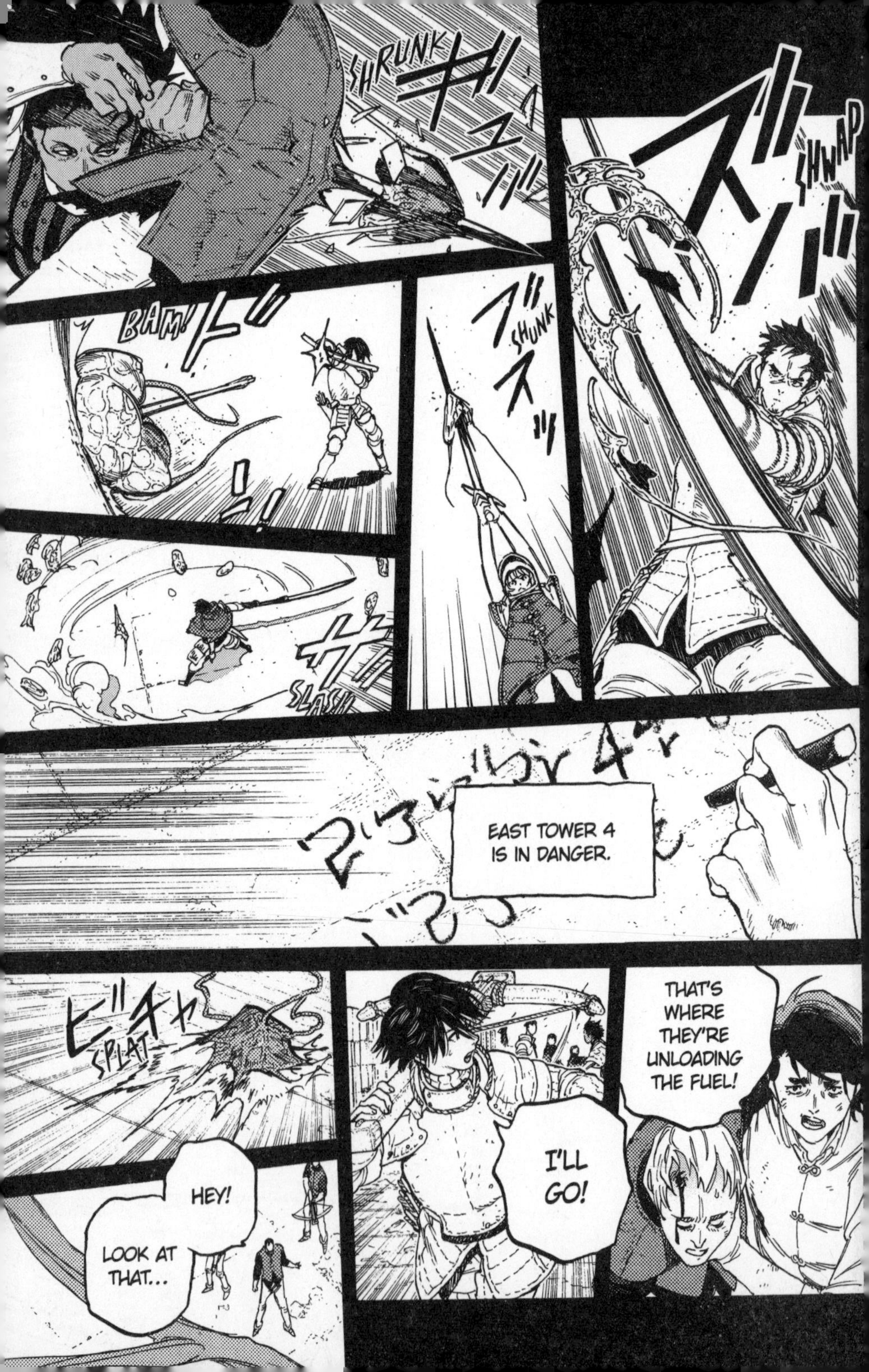
SHWAP
SHRUNK
SHUNK
BAM!
SLASH
EAST TOWER 4 IS IN DANGER.
THAT'S WHERE THEY'RE UNLOADING THE FUEL!
I'LL GO!
SPLAT
HEY!
LOOK AT THAT...

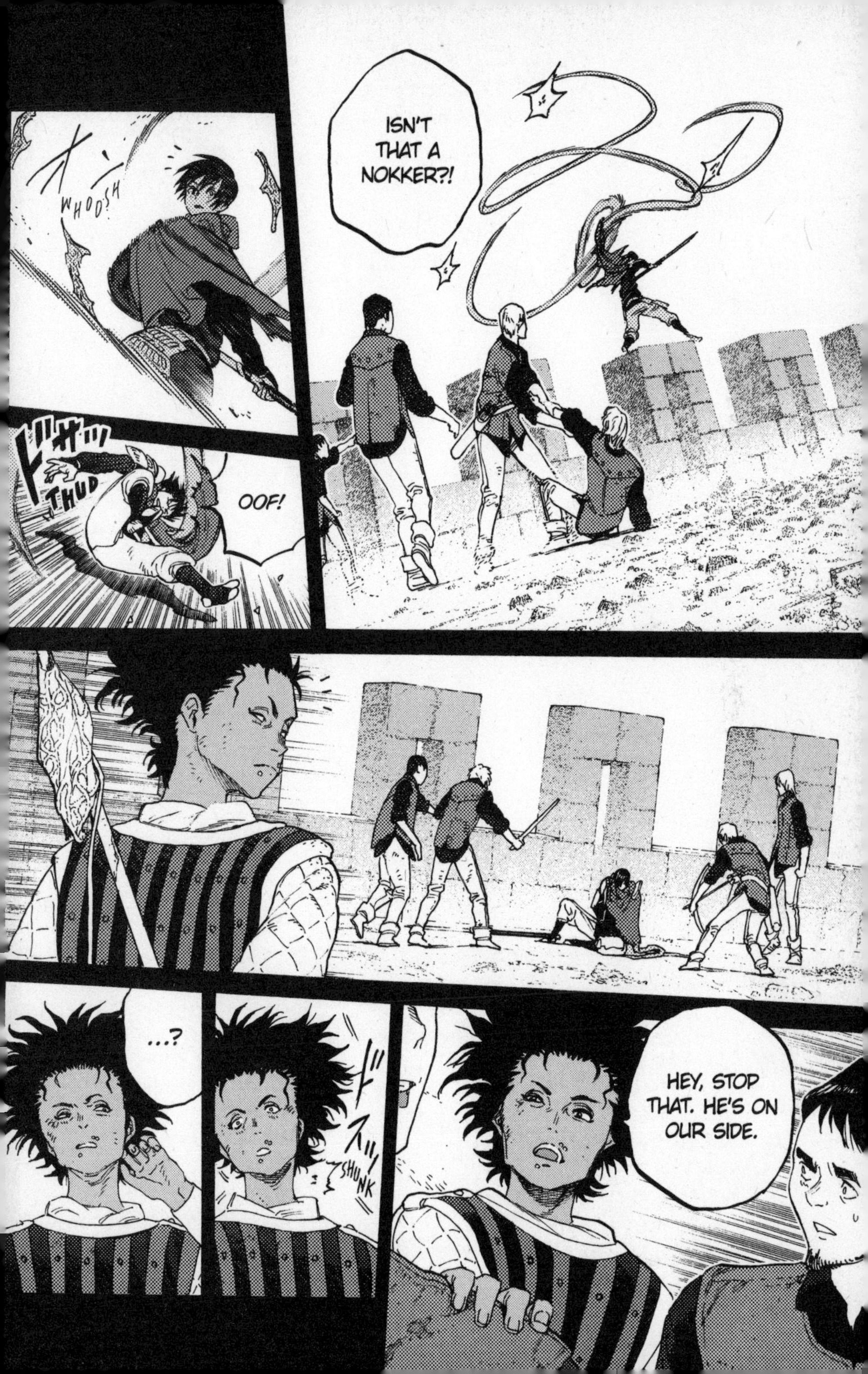
ISN'T THAT A NOKKER?!
WHOOSH
THUD
OOF!
HEY, STOP THAT. HE'S ON OUR SIDE.
SHUNK
...?

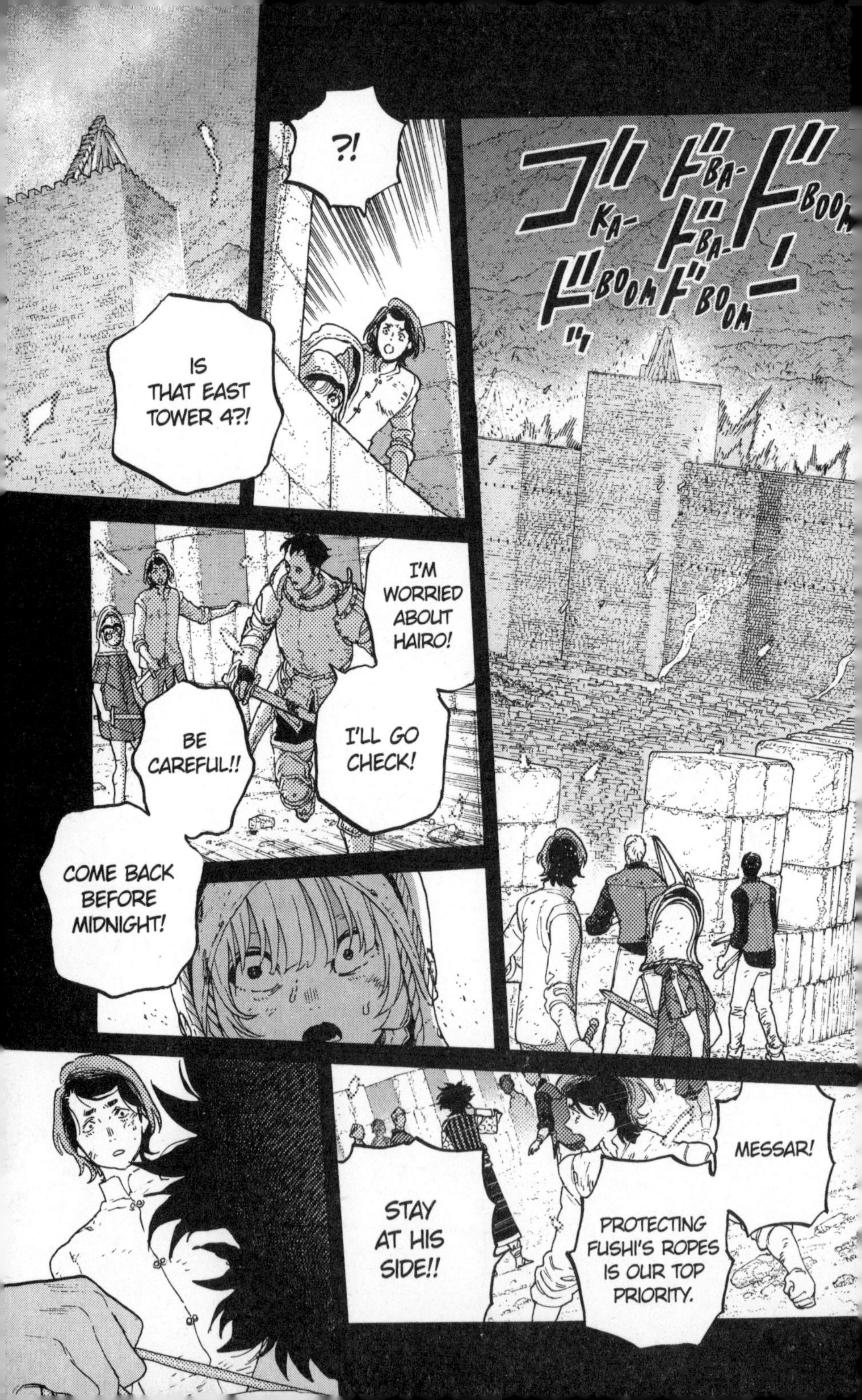
BOOM
BA-
BA-
KA-
BOOM
BOOM
BOOM
?!
IS THAT EAST TOWER 4?!
I'M WORRIED ABOUT HAIRO!
I'LL GO CHECK!
BE CAREFUL!!
COME BACK BEFORE MIDNIGHT!
MESSAR!
PROTECTING FUSHI'S ROPES IS OUR TOP PRIORITY.
STAY AT HIS SIDE!!

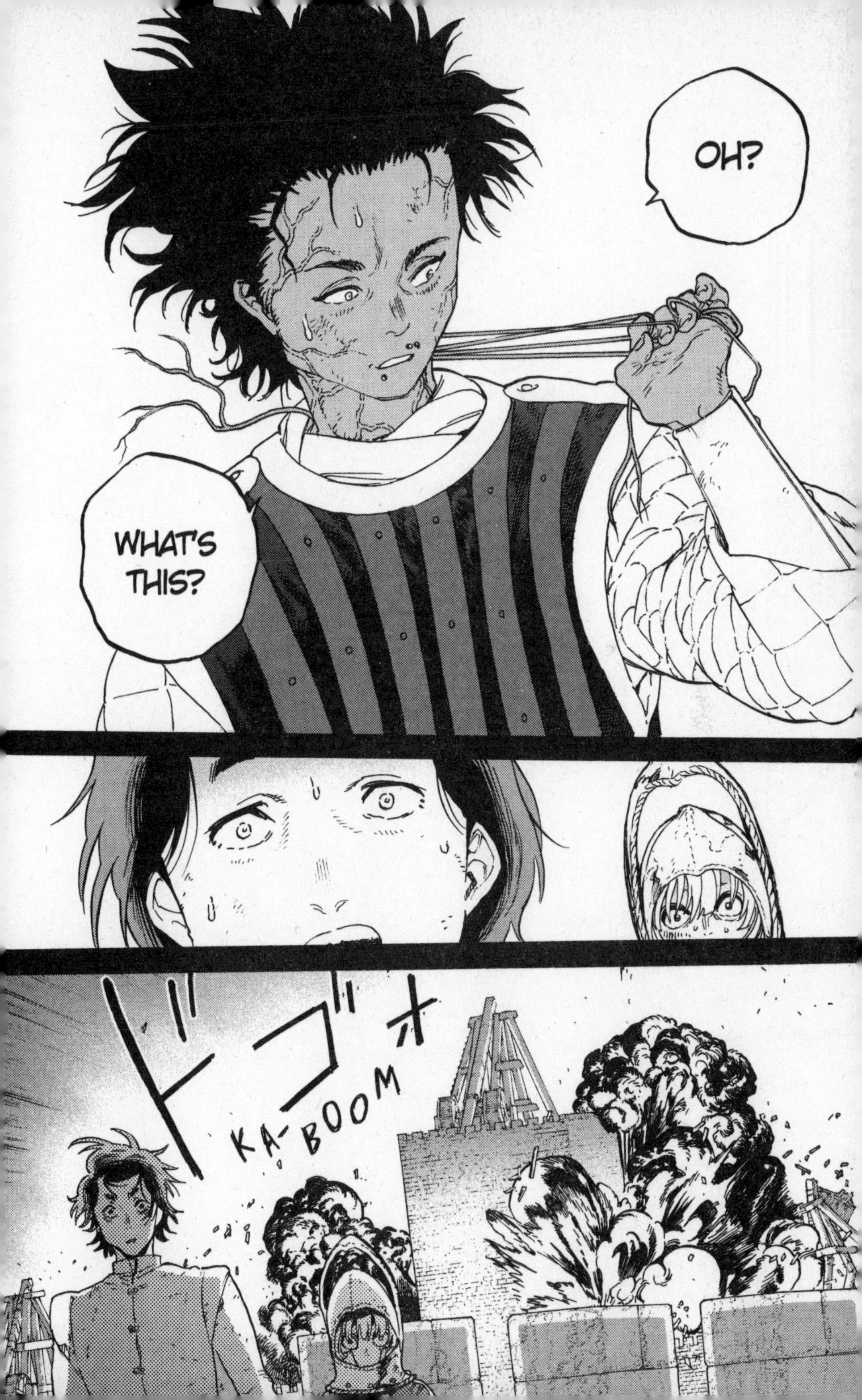
OH?
WHAT'S THIS?
ドゴォ
KA-BOOM

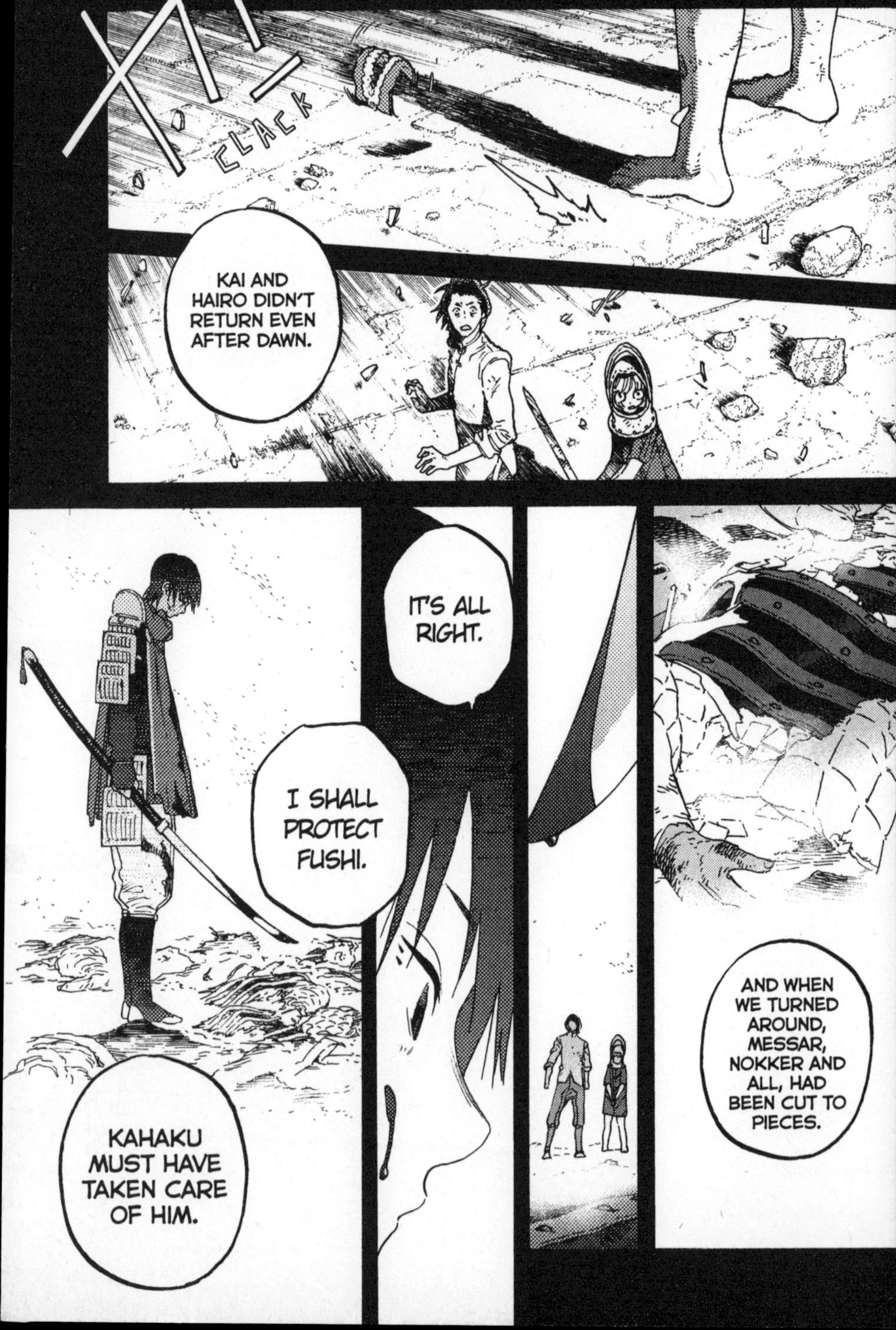
CLACK
KAI AND HAIRO DIDN'T RETURN EVEN AFTER DAWN.
AND WHEN WE TURNED AROUND, MESSAR, NOKKER AND ALL, HAD BEEN CUT TO PIECES.
IT'S ALL RIGHT.
I SHALL PROTECT FUSHI.
KAHAKU MUST HAVE TAKEN CARE OF HIM.

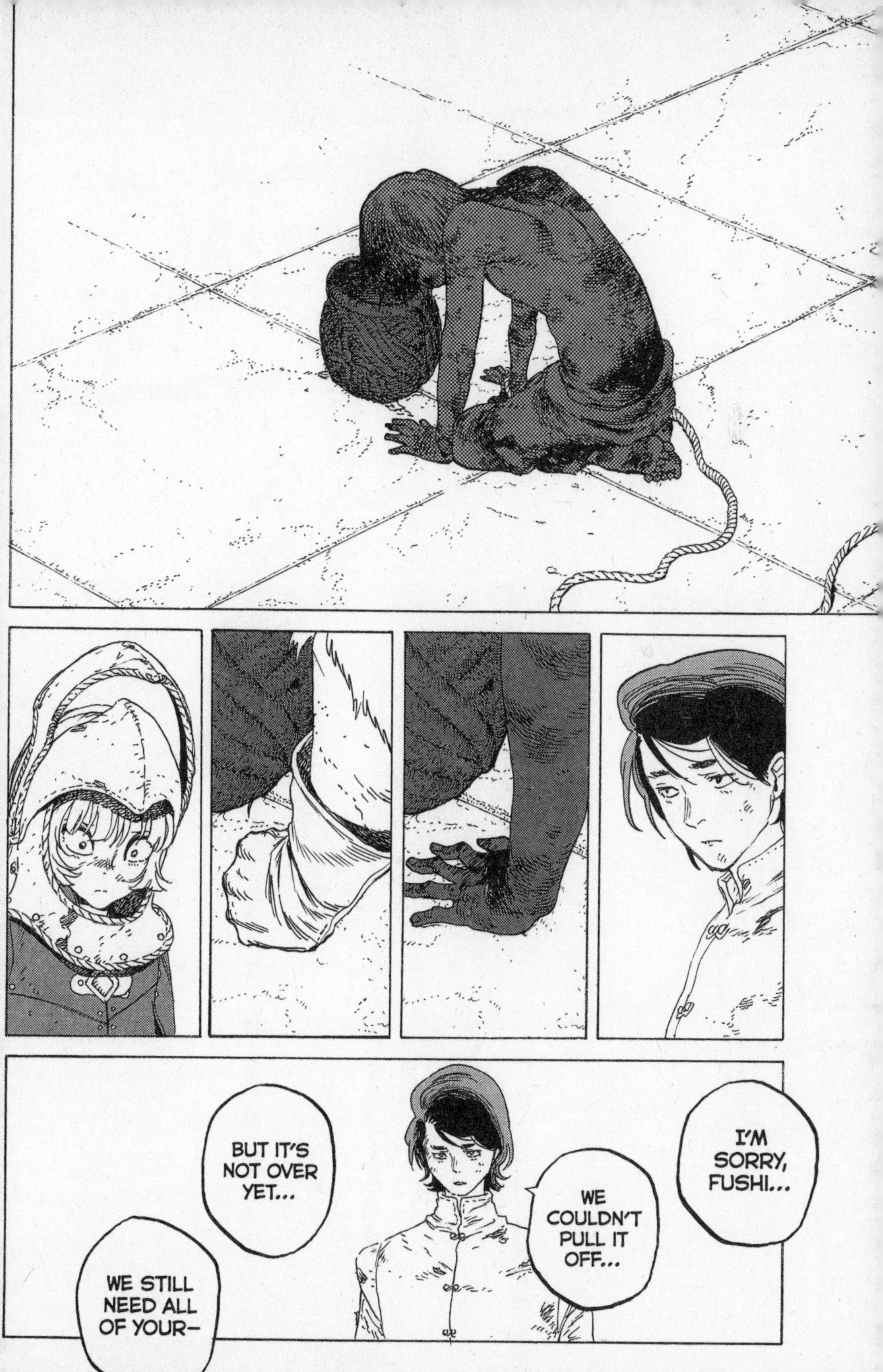
I'M SORRY, FUSHI...
WE COULDN'T PULL IT OFF...
BUT IT'S NOT OVER YET...
WE STILL NEED ALL OF YOUR—

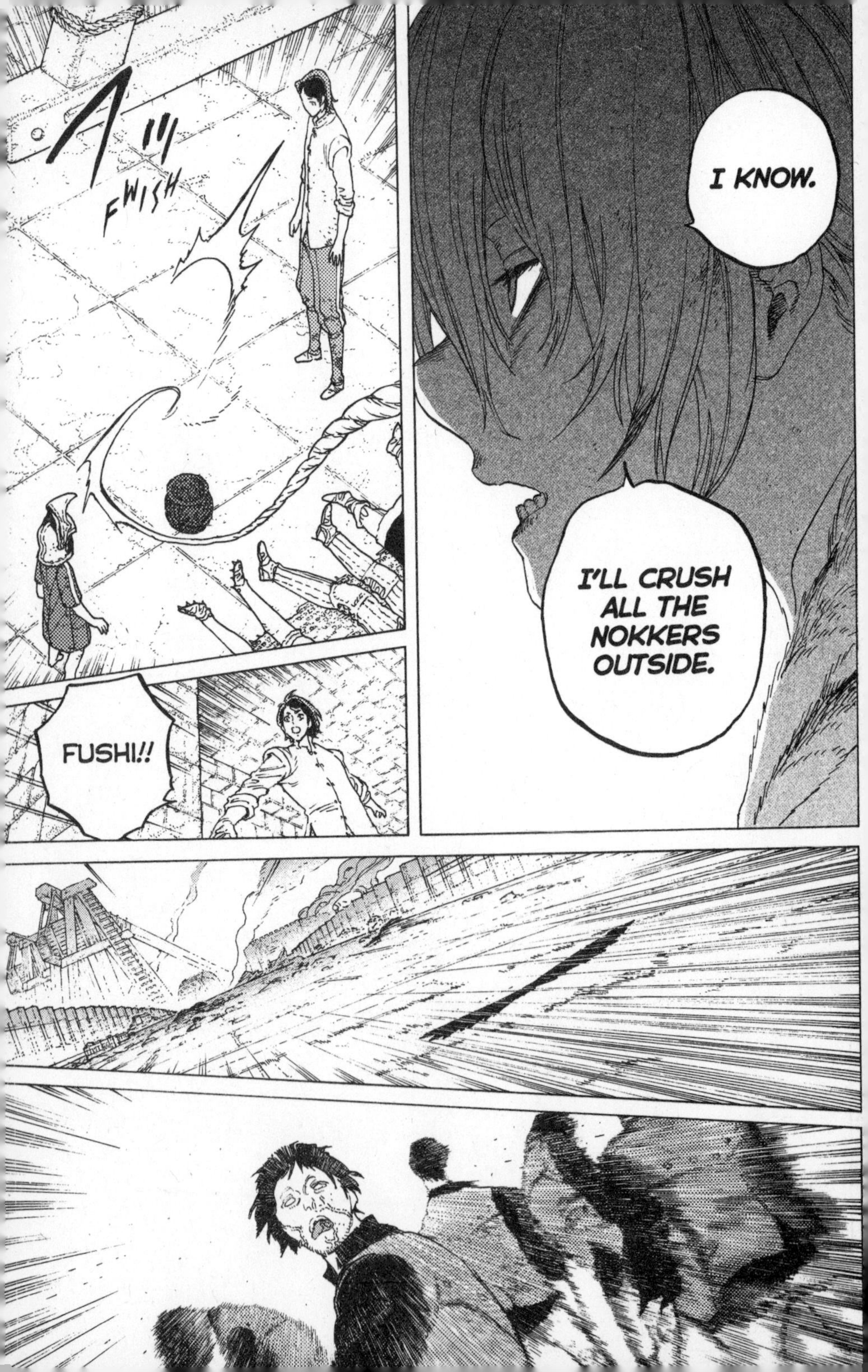
I KNOW.
I'LL CRUSH ALL THE NOKKERS OUTSIDE.
FWISH
FUSHI!!

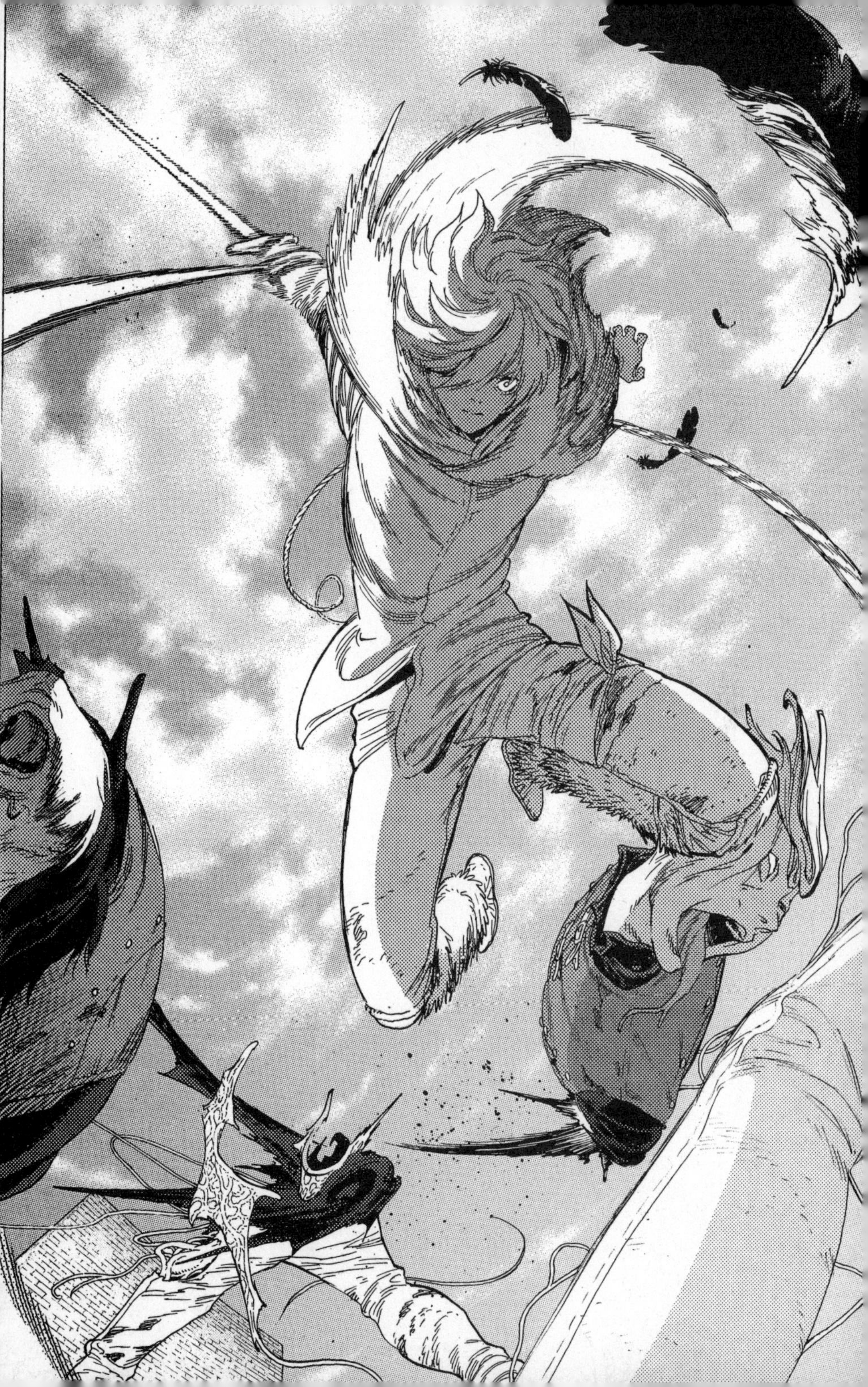

#100 The Immortal Army

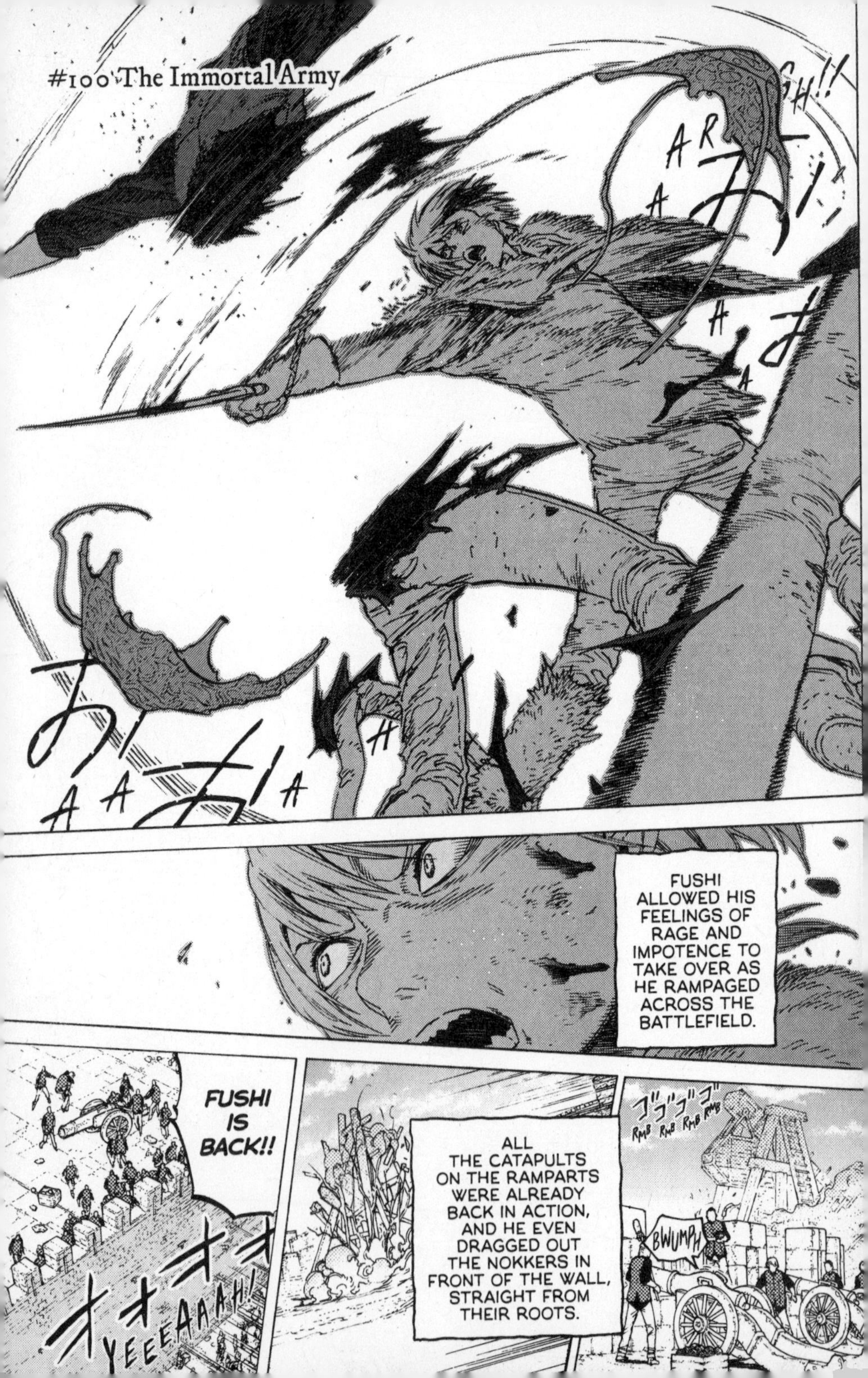
FUSHI ALLOWED HIS FEELINGS OF RAGE AND IMPOTENCE TO TAKE OVER AS HE RAMPAGED ACROSS THE BATTLEFIELD.
RMB RMB RMB RMB
BWUMPH
ALL THE CATAPULTS ON THE RAMPARTS WERE ALREADY BACK IN ACTION, AND HE EVEN DRAGGED OUT THE NOKKERS IN FRONT OF THE WALL, STRAIGHT FROM THEIR ROOTS.
FUSHI IS BACK!!
YEEEAAAAH!

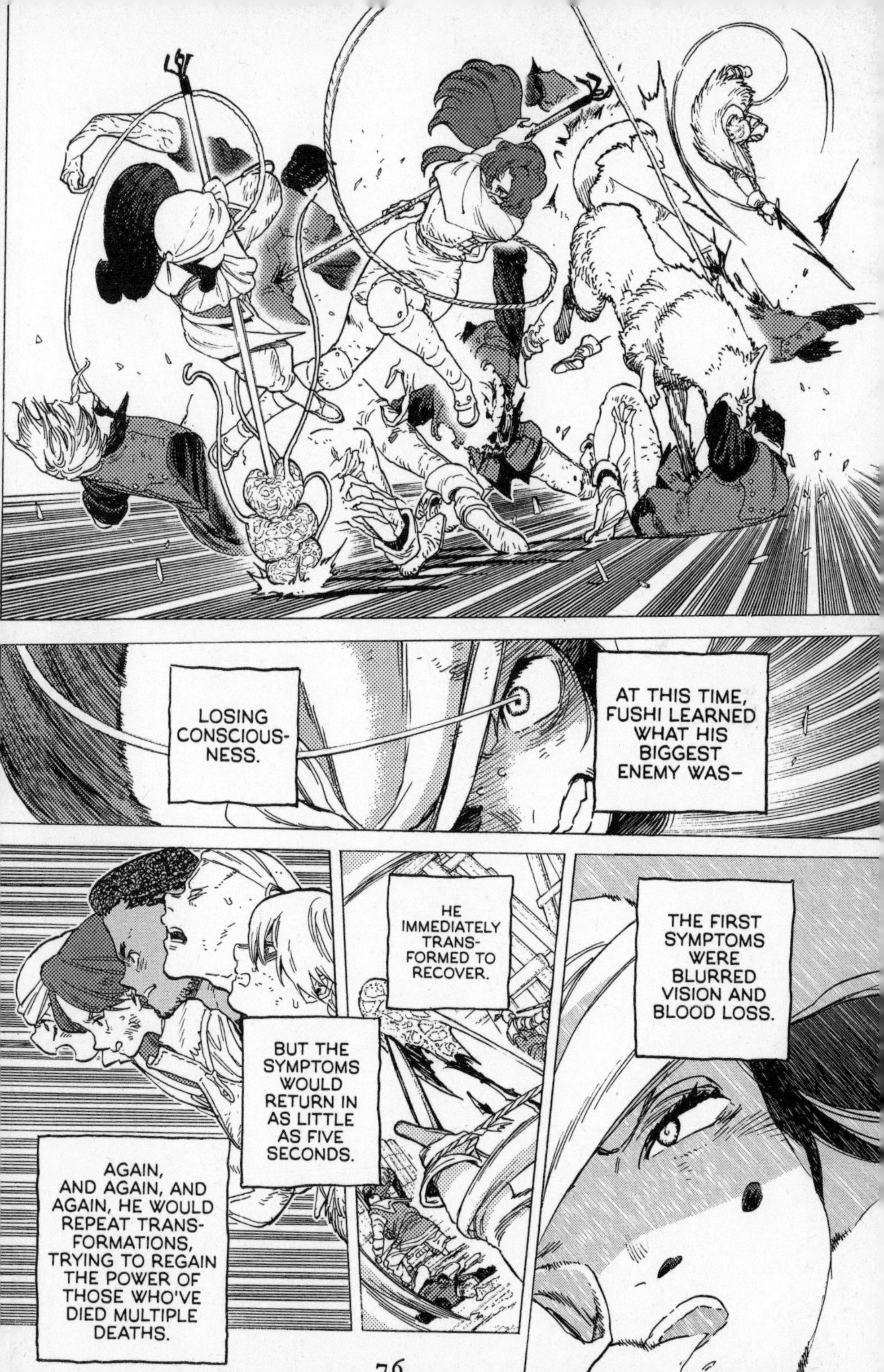
AT THIS TIME, FUSHI LEARNED WHAT HIS BIGGEST ENEMY WAS–
LOSING CONSCIOUS-NESS.
THE FIRST SYMPTOMS WERE BLURRED VISION AND BLOOD LOSS.
HE IMMEDIATELY TRANS-FORMED TO RECOVER.
BUT THE SYMPTOMS WOULD RETURN IN AS LITTLE AS FIVE SECONDS.
AGAIN, AND AGAIN, AND AGAIN, HE WOULD REPEAT TRANS-FORMATIONS, TRYING TO REGAIN THE POWER OF THOSE WHO'VE DIED MULTIPLE DEATHS.

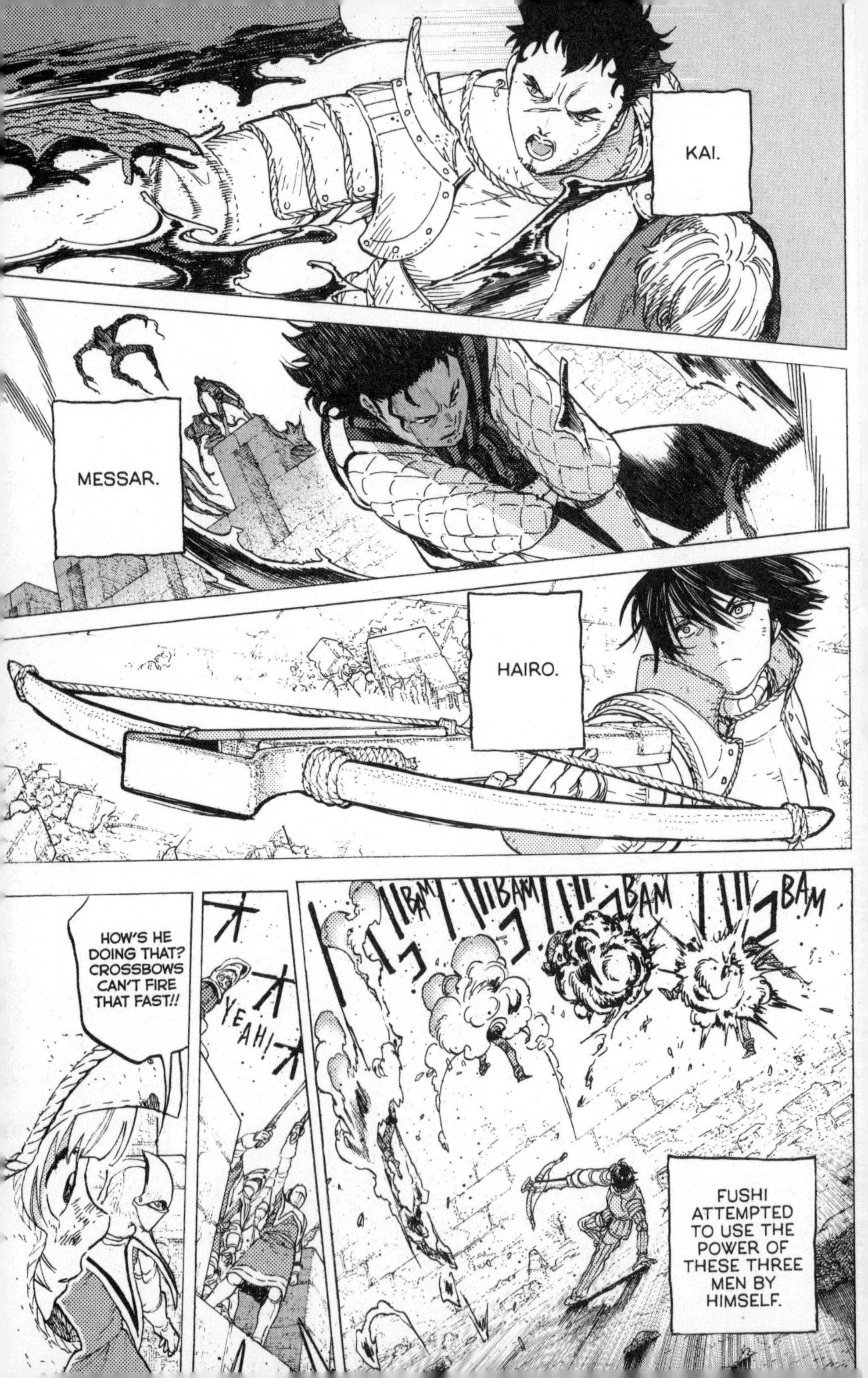
KAI.
MESSAR.
HAIRO.
BAM
BAM
BAM
BAM
FUSHI ATTEMPTED TO USE THE POWER OF THESE THREE MEN BY HIMSELF.
YEAH!
HOW'S HE DOING THAT? CROSSBOWS CAN'T FIRE THAT FAST!!

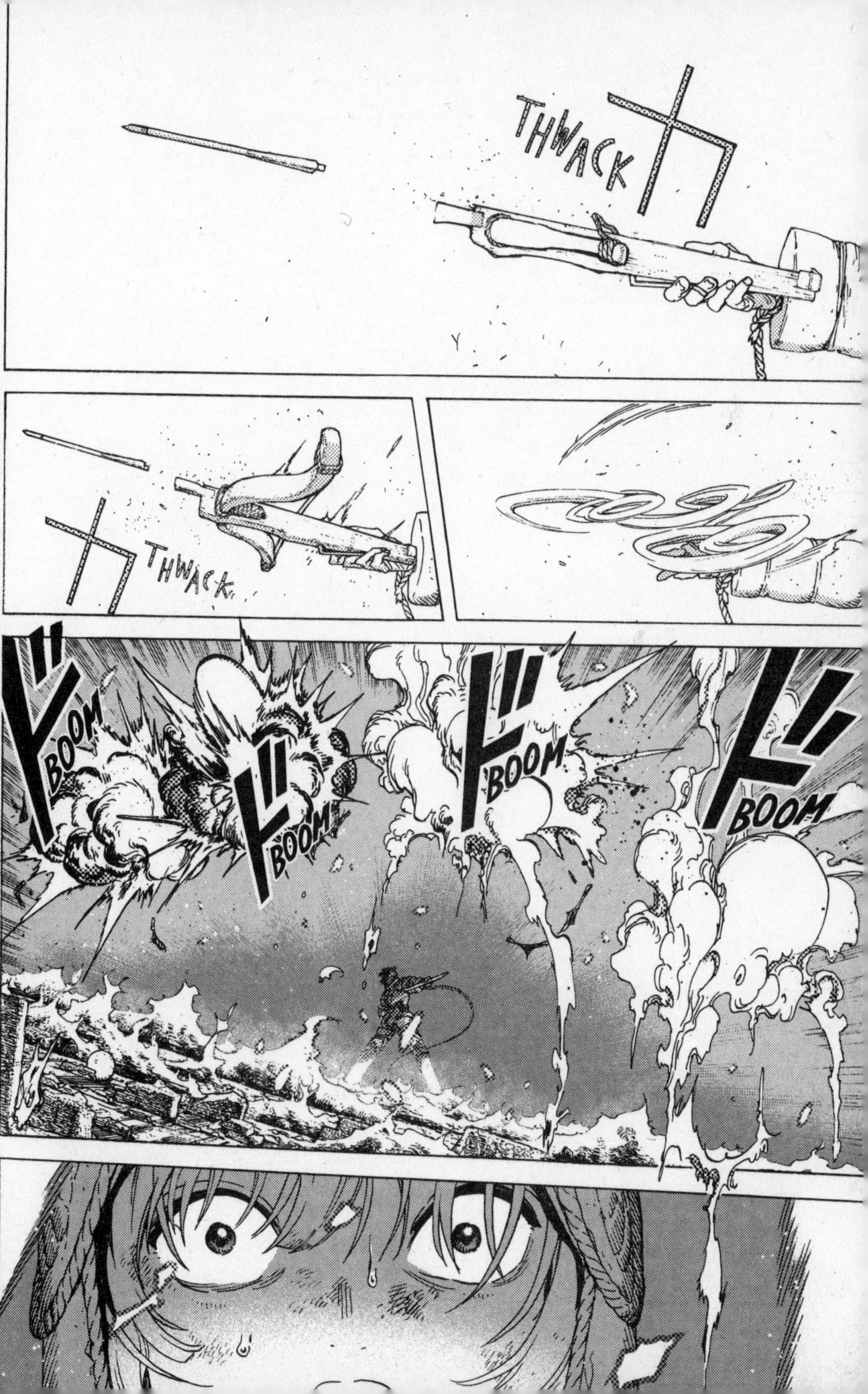
THWACK
THWACK
ド
BOOM
ド
BOOM
ド
BOOM
ド
BOOM

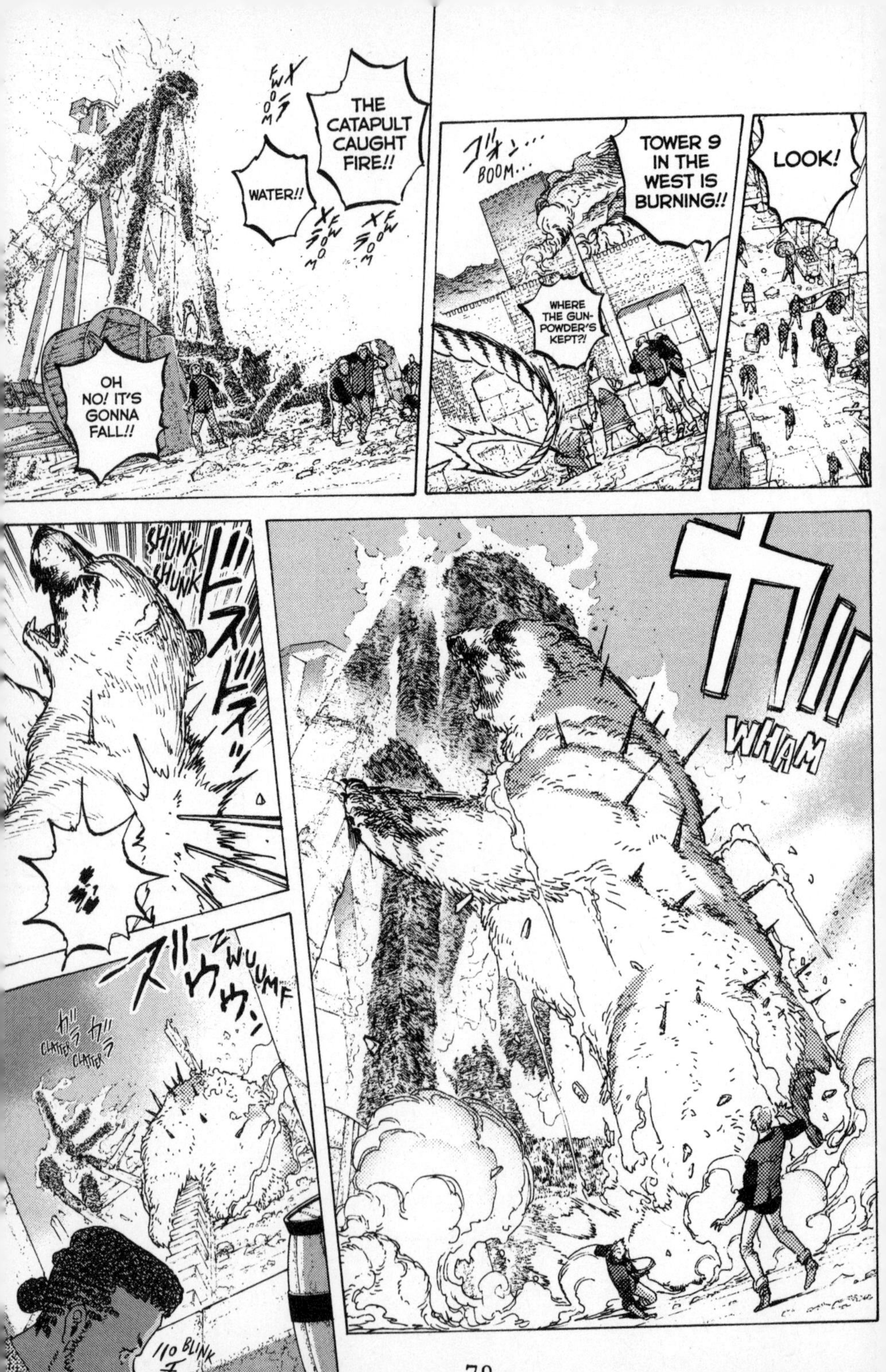
LOOK!
TOWER 9 IN THE WEST IS BURNING!!
BOOM...
WHERE THE GUN-POWDER'S KEPT?!
FWOOM
THE CATAPULT CAUGHT FIRE!!
WATER!!
FWOOM
FWOOM
OH NO! IT'S GONNA FALL!!
WHAM
SHUNK SHUNK
WUUMF
CLATTER CLATTER
BLINK

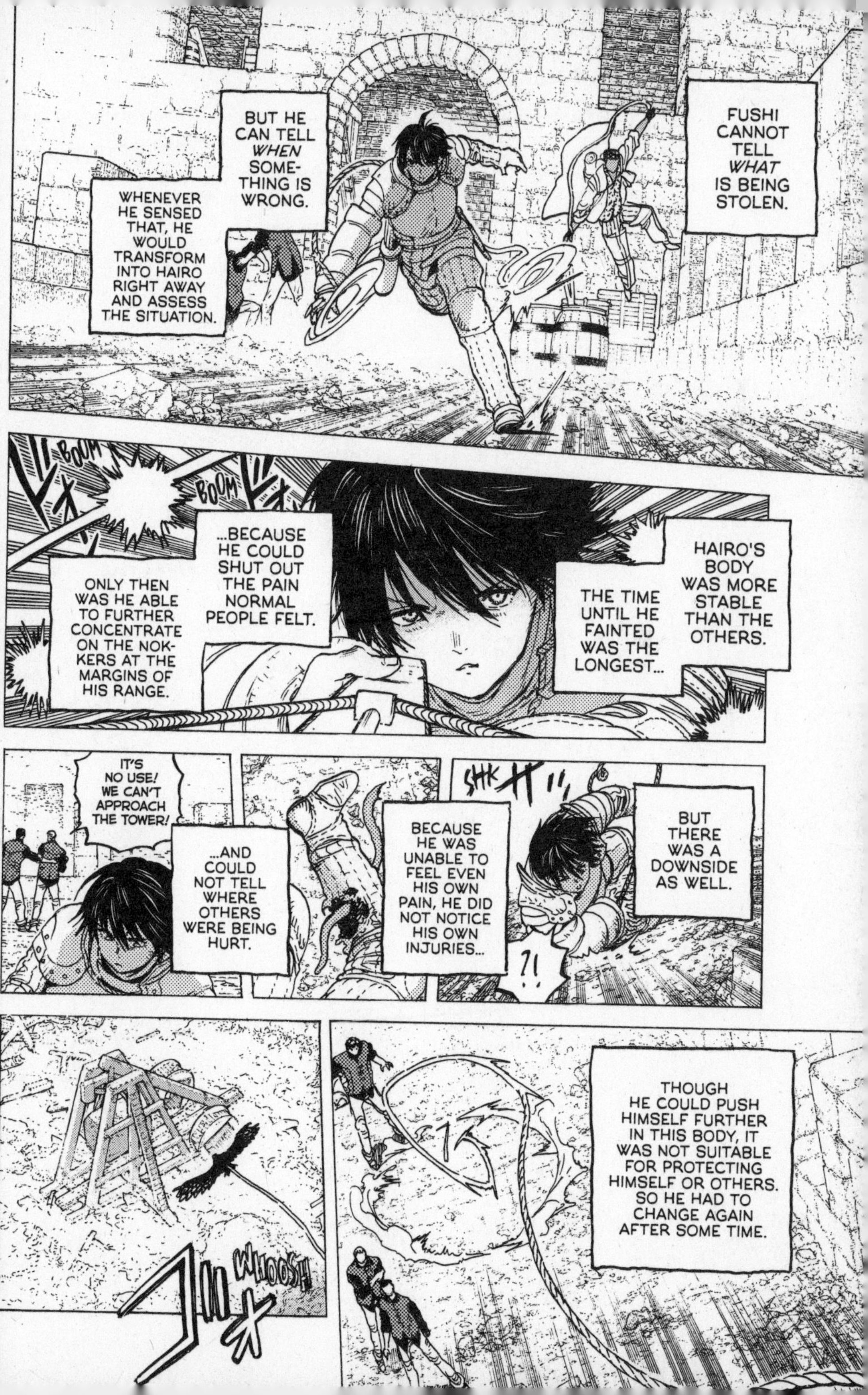
FUSHI CANNOT TELL *WHAT* IS BEING STOLEN.
BUT HE CAN TELL *WHEN* SOMETHING IS WRONG.
WHENEVER HE SENSED THAT, HE WOULD TRANSFORM INTO HAIRO RIGHT AWAY AND ASSESS THE SITUATION.
BOOM
BOOM
HAIRO'S BODY WAS MORE STABLE THAN THE OTHERS.
THE TIME UNTIL HE FAINTED WAS THE LONGEST...
...BECAUSE HE COULD SHUT OUT THE PAIN NORMAL PEOPLE FELT.
ONLY THEN WAS HE ABLE TO FURTHER CONCENTRATE ON THE NOKKERS AT THE MARGINS OF HIS RANGE.
SHK
BUT THERE WAS A DOWNSIDE AS WELL.
?!
BECAUSE HE WAS UNABLE TO FEEL EVEN HIS OWN PAIN, HE DID NOT NOTICE HIS OWN INJURIES...
IT'S NO USE! WE CAN'T APPROACH THE TOWER!
...AND COULD NOT TELL WHERE OTHERS WERE BEING HURT.
THOUGH HE COULD PUSH HIMSELF FURTHER IN THIS BODY, IT WAS NOT SUITABLE FOR PROTECTING HIMSELF OR OTHERS. SO HE HAD TO CHANGE AGAIN AFTER SOME TIME.
WHOOSH

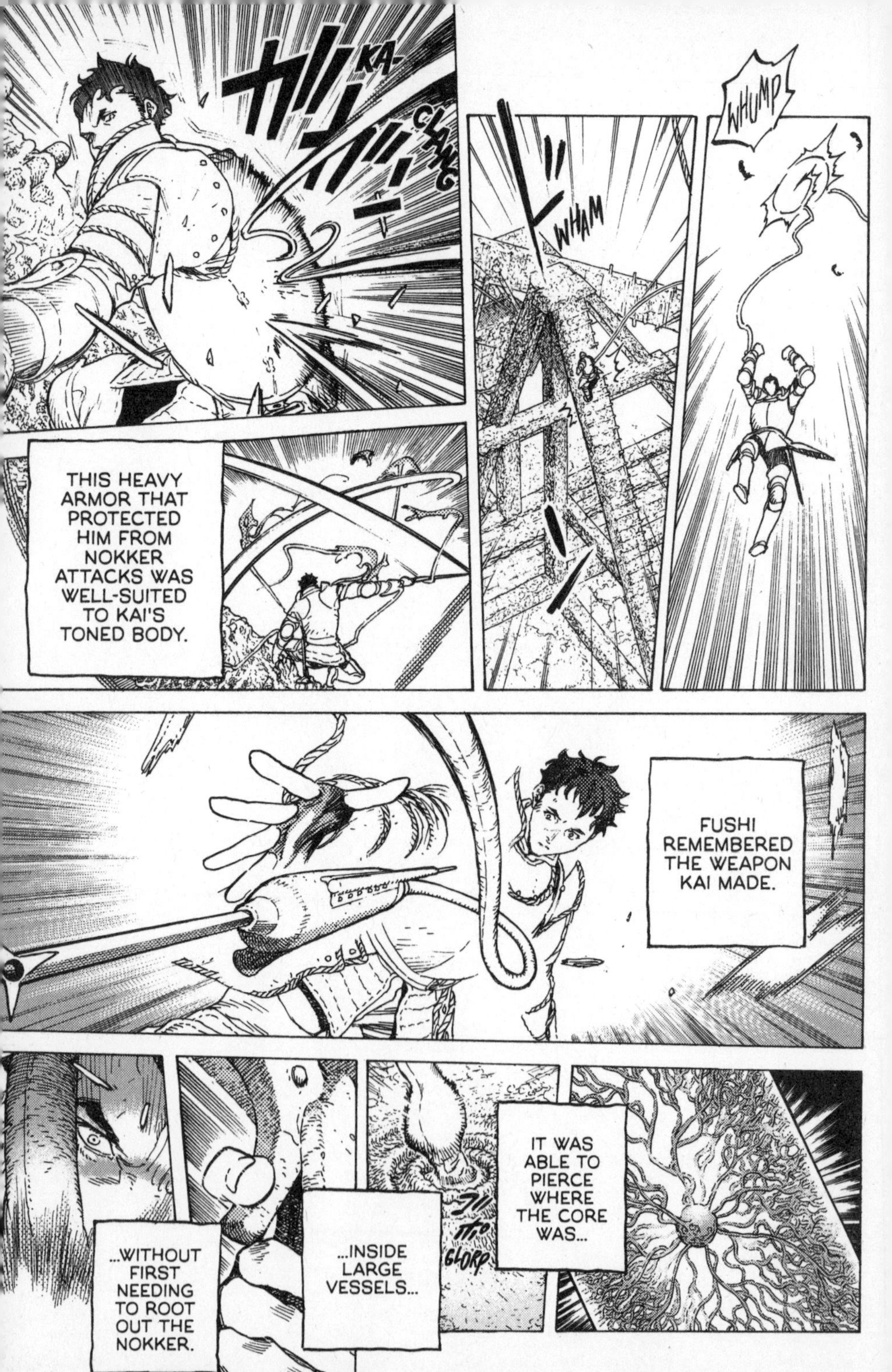
WHUMP
WHAM
KA-
CLANG
THIS HEAVY ARMOR THAT PROTECTED HIM FROM NOKKER ATTACKS WAS WELL-SUITED TO KAI'S TONED BODY.
FUSHI REMEMBERED THE WEAPON KAI MADE.
IT WAS ABLE TO PIERCE WHERE THE CORE WAS...
GLORP
...INSIDE LARGE VESSELS...
...WITHOUT FIRST NEEDING TO ROOT OUT THE NOKKER.

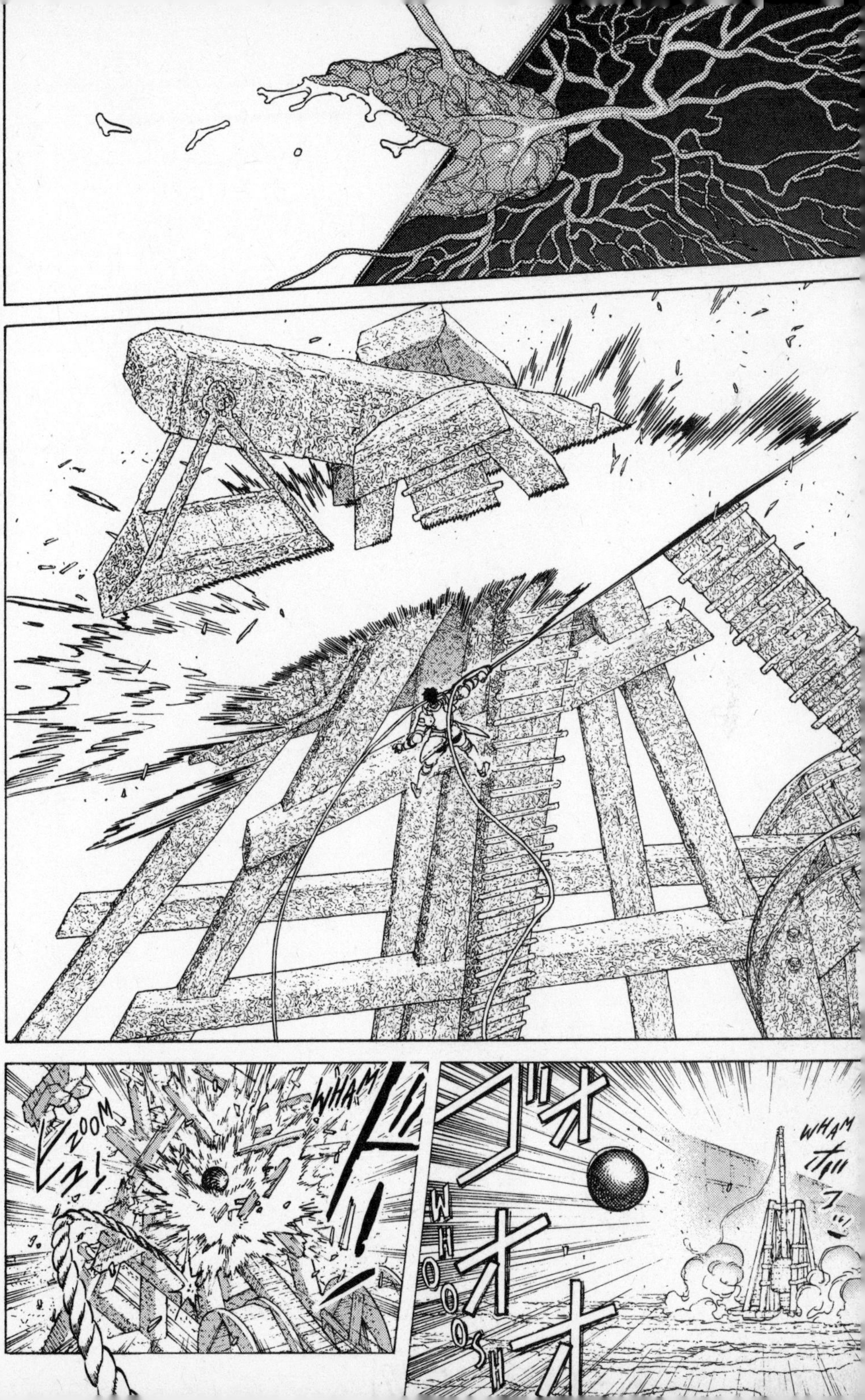
WHAM
WHOOOOSH
WHAM
ZOOM

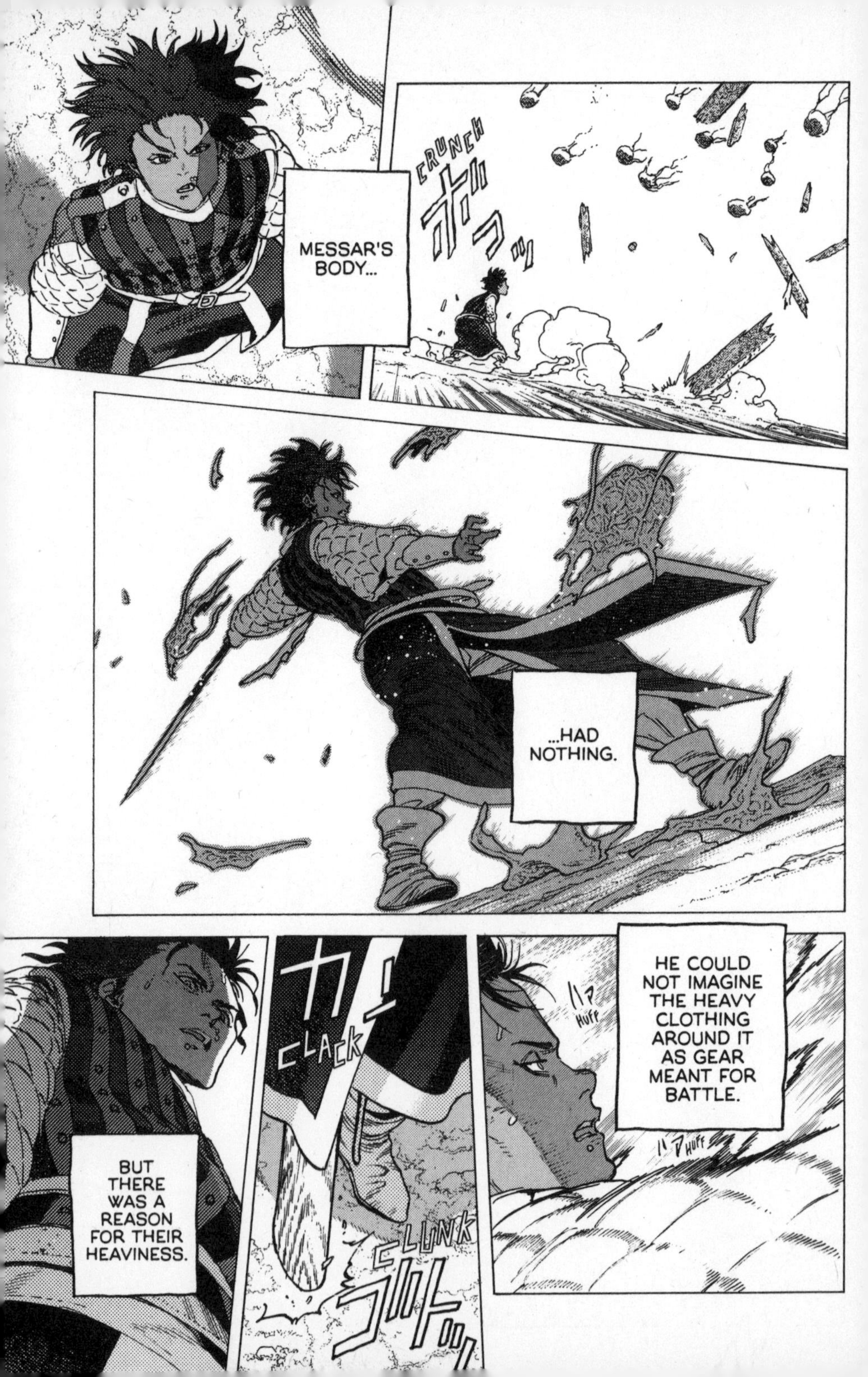
CRUNCH
MESSAR'S BODY...
...HAD NOTHING.
HUFF
HE COULD NOT IMAGINE THE HEAVY CLOTHING AROUND IT AS GEAR MEANT FOR BATTLE.
HUFF
CLACK
CLUNK
BUT THERE WAS A REASON FOR THEIR HEAVINESS.

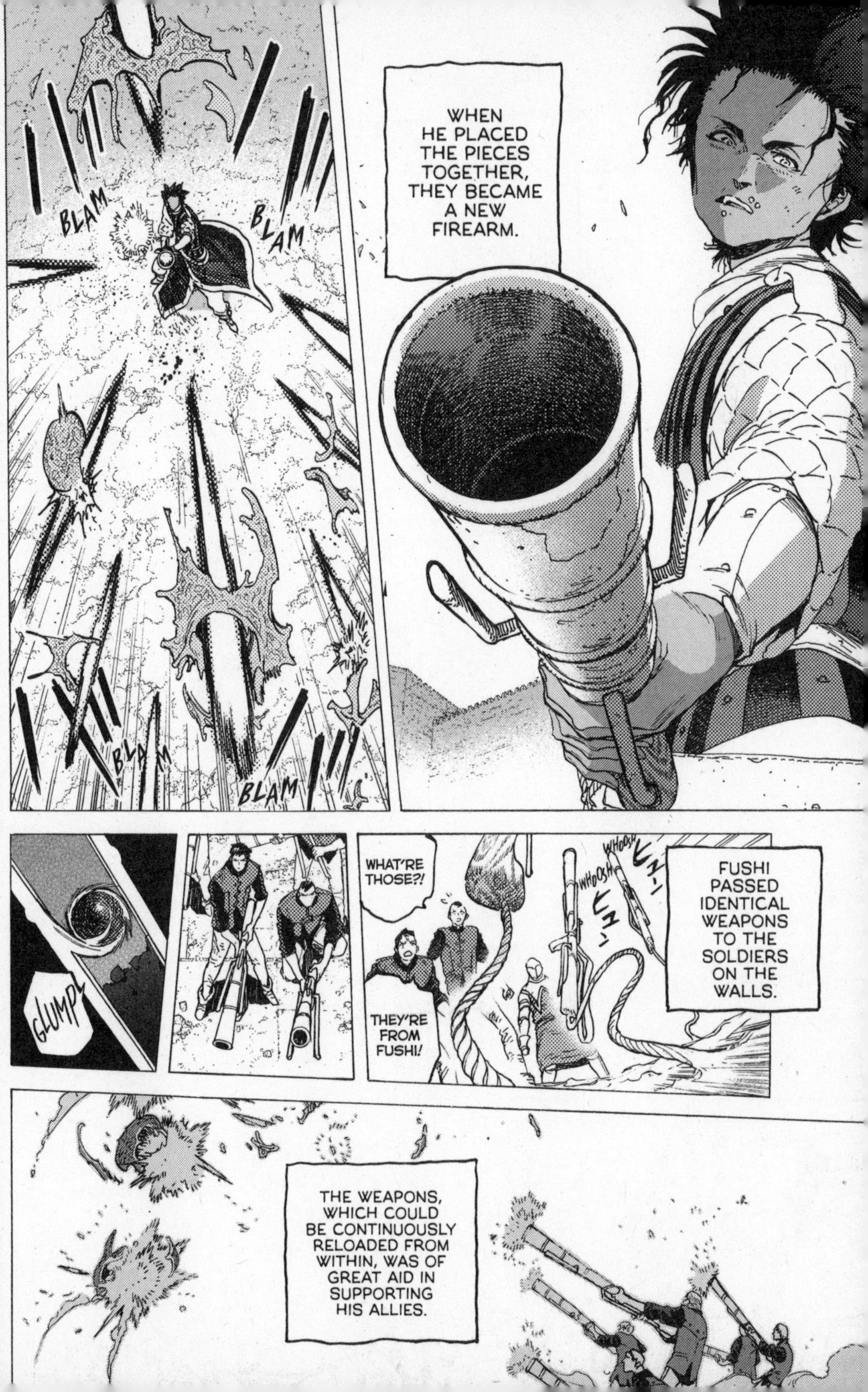
WHEN HE PLACED THE PIECES TOGETHER, THEY BECAME A NEW FIREARM.
BLAM
BLAM
BLAM
BLAM
FUSHI PASSED IDENTICAL WEAPONS TO THE SOLDIERS ON THE WALLS.
WHOOSH
WHOOSH
WHAT'RE THOSE?!
THEY'RE FROM FUSHI!
GLUMP
THE WEAPONS, WHICH COULD BE CONTINUOUSLY RELOADED FROM WITHIN, WAS OF GREAT AID IN SUPPORTING HIS ALLIES.

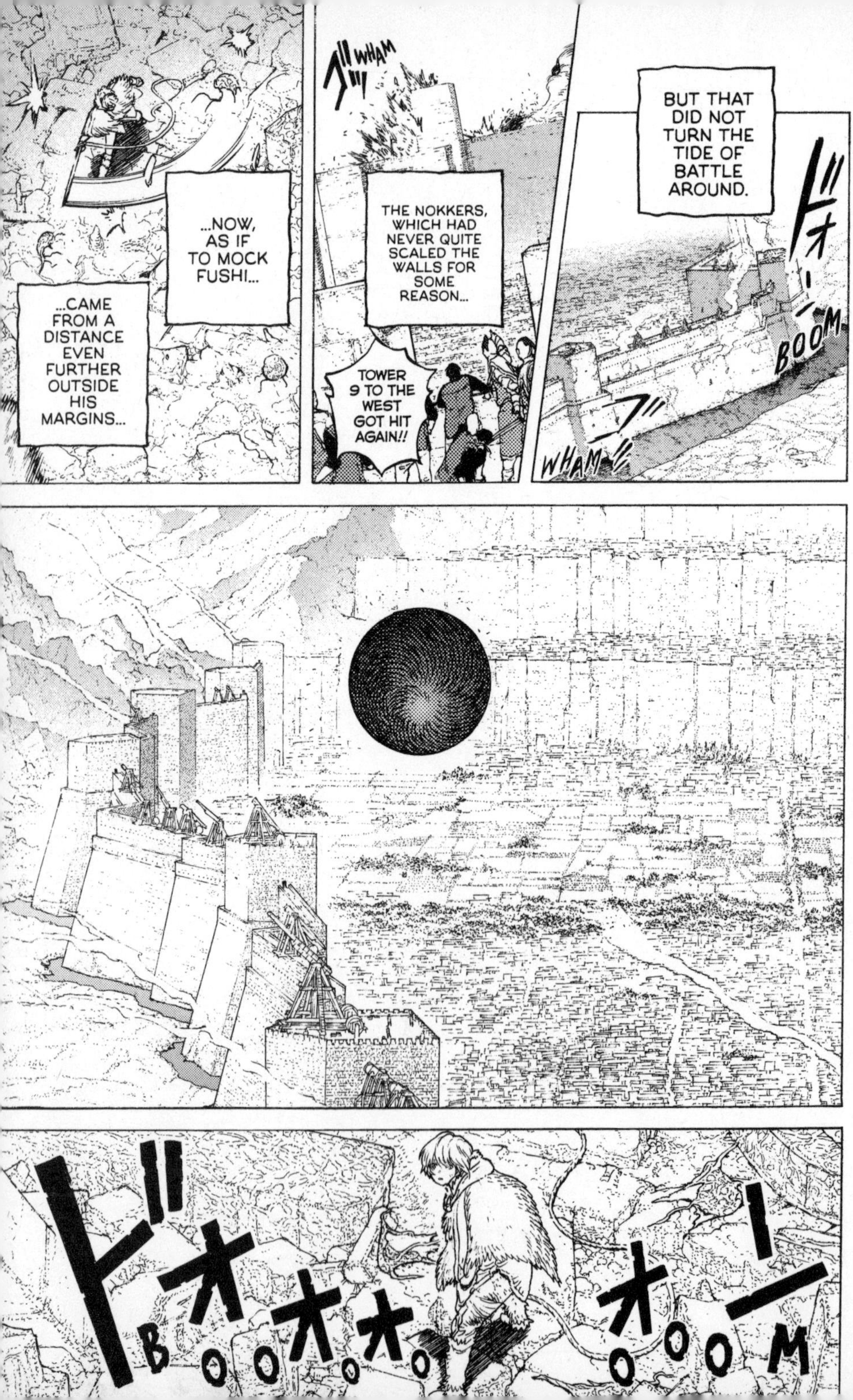
BUT THAT DID NOT TURN THE TIDE OF BATTLE AROUND.
BOOM
WHAM
WHAM
THE NOKKERS, WHICH HAD NEVER QUITE SCALED THE WALLS FOR SOME REASON...
TOWER 9 TO THE WEST GOT HIT AGAIN!!
...NOW, AS IF TO MOCK FUSHI...
...CAME FROM A DISTANCE EVEN FURTHER OUTSIDE HIS MARGINS...
BOOOOOOOM

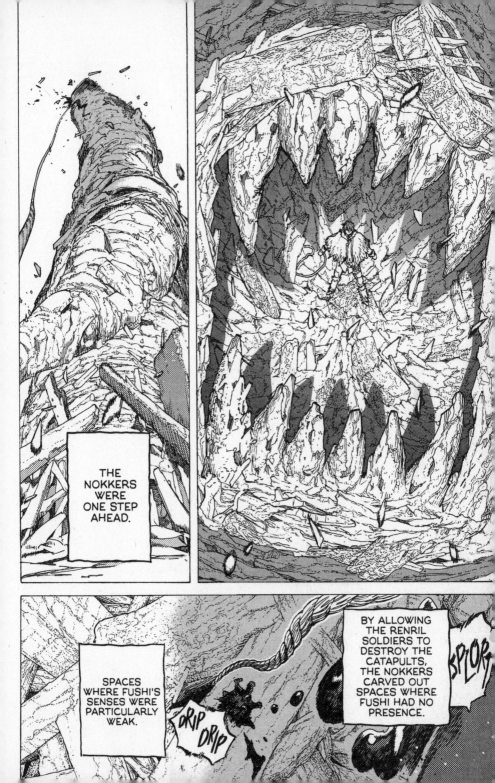

THE NOKKERS WERE ONE STEP AHEAD.

BY ALLOWING THE RENRIL SOLDIERS TO DESTROY THE CATAPULTS, THE NOKKERS CARVED OUT SPACES WHERE FUSHI HAD NO PRESENCE.

SPACES WHERE FUSHI'S SENSES WERE PARTICULARLY WEAK.

SPLORT

DRIP DRIP

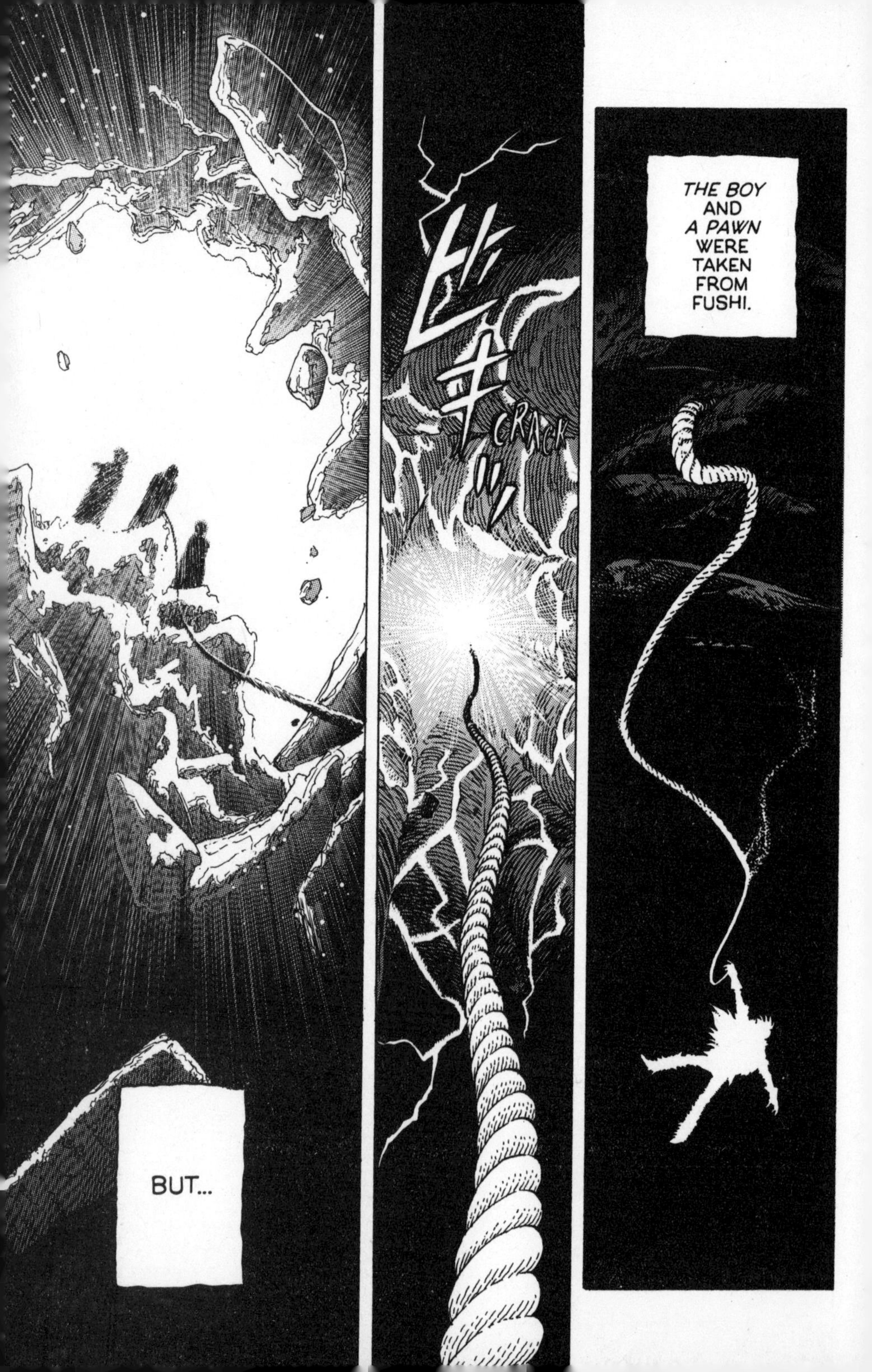
THE BOY AND A PAWN WERE TAKEN FROM FUSHI.
ビキッ
CRACK
BUT...

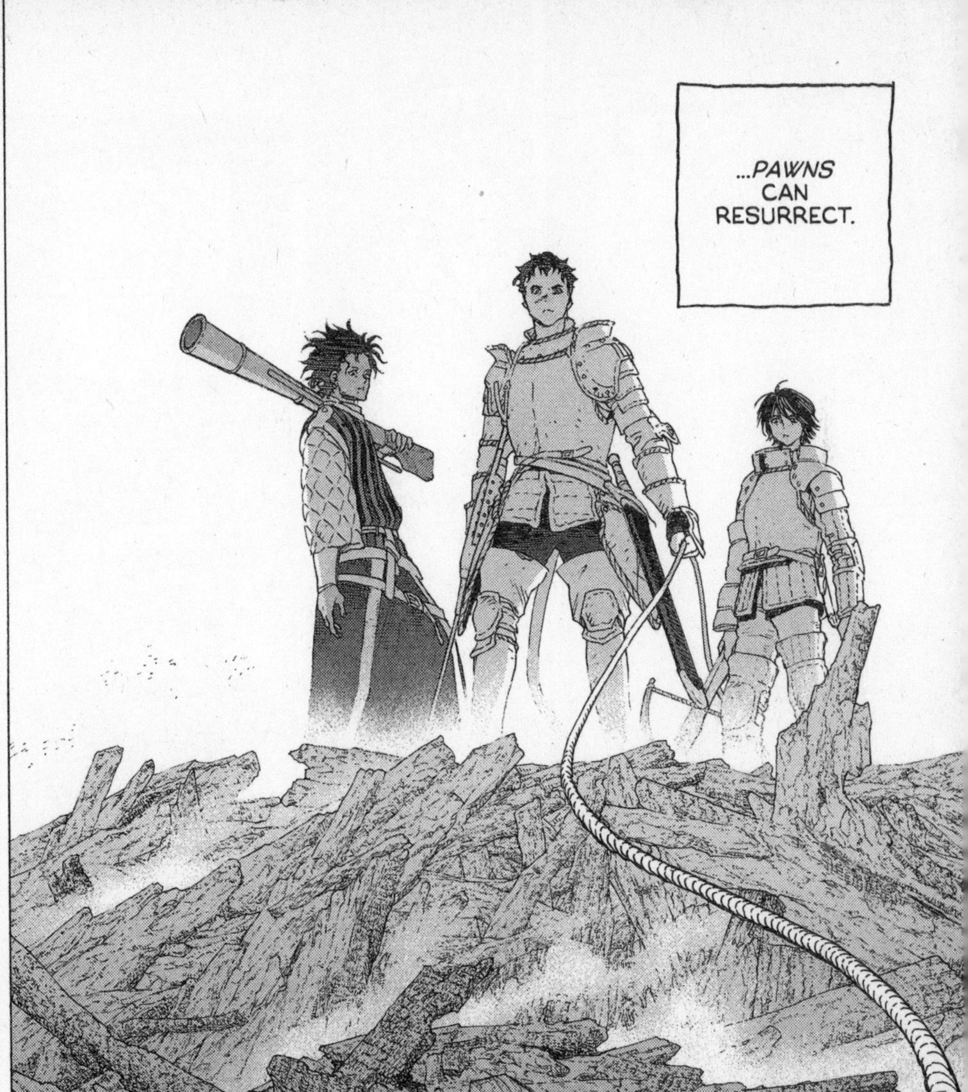
...PAWNS CAN RESURRECT.
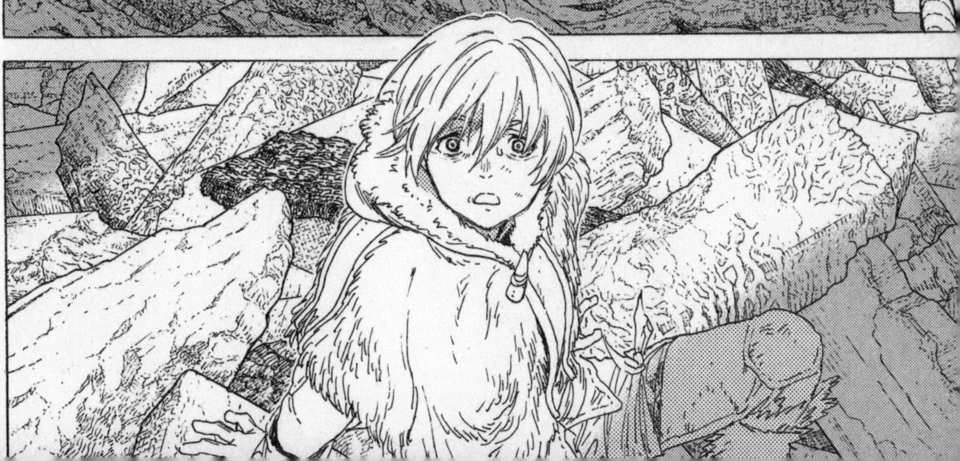

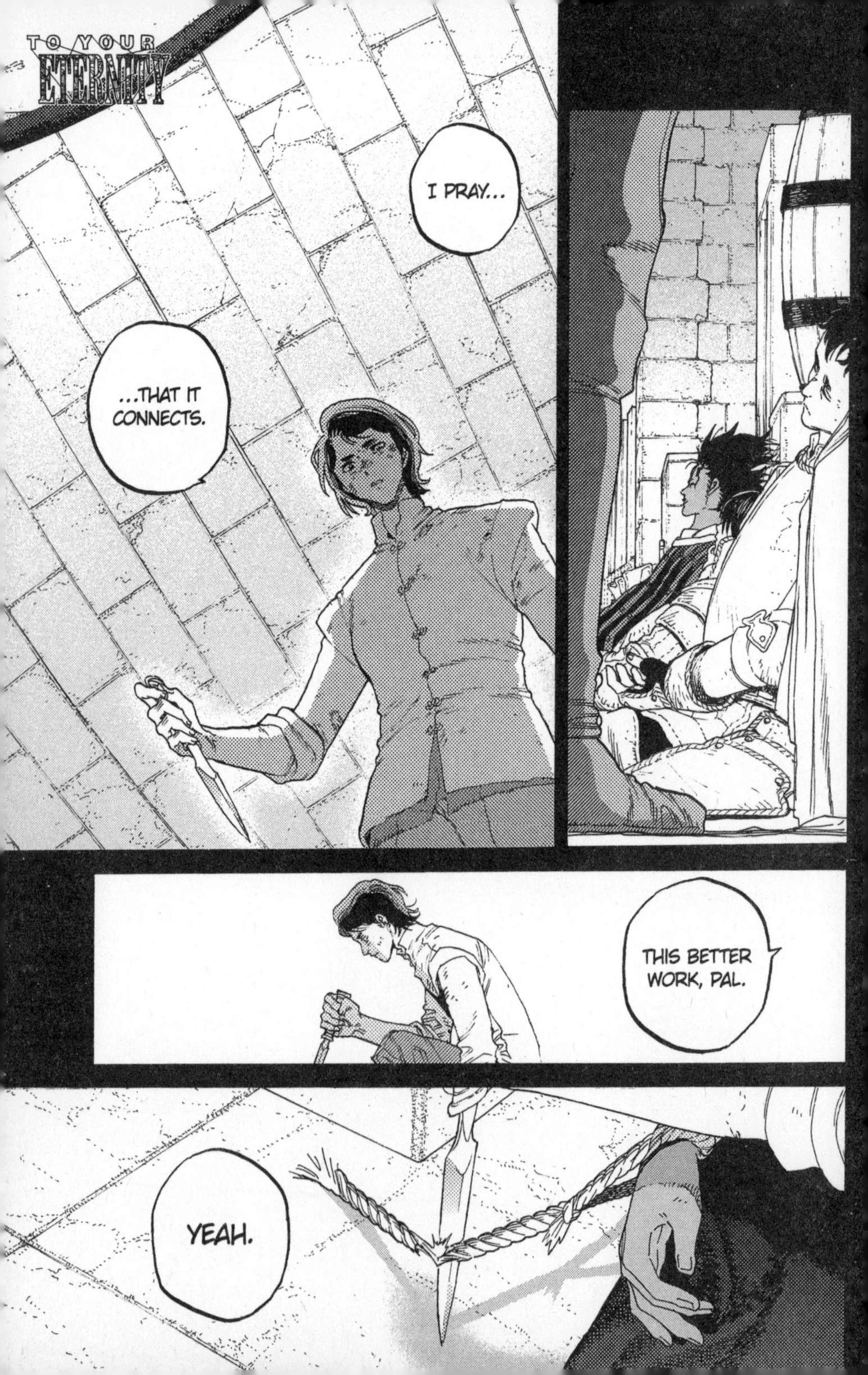
I PRAY...
...THAT IT CONNECTS.
THIS BETTER WORK, PAL.
YEAH.

#101 Rope of Life

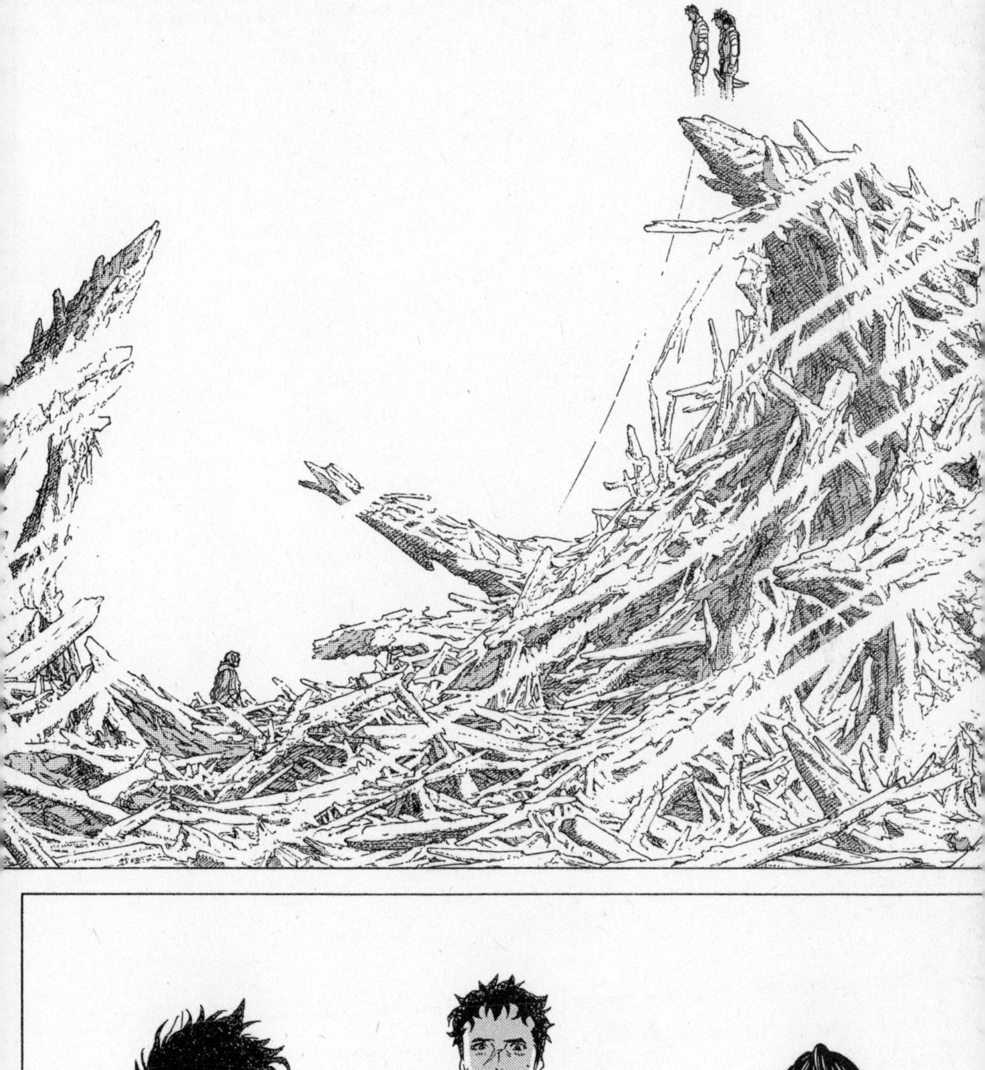

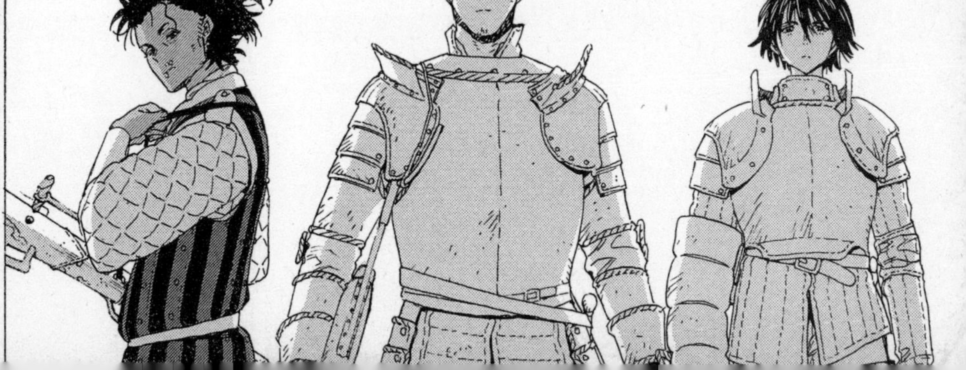

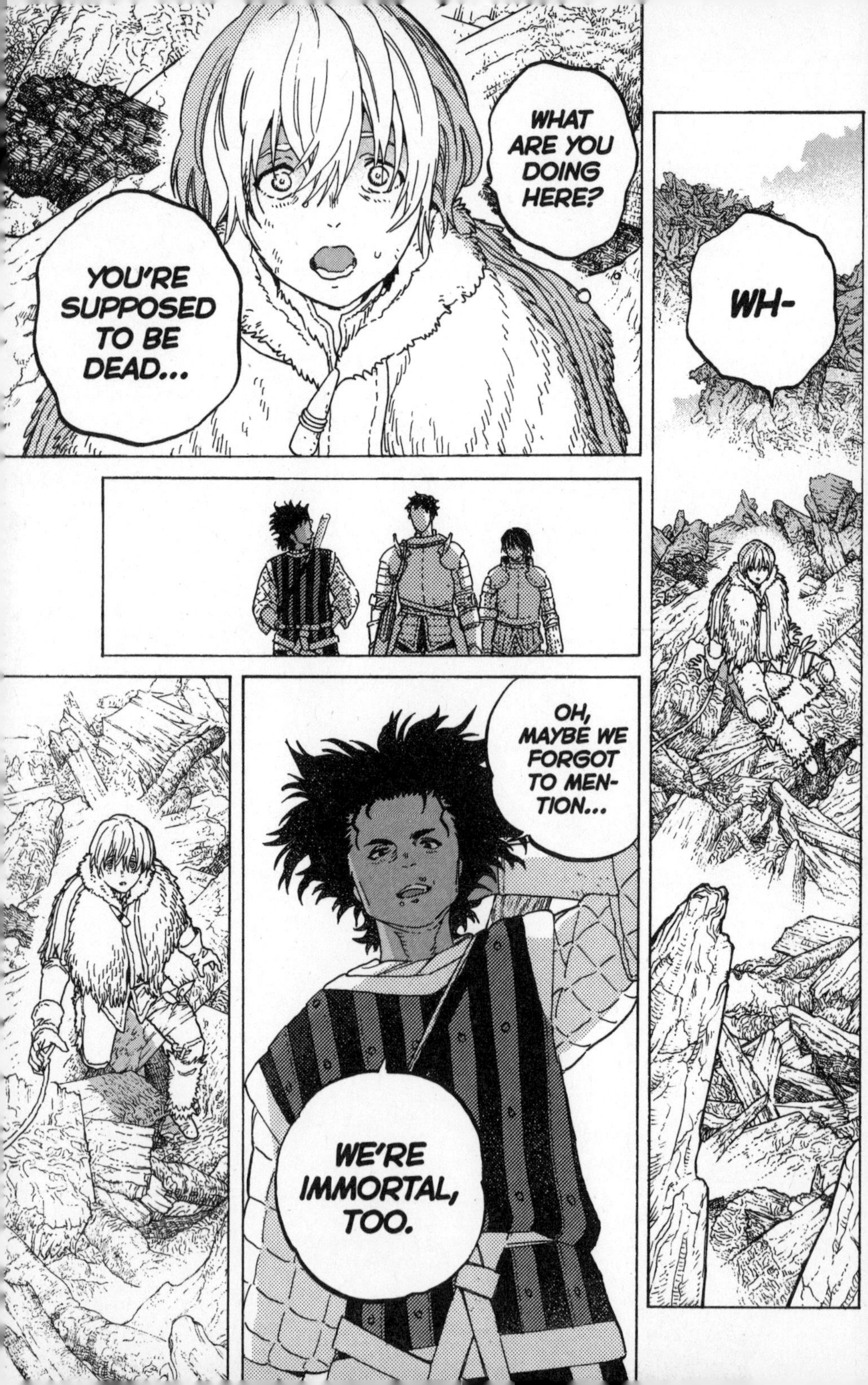
WH-
WHAT ARE YOU DOING HERE?
YOU'RE SUPPOSED TO BE DEAD...
OH, MAYBE WE FORGOT TO MEN-TION...
WE'RE IMMORTAL, TOO.

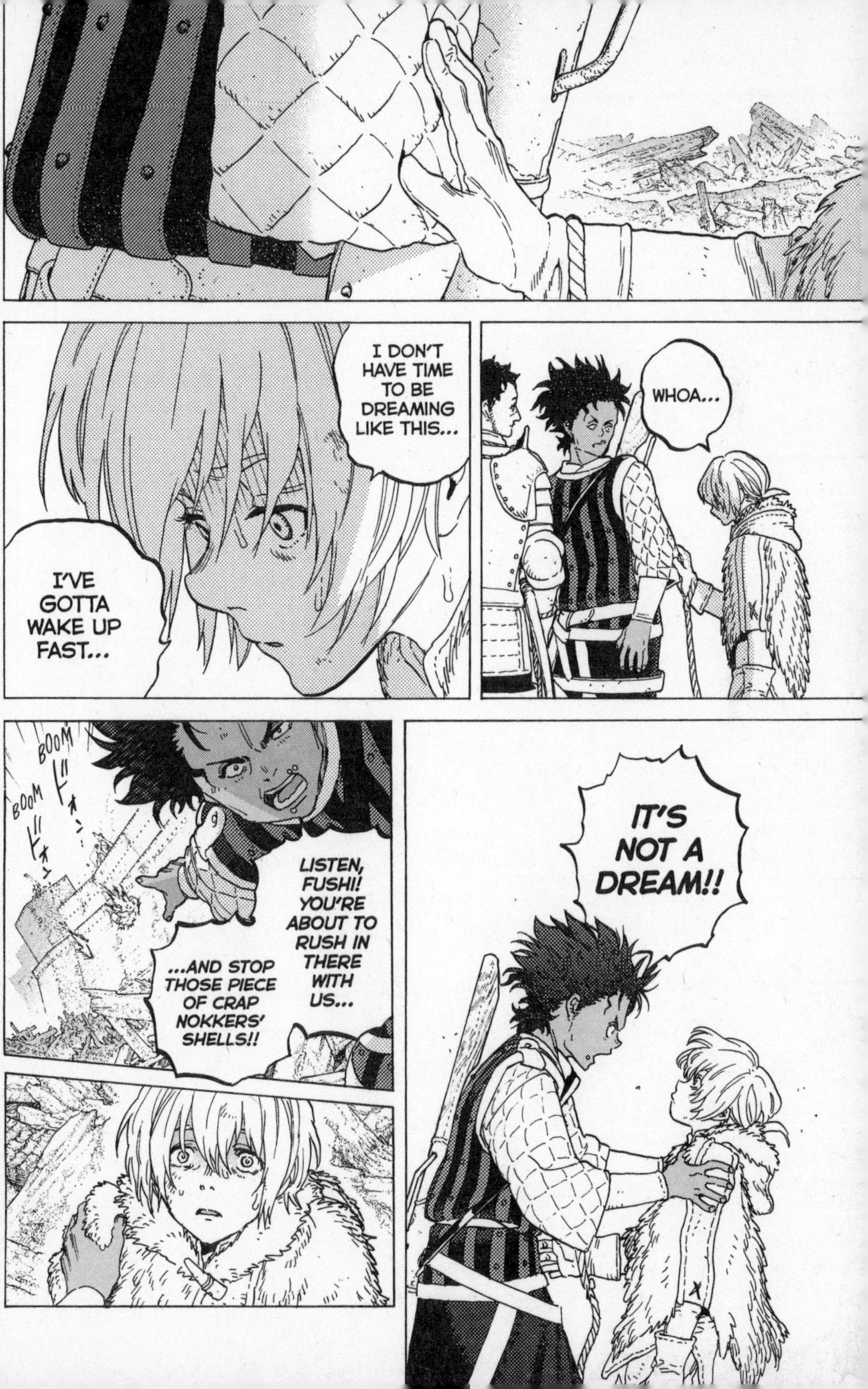
WHOA...
I DON'T HAVE TIME TO BE DREAMING LIKE THIS...
I'VE GOTTA WAKE UP FAST...
IT'S NOT A DREAM!!
BOOM
BOOM
LISTEN, FUSHI! YOU'RE ABOUT TO RUSH IN THERE WITH US...
...AND STOP THOSE PIECE OF CRAP NOKKERS' SHELLS!!

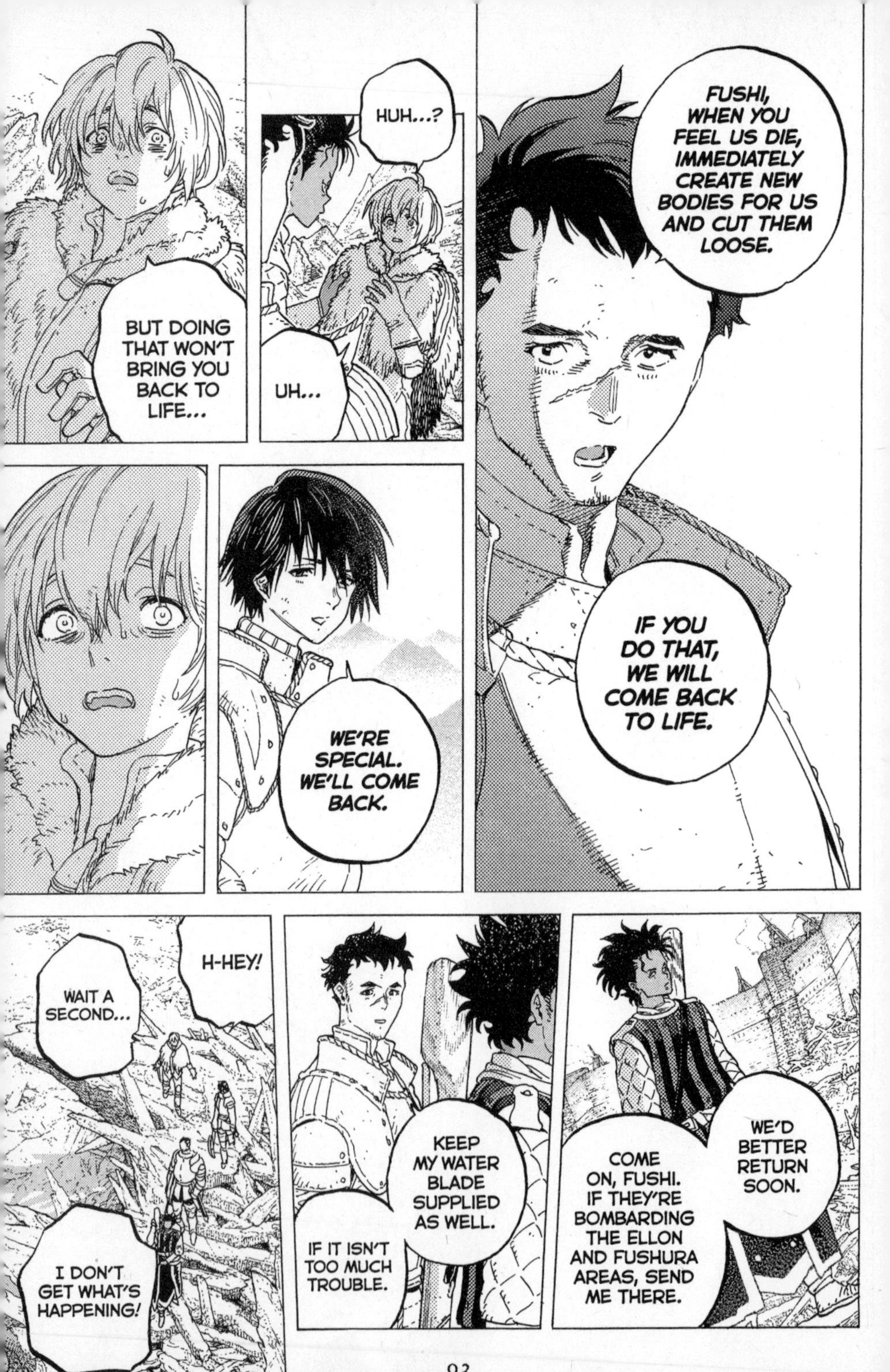
FUSHI, WHEN YOU FEEL US DIE, IMMEDIATELY CREATE NEW BODIES FOR US AND CUT THEM LOOSE.
IF YOU DO THAT, WE WILL COME BACK TO LIFE.
HUH...?
UH...
BUT DOING THAT WON'T BRING YOU BACK TO LIFE...
WE'RE SPECIAL. WE'LL COME BACK.
WE'D BETTER RETURN SOON.
COME ON, FUSHI. IF THEY'RE BOMBARDING THE ELLON AND FUSHURA AREAS, SEND ME THERE.
KEEP MY WATER BLADE SUPPLIED AS WELL.
IF IT ISN'T TOO MUCH TROUBLE.
H-HEY!
WAIT A SECOND...
I DON'T GET WHAT'S HAPPENING!

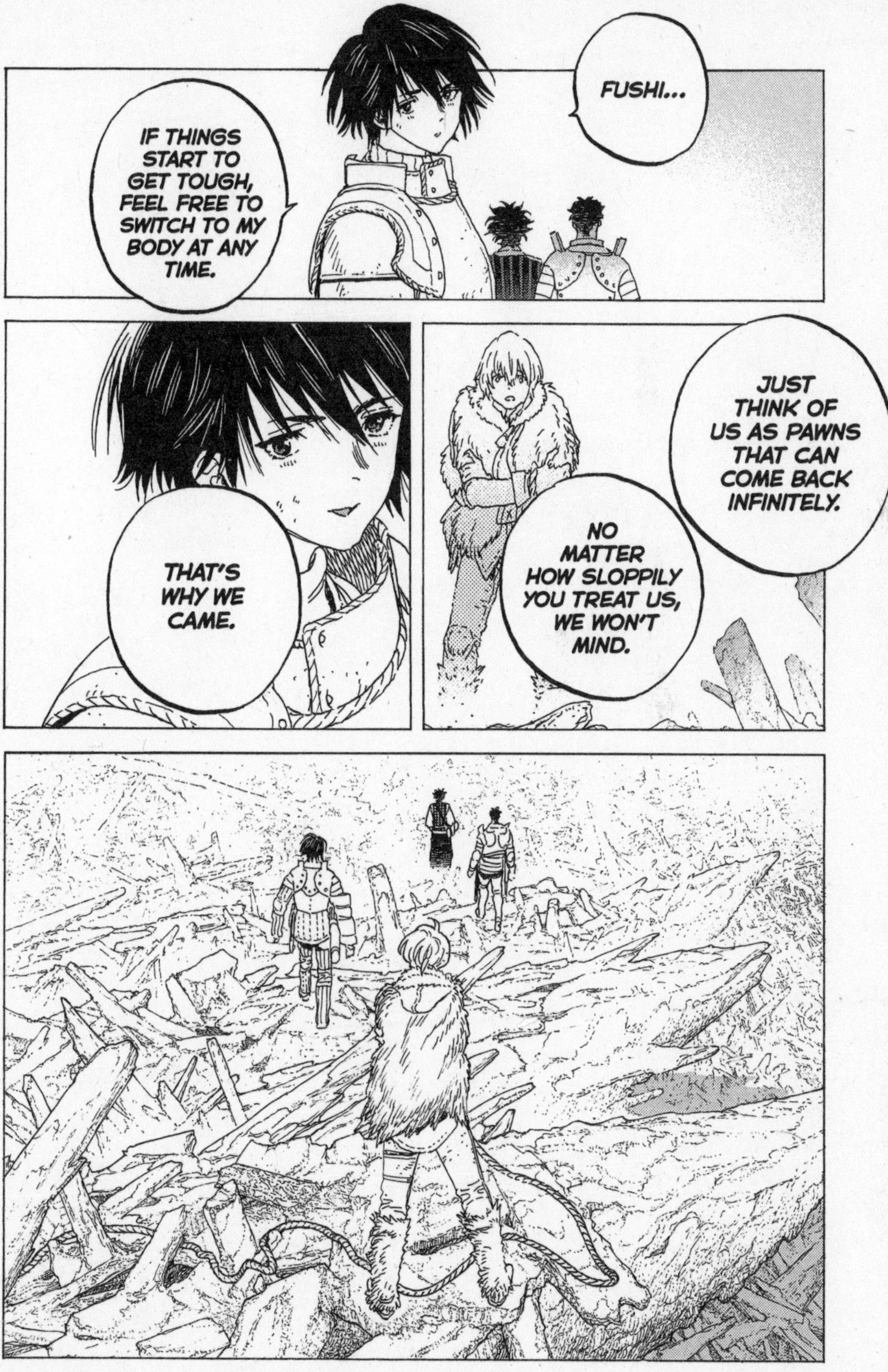
FUSHI...
IF THINGS START TO GET TOUGH, FEEL FREE TO SWITCH TO MY BODY AT ANY TIME.
JUST THINK OF US AS PAWNS THAT CAN COME BACK INFINITELY.
NO MATTER HOW SLOPPILY YOU TREAT US, WE WON'T MIND.
THAT'S WHY WE CAME.

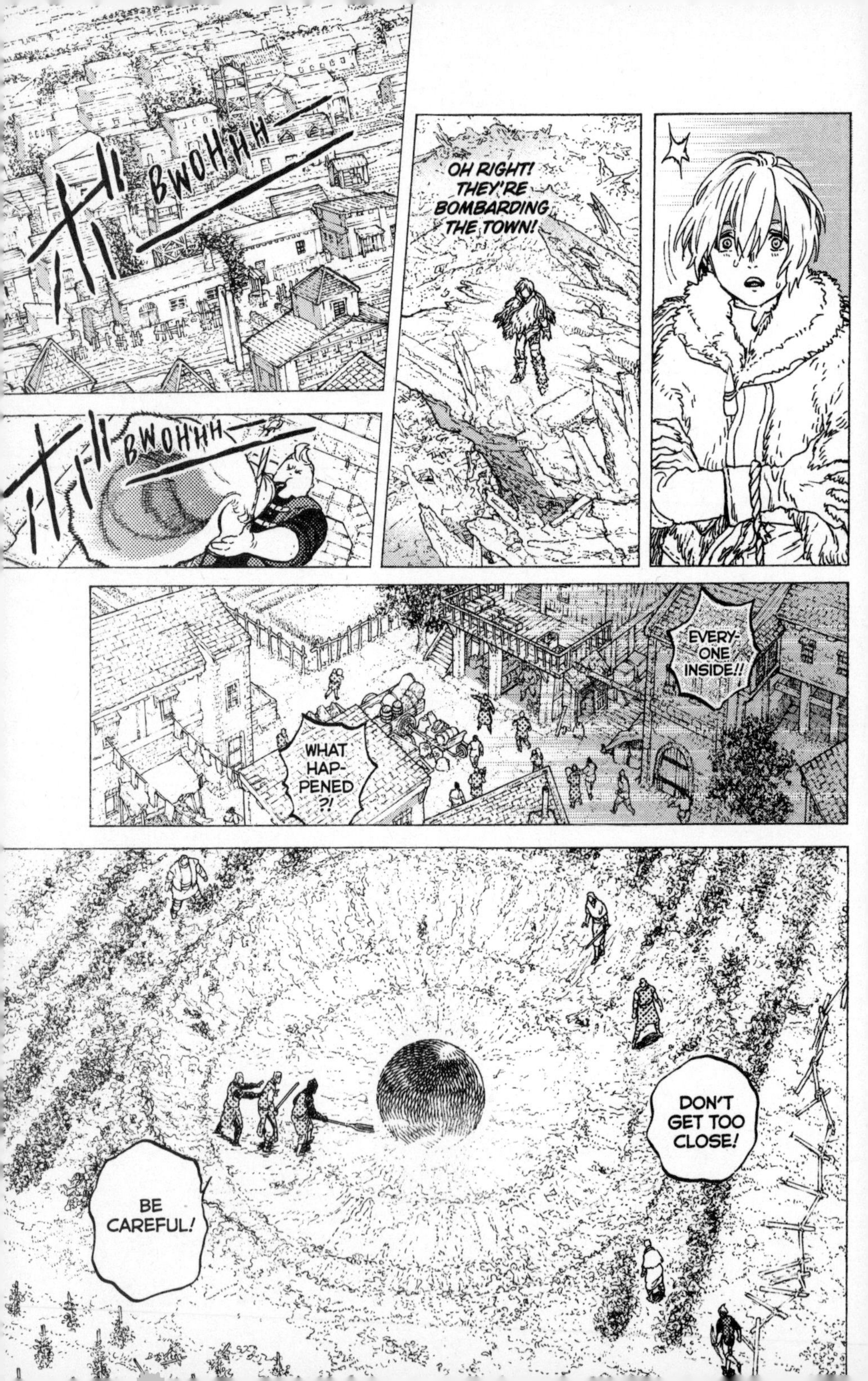
OH RIGHT! THEY'RE BOMBARDING THE TOWN!
BWOHHH
BWOHHH
EVERY-ONE INSIDE!!
WHAT HAP-PENED ?!
DON'T GET TOO CLOSE!
BE CAREFUL!

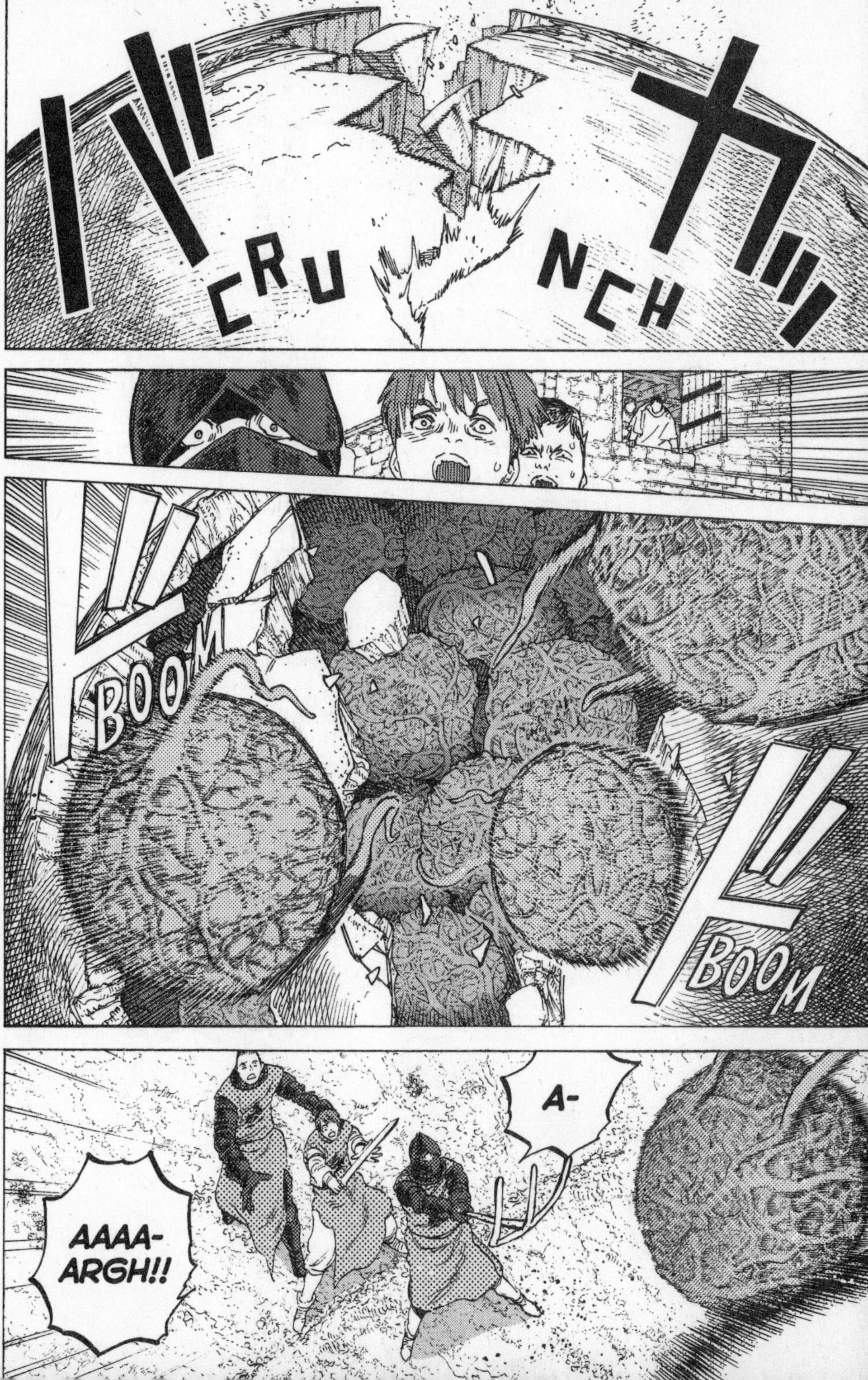
CRUNCH
BOOM
BOOM
A-
AAAA-ARGH!!

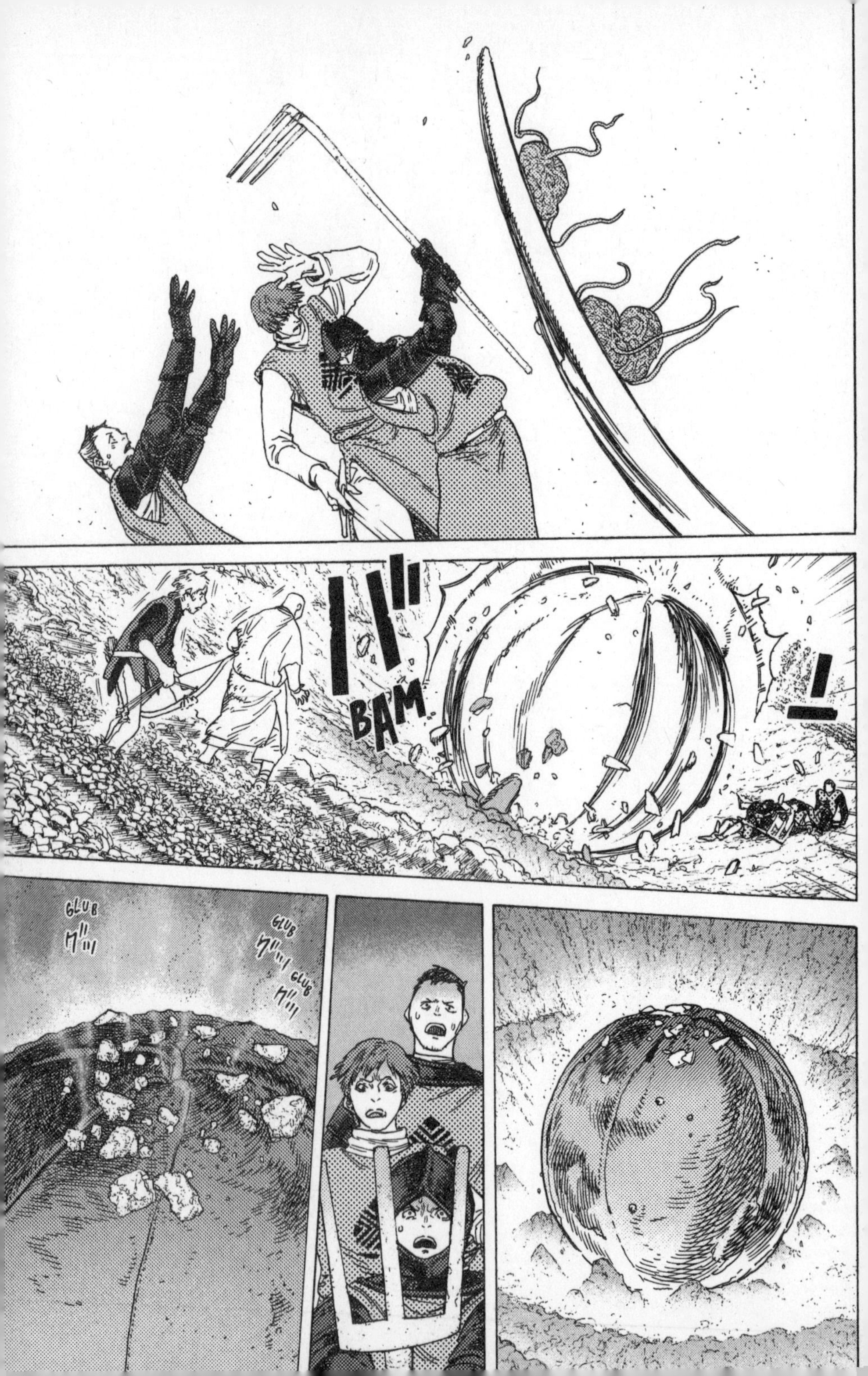
!
バ
BAM
GLUB
GLUB
GLUB

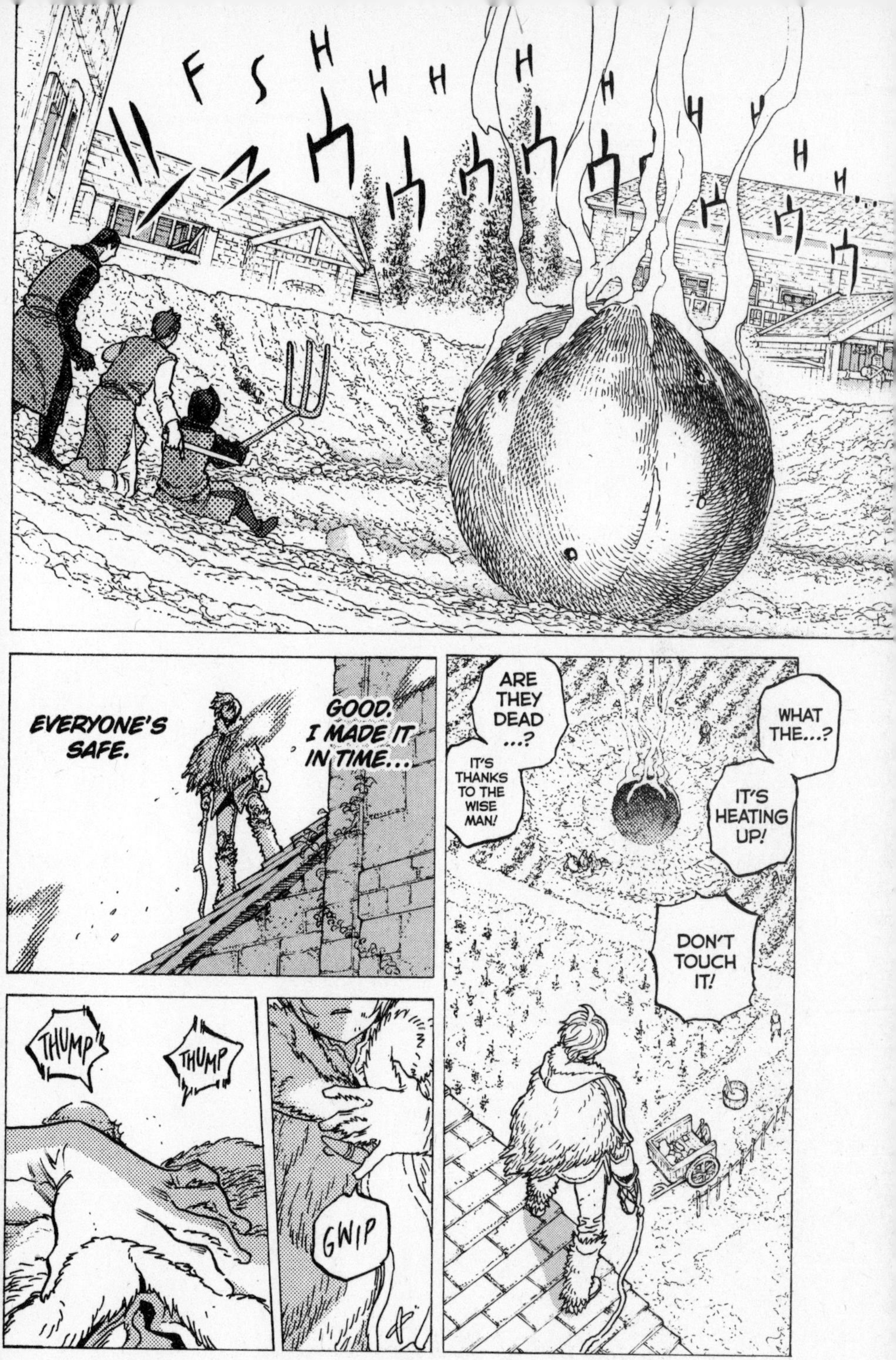
FSHHHHHHHHH
WHAT THE...?
ARE THEY DEAD ...?
IT'S HEATING UP!
IT'S THANKS TO THE WISE MAN!
DON'T TOUCH IT!
GOOD. I MADE IT IN TIME...
EVERYONE'S SAFE.
GWIP
THUMP
THUMP

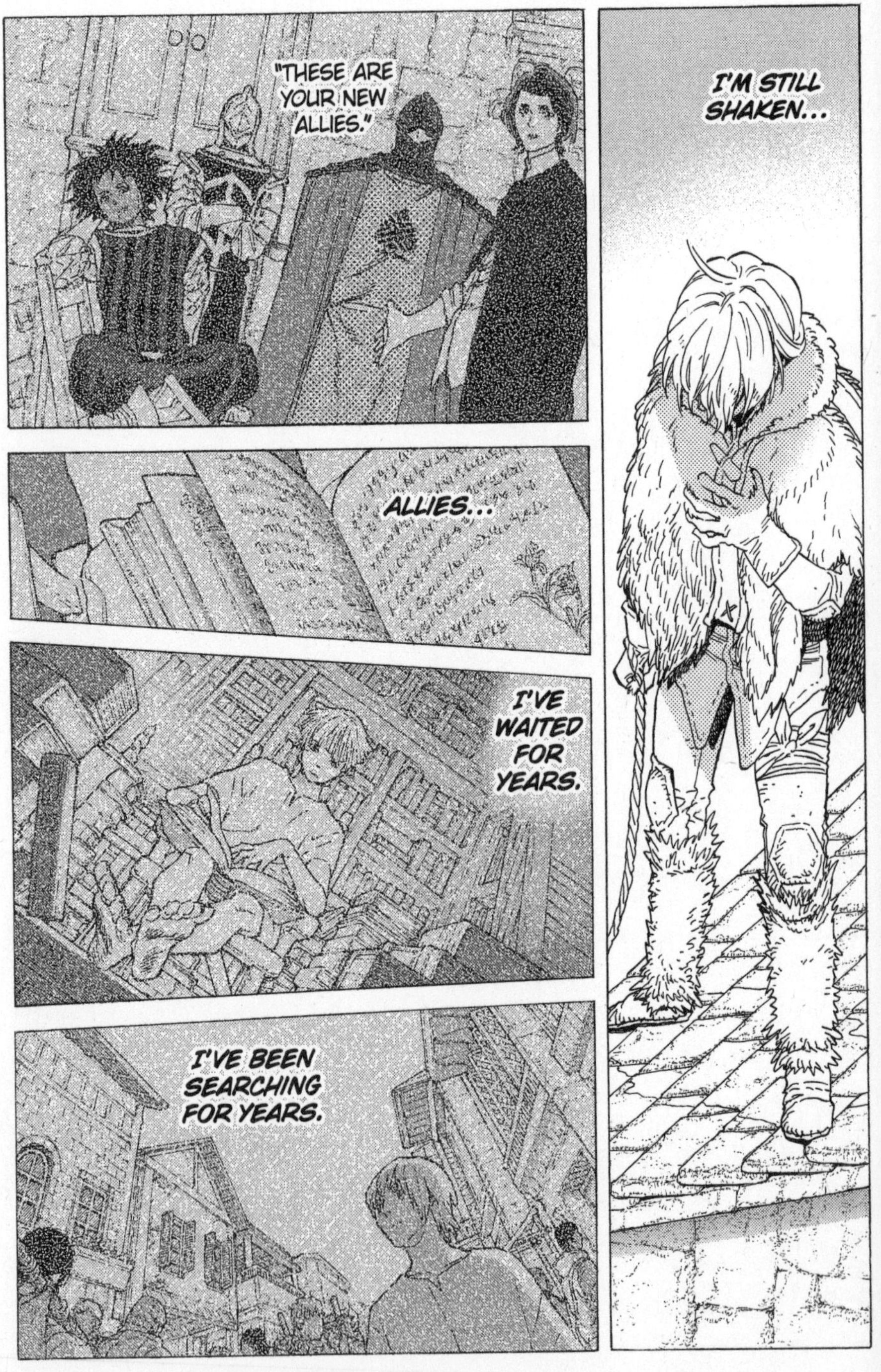
I'M STILL SHAKEN...
"THESE ARE YOUR NEW ALLIES."
ALLIES...
I'VE WAITED FOR YEARS.
I'VE BEEN SEARCHING FOR YEARS.

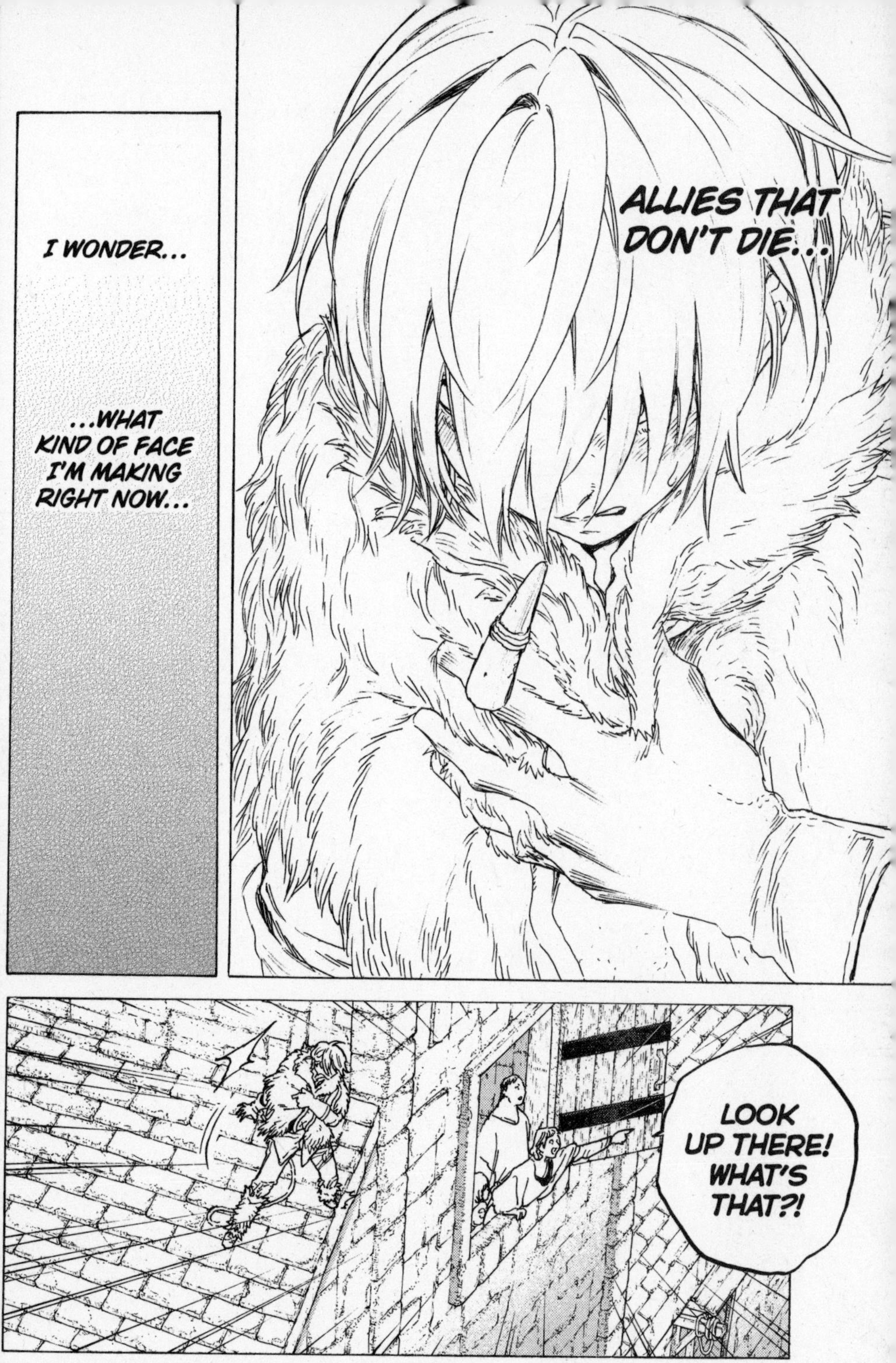
ALLIES THAT DON'T DIE...
I WONDER...
...WHAT KIND OF FACE I'M MAKING RIGHT NOW...
LOOK UP THERE! WHAT'S THAT?!

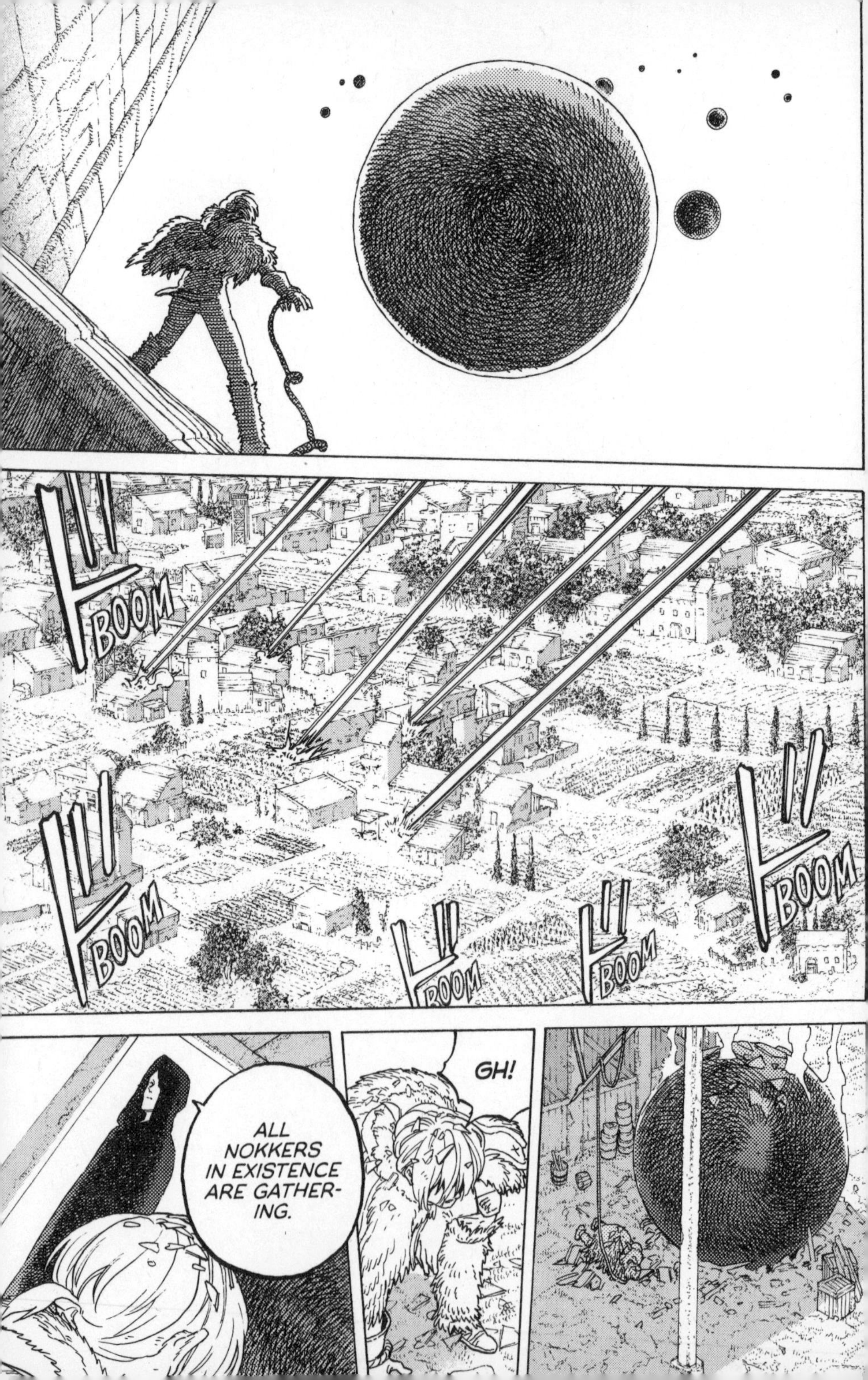
BOOM
BOOM
BOOM
BOOM
BOOM
BOOM
GH!
ALL NOKKERS IN EXISTENCE ARE GATHER-ING.

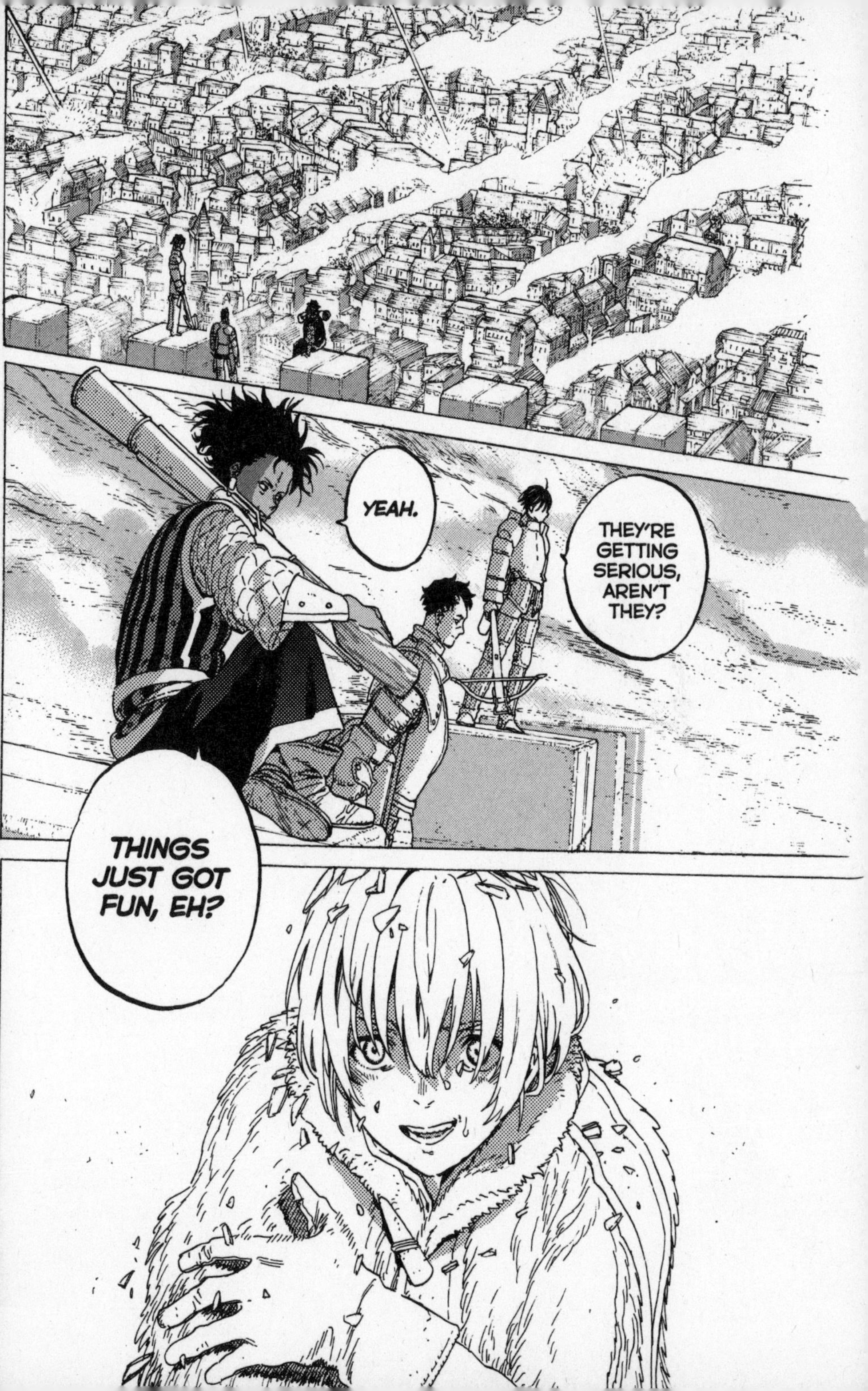
THEY'RE GETTING SERIOUS, AREN'T THEY?
YEAH.
THINGS JUST GOT FUN, EH?

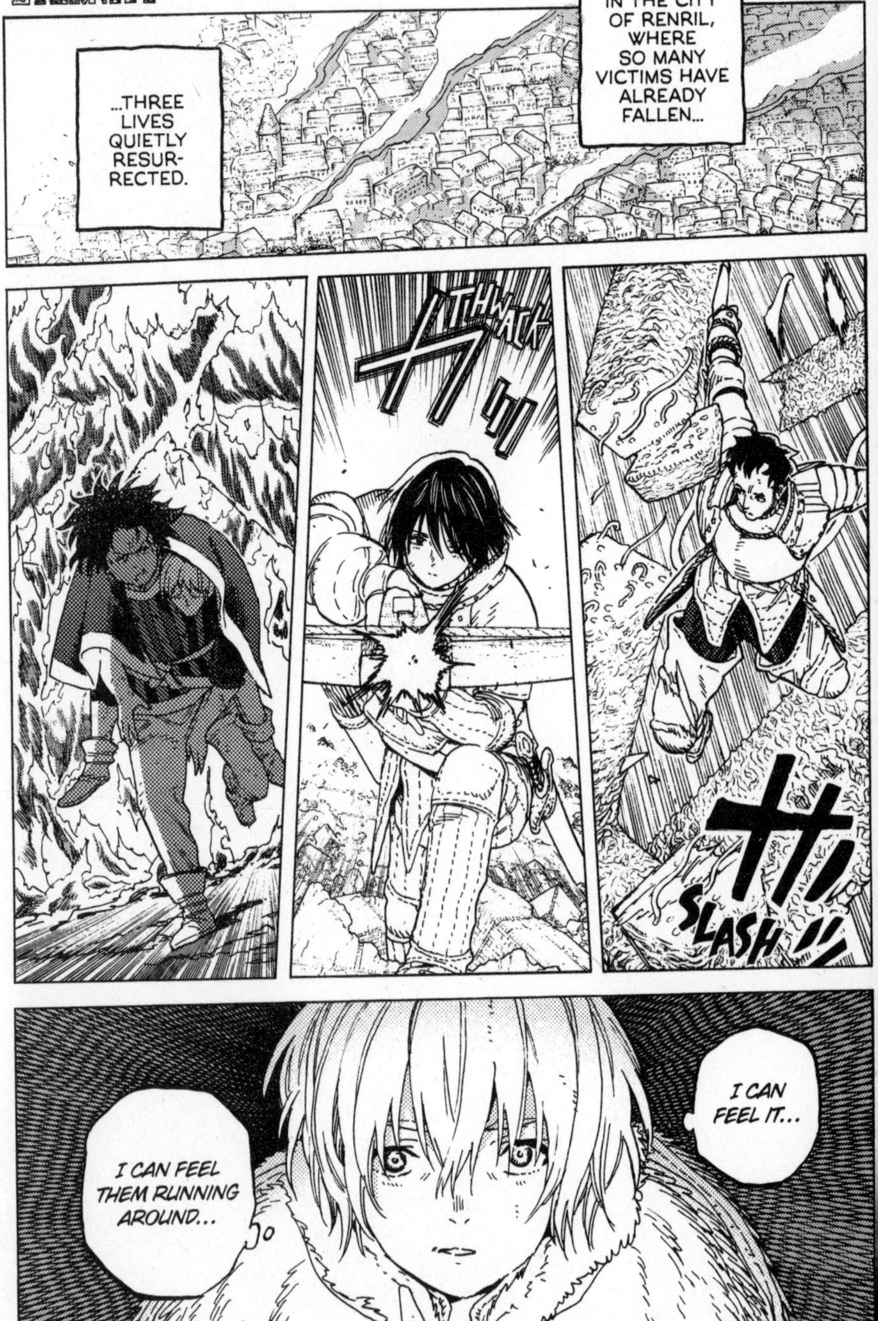
IN THE CITY OF RENRIL, WHERE SO MANY VICTIMS HAVE ALREADY FALLEN...
...THREE LIVES QUIETLY RESURRECTED.
SLASH
THWACK
I CAN FEEL IT...
I CAN FEEL THEM RUNNING AROUND...

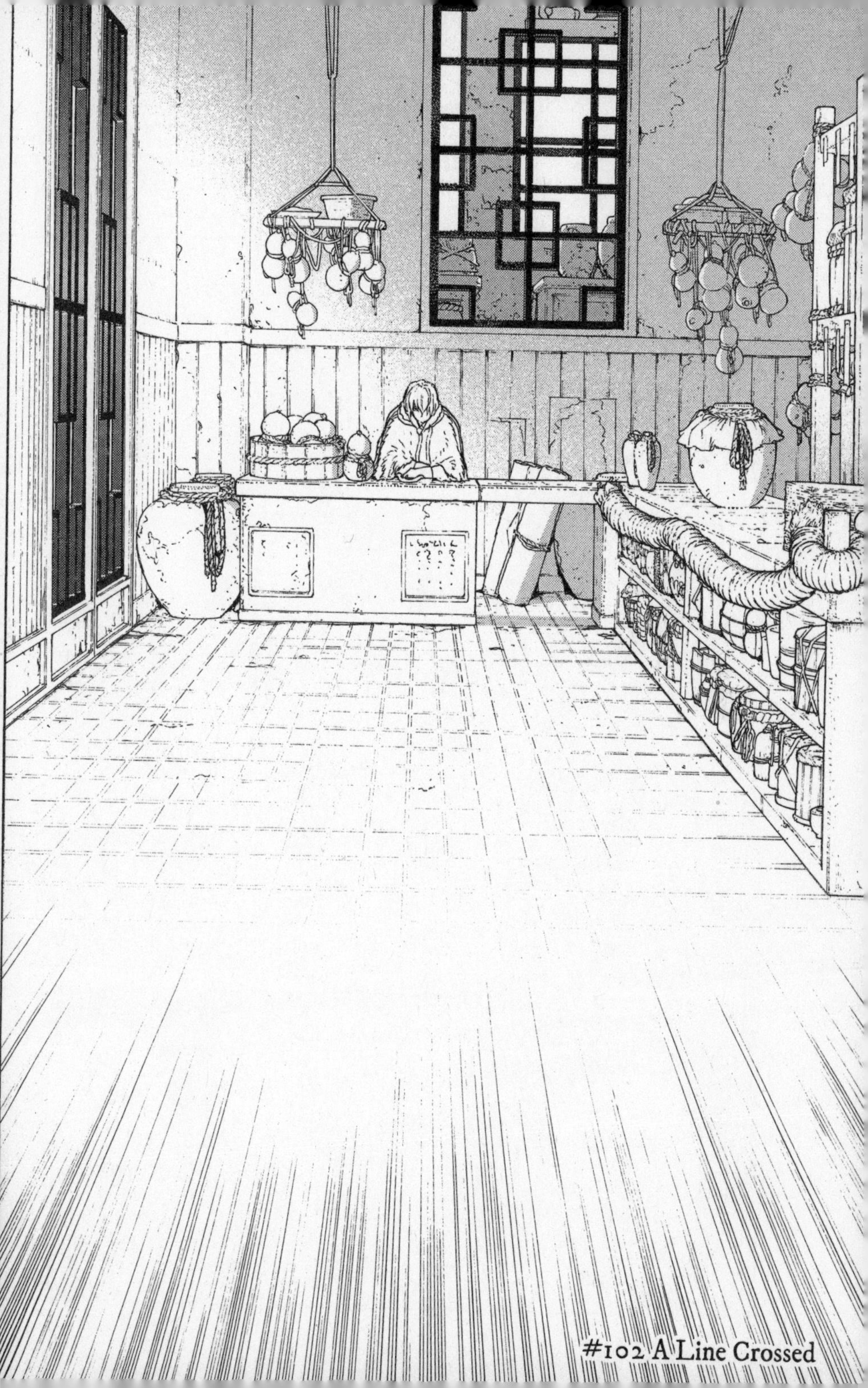

#102 A Line Crossed

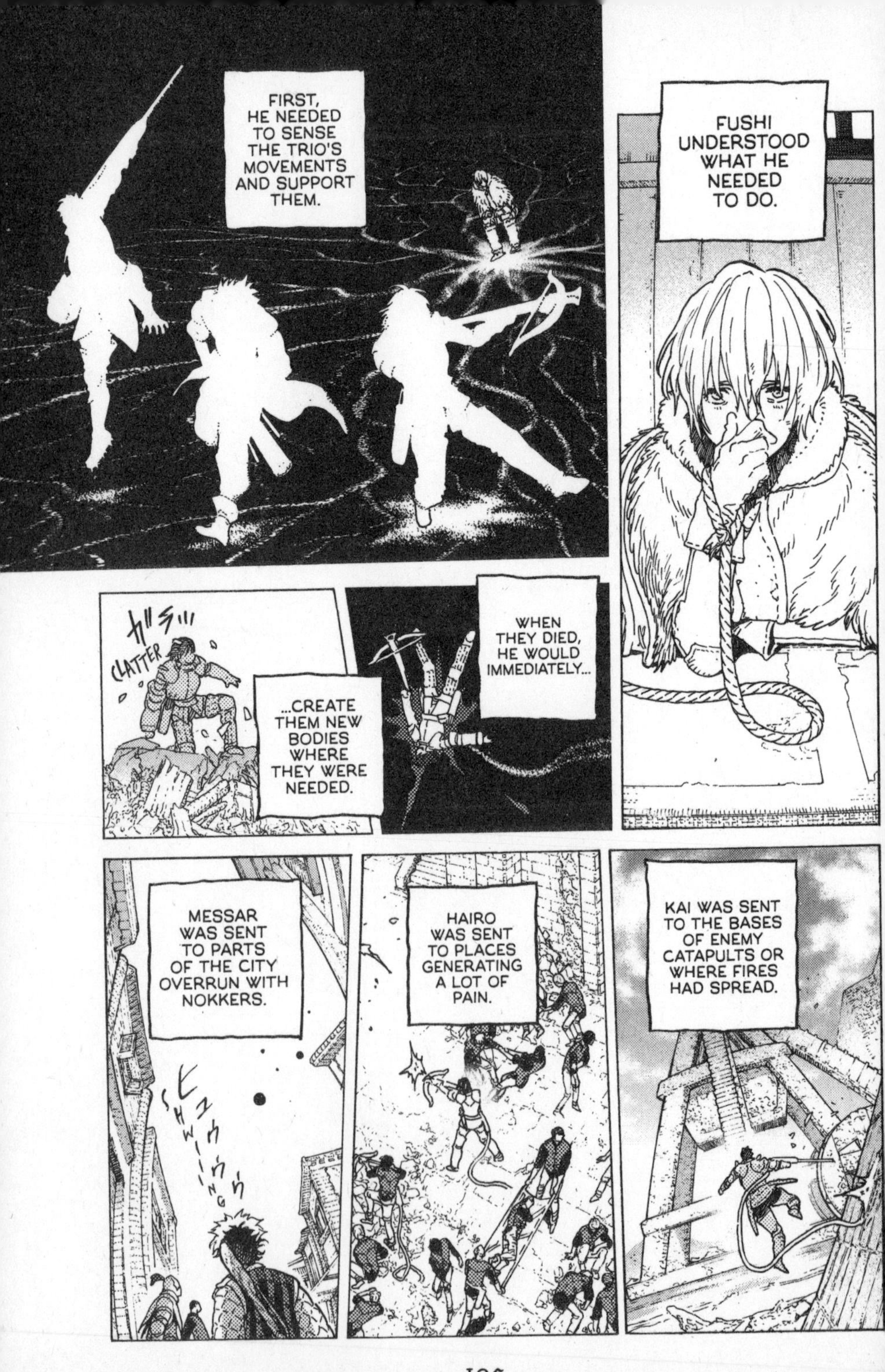
FUSHI UNDERSTOOD WHAT HE NEEDED TO DO.
FIRST, HE NEEDED TO SENSE THE TRIO'S MOVEMENTS AND SUPPORT THEM.
WHEN THEY DIED, HE WOULD IMMEDIATELY...
...CREATE THEM NEW BODIES WHERE THEY WERE NEEDED.
CLATTER
KAI WAS SENT TO THE BASES OF ENEMY CATAPULTS OR WHERE FIRES HAD SPREAD.
HAIRO WAS SENT TO PLACES GENERATING A LOT OF PAIN.
MESSAR WAS SENT TO PARTS OF THE CITY OVERRUN WITH NOKKERS.
SHWIIING

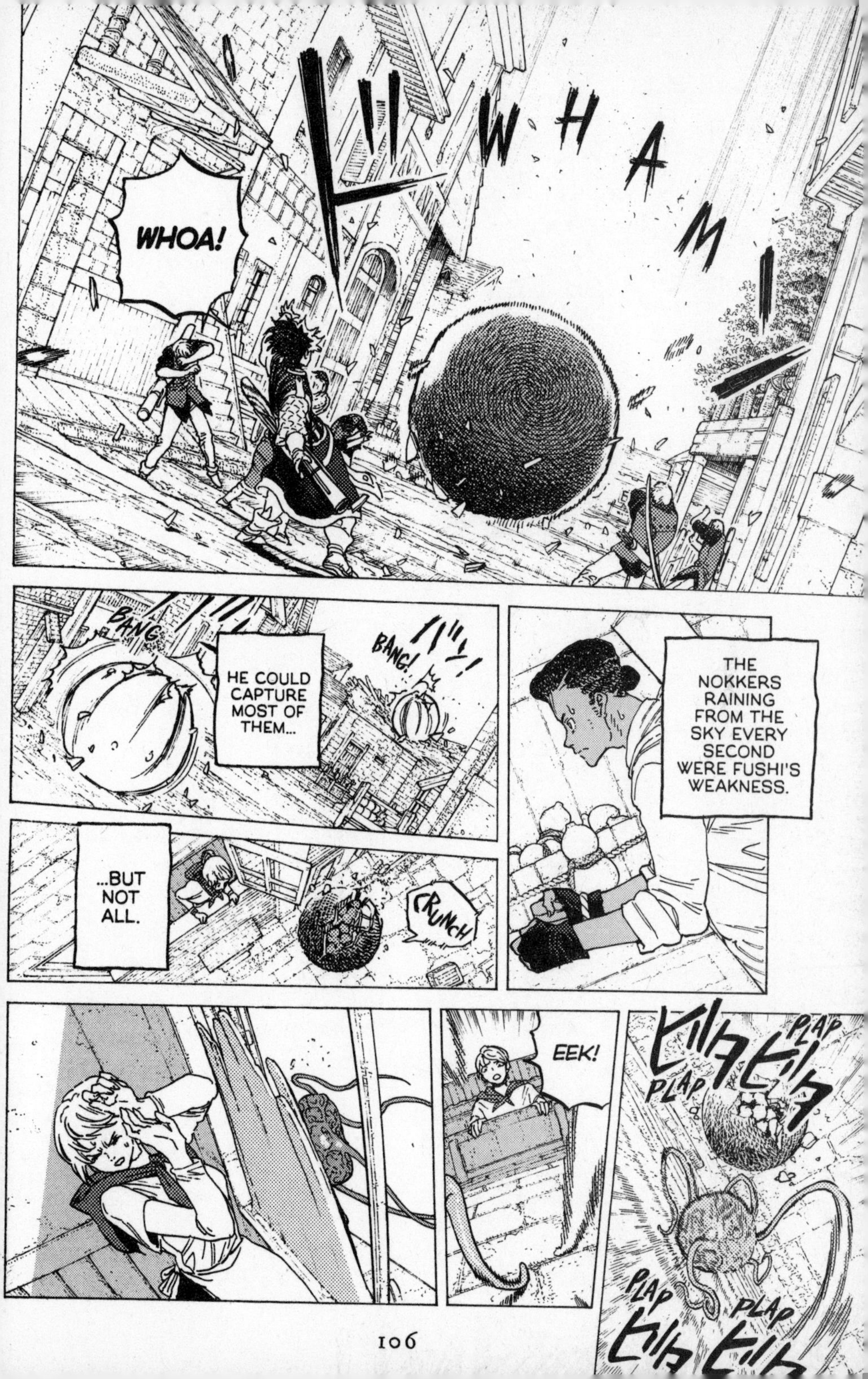
WHAM!
WHOA!
THE NOKKERS RAINING FROM THE SKY EVERY SECOND WERE FUSHI'S WEAKNESS.
BANG!
HE COULD CAPTURE MOST OF THEM...
BANG
CRUNCH
...BUT NOT ALL.
PLAP
PLAP
PLAP
PLAP
EEK!

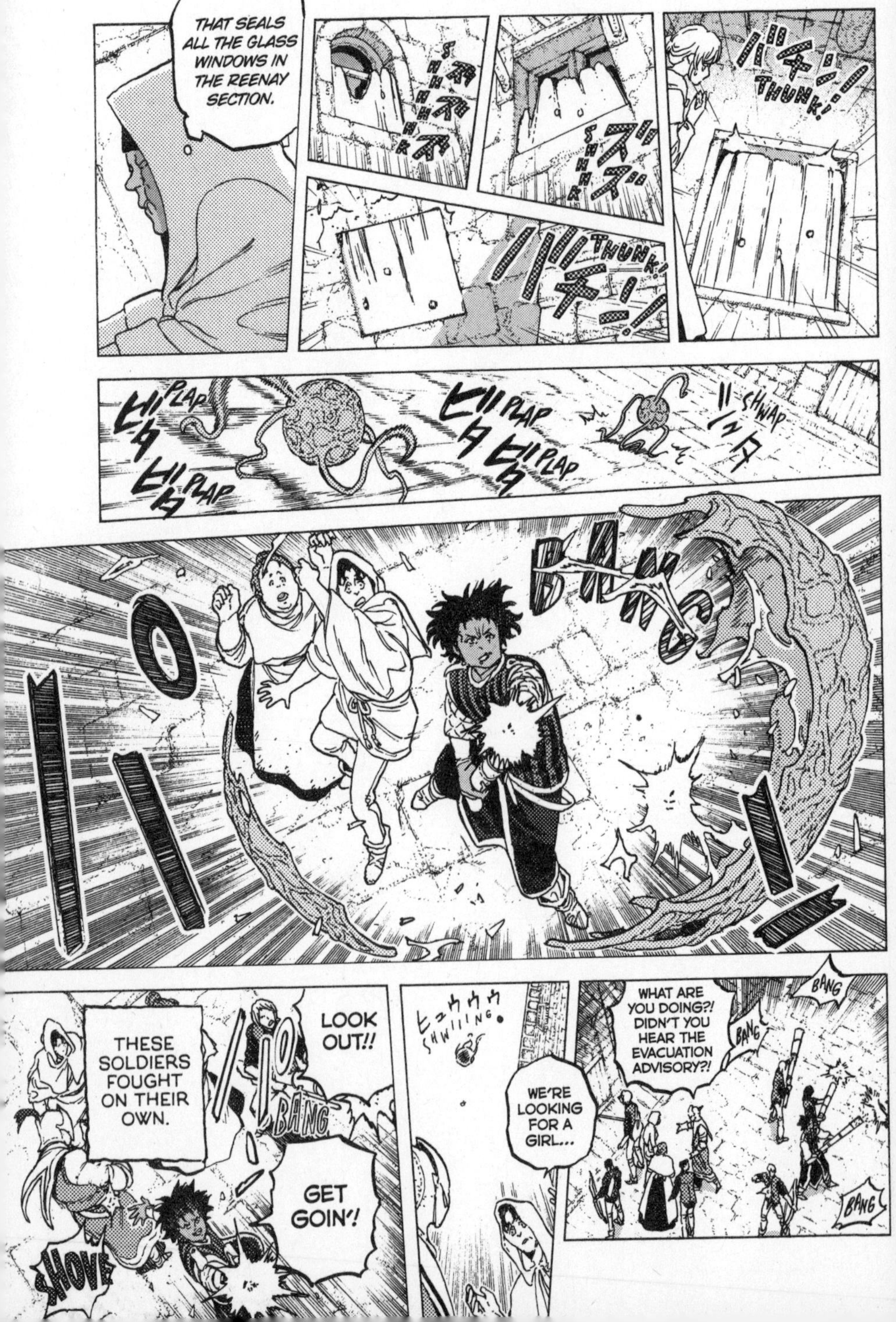
THUNK!
SHHHHK
SHHHHK
THUNK!
THAT SEALS ALL THE GLASS WINDOWS IN THE REENAY SECTION.
SHWAP
PLAP
PLAP
PLAP
PLAP
WHAT ARE YOU DOING?! DIDN'T YOU HEAR THE EVACUATION ADVISORY?!
BANG
BANG
BANG
SHWIIING
WE'RE LOOKING FOR A GIRL...
LOOK OUT!!
THESE SOLDIERS FOUGHT ON THEIR OWN.
BANG
GET GOIN'!
SHOVE

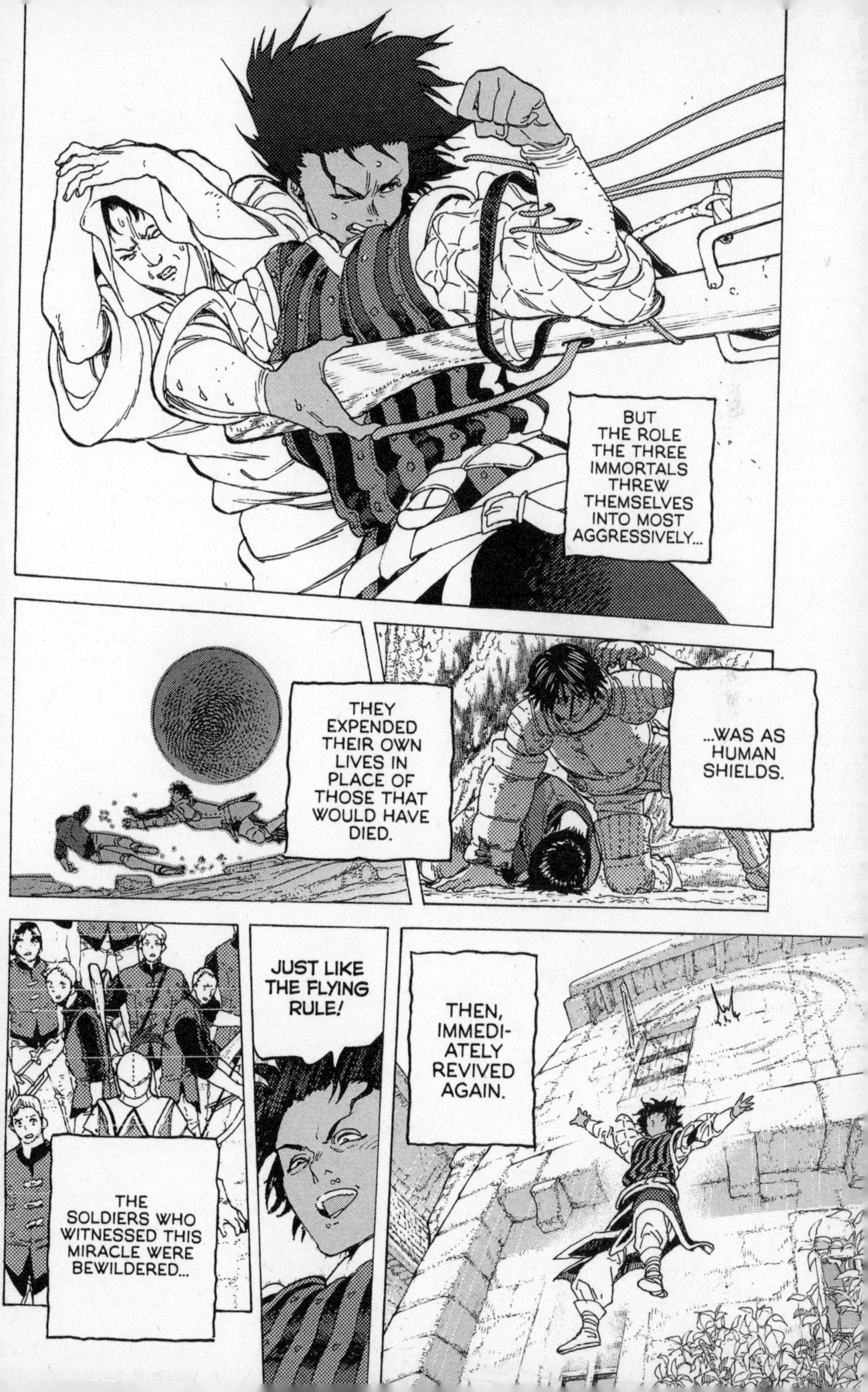
BUT THE ROLE THE THREE IMMORTALS THREW THEMSELVES INTO MOST AGGRESSIVELY...
...WAS AS HUMAN SHIELDS.
THEY EXPENDED THEIR OWN LIVES IN PLACE OF THOSE THAT WOULD HAVE DIED.
THEN, IMMEDI-ATELY REVIVED AGAIN.
JUST LIKE THE FLYING RULE!
THE SOLDIERS WHO WITNESSED THIS MIRACLE WERE BEWILDERED...

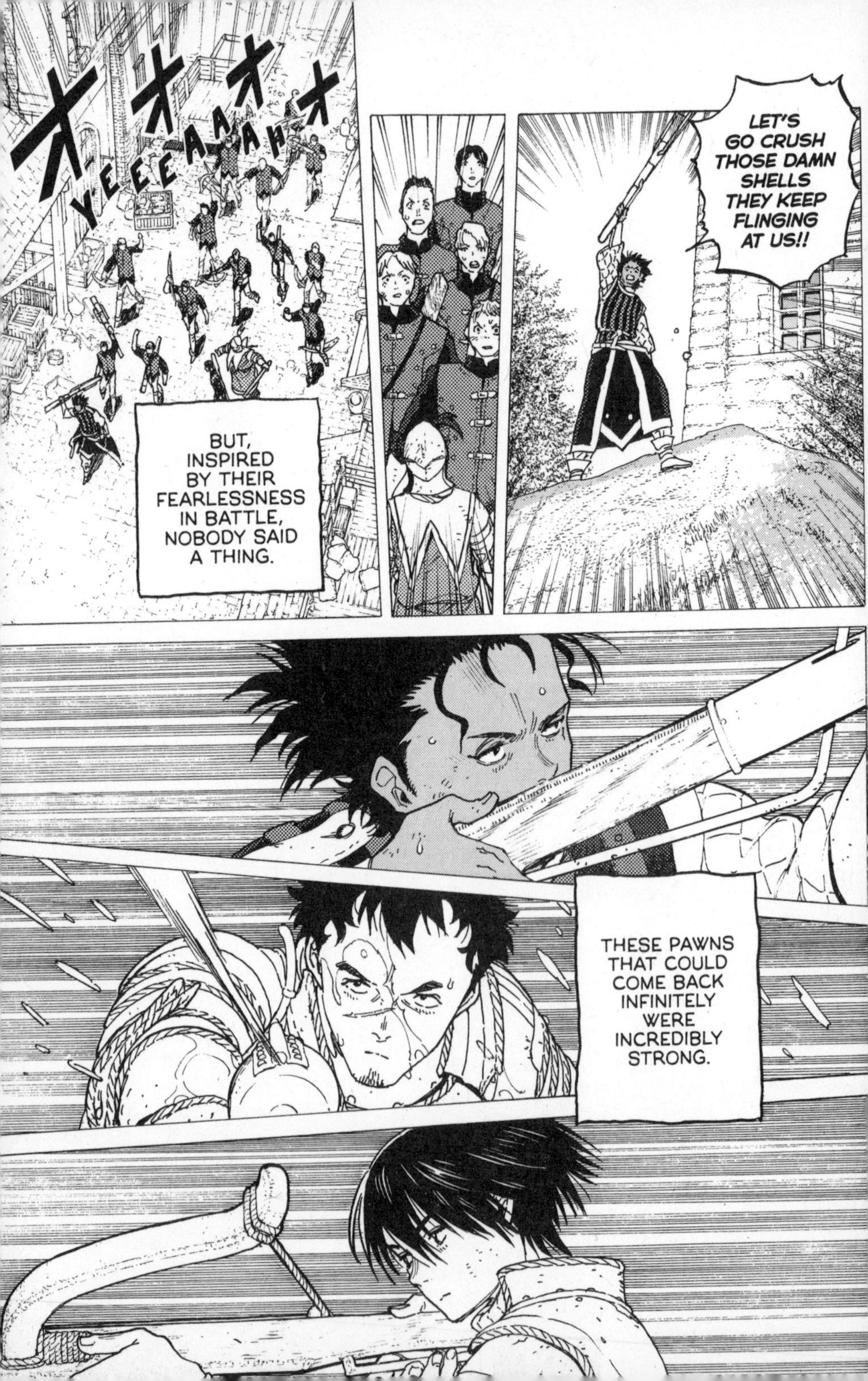
LET'S GO CRUSH THOSE DAMN SHELLS THEY KEEP FLINGING AT US!!
オオオオ
YEEEAAAH
BUT, INSPIRED BY THEIR FEARLESSNESS IN BATTLE, NOBODY SAID A THING.
THESE PAWNS THAT COULD COME BACK INFINITELY WERE INCREDIBLY STRONG.

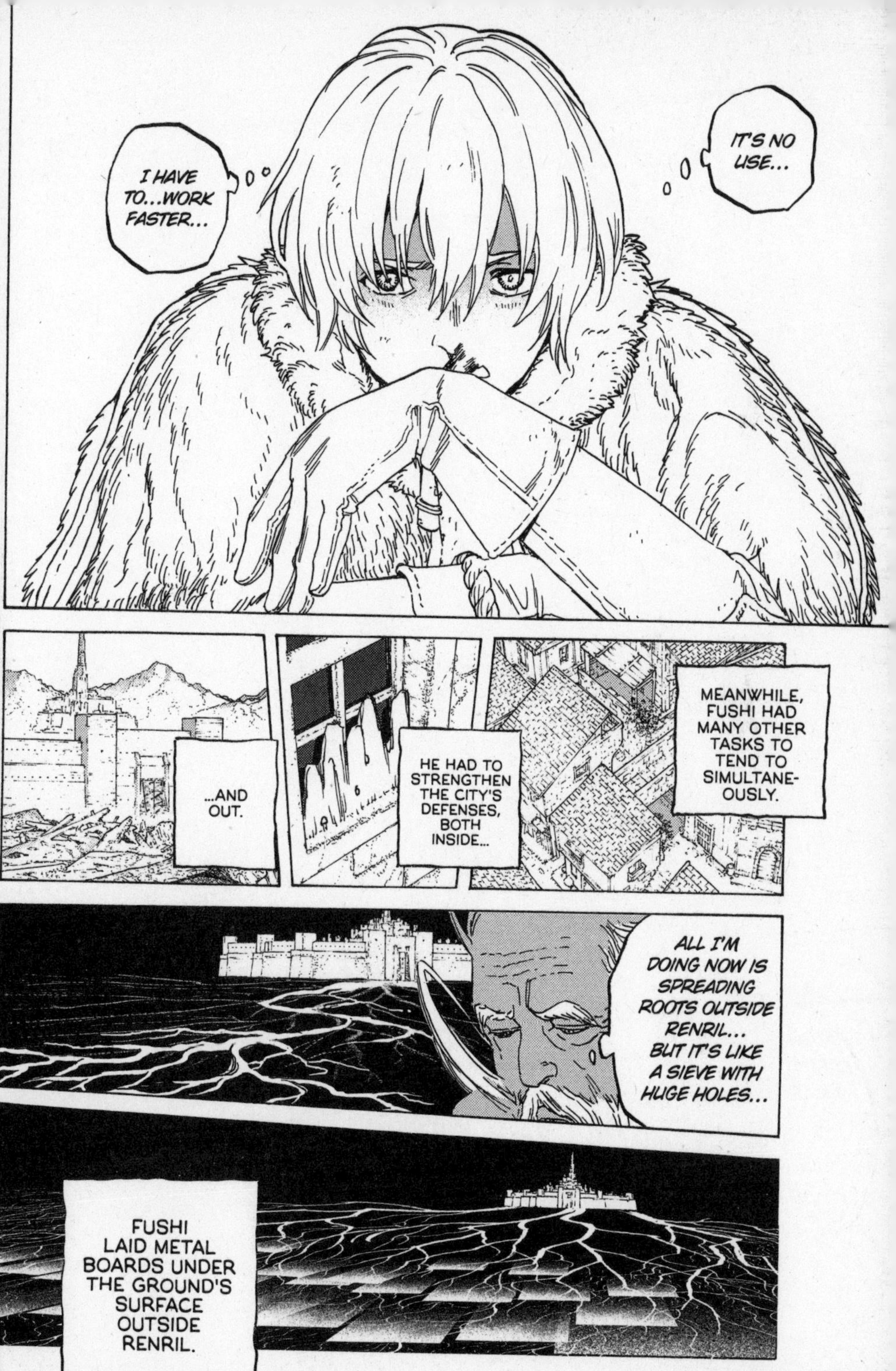
IT'S NO USE...
I HAVE TO...WORK FASTER...
MEANWHILE, FUSHI HAD MANY OTHER TASKS TO TEND TO SIMULTANE-OUSLY.
HE HAD TO STRENGTHEN THE CITY'S DEFENSES, BOTH INSIDE...
...AND OUT.
ALL I'M DOING NOW IS SPREADING ROOTS OUTSIDE RENRIL... BUT IT'S LIKE A SIEVE WITH HUGE HOLES...
FUSHI LAID METAL BOARDS UNDER THE GROUND'S SURFACE OUTSIDE RENRIL.

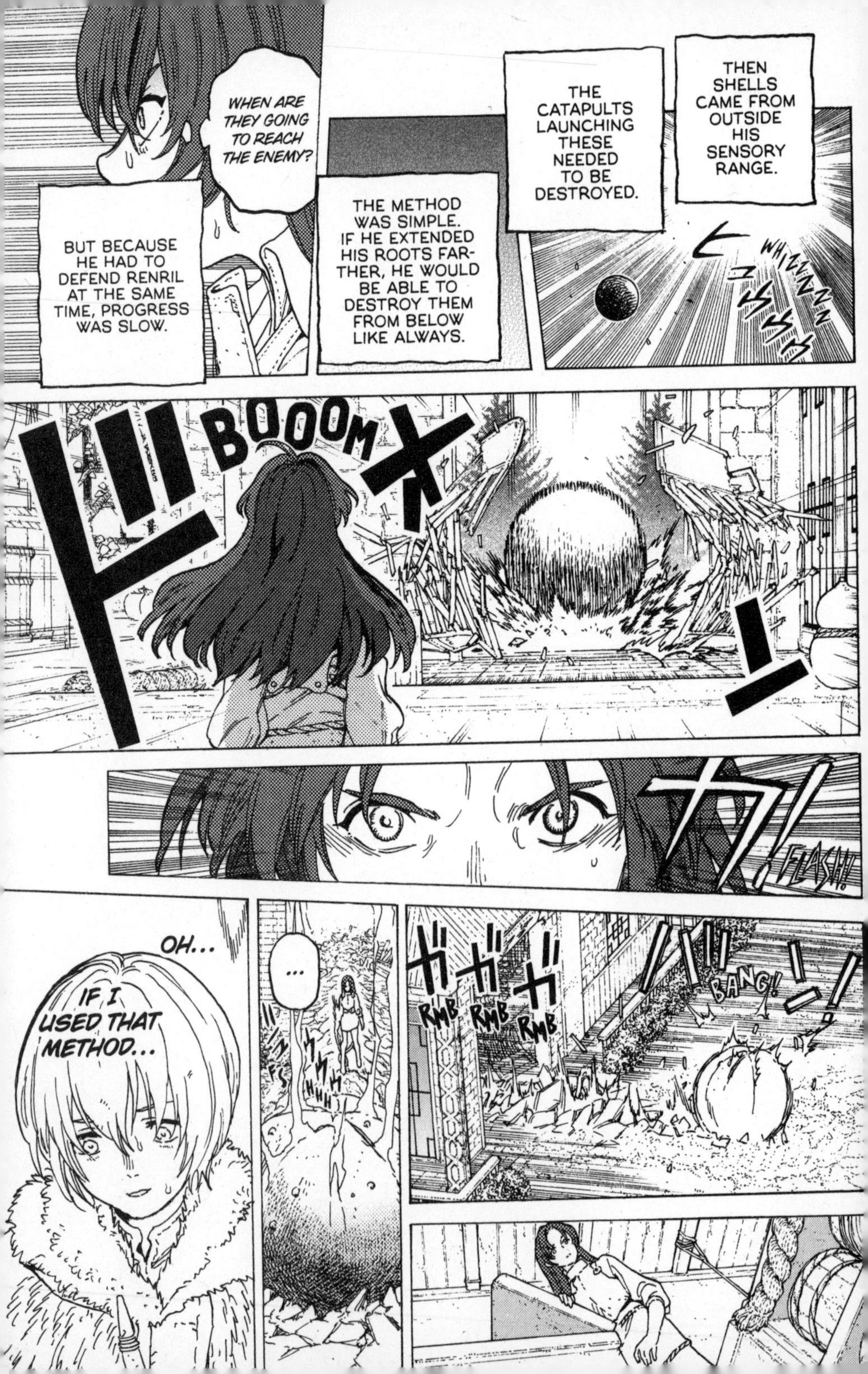
THEN SHELLS CAME FROM OUTSIDE HIS SENSORY RANGE.
THE CATAPULTS LAUNCHING THESE NEEDED TO BE DESTROYED.
WHIZZZZZZ
THE METHOD WAS SIMPLE. IF HE EXTENDED HIS ROOTS FARTHER, HE WOULD BE ABLE TO DESTROY THEM FROM BELOW LIKE ALWAYS.
WHEN ARE THEY GOING TO REACH THE ENEMY?
BUT BECAUSE HE HAD TO DEFEND RENRIL AT THE SAME TIME, PROGRESS WAS SLOW.
BOOOM
FLASH!
BANG!
RMB
RMB
RMB
...
OH...
IF I USED THAT METHOD...

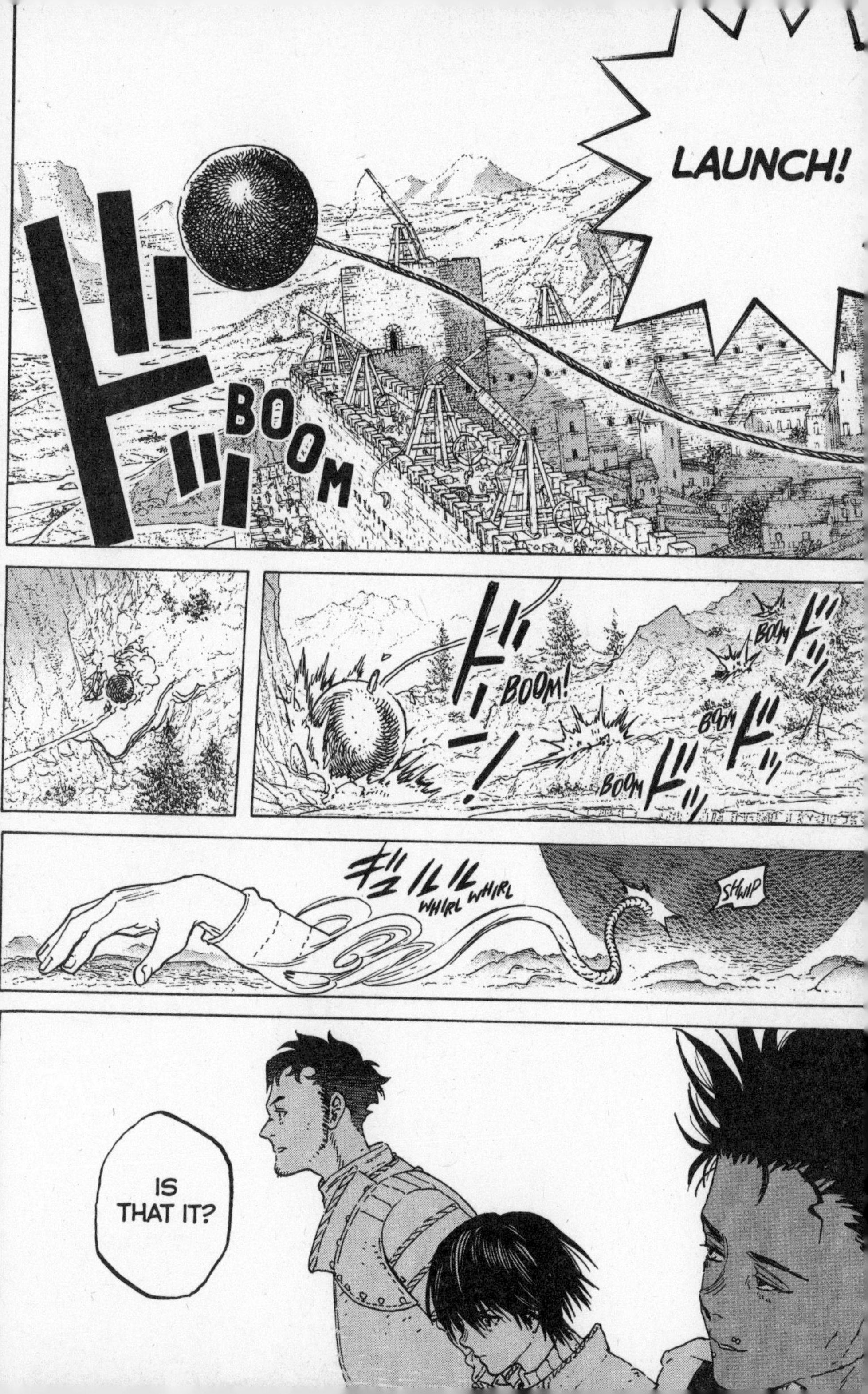
LAUNCH!
BOOM
BOOM
BOOM!
BOOM
BOOM
SHWIP
ギュルル
WHIRL WHIRL
IS THAT IT?

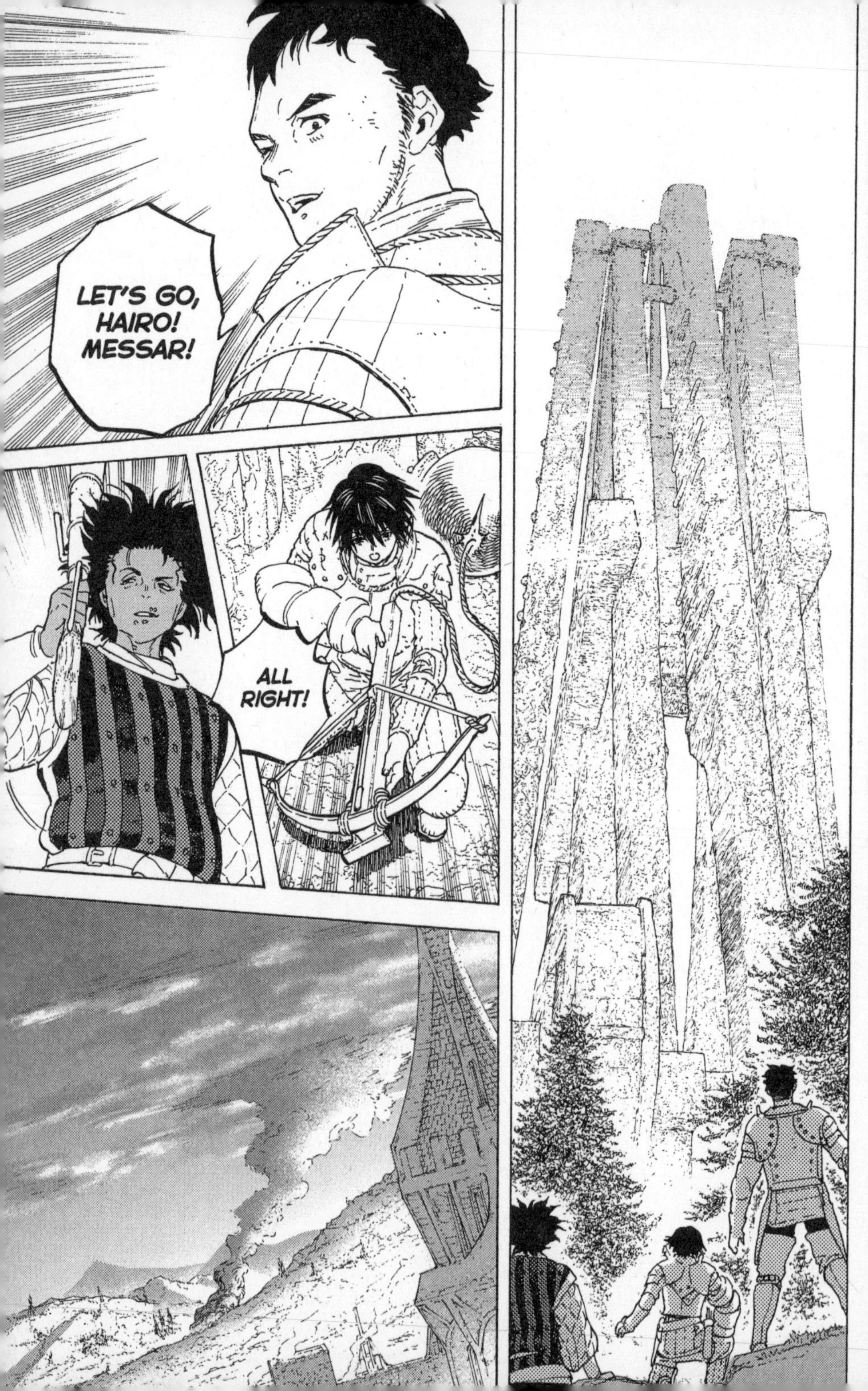
LET'S GO, HAIRO! MESSAR!
ALL RIGHT!

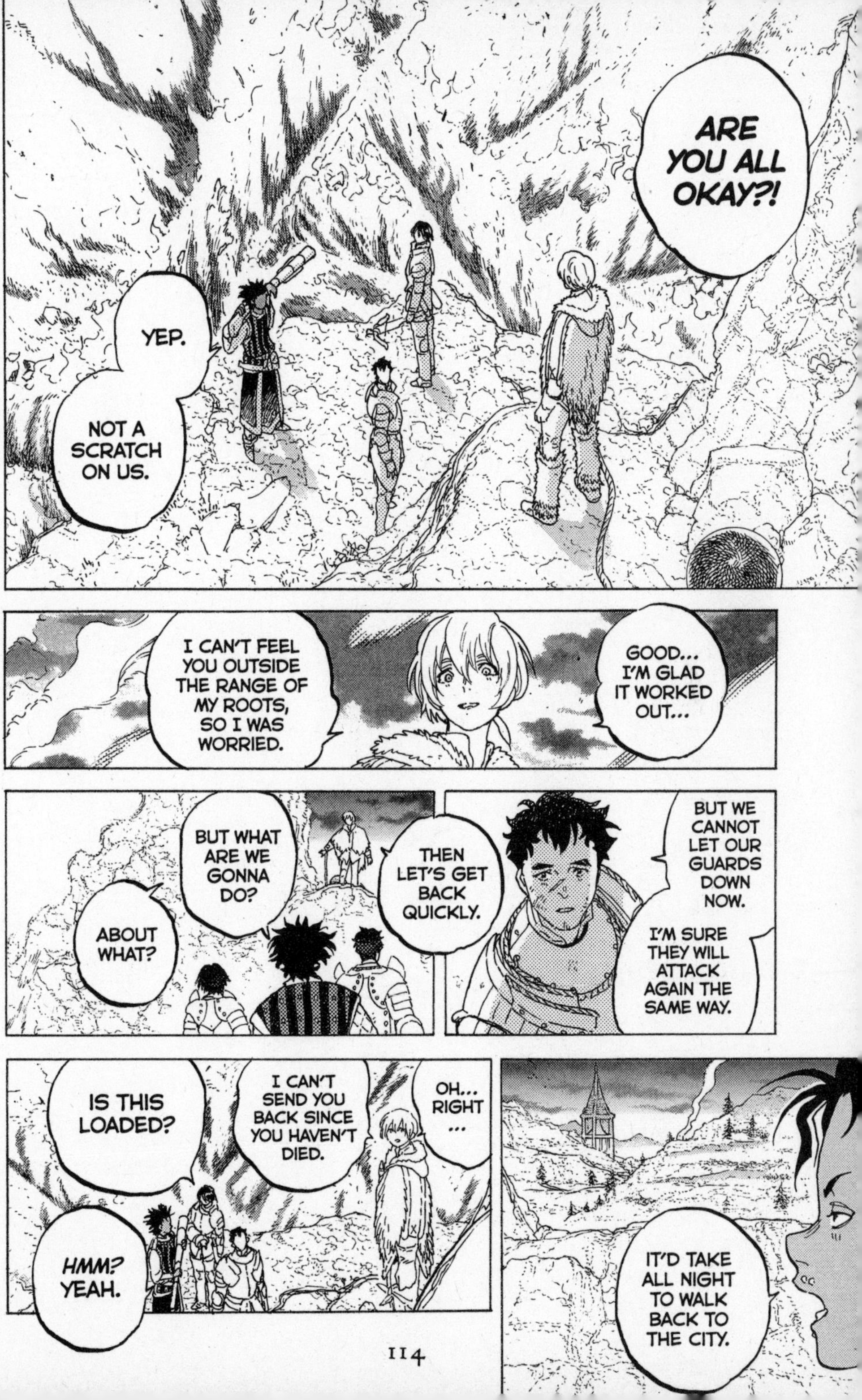
ARE YOU ALL OKAY?!
YEP.
NOT A SCRATCH ON US.
GOOD... I'M GLAD IT WORKED OUT...
I CAN'T FEEL YOU OUTSIDE THE RANGE OF MY ROOTS, SO I WAS WORRIED.
BUT WE CANNOT LET OUR GUARDS DOWN NOW.
I'M SURE THEY WILL ATTACK AGAIN THE SAME WAY.
THEN LET'S GET BACK QUICKLY.
BUT WHAT ARE WE GONNA DO?
ABOUT WHAT?
IT'D TAKE ALL NIGHT TO WALK BACK TO THE CITY.
OH... RIGHT...
I CAN'T SEND YOU BACK SINCE YOU HAVEN'T DIED.
IS THIS LOADED?
HMM? YEAH.

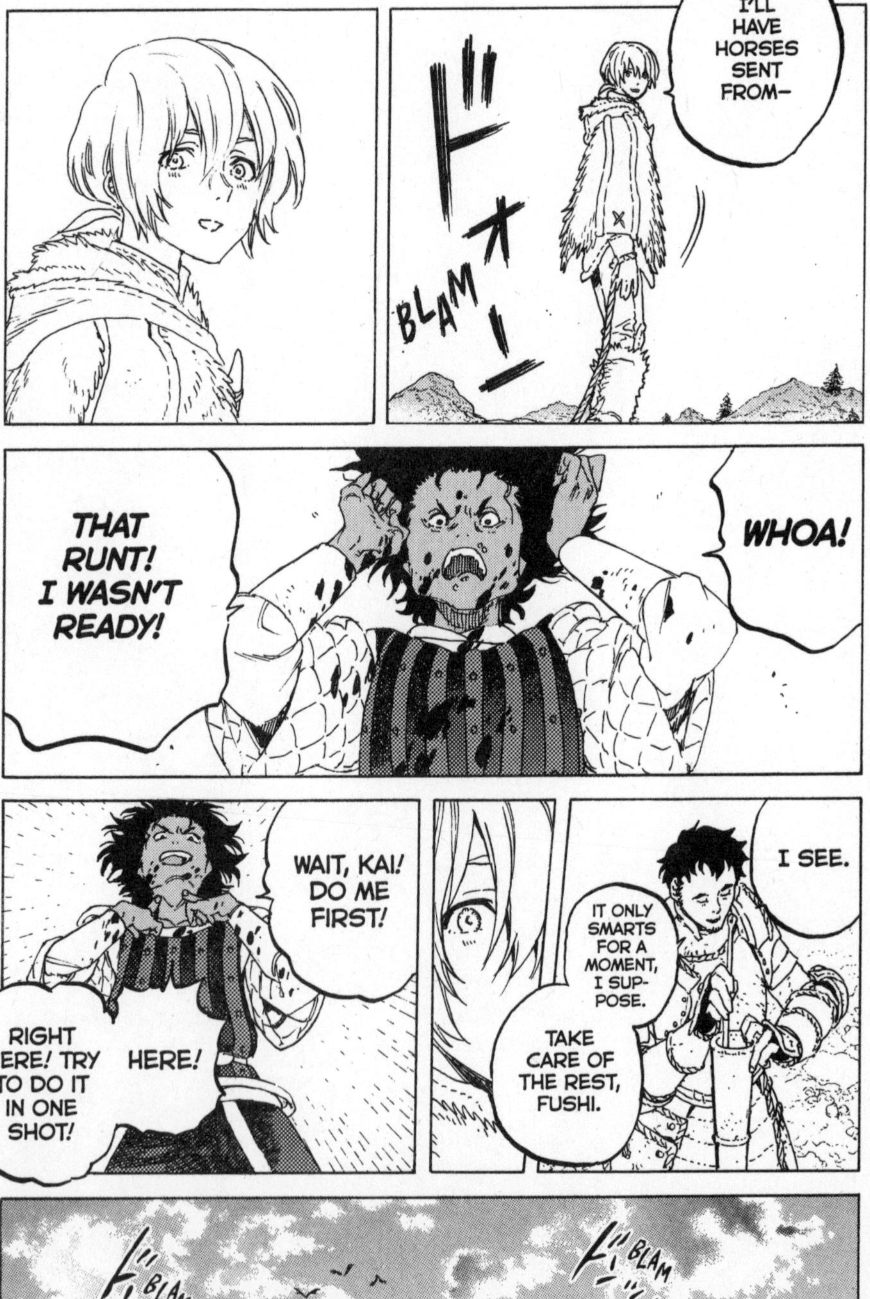
I'LL HAVE HORSES SENT FROM—
BLAM
WHOA!
THAT RUNT! I WASN'T READY!
I SEE.
IT ONLY SMARTS FOR A MOMENT, I SUPPOSE.
TAKE CARE OF THE REST, FUSHI.
WAIT, KAI! DO ME FIRST!
HERE!
RIGHT HERE! TRY TO DO IT IN ONE SHOT!
BLAM
BLAM

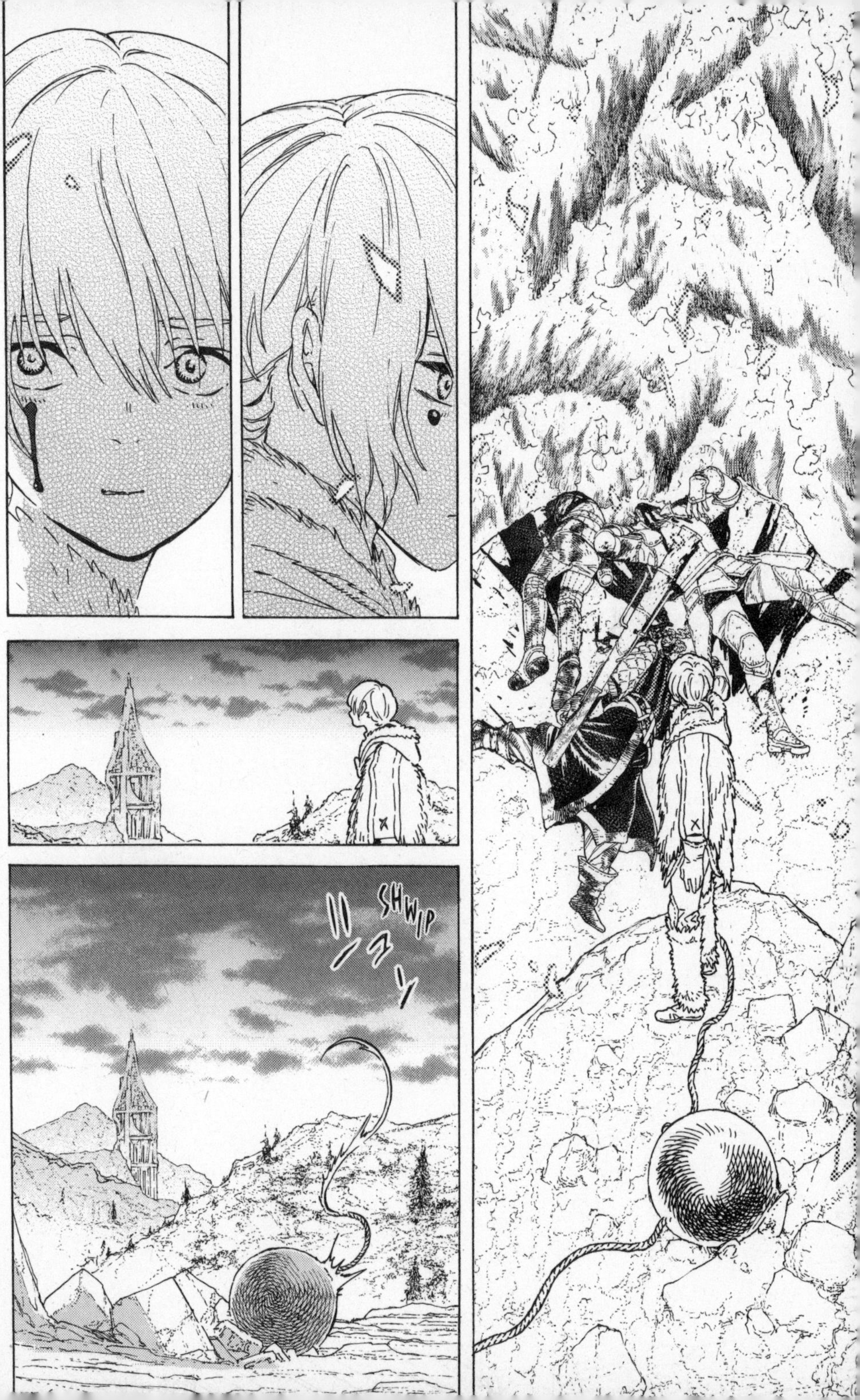
SHWIP

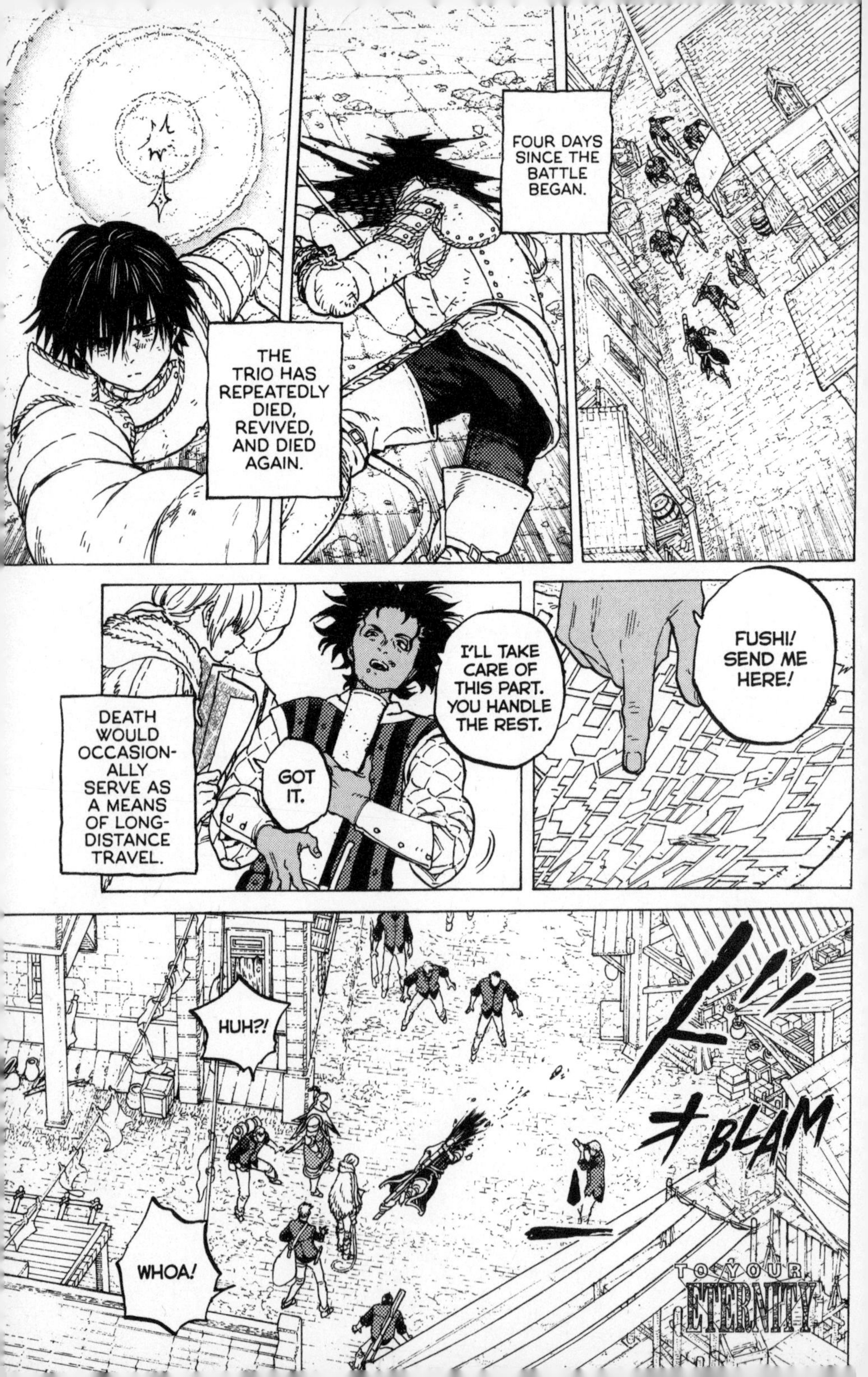
FOUR DAYS SINCE THE BATTLE BEGAN.
THE TRIO HAS REPEATEDLY DIED, REVIVED, AND DIED AGAIN.
FUSHI! SEND ME HERE!
I'LL TAKE CARE OF THIS PART. YOU HANDLE THE REST.
GOT IT.
DEATH WOULD OCCASION-ALLY SERVE AS A MEANS OF LONG-DISTANCE TRAVEL.
BLAM
HUH?!
WHOA!

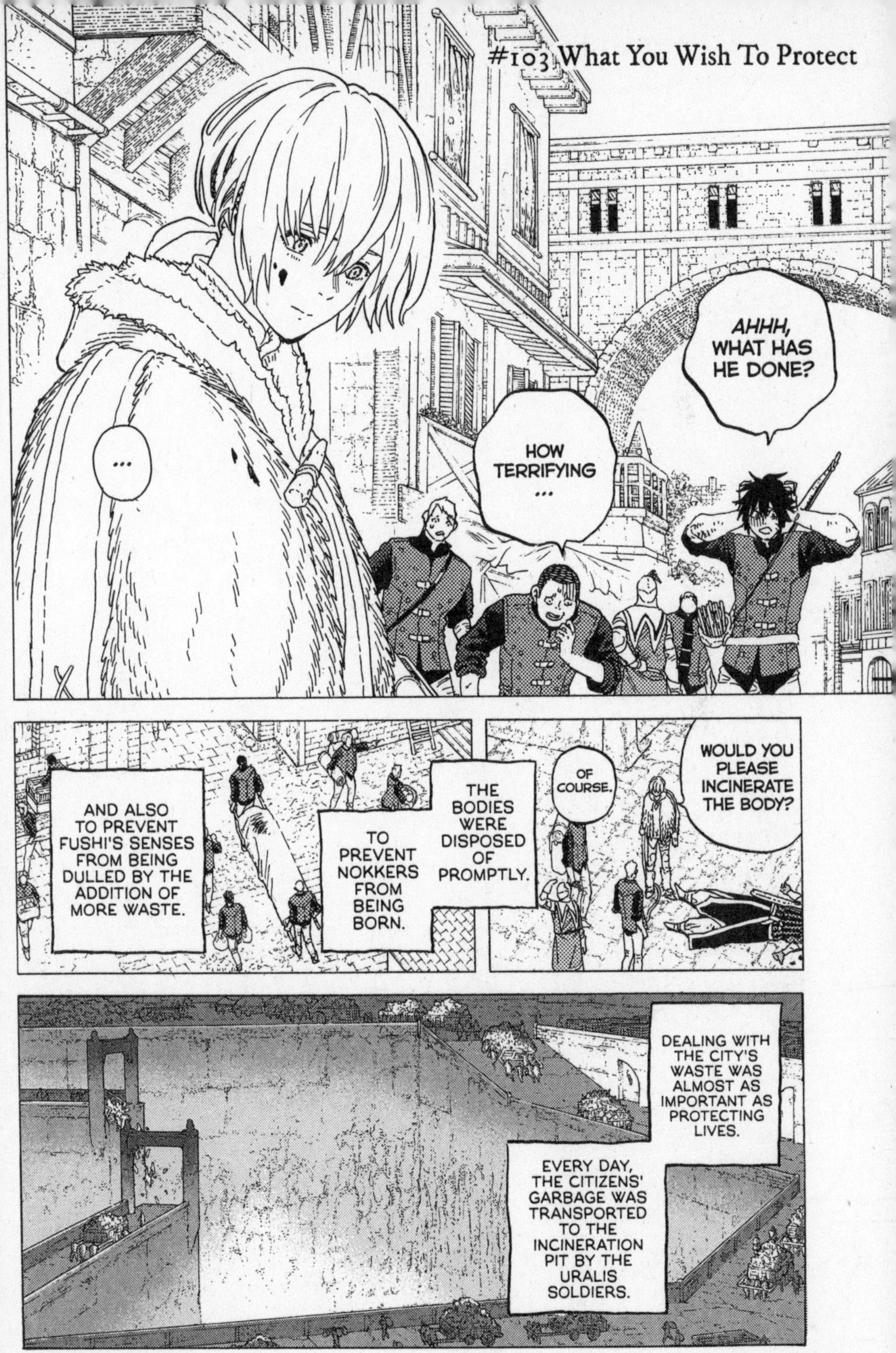
#103 What You Wish To Protect
AHHH, WHAT HAS HE DONE?
HOW TERRIFYING ...
...
WOULD YOU PLEASE INCINERATE THE BODY?
OF COURSE.
THE BODIES WERE DISPOSED OF PROMPTLY.
TO PREVENT NOKKERS FROM BEING BORN.
AND ALSO TO PREVENT FUSHI'S SENSES FROM BEING DULLED BY THE ADDITION OF MORE WASTE.
DEALING WITH THE CITY'S WASTE WAS ALMOST AS IMPORTANT AS PROTECTING LIVES.
EVERY DAY, THE CITIZENS' GARBAGE WAS TRANSPORTED TO THE INCINERATION PIT BY THE URALIS SOLDIERS.

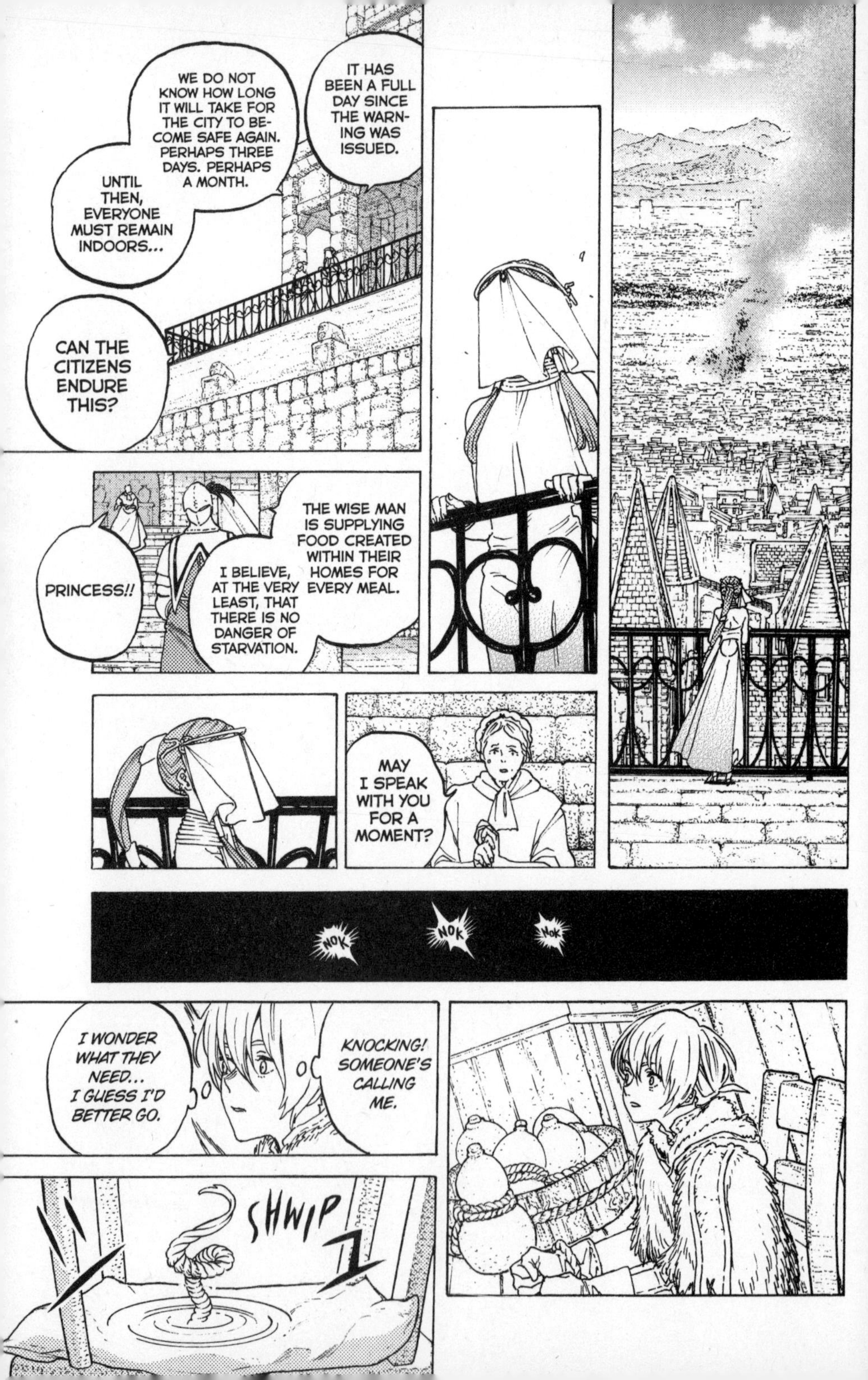
IT HAS BEEN A FULL DAY SINCE THE WARNING WAS ISSUED.
WE DO NOT KNOW HOW LONG IT WILL TAKE FOR THE CITY TO BECOME SAFE AGAIN. PERHAPS THREE DAYS. PERHAPS A MONTH.
UNTIL THEN, EVERYONE MUST REMAIN INDOORS...
CAN THE CITIZENS ENDURE THIS?
THE WISE MAN IS SUPPLYING FOOD CREATED WITHIN THEIR HOMES FOR EVERY MEAL.
I BELIEVE, AT THE VERY LEAST, THAT THERE IS NO DANGER OF STARVATION.
PRINCESS!!
MAY I SPEAK WITH YOU FOR A MOMENT?
NOK
NOK
NOK
KNOCKING! SOMEONE'S CALLING ME.
I WONDER WHAT THEY NEED... I GUESS I'D BETTER GO.
SHWIP

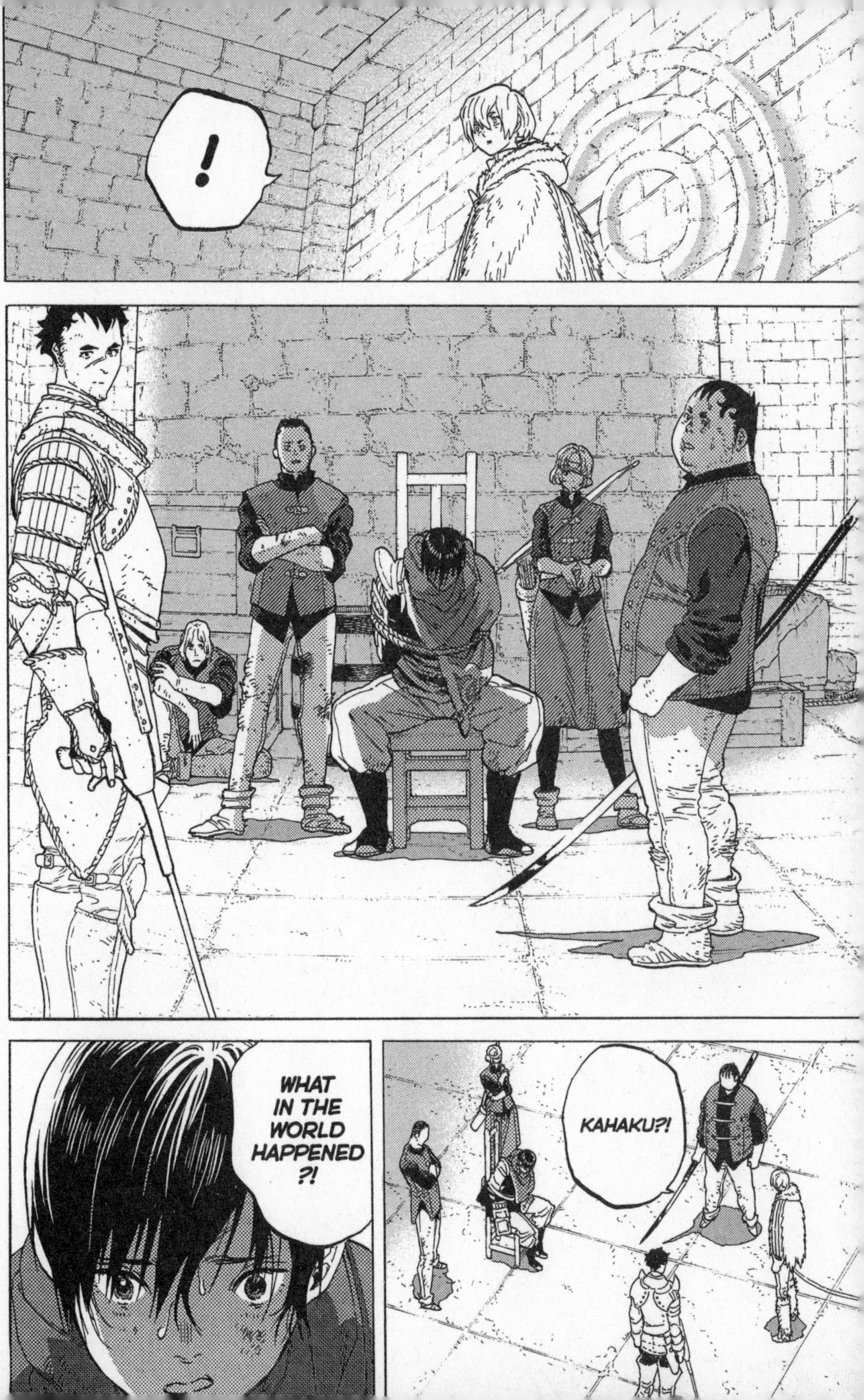
!
KAHAKU?!
WHAT IN THE WORLD HAPPENED?!

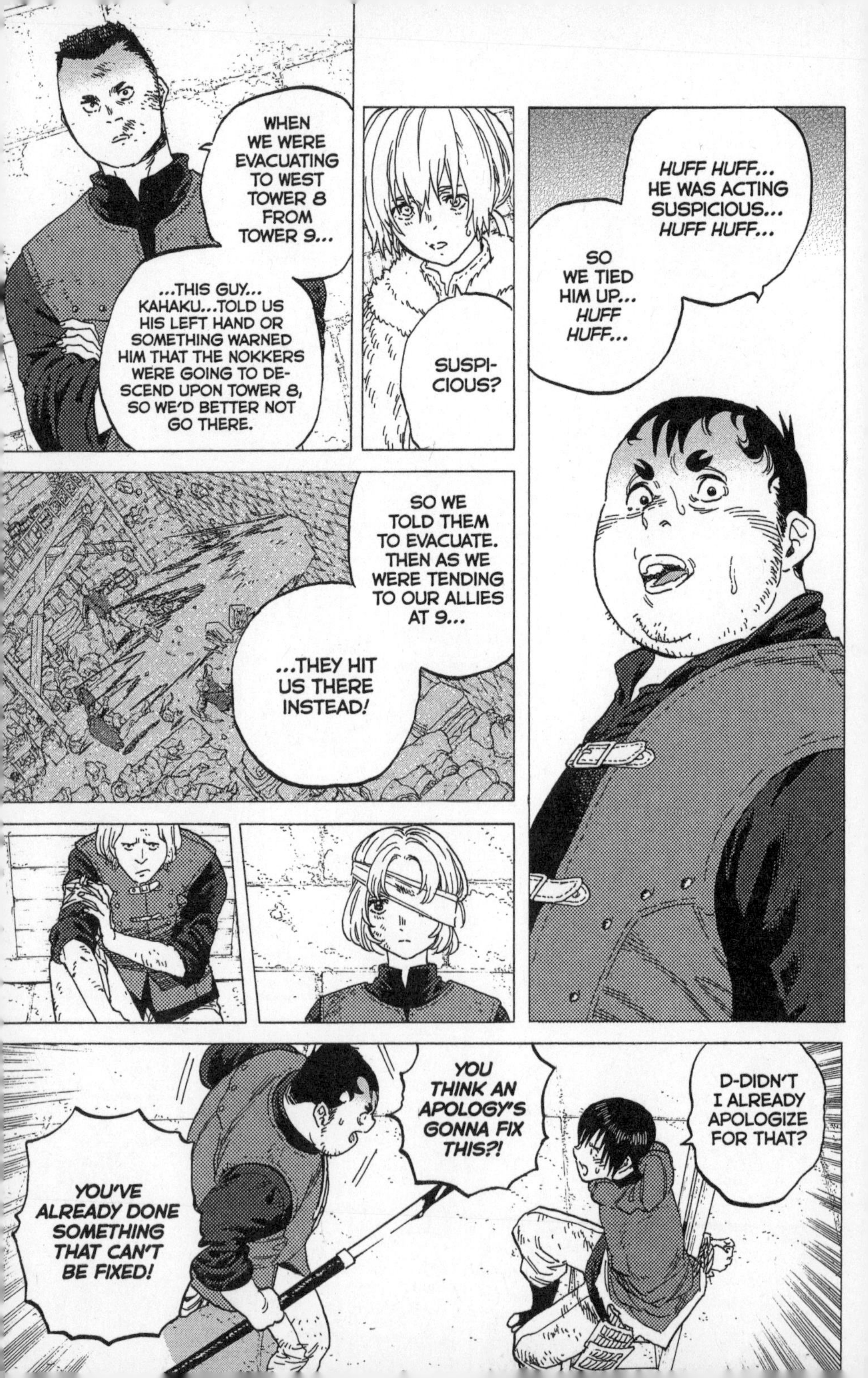
HUFF HUFF... HE WAS ACTING SUSPICIOUS... HUFF HUFF...
SO WE TIED HIM UP... HUFF HUFF...
SUSPICIOUS?
WHEN WE WERE EVACUATING TO WEST TOWER 8 FROM TOWER 9...
...THIS GUY... KAHAKU...TOLD US HIS LEFT HAND OR SOMETHING WARNED HIM THAT THE NOKKERS WERE GOING TO DESCEND UPON TOWER 8, SO WE'D BETTER NOT GO THERE.
SO WE TOLD THEM TO EVACUATE. THEN AS WE WERE TENDING TO OUR ALLIES AT 9...
...THEY HIT US THERE INSTEAD!
D-DIDN'T I ALREADY APOLOGIZE FOR THAT?
YOU THINK AN APOLOGY'S GONNA FIX THIS?!
YOU'VE ALREADY DONE SOMETHING THAT CAN'T BE FIXED!

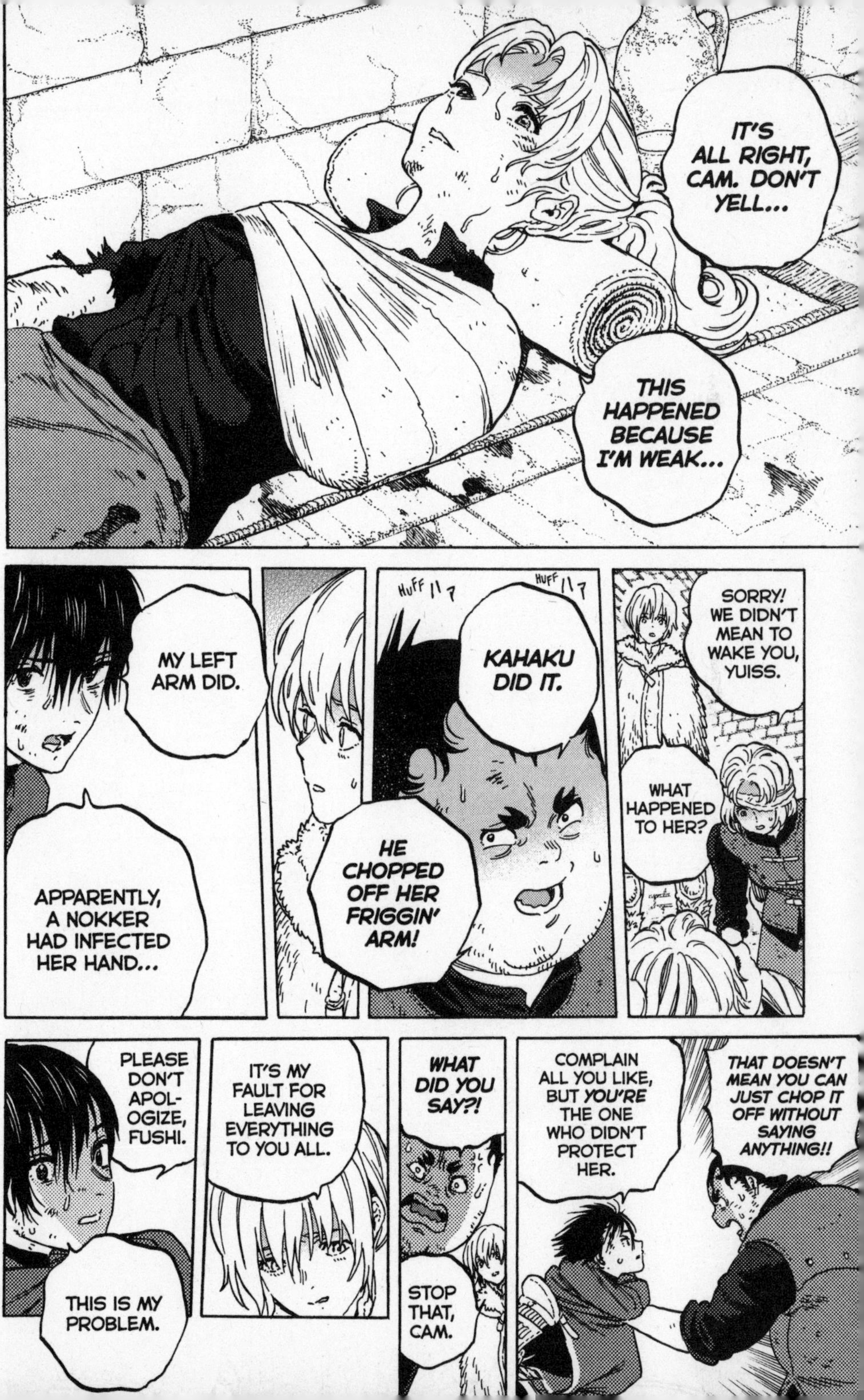
IT'S ALL RIGHT, CAM. DON'T YELL...
THIS HAPPENED BECAUSE I'M WEAK...
SORRY! WE DIDN'T MEAN TO WAKE YOU, YUISS.
WHAT HAPPENED TO HER?
HUFF ハァ
HUFF ハァ
KAHAKU DID IT.
HE CHOPPED OFF HER FRIGGIN' ARM!
MY LEFT ARM DID.
APPARENTLY, A NOKKER HAD INFECTED HER HAND...
THAT DOESN'T MEAN YOU CAN JUST CHOP IT OFF WITHOUT SAYING ANYTHING!!
COMPLAIN ALL YOU LIKE, BUT YOU'RE THE ONE WHO DIDN'T PROTECT HER.
WHAT DID YOU SAY?!
STOP THAT, CAM.
IT'S MY FAULT FOR LEAVING EVERYTHING TO YOU ALL.
PLEASE DON'T APOLOGIZE, FUSHI.
THIS IS MY PROBLEM.

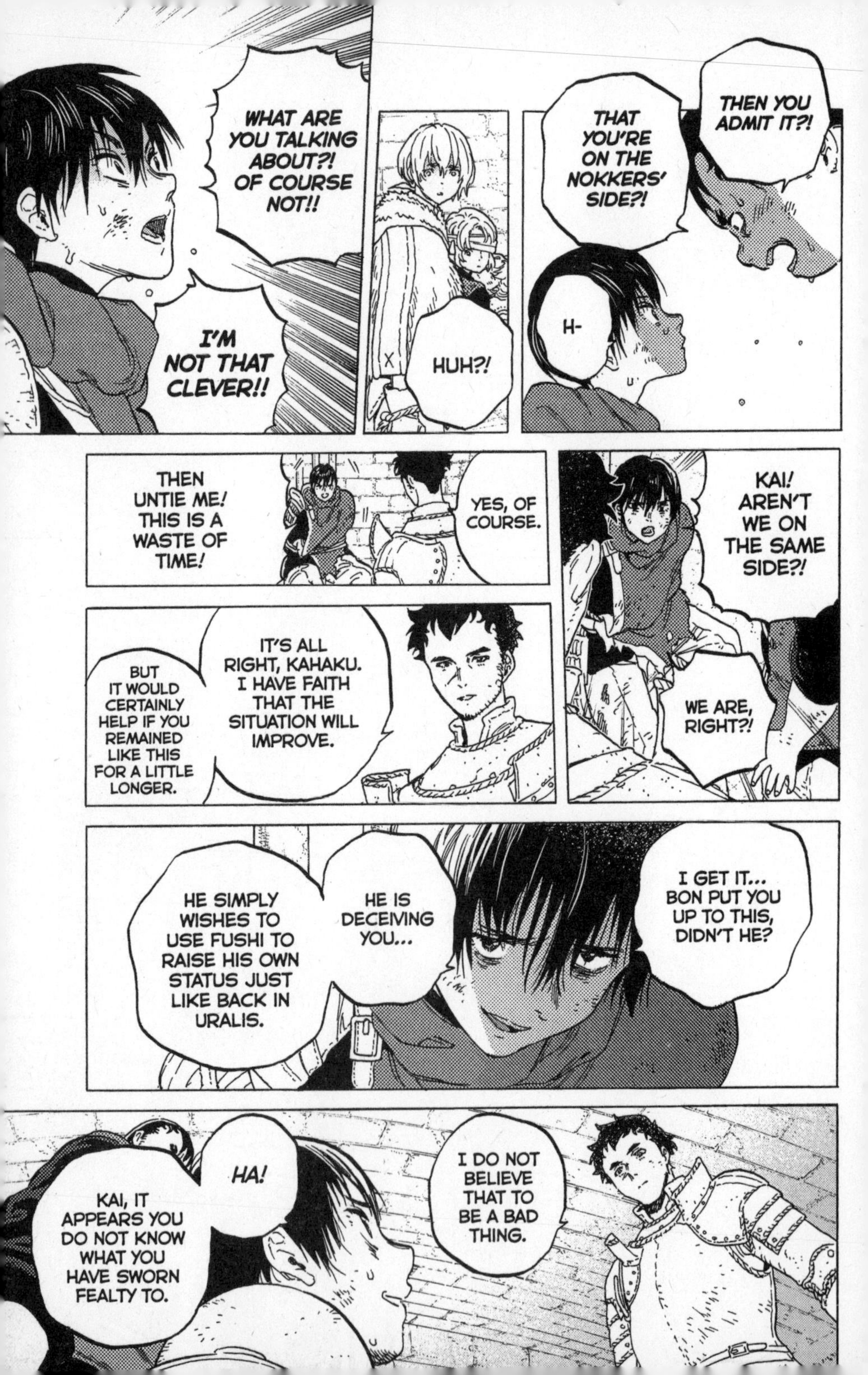
THEN YOU ADMIT IT?!
THAT YOU'RE ON THE NOKKERS' SIDE?!
H-
HUH?!
WHAT ARE YOU TALKING ABOUT?! OF COURSE NOT!!
I'M NOT THAT CLEVER!!
KAI! AREN'T WE ON THE SAME SIDE?!
WE ARE, RIGHT?!
YES, OF COURSE.
THEN UNTIE ME! THIS IS A WASTE OF TIME!
IT'S ALL RIGHT, KAHAKU. I HAVE FAITH THAT THE SITUATION WILL IMPROVE.
BUT IT WOULD CERTAINLY HELP IF YOU REMAINED LIKE THIS FOR A LITTLE LONGER.
I GET IT... BON PUT YOU UP TO THIS, DIDN'T HE?
HE IS DECEIVING YOU...
HE SIMPLY WISHES TO USE FUSHI TO RAISE HIS OWN STATUS JUST LIKE BACK IN URALIS.
I DO NOT BELIEVE THAT TO BE A BAD THING.
HA!
KAI, IT APPEARS YOU DO NOT KNOW WHAT YOU HAVE SWORN FEALTY TO.

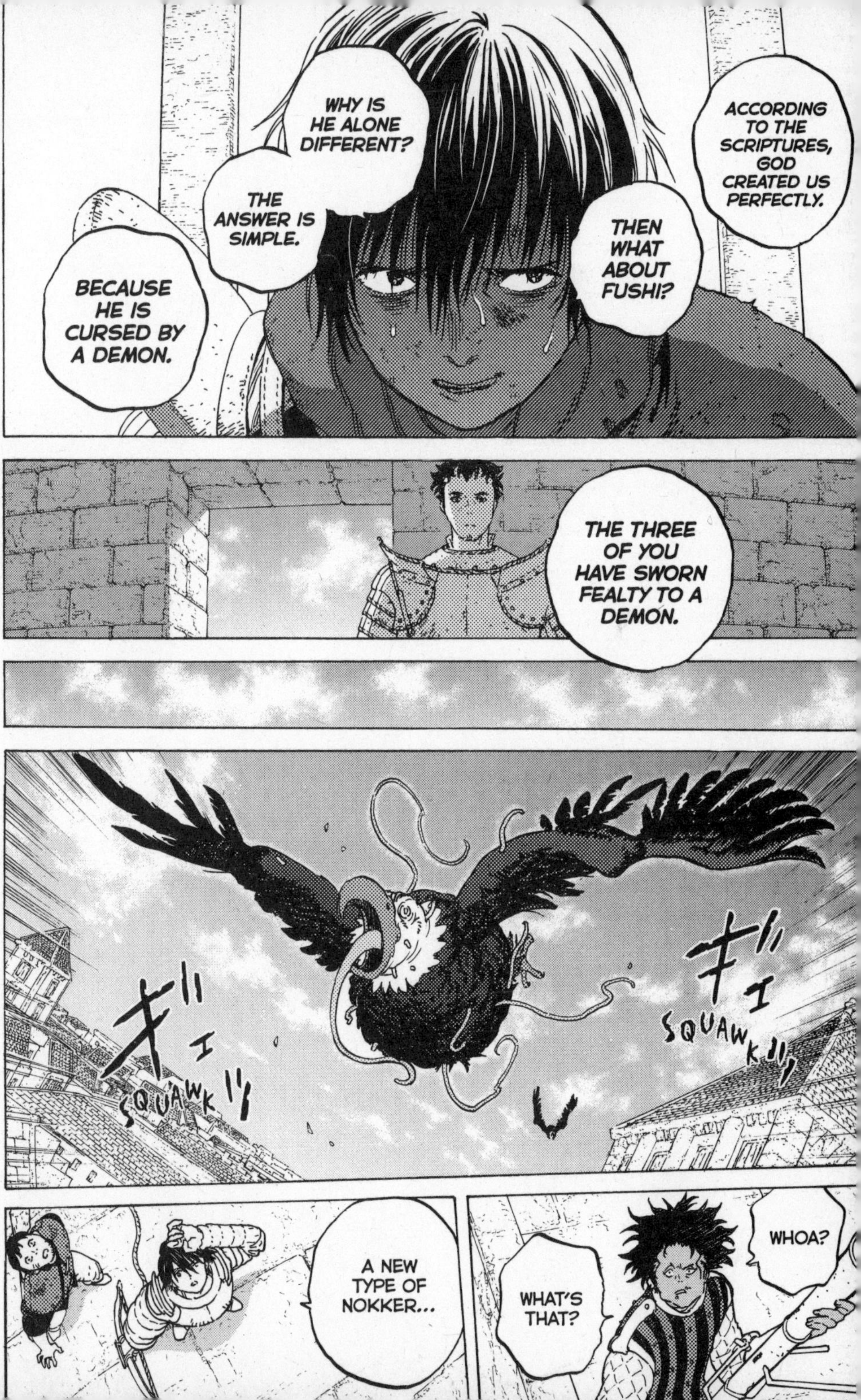
ACCORDING TO THE SCRIPTURES, GOD CREATED US PERFECTLY.
THEN WHAT ABOUT FUSHI?
WHY IS HE ALONE DIFFERENT?
THE ANSWER IS SIMPLE.
BECAUSE HE IS CURSED BY A DEMON.
THE THREE OF YOU HAVE SWORN FEALTY TO A DEMON.
SQUAWK
SQUAWK
WHOA?
WHAT'S THAT?
A NEW TYPE OF NOKKER...

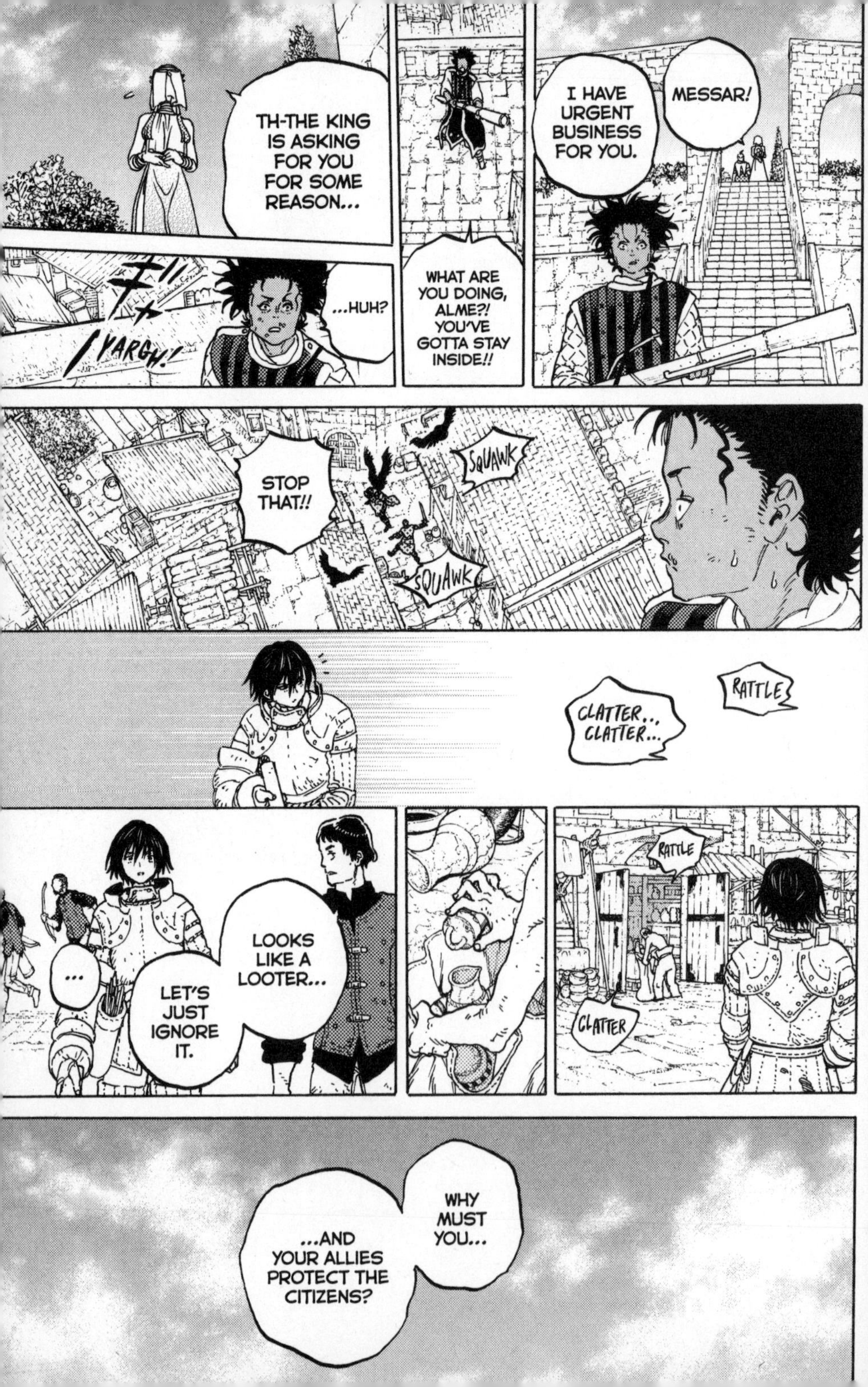
MESSAR!
I HAVE URGENT BUSINESS FOR YOU.
WHAT ARE YOU DOING, ALME?! YOU'VE GOTTA STAY INSIDE!!
TH-THE KING IS ASKING FOR YOU FOR SOME REASON...
...HUH?
YARGH!
SQUAWK
STOP THAT!!
SQUAWK
RATTLE
CLATTER... CLATTER...
RATTLE
CLATTER
LOOKS LIKE A LOOTER...
LET'S JUST IGNORE IT.
...
WHY MUST YOU...
...AND YOUR ALLIES PROTECT THE CITIZENS?

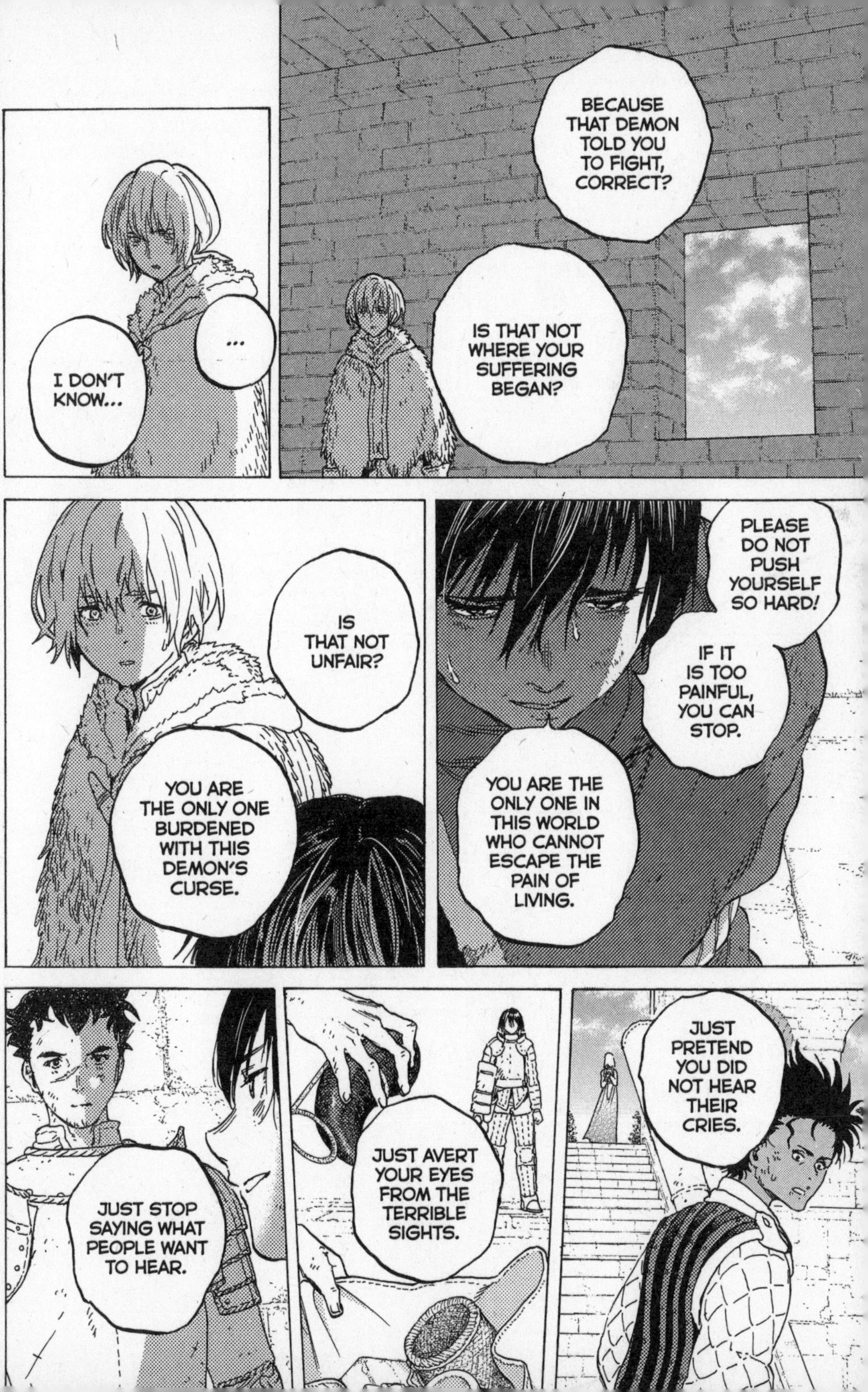
BECAUSE THAT DEMON TOLD YOU TO FIGHT, CORRECT?
IS THAT NOT WHERE YOUR SUFFERING BEGAN?
...
I DON'T KNOW...
PLEASE DO NOT PUSH YOURSELF SO HARD!
IF IT IS TOO PAINFUL, YOU CAN STOP.
YOU ARE THE ONLY ONE IN THIS WORLD WHO CANNOT ESCAPE THE PAIN OF LIVING.
IS THAT NOT UNFAIR?
YOU ARE THE ONLY ONE BURDENED WITH THIS DEMON'S CURSE.
JUST PRETEND YOU DID NOT HEAR THEIR CRIES.
JUST AVERT YOUR EYES FROM THE TERRIBLE SIGHTS.
JUST STOP SAYING WHAT PEOPLE WANT TO HEAR.

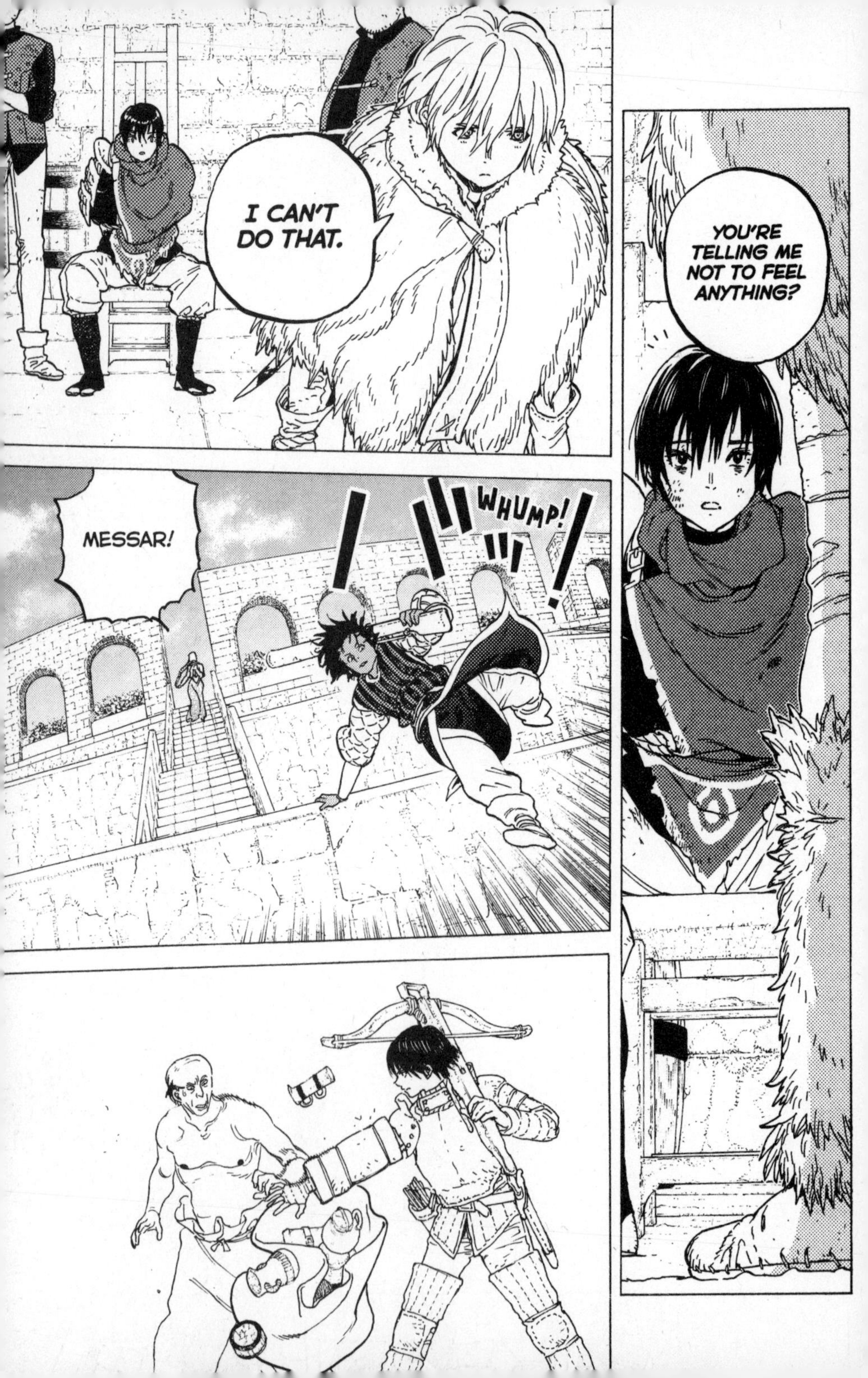
YOU'RE TELLING ME NOT TO FEEL ANYTHING?
I CAN'T DO THAT.
WHUMP!
MESSAR!

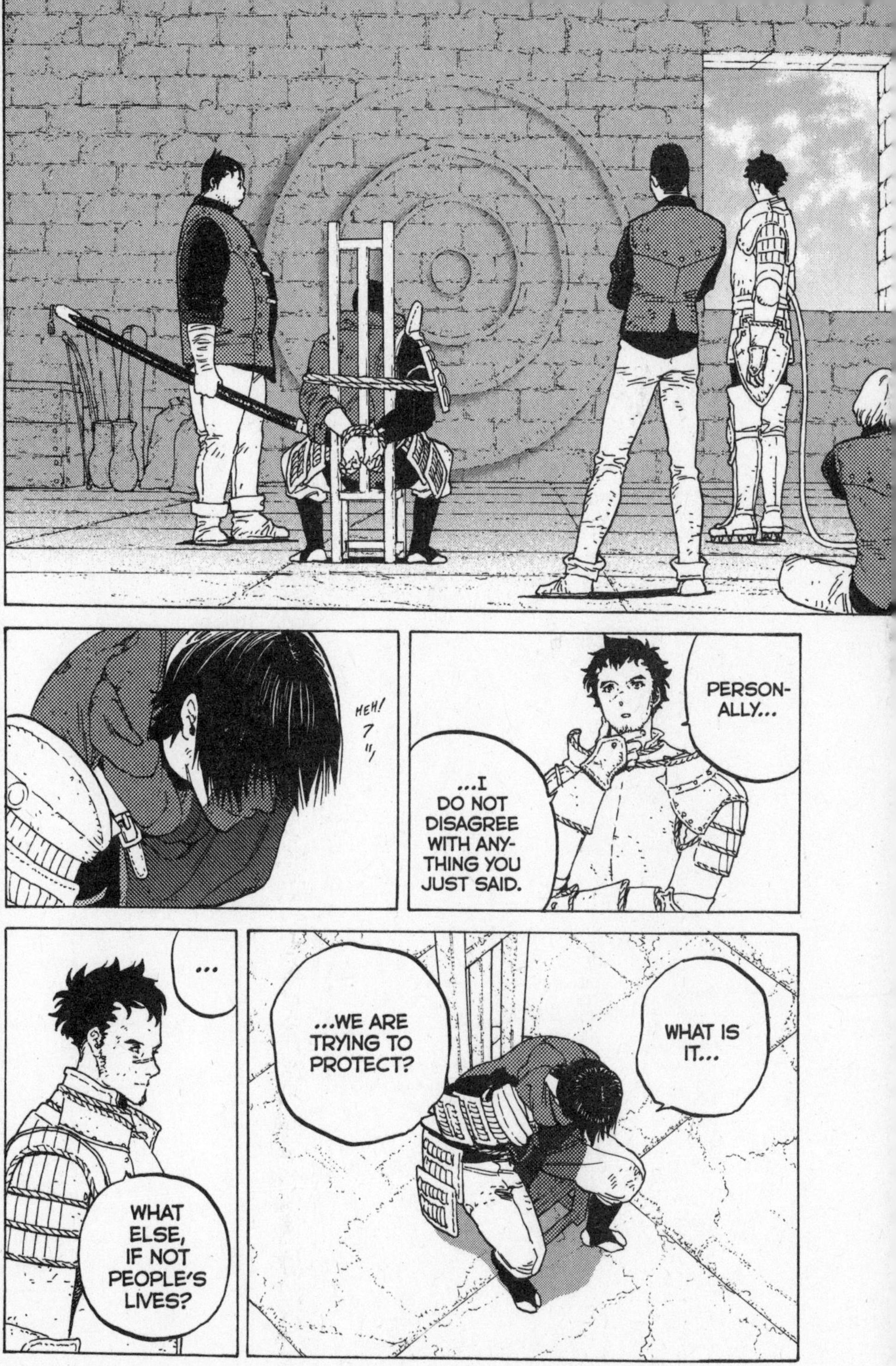
PERSON-ALLY...
...I DO NOT DISAGREE WITH ANY-THING YOU JUST SAID.
HEH!
WHAT IS IT...
...WE ARE TRYING TO PROTECT?
...
WHAT ELSE, IF NOT PEOPLE'S LIVES?

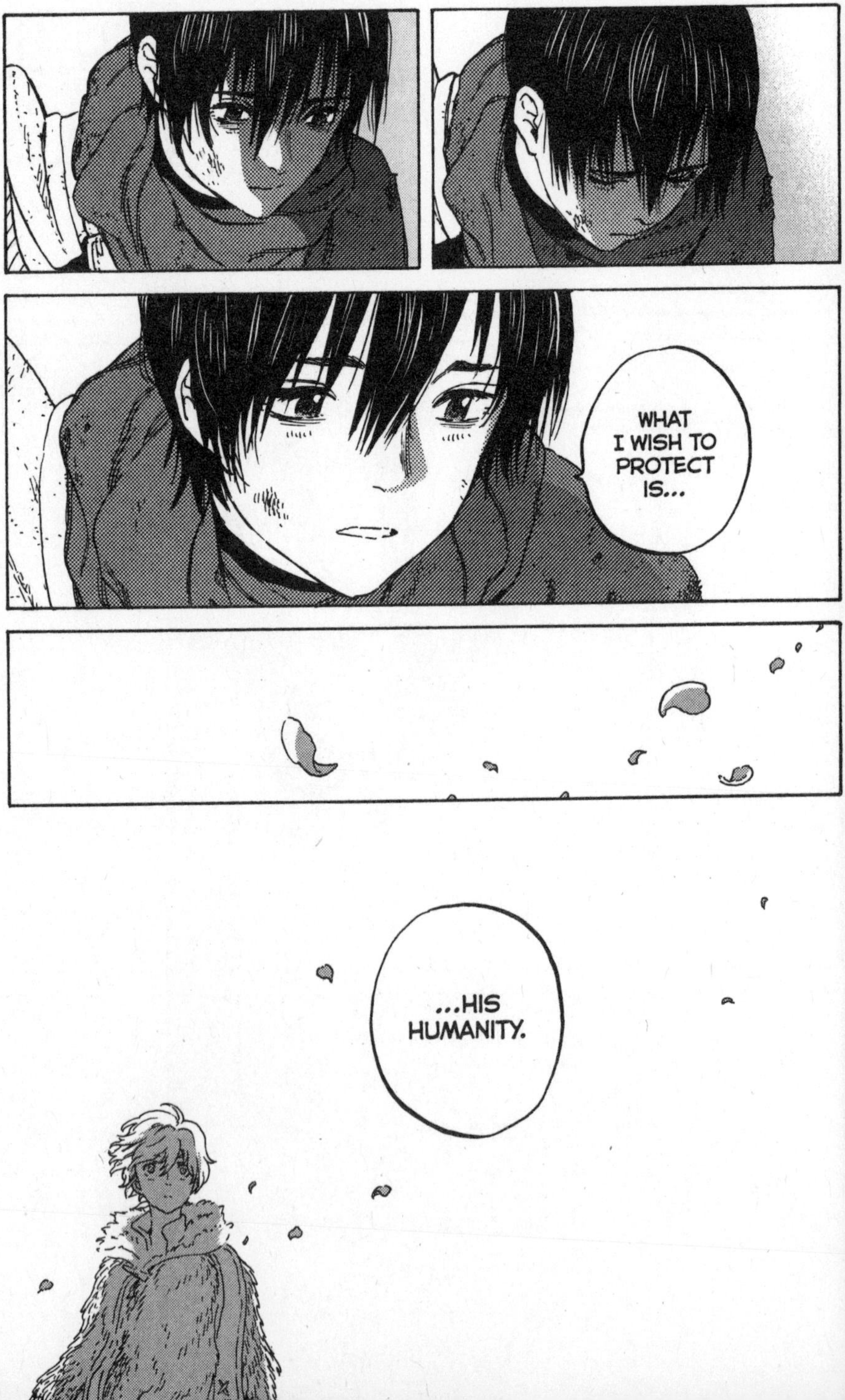
WHAT I WISH TO PROTECT IS...
...HIS HUMANITY.

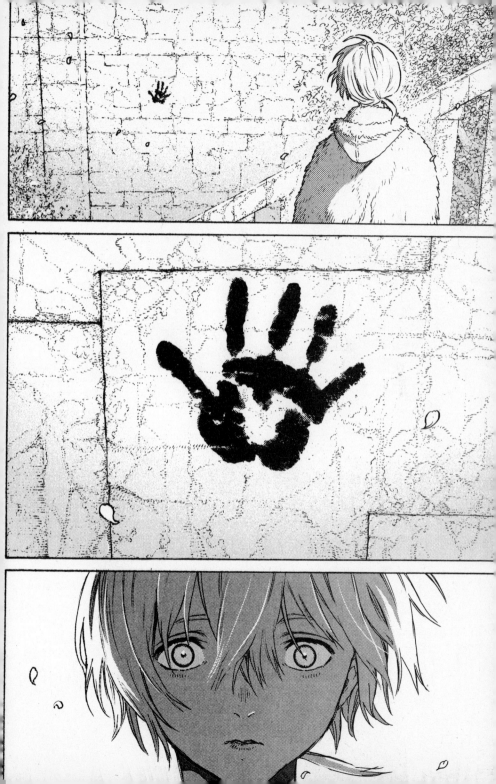

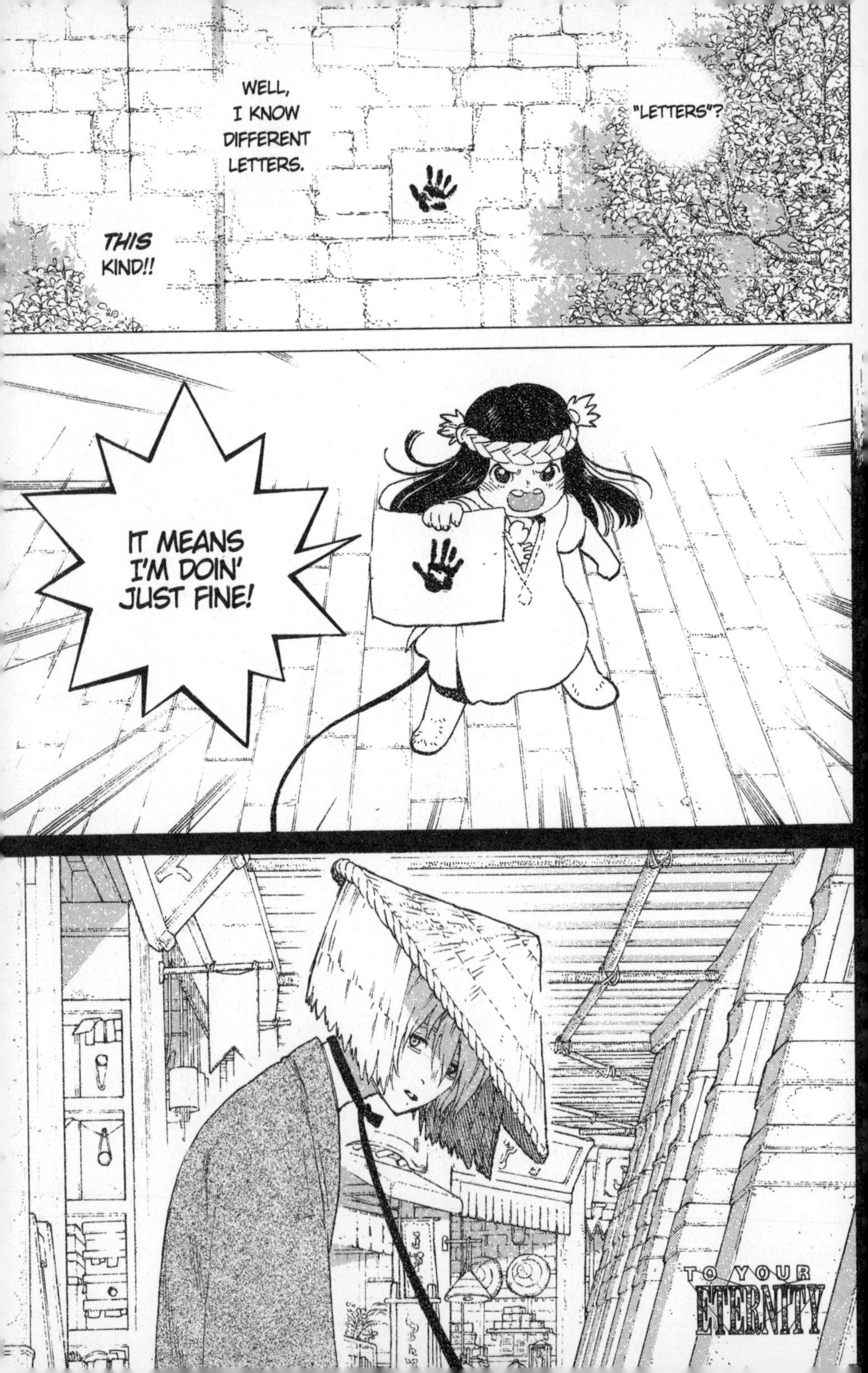
"LETTERS"?
WELL, I KNOW DIFFERENT LETTERS.
THIS KIND!!
IT MEANS I'M DOIN' JUST FINE!
TO YOUR ETERNITY

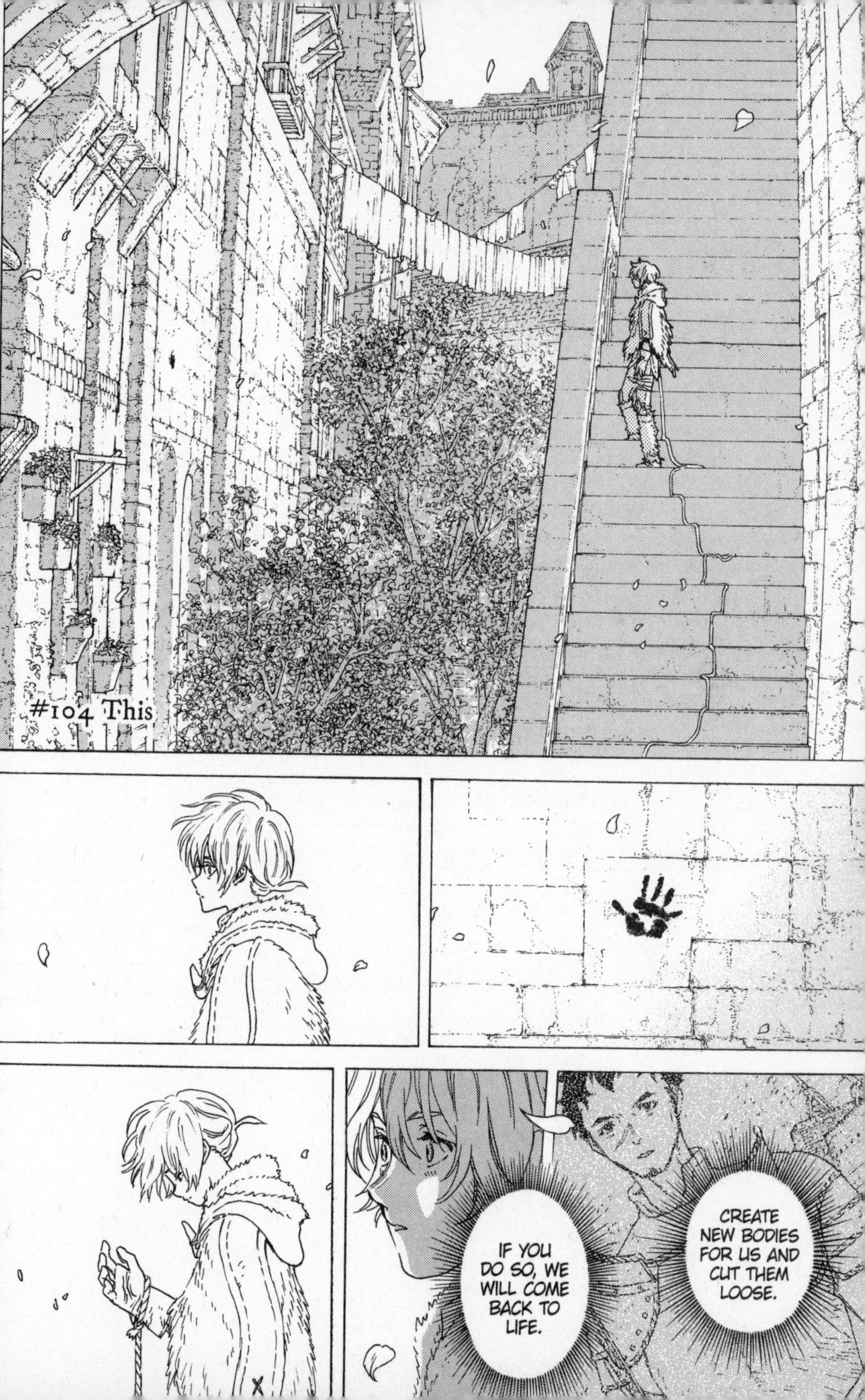
#104 This
CREATE NEW BODIES FOR US AND CUT THEM LOOSE.
IF YOU DO SO, WE WILL COME BACK TO LIFE.

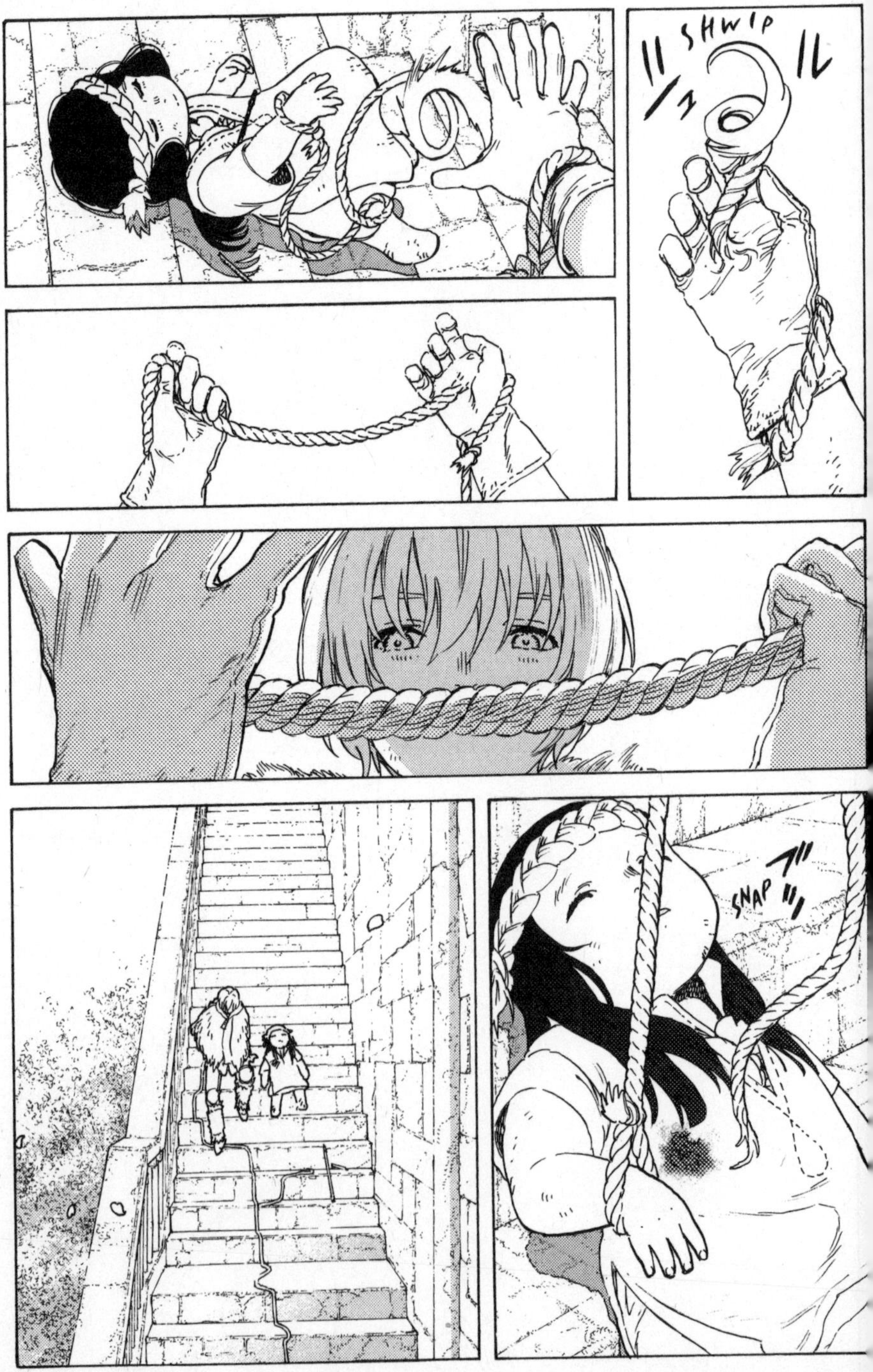
SHWIP
SNAP

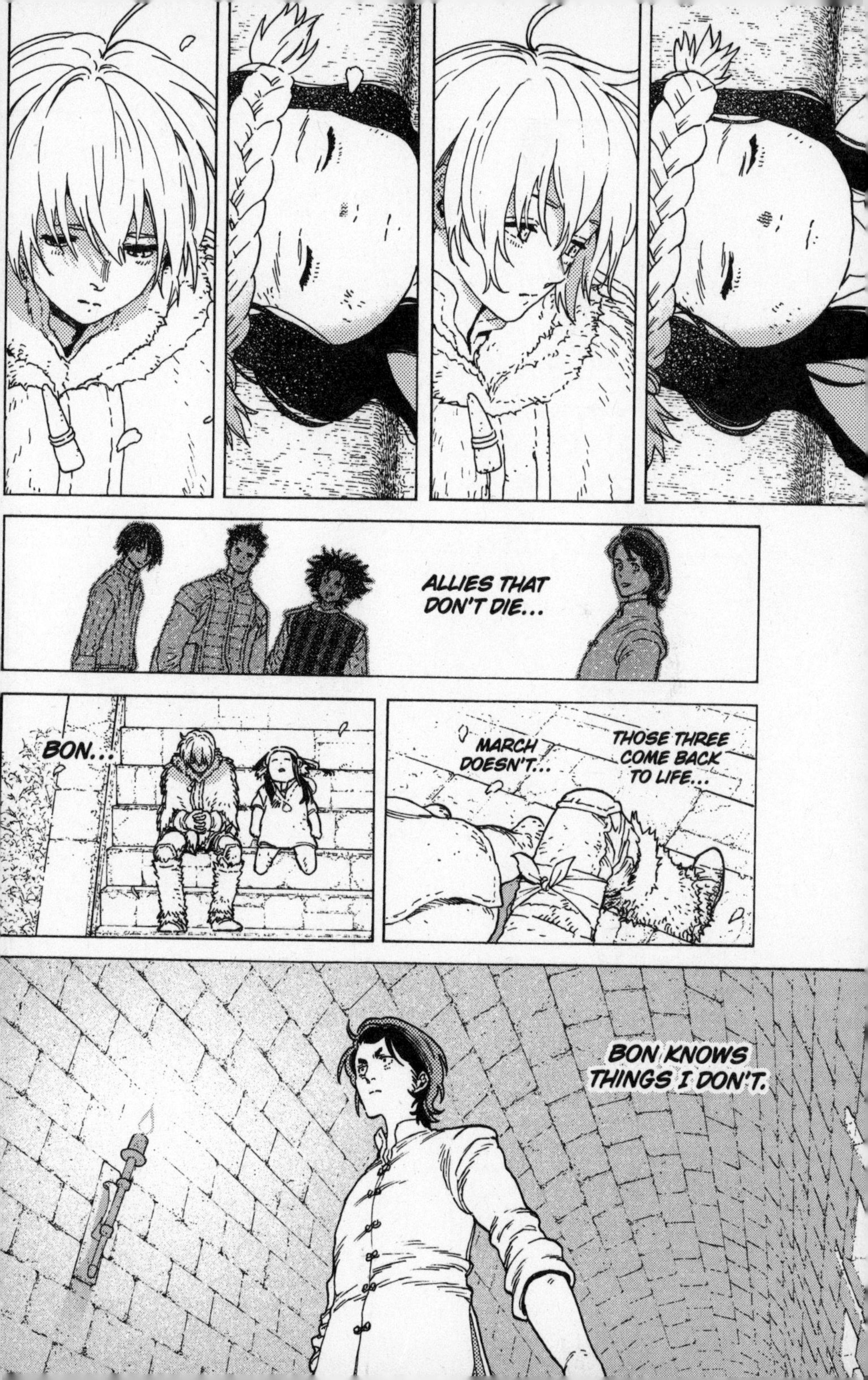
ALLIES THAT DON'T DIE...
THOSE THREE COME BACK TO LIFE...
MARCH DOESN'T...
BON...
BON KNOWS THINGS I DON'T.

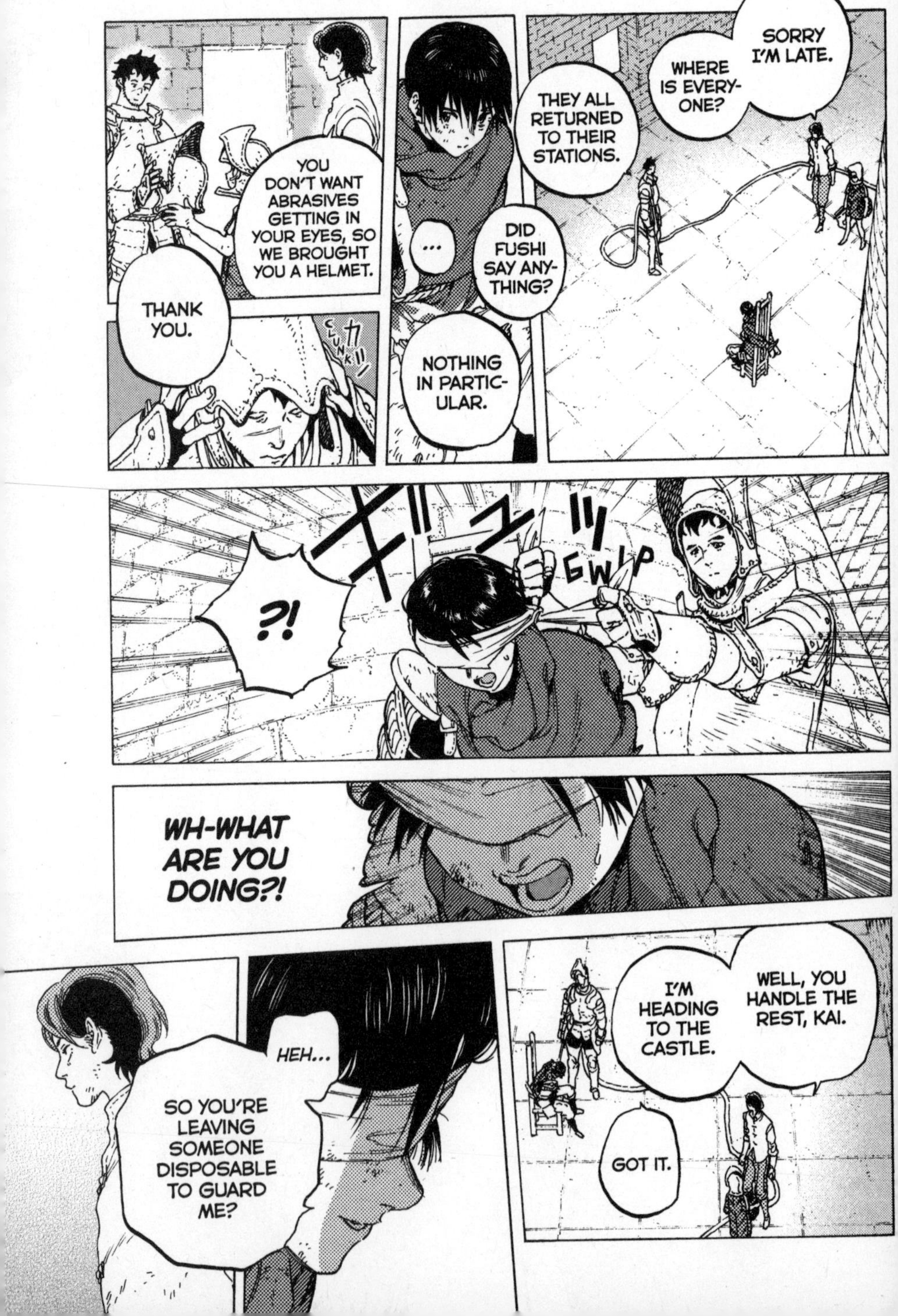
SORRY I'M LATE.
WHERE IS EVERY-ONE?
THEY ALL RETURNED TO THEIR STATIONS.
DID FUSHI SAY ANY-THING?
...
NOTHING IN PARTIC-ULAR.
YOU DON'T WANT ABRASIVES GETTING IN YOUR EYES, SO WE BROUGHT YOU A HELMET.
THANK YOU.
CLUNK
GWIP
?!
WH-WHAT ARE YOU DOING?!
WELL, YOU HANDLE THE REST, KAI.
I'M HEADING TO THE CASTLE.
GOT IT.
HEH...
SO YOU'RE LEAVING SOMEONE DISPOSABLE TO GUARD ME?

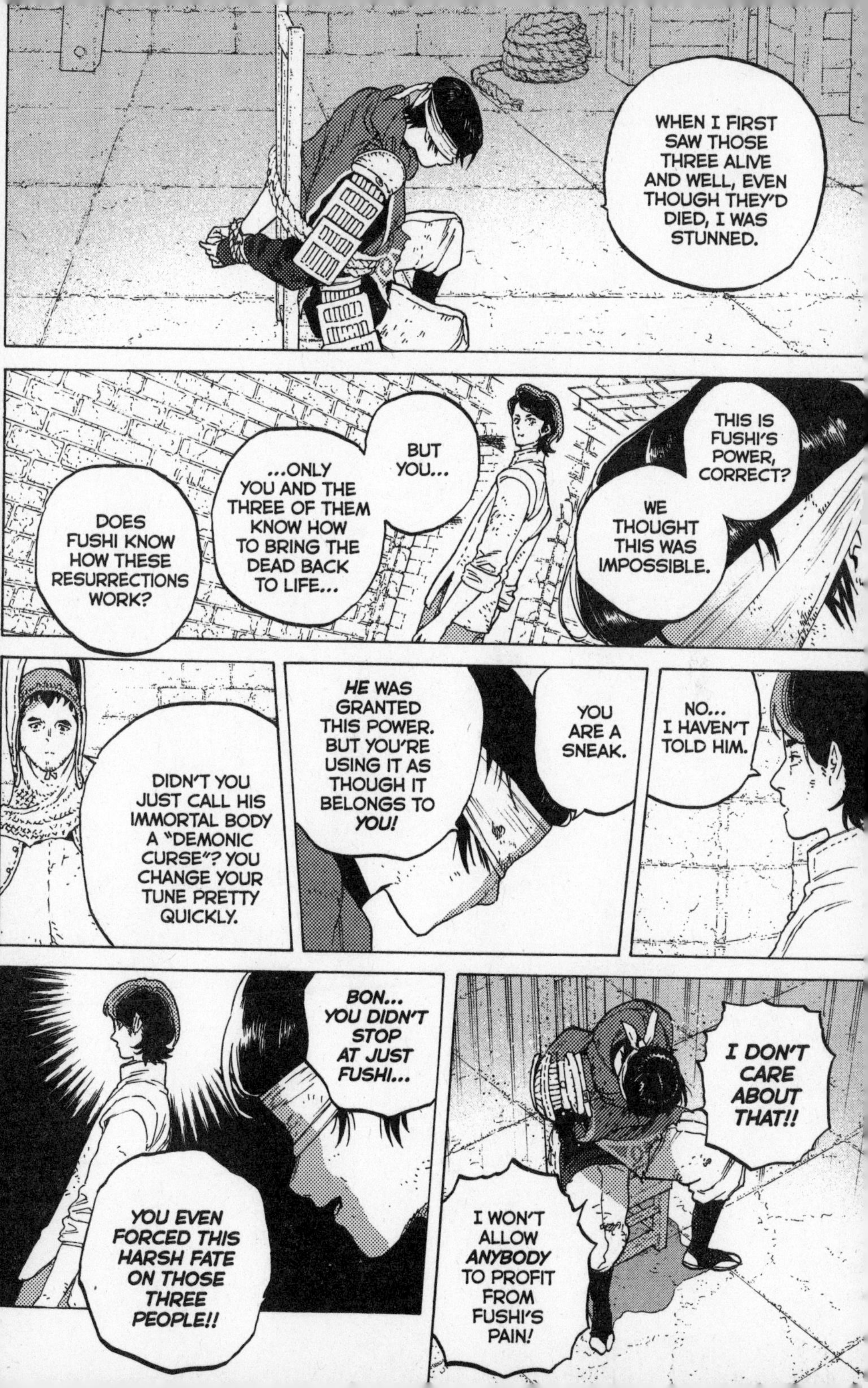
WHEN I FIRST SAW THOSE THREE ALIVE AND WELL, EVEN THOUGH THEY'D DIED, I WAS STUNNED.
THIS IS FUSHI'S POWER, CORRECT?
WE THOUGHT THIS WAS IMPOSSIBLE.
BUT YOU...
...ONLY YOU AND THE THREE OF THEM KNOW HOW TO BRING THE DEAD BACK TO LIFE...
DOES FUSHI KNOW HOW THESE RESURRECTIONS WORK?
NO... I HAVEN'T TOLD HIM.
YOU ARE A SNEAK.
HE WAS GRANTED THIS POWER. BUT YOU'RE USING IT AS THOUGH IT BELONGS TO *YOU!*
DIDN'T YOU JUST CALL HIS IMMORTAL BODY A "DEMONIC CURSE"? YOU CHANGE YOUR TUNE PRETTY QUICKLY.
I DON'T CARE ABOUT THAT!!
I WON'T ALLOW *ANYBODY* TO PROFIT FROM FUSHI'S PAIN!
BON... YOU DIDN'T STOP AT JUST FUSHI...
YOU EVEN FORCED THIS HARSH FATE ON THOSE THREE PEOPLE!!

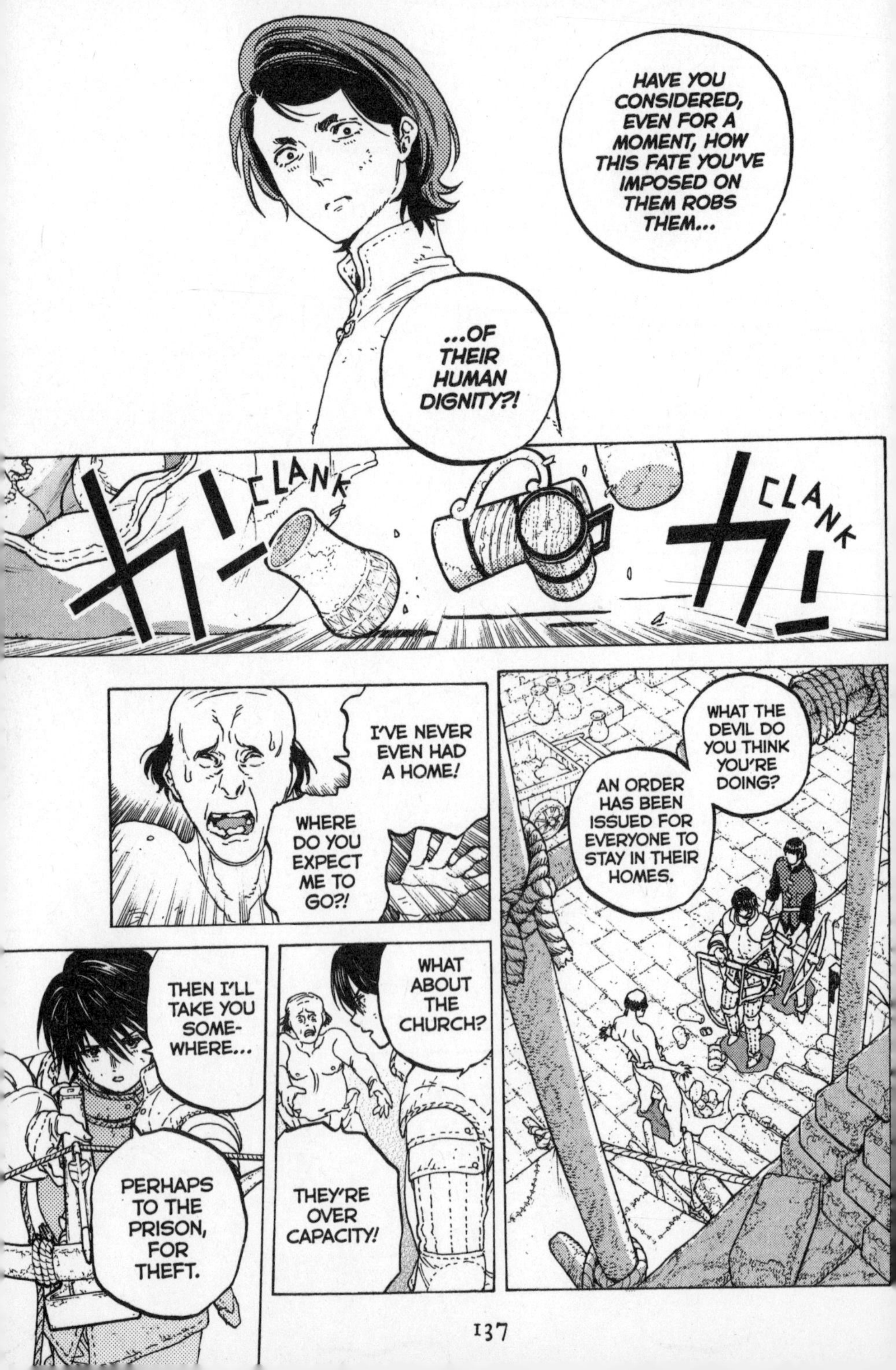
HAVE YOU CONSIDERED, EVEN FOR A MOMENT, HOW THIS FATE YOU'VE IMPOSED ON THEM ROBS THEM...
...OF THEIR HUMAN DIGNITY?!
CLANK
CLANK
WHAT THE DEVIL DO YOU THINK YOU'RE DOING?
AN ORDER HAS BEEN ISSUED FOR EVERYONE TO STAY IN THEIR HOMES.
I'VE NEVER EVEN HAD A HOME!
WHERE DO YOU EXPECT ME TO GO?!
WHAT ABOUT THE CHURCH?
THEY'RE OVER CAPACITY!
THEN I'LL TAKE YOU SOME-WHERE...
PERHAPS TO THE PRISON, FOR THEFT.

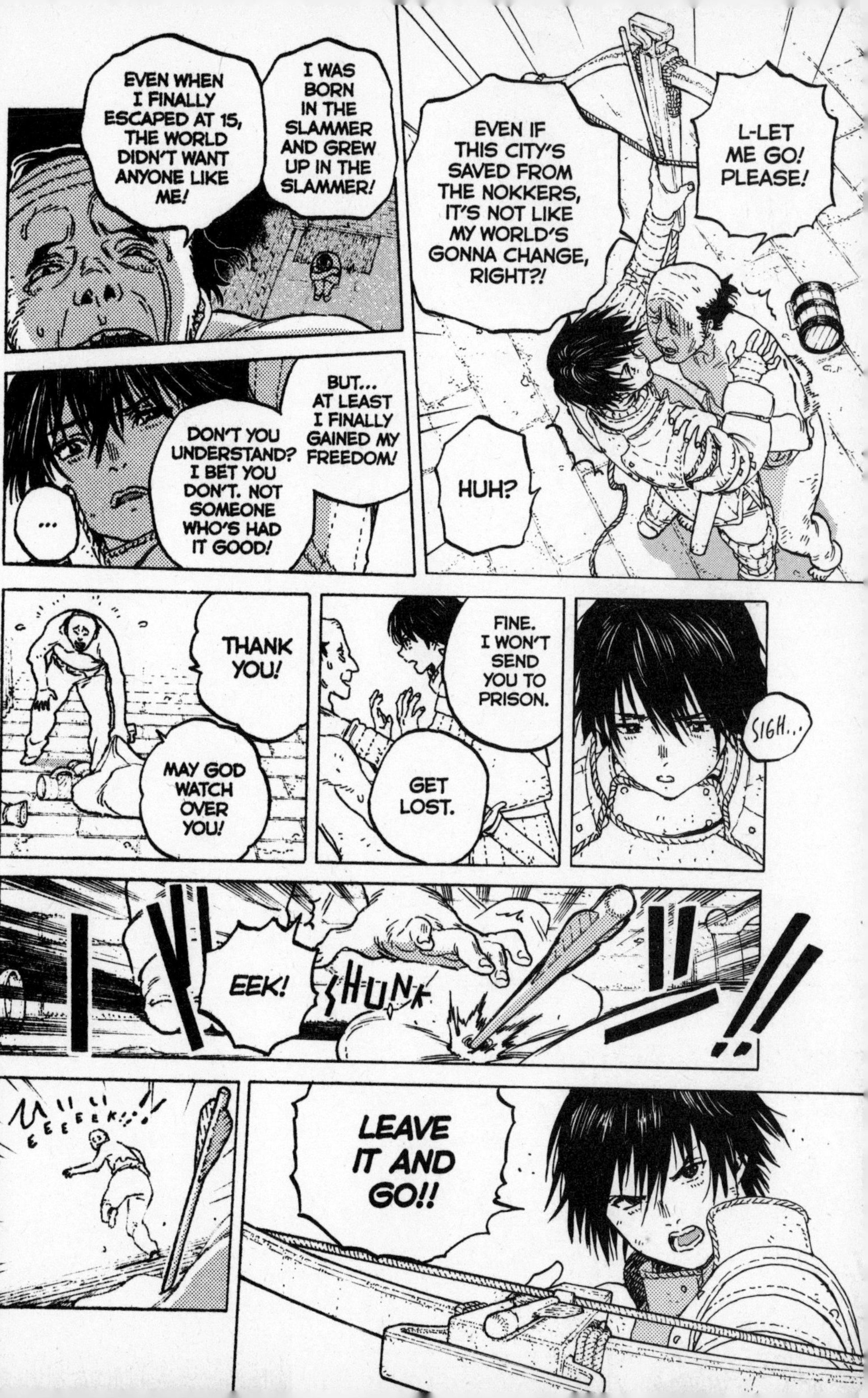
L-LET ME GO! PLEASE!
EVEN IF THIS CITY'S SAVED FROM THE NOKKERS, IT'S NOT LIKE MY WORLD'S GONNA CHANGE, RIGHT?!
HUH?
I WAS BORN IN THE SLAMMER AND GREW UP IN THE SLAMMER!
EVEN WHEN I FINALLY ESCAPED AT 15, THE WORLD DIDN'T WANT ANYONE LIKE ME!
BUT... AT LEAST I FINALLY GAINED MY FREEDOM!
DON'T YOU UNDERSTAND? I BET YOU DON'T. NOT SOMEONE WHO'S HAD IT GOOD!
...
SIGH...
FINE. I WON'T SEND YOU TO PRISON.
GET LOST.
THANK YOU!
MAY GOD WATCH OVER YOU!
SHUNK
EEK!
LEAVE IT AND GO!!
EEEEEK!!

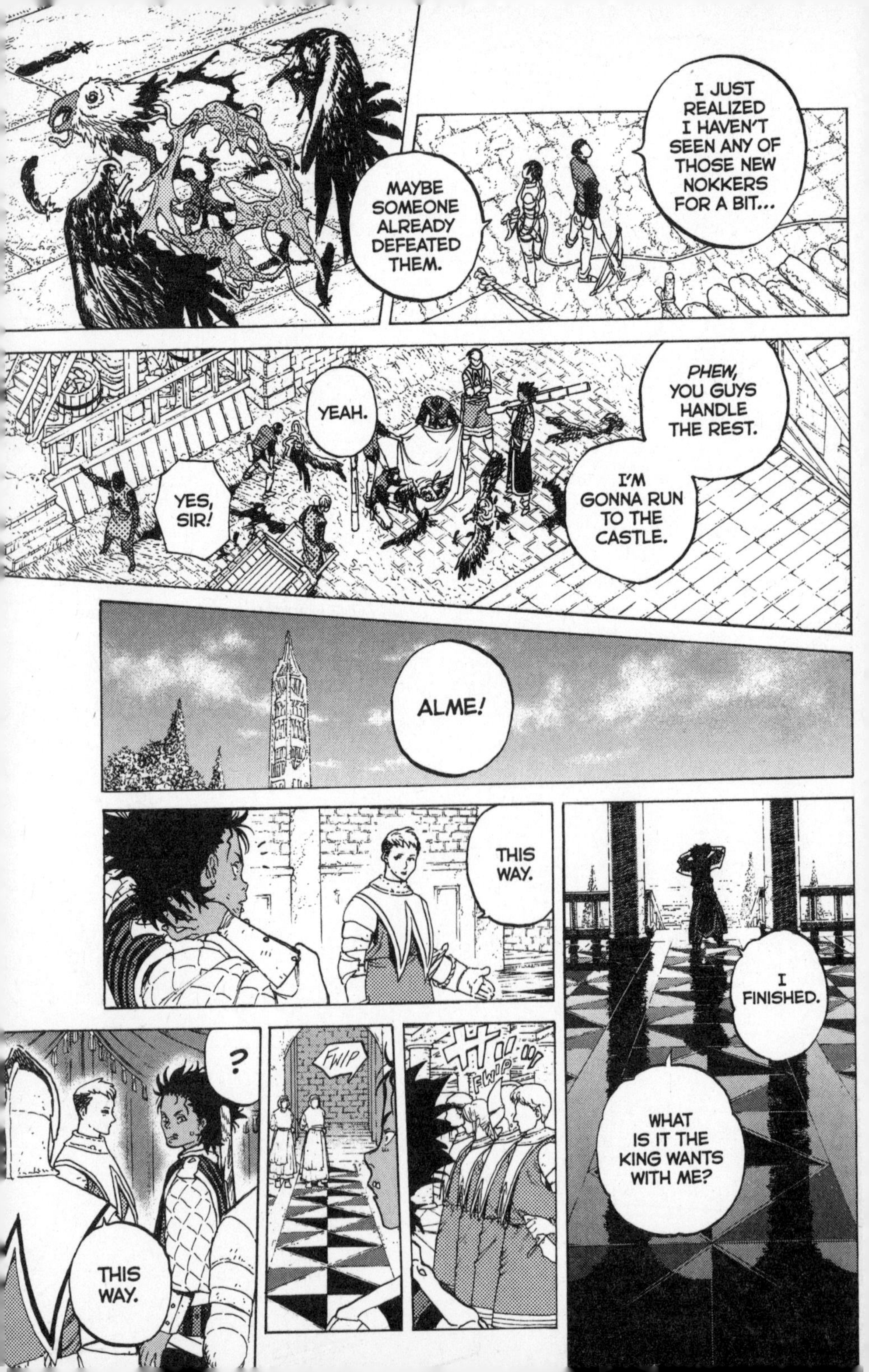
I JUST REALIZED I HAVEN'T SEEN ANY OF THOSE NEW NOKKERS FOR A BIT...
MAYBE SOMEONE ALREADY DEFEATED THEM.
PHEW, YOU GUYS HANDLE THE REST.
I'M GONNA RUN TO THE CASTLE.
YEAH.
YES, SIR!
ALME!
I FINISHED.
WHAT IS IT THE KING WANTS WITH ME?
THIS WAY.
FWIP
FWIP
?
THIS WAY.

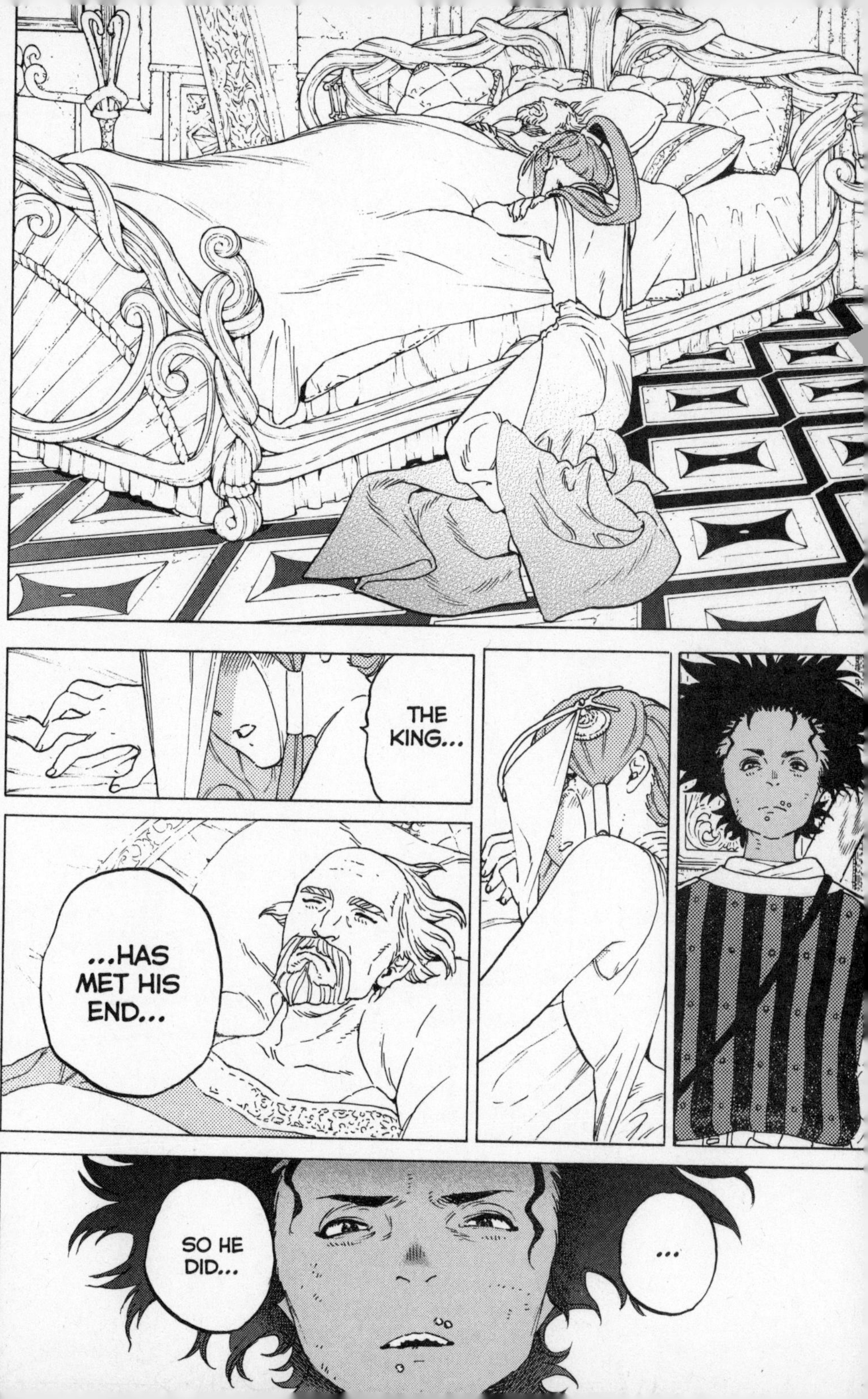
THE KING...
...HAS MET HIS END...
...
SO HE DID...

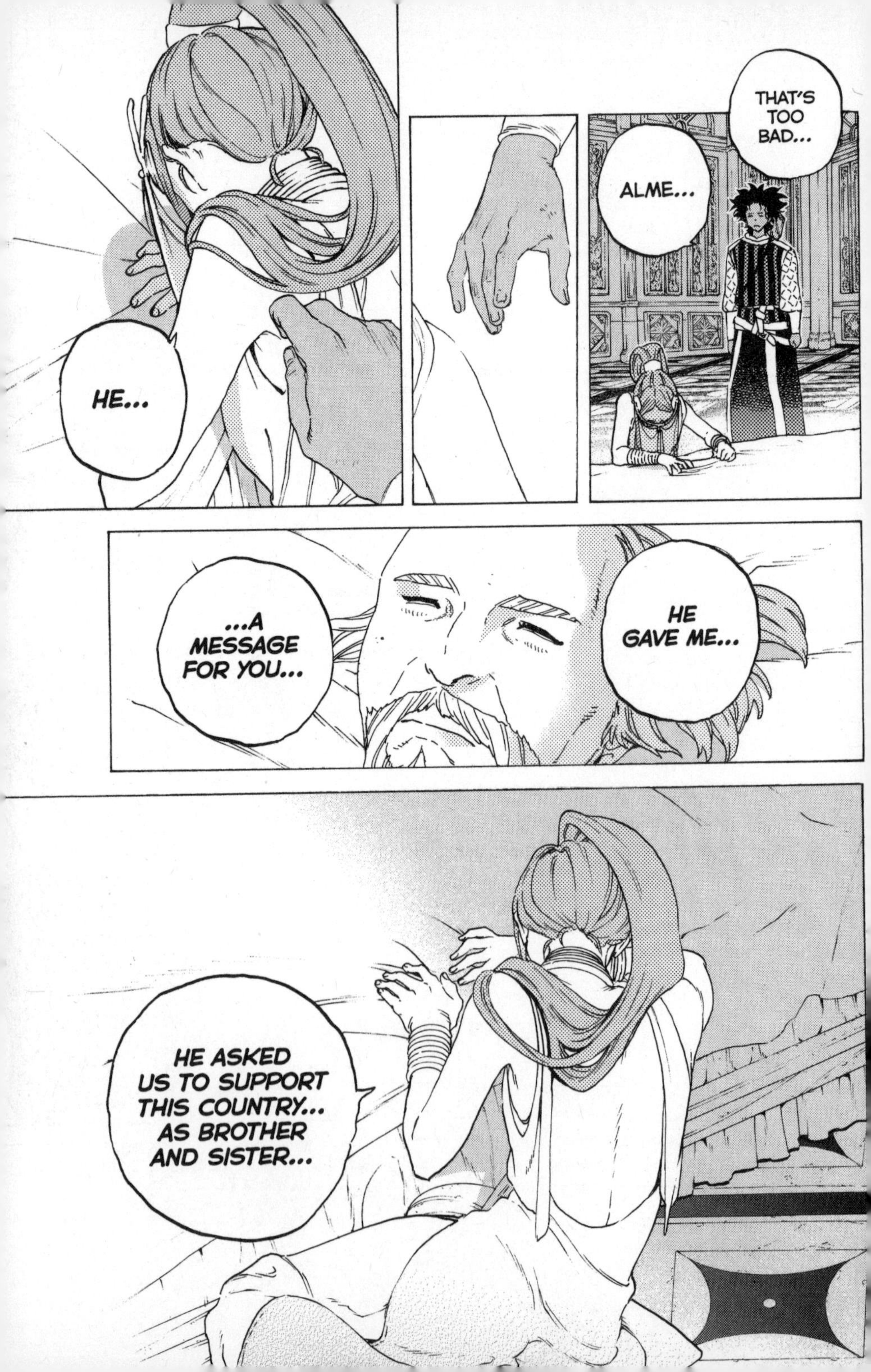
THAT'S TOO BAD...
ALME...
HE...
HE GAVE ME...
...A MESSAGE FOR YOU...
HE ASKED US TO SUPPORT THIS COUNTRY... AS BROTHER AND SISTER...

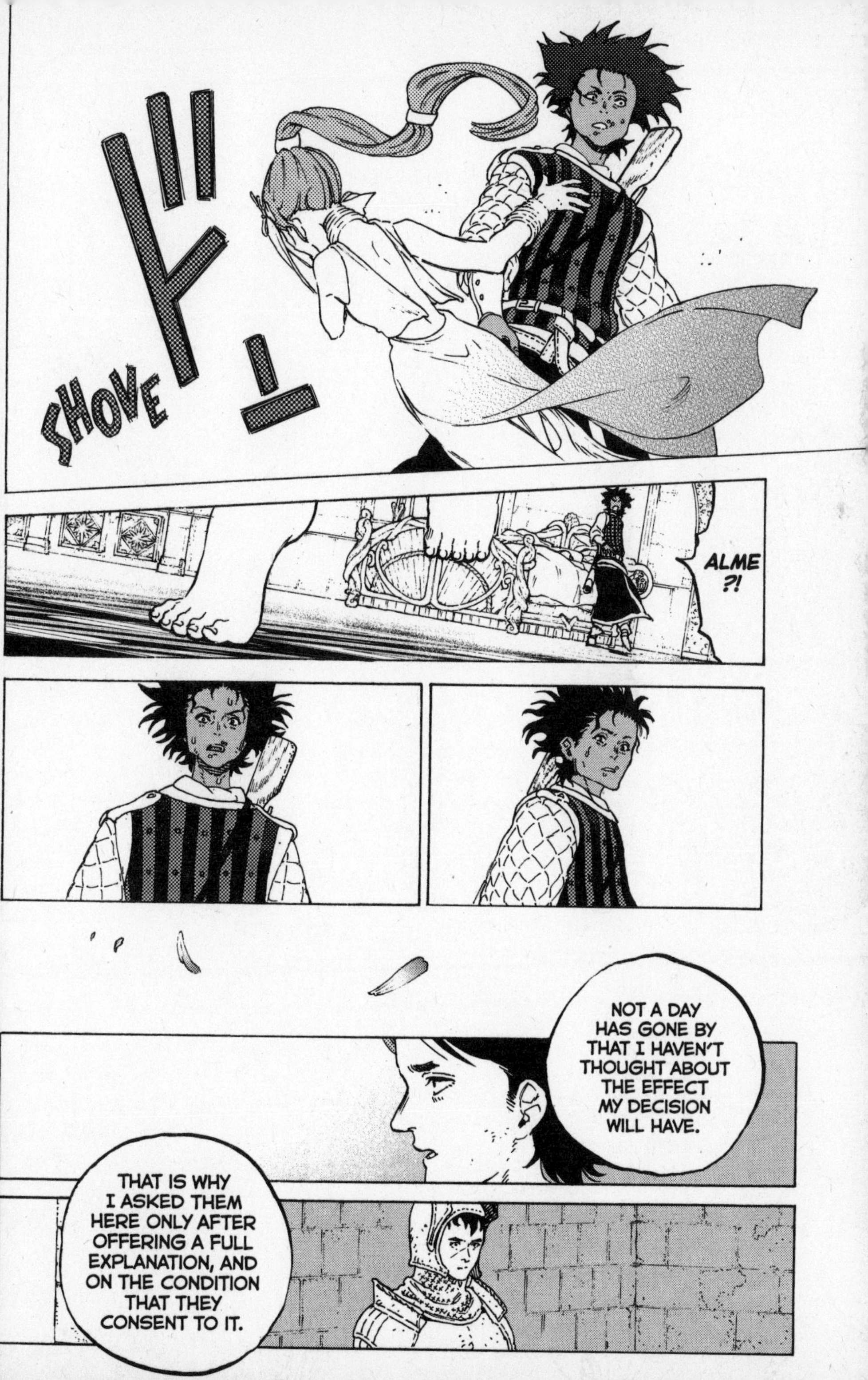
SHOVE
ALME ?!
NOT A DAY HAS GONE BY THAT I HAVEN'T THOUGHT ABOUT THE EFFECT MY DECISION WILL HAVE.
THAT IS WHY I ASKED THEM HERE ONLY AFTER OFFERING A FULL EXPLANATION, AND ON THE CONDITION THAT THEY CONSENT TO IT.

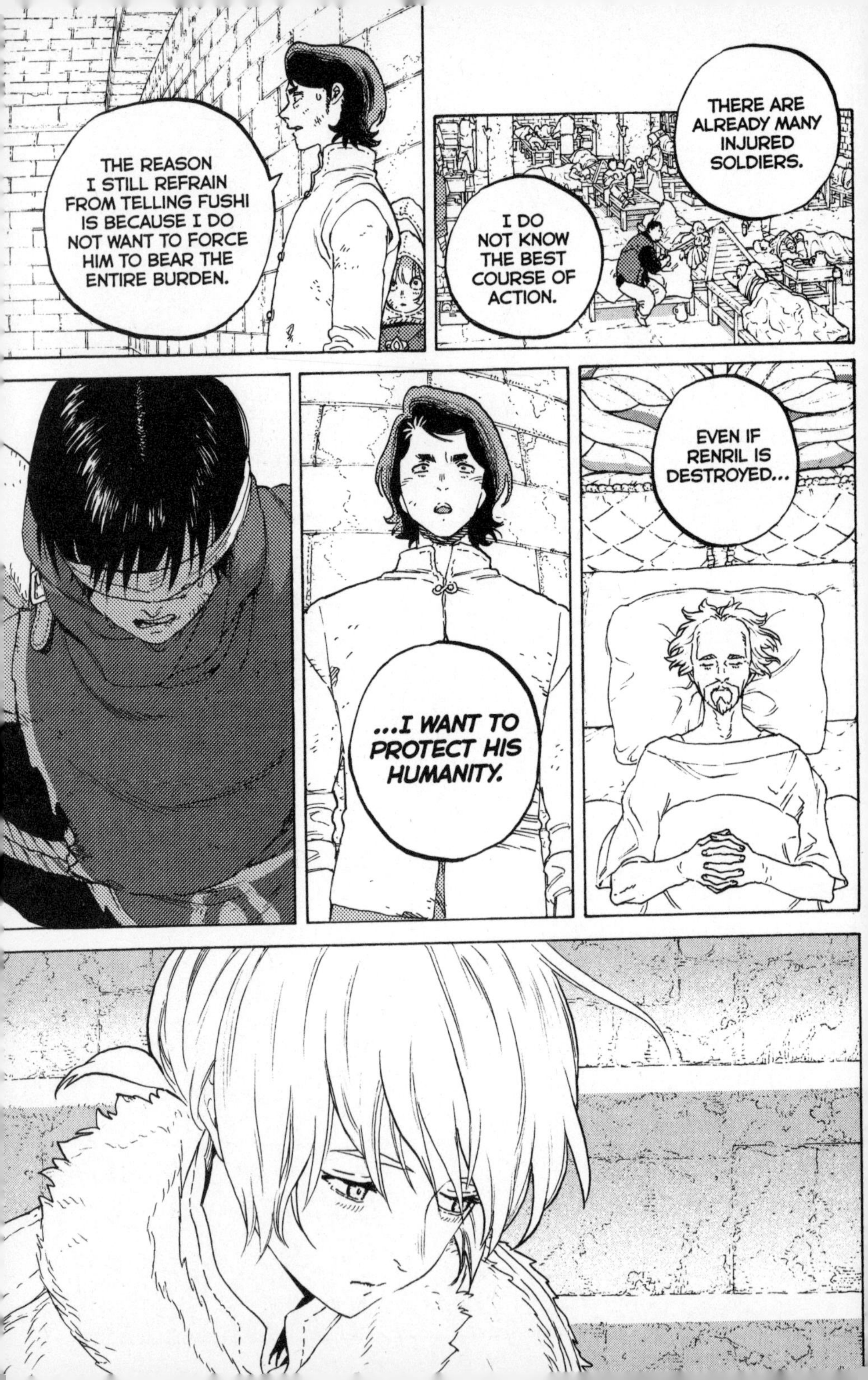
THERE ARE ALREADY MANY INJURED SOLDIERS.
I DO NOT KNOW THE BEST COURSE OF ACTION.
THE REASON I STILL REFRAIN FROM TELLING FUSHI IS BECAUSE I DO NOT WANT TO FORCE HIM TO BEAR THE ENTIRE BURDEN.
EVEN IF RENRIL IS DESTROYED...
...I WANT TO PROTECT HIS HUMANITY.

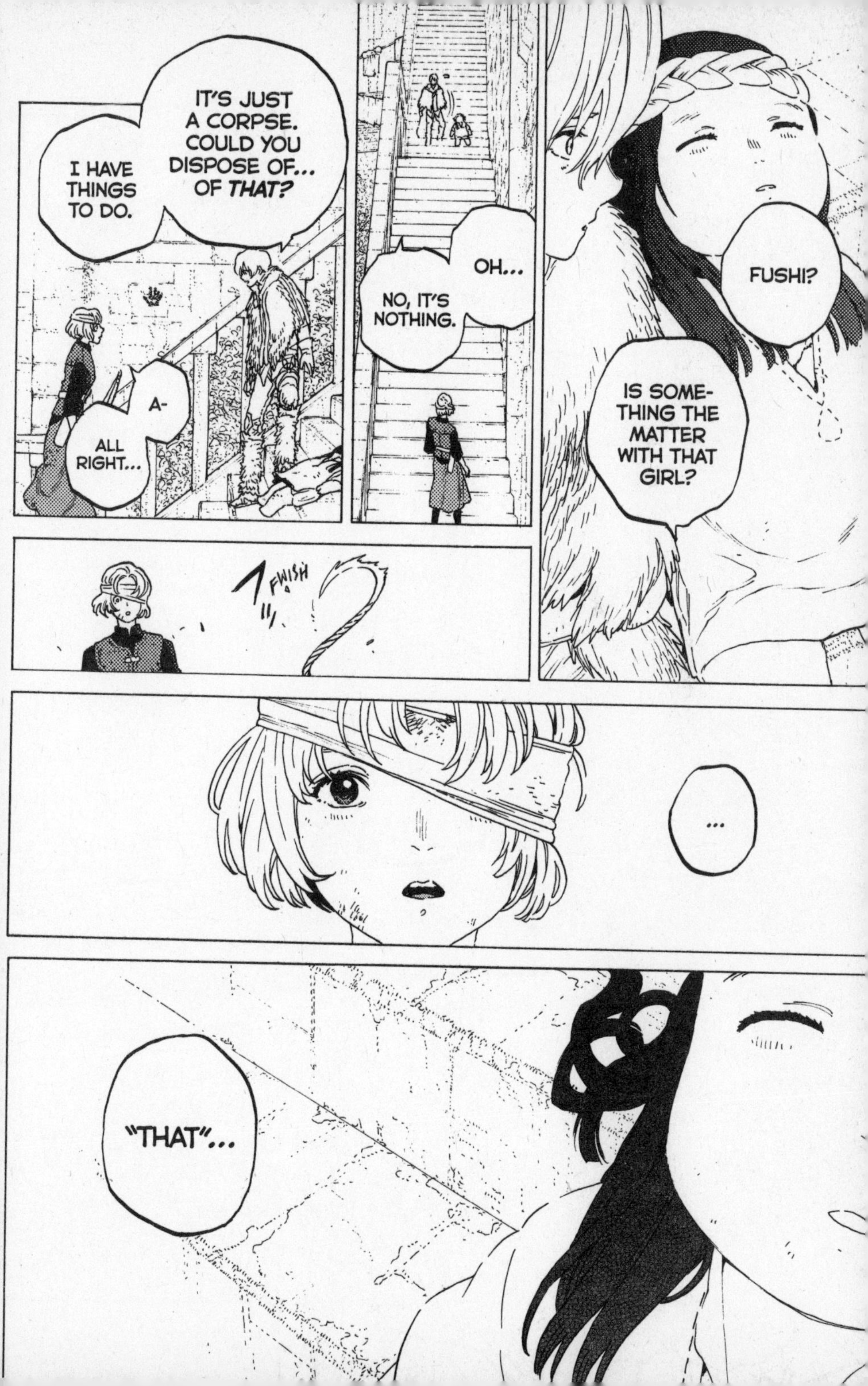
FUSHI?
IS SOMETHING THE MATTER WITH THAT GIRL?
OH...
NO, IT'S NOTHING.
IT'S JUST A CORPSE. COULD YOU DISPOSE OF... OF *THAT?*
I HAVE THINGS TO DO.
A-
ALL RIGHT...
FWISH
...
"THAT"...

#105 Setting Sun

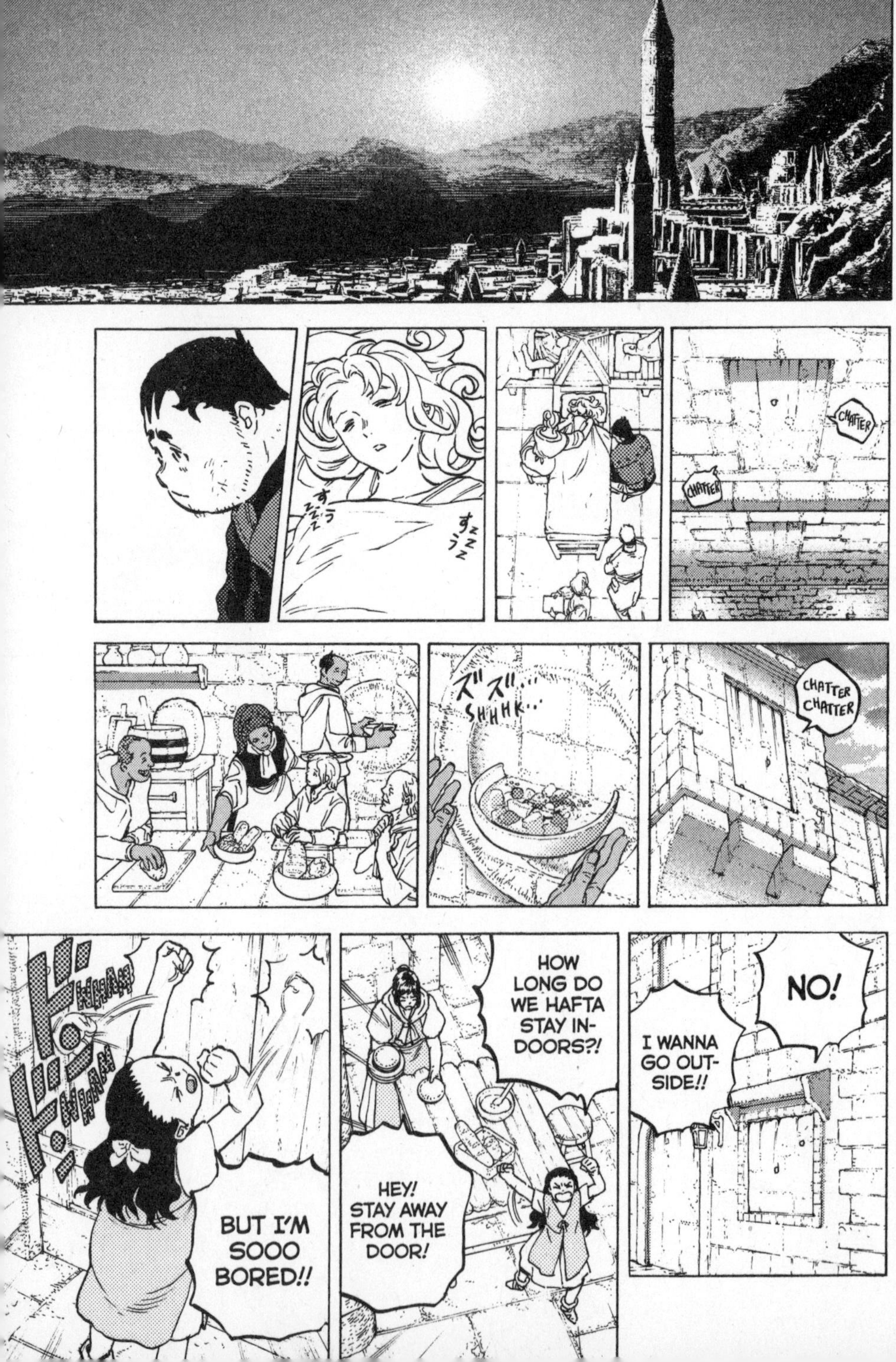
CHATTER
CHATTER
CHATTER CHATTER
ズズ… SHHHK…
NO!
I WANNA GO OUTSIDE!!
HOW LONG DO WE HAFTA STAY INDOORS?!
HEY! STAY AWAY FROM THE DOOR!
BUT I'M SOOO BORED!!

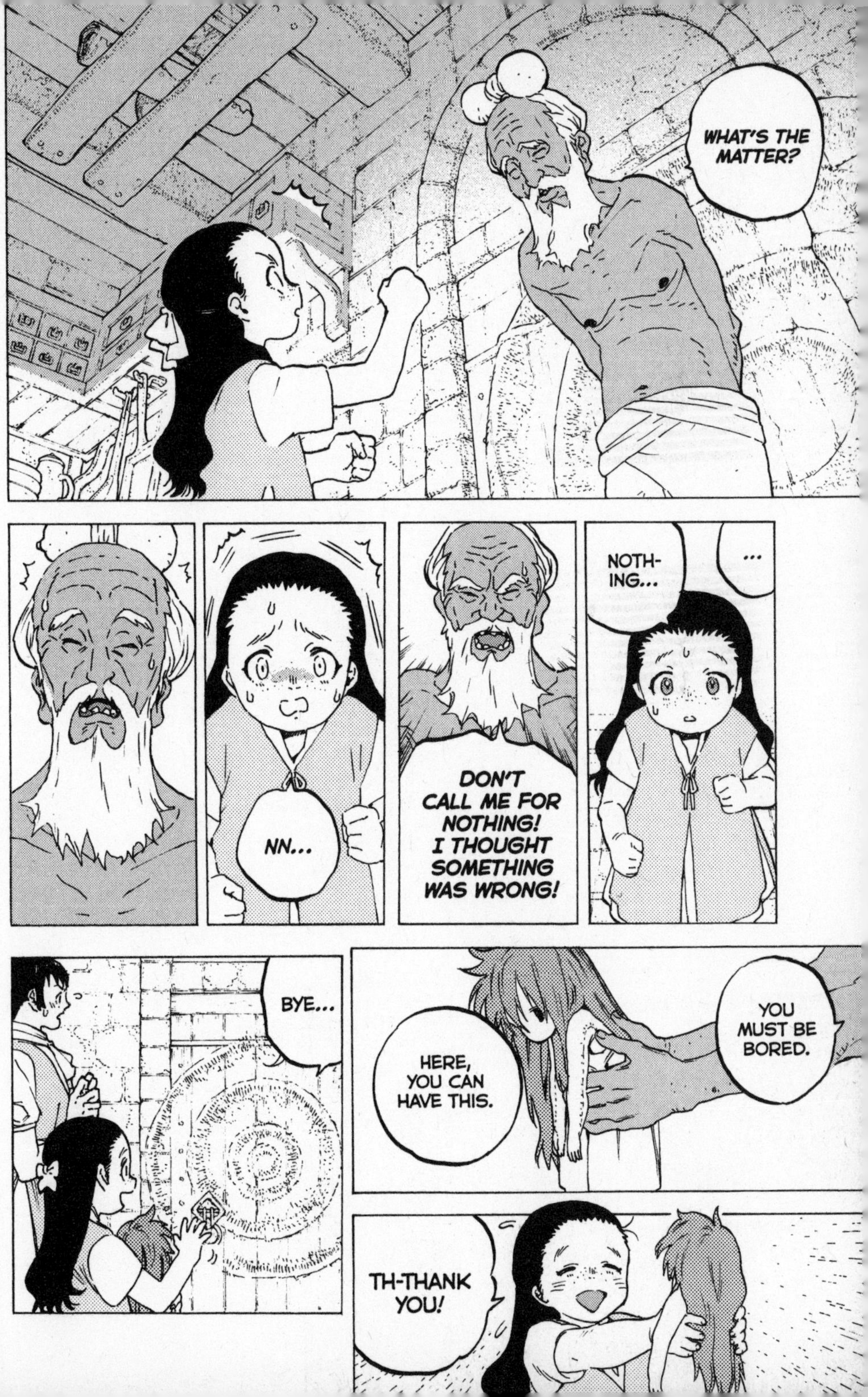
WHAT'S THE MATTER?
...
NOTH-ING...
DON'T CALL ME FOR NOTHING! I THOUGHT SOMETHING WAS WRONG!
NN...
YOU MUST BE BORED.
HERE, YOU CAN HAVE THIS.
TH-THANK YOU!
BYE...

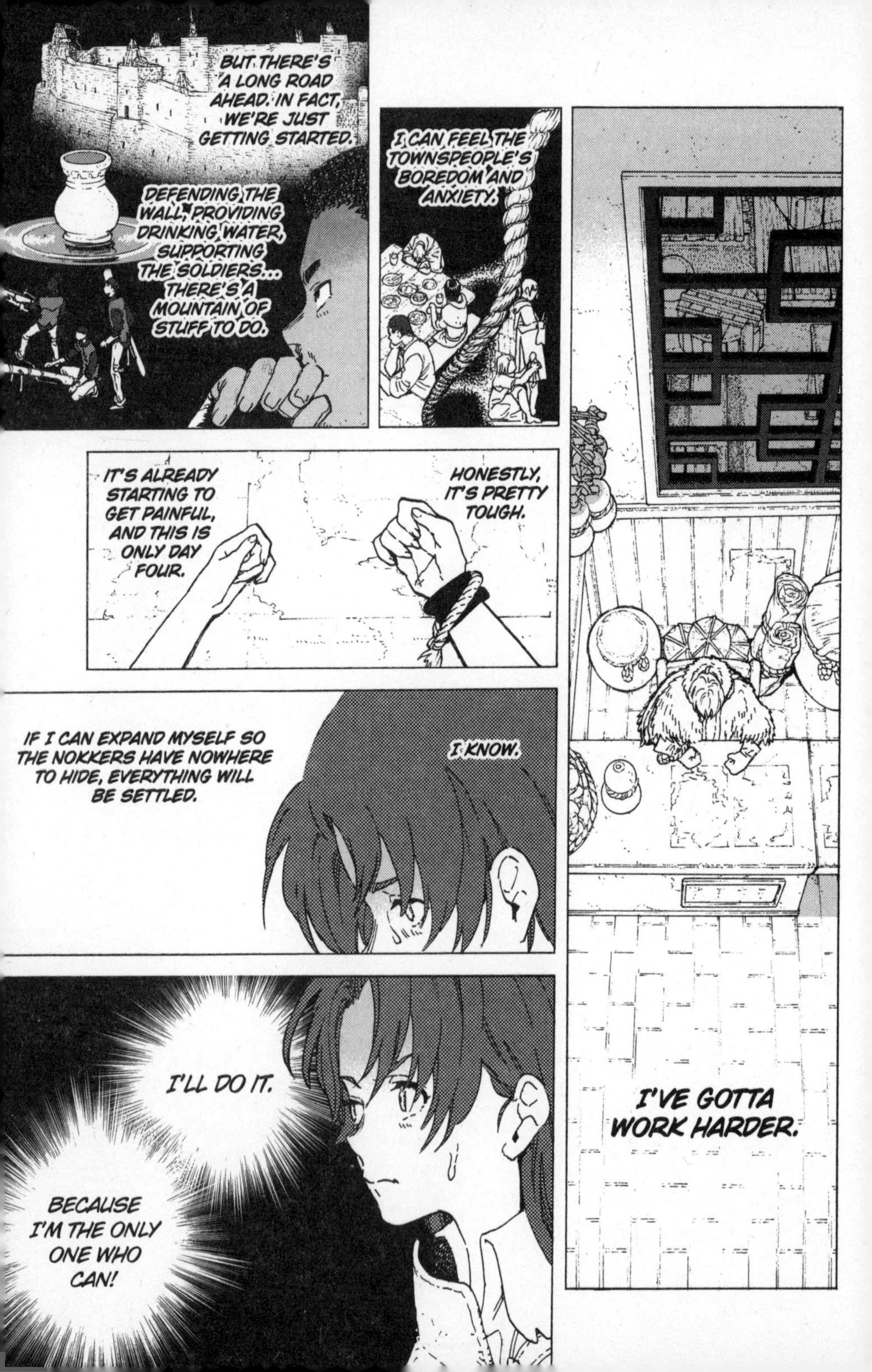
I'VE GOTTA WORK HARDER.
BUT THERE'S A LONG ROAD AHEAD. IN FACT, WE'RE JUST GETTING STARTED.
DEFENDING THE WALL, PROVIDING DRINKING WATER, SUPPORTING THE SOLDIERS... THERE'S A MOUNTAIN OF STUFF TO DO.
I CAN FEEL THE TOWNSPEOPLE'S BOREDOM AND ANXIETY.
HONESTLY, IT'S PRETTY TOUGH.
IT'S ALREADY STARTING TO GET PAINFUL, AND THIS IS ONLY DAY FOUR.
I KNOW.
IF I CAN EXPAND MYSELF SO THE NOKKERS HAVE NOWHERE TO HIDE, EVERYTHING WILL BE SETTLED.
I'LL DO IT.
BECAUSE I'M THE ONLY ONE WHO CAN!

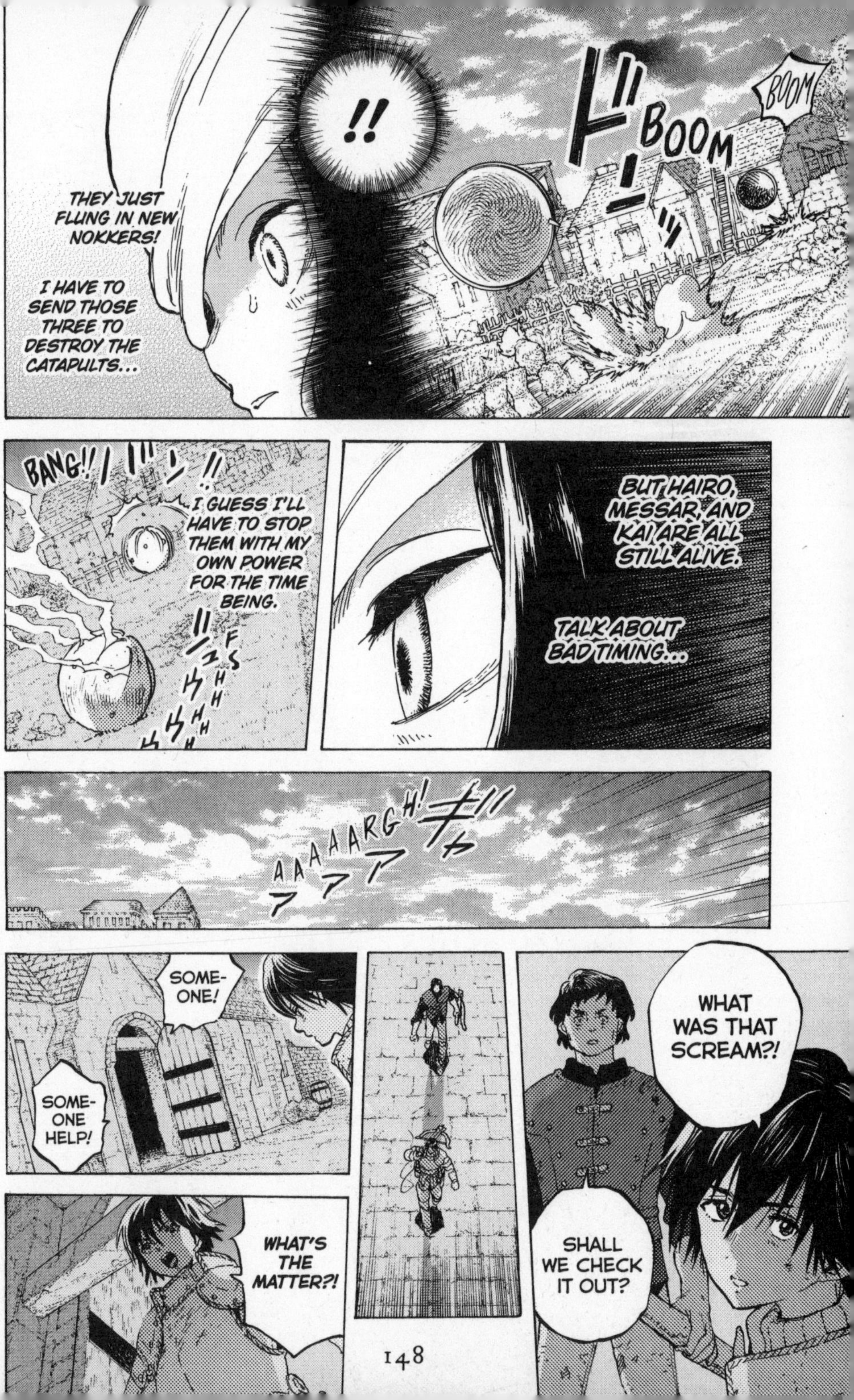
!!
BOOM
BOOM
THEY JUST FLUNG IN NEW NOKKERS!
I HAVE TO SEND THOSE THREE TO DESTROY THE CATAPULTS...
BUT HAIRO, MESSAR, AND KAI ARE ALL STILL ALIVE.
TALK ABOUT BAD TIMING...
BANG!!
I GUESS I'LL HAVE TO STOP THEM WITH MY OWN POWER FOR THE TIME BEING.
FSHHHHH
AAAAAARGH!
WHAT WAS THAT SCREAM?!
SHALL WE CHECK IT OUT?
SOME-ONE!
SOME-ONE HELP!
WHAT'S THE MATTER?!

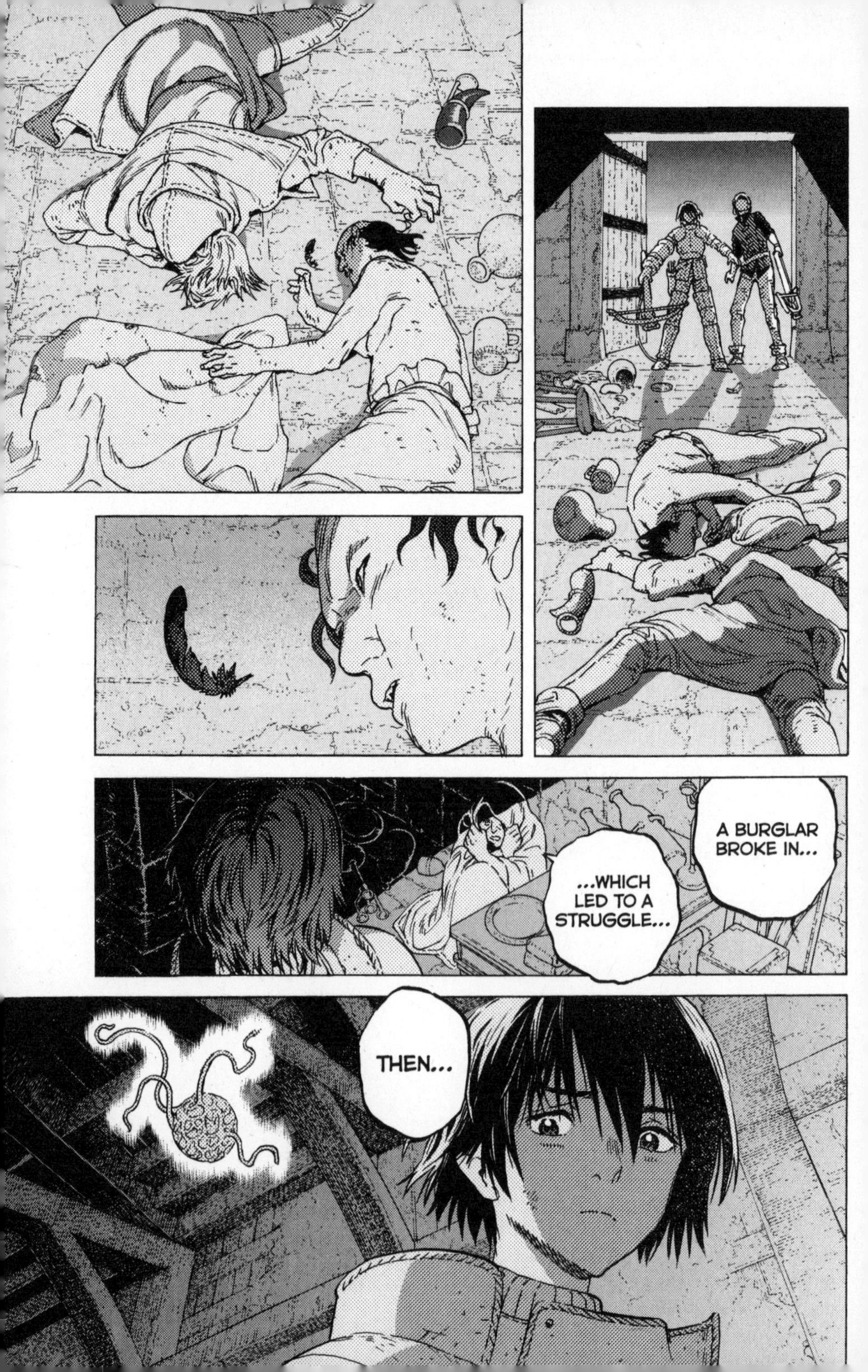
A BURGLAR BROKE IN...
...WHICH LED TO A STRUGGLE...
THEN...

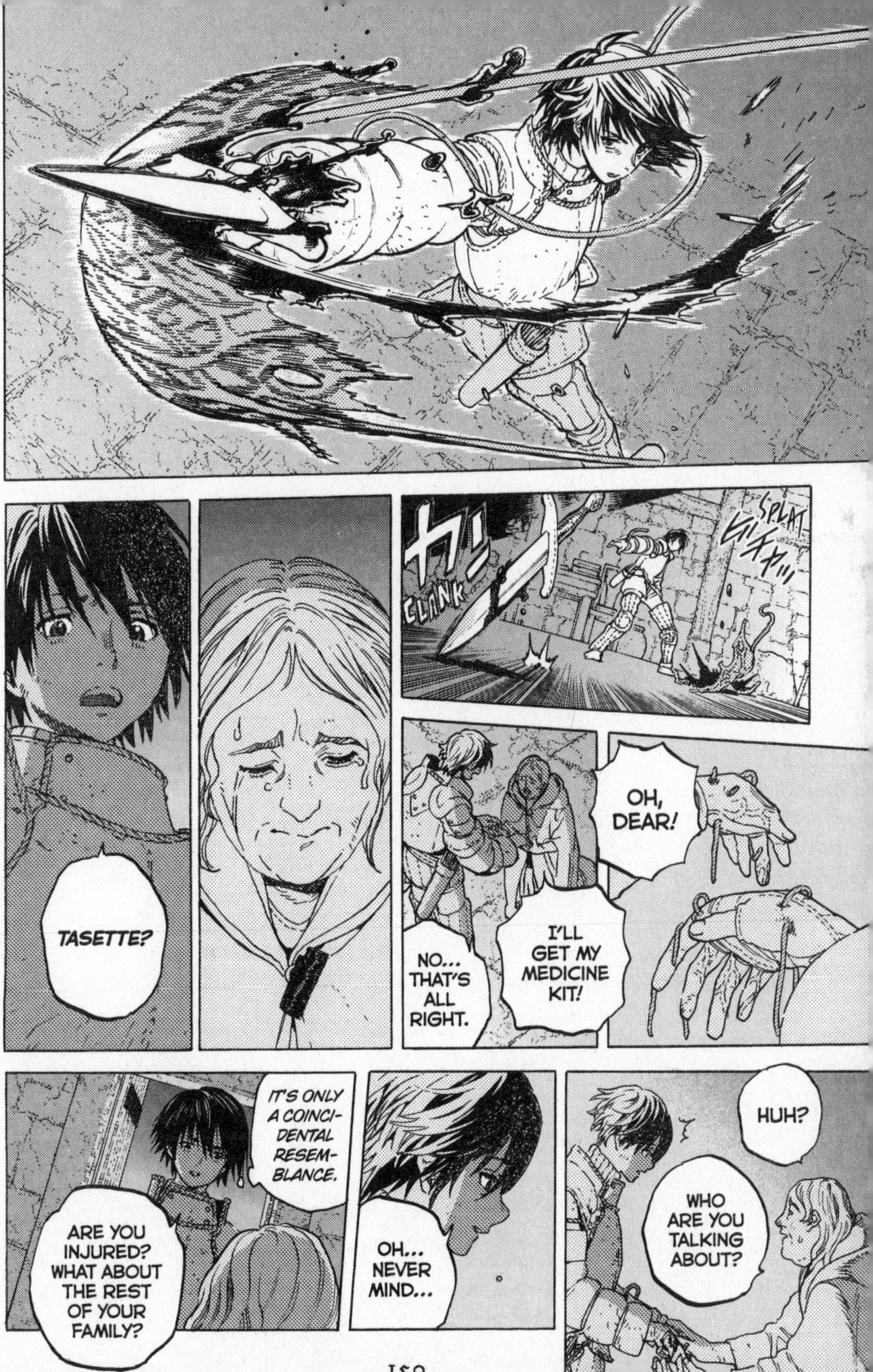
SPLAT
CLANK
OH, DEAR!
I'LL GET MY MEDICINE KIT!
NO... THAT'S ALL RIGHT.
TASETTE?
HUH?
WHO ARE YOU TALKING ABOUT?
OH... NEVER MIND...
IT'S ONLY A COINCIDENTAL RESEMBLANCE.
ARE YOU INJURED? WHAT ABOUT THE REST OF YOUR FAMILY?

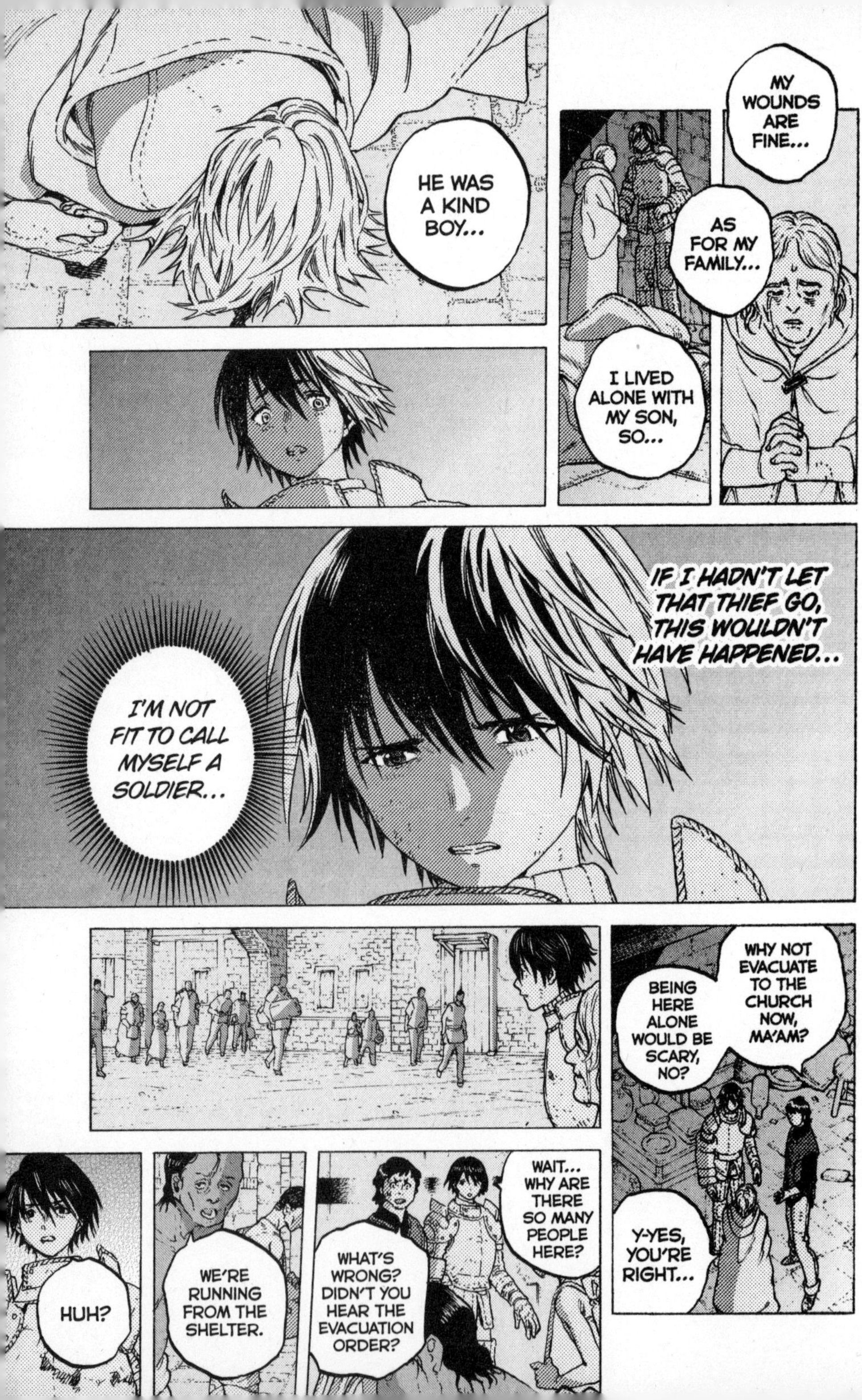
MY WOUNDS ARE FINE...
AS FOR MY FAMILY...
I LIVED ALONE WITH MY SON, SO...
HE WAS A KIND BOY...
IF I HADN'T LET THAT THIEF GO, THIS WOULDN'T HAVE HAPPENED...
I'M NOT FIT TO CALL MYSELF A SOLDIER...
WHY NOT EVACUATE TO THE CHURCH NOW, MA'AM?
BEING HERE ALONE WOULD BE SCARY, NO?
Y-YES, YOU'RE RIGHT...
WAIT... WHY ARE THERE SO MANY PEOPLE HERE?
WHAT'S WRONG? DIDN'T YOU HEAR THE EVACUATION ORDER?
WE'RE RUNNING FROM THE SHELTER.
HUH?

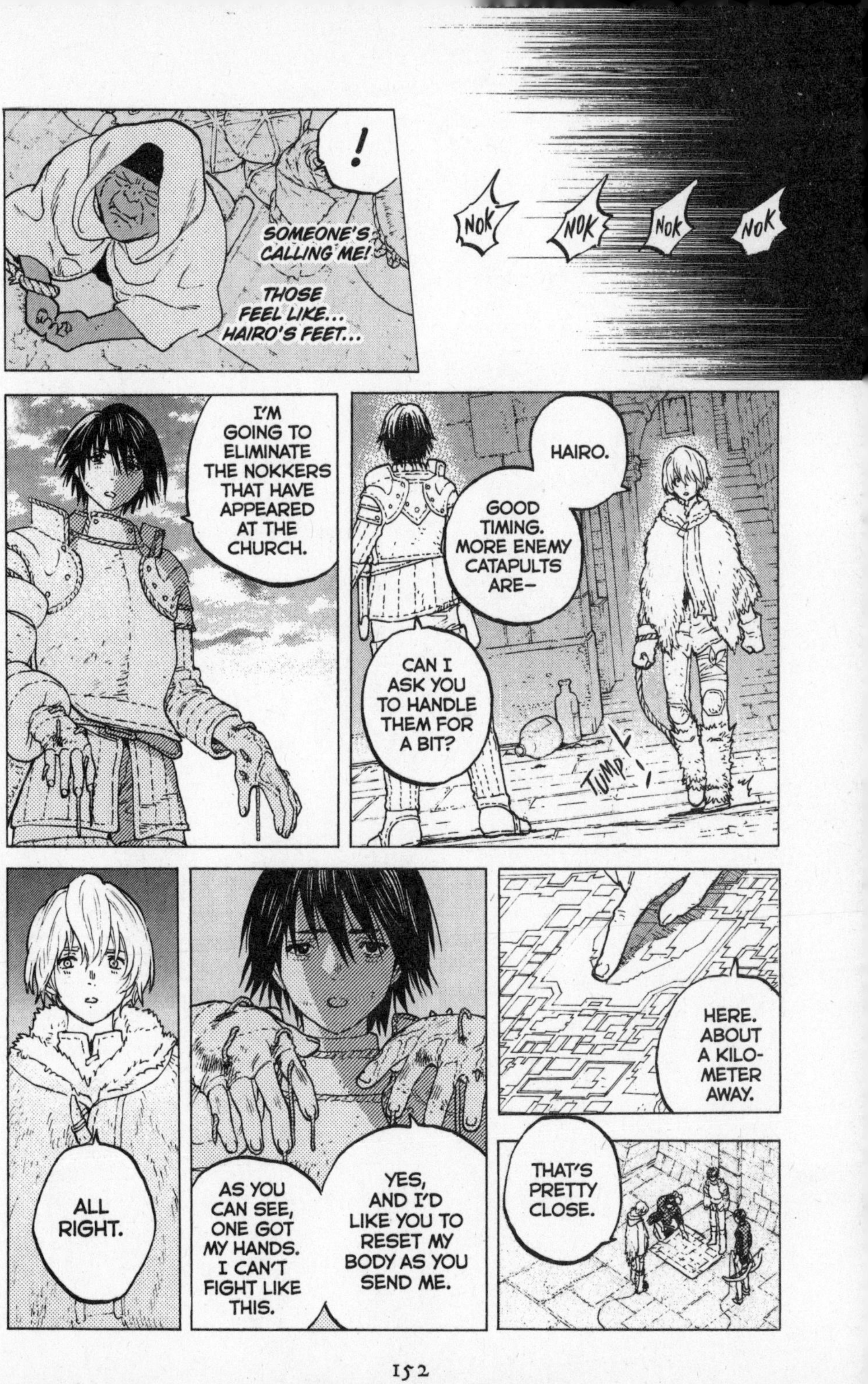
NOK
NOK
NOK
NOK
!
SOMEONE'S CALLING ME!
THOSE FEEL LIKE... HAIRO'S FEET...
HAIRO.
GOOD TIMING. MORE ENEMY CATAPULTS ARE—
CAN I ASK YOU TO HANDLE THEM FOR A BIT?
TUMP
I'M GOING TO ELIMINATE THE NOKKERS THAT HAVE APPEARED AT THE CHURCH.
HERE. ABOUT A KILO-METER AWAY.
THAT'S PRETTY CLOSE.
YES, AND I'D LIKE YOU TO RESET MY BODY AS YOU SEND ME.
AS YOU CAN SEE, ONE GOT MY HANDS. I CAN'T FIGHT LIKE THIS.
ALL RIGHT.

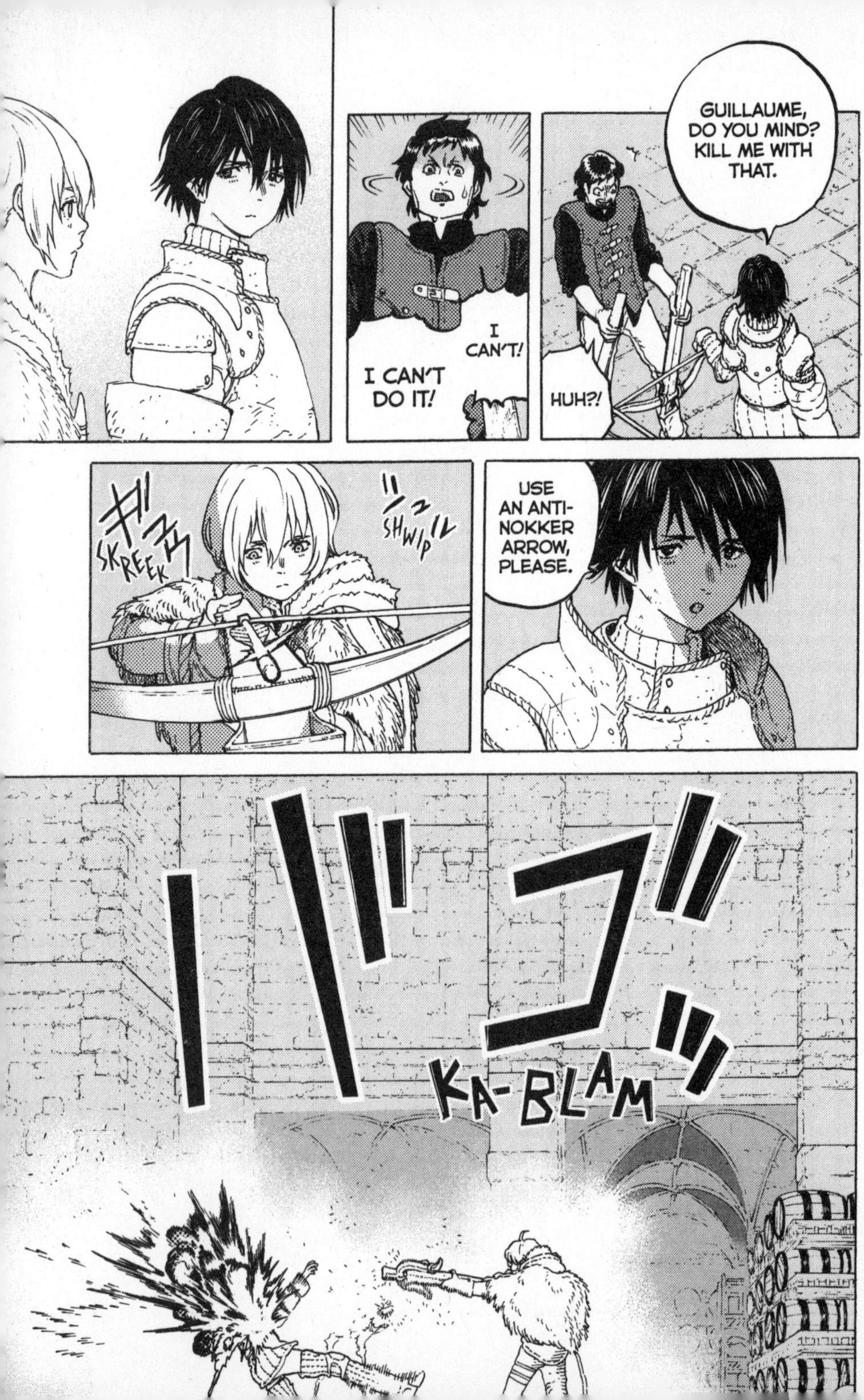
GUILLAUME, DO YOU MIND? KILL ME WITH THAT.
HUH?!
I CAN'T!
I CAN'T DO IT!
USE AN ANTI-NOKKER ARROW, PLEASE.
SHWIP
SKREEEK
KA-BLAM

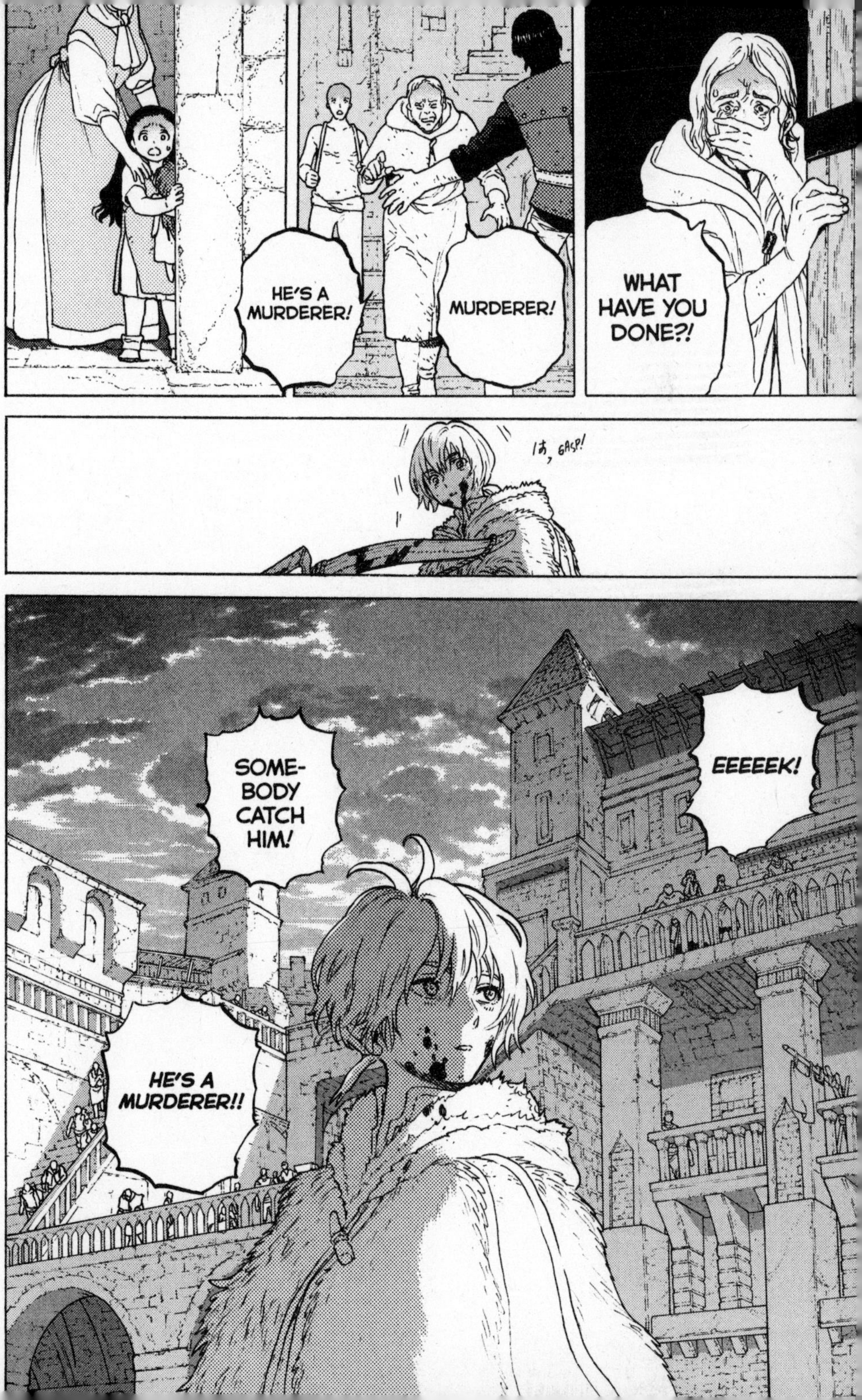
WHAT HAVE YOU DONE?!
MURDERER!
HE'S A MURDERER!
は, GASP!
EEEEEK!
SOME-BODY CATCH HIM!
HE'S A MURDERER!!

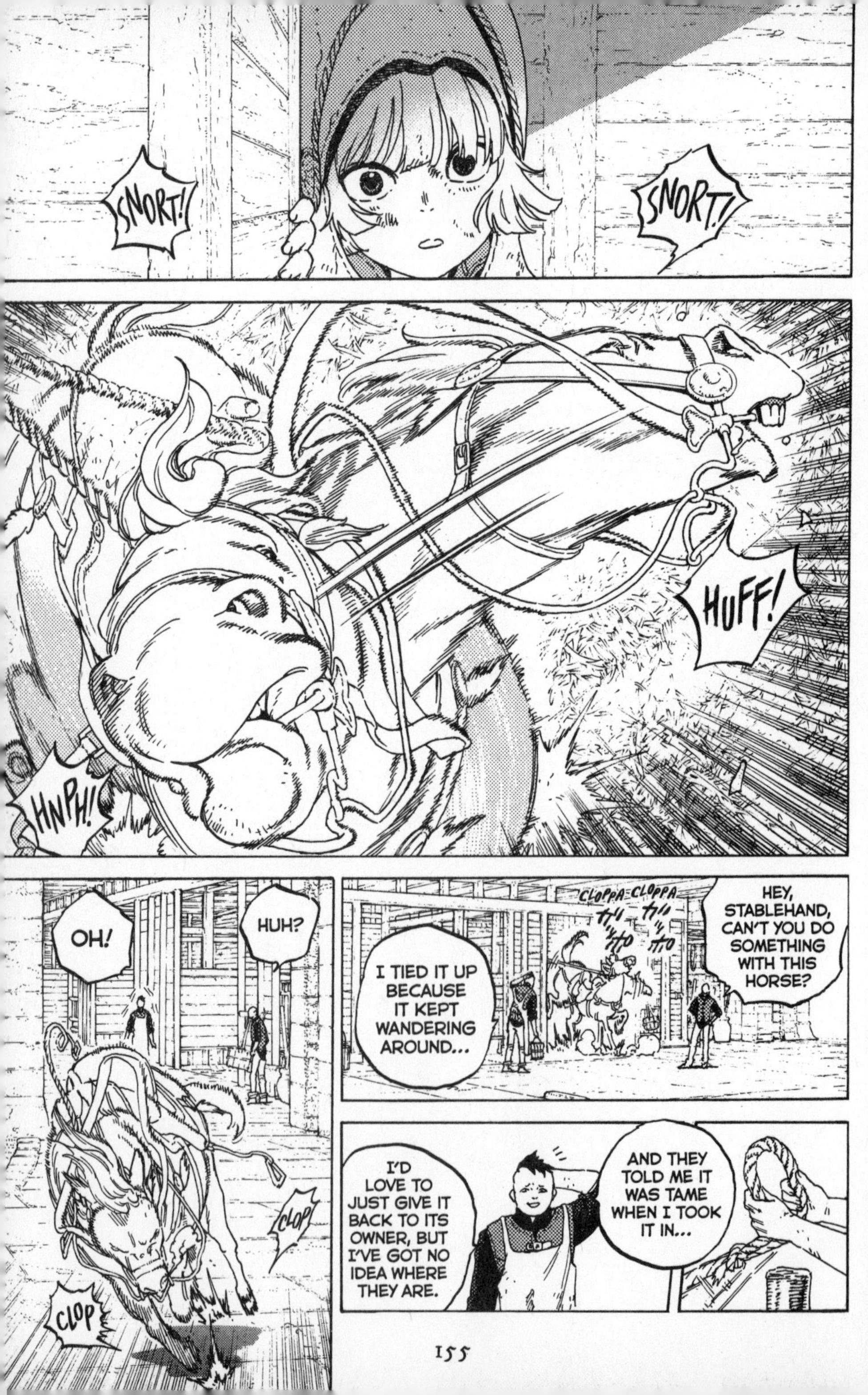
SNORT!
SNORT!
HUFF!
HNPH!
CLOPPA CLOPPA
HEY, STABLEHAND, CAN'T YOU DO SOMETHING WITH THIS HORSE?
I TIED IT UP BECAUSE IT KEPT WANDERING AROUND...
AND THEY TOLD ME IT WAS TAME WHEN I TOOK IT IN...
I'D LOVE TO JUST GIVE IT BACK TO ITS OWNER, BUT I'VE GOT NO IDEA WHERE THEY ARE.
HUH?
OH!
CLOP
CLOP

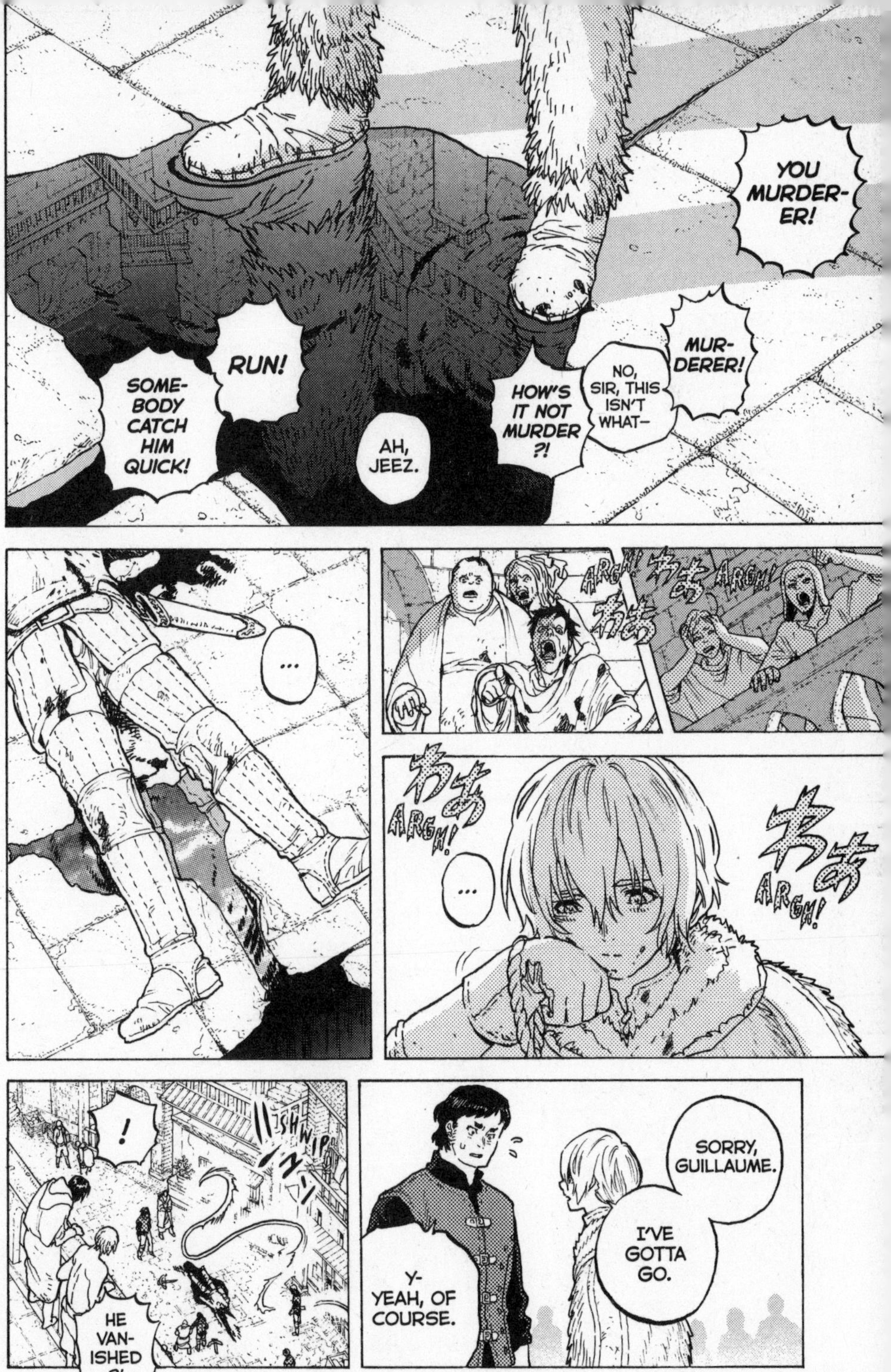

YOU MURDERER!
MURDERER!
NO, SIR, THIS ISN'T WHAT—
HOW'S IT NOT MURDER?!
AH, JEEZ.
RUN!
SOMEBODY CATCH HIM QUICK!
ARGH! わあ ARGH! わあ
わあ ARGH!
...
わあ ARGH!
...
SORRY, GUILLAUME.
I'VE GOTTA GO.
Y-YEAH, OF COURSE.
!
SHWIP
HE VANISHED?!

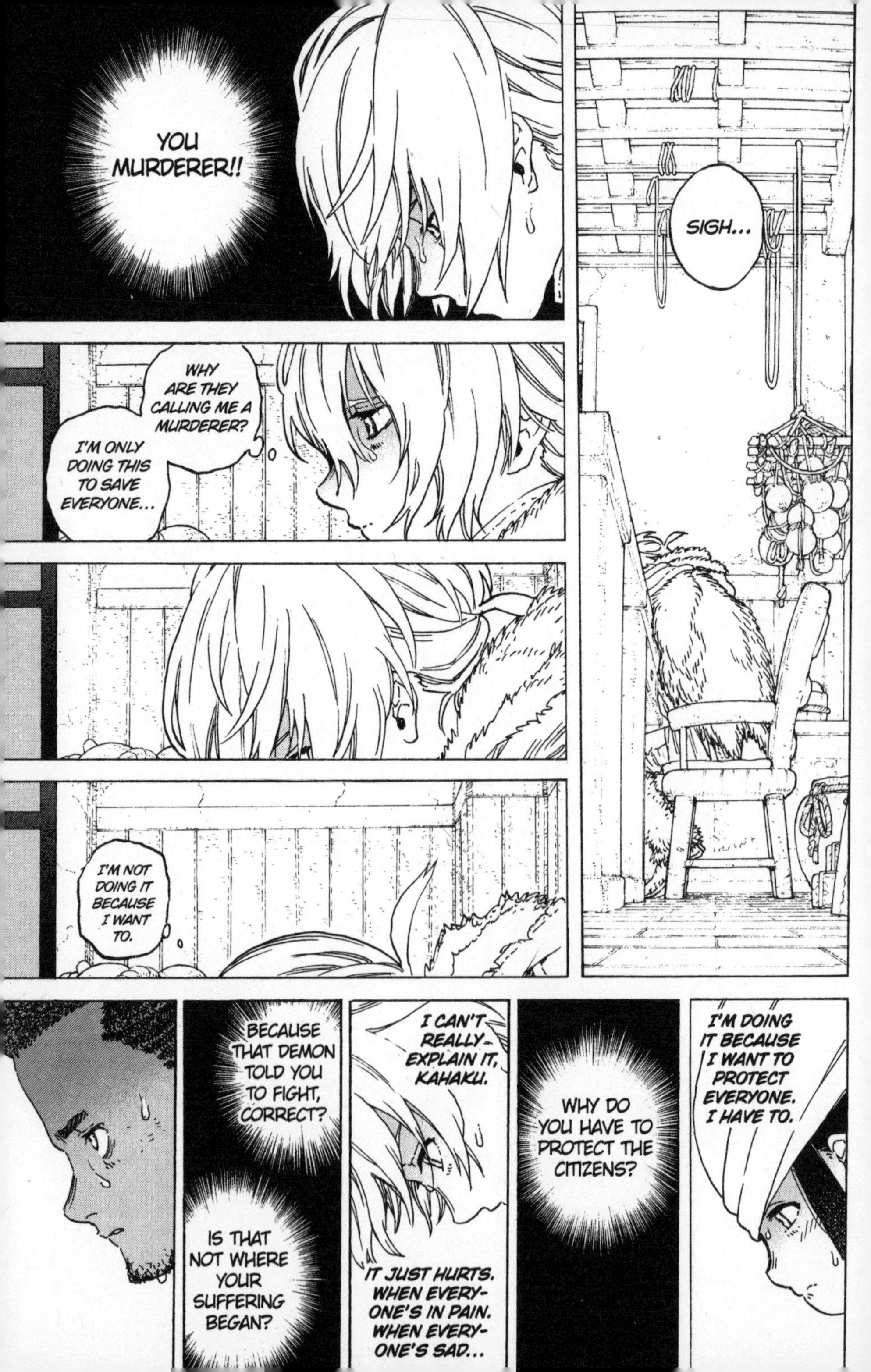
SIGH...
YOU MURDERER!!
WHY ARE THEY CALLING ME A MURDERER?
I'M ONLY DOING THIS TO SAVE EVERYONE...
I'M NOT DOING IT BECAUSE I WANT TO.
I'M DOING IT BECAUSE I WANT TO PROTECT EVERYONE. I HAVE TO.
WHY DO YOU HAVE TO PROTECT THE CITIZENS?
I CAN'T REALLY EXPLAIN IT, KAHAKU.
IT JUST HURTS. WHEN EVERYONE'S IN PAIN. WHEN EVERYONE'S SAD...
BECAUSE THAT DEMON TOLD YOU TO FIGHT, CORRECT?
IS THAT NOT WHERE YOUR SUFFERING BEGAN?

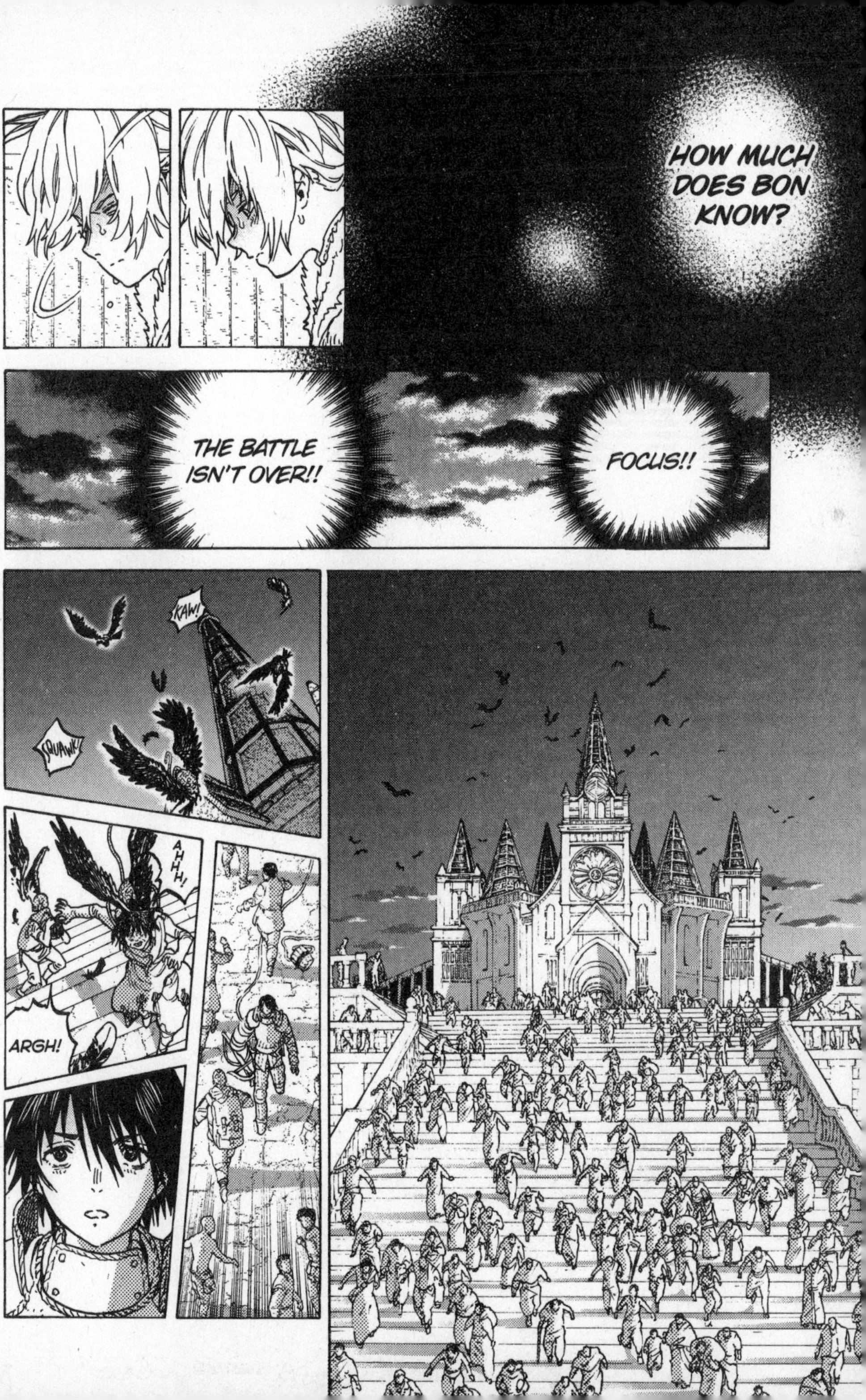
HOW MUCH DOES BON KNOW?
FOCUS!!
THE BATTLE ISN'T OVER!!
KAW!
SQUAWK!
AHHH!
ARGH!

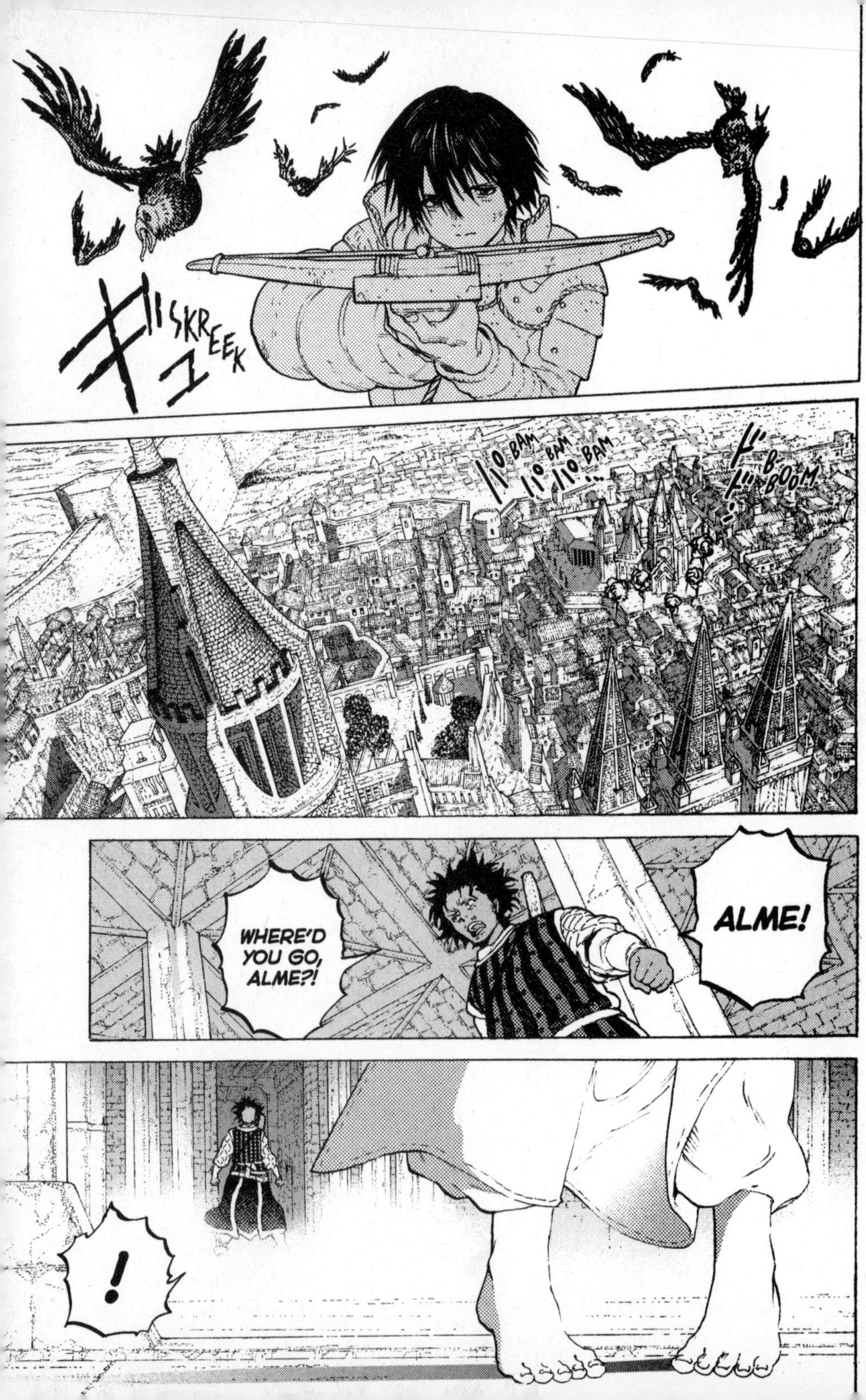
SKREEEK
B-BOOM
BAM BAM BAM...
ALME!
WHERE'D YOU GO, ALME?!
!

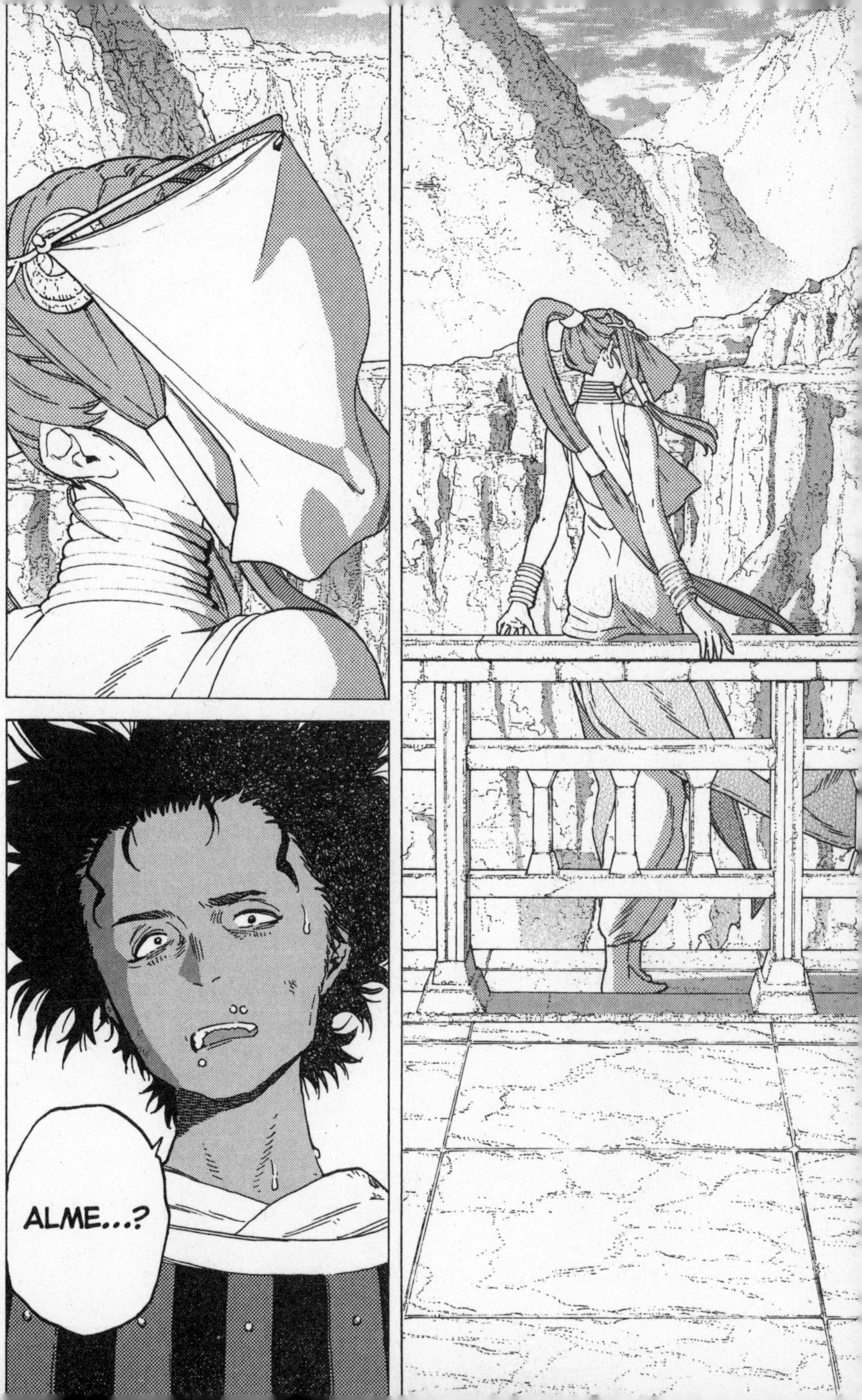
ALME...?

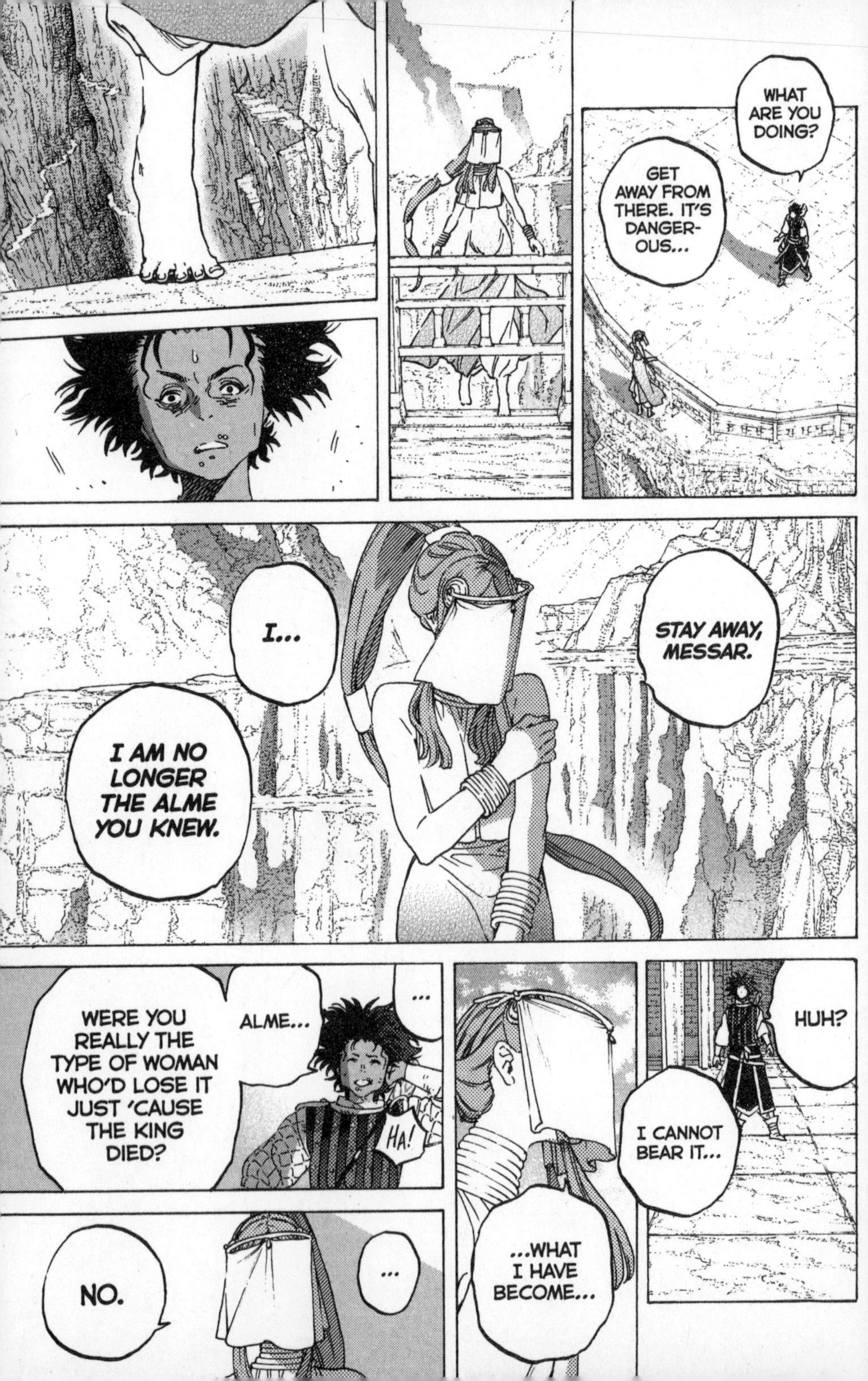
WHAT ARE YOU DOING?
GET AWAY FROM THERE. IT'S DANGER-OUS...
STAY AWAY, MESSAR.
I...
I AM NO LONGER THE ALME YOU KNEW.
HUH?
I CANNOT BEAR IT...
...WHAT I HAVE BECOME...
...
ALME...
WERE YOU REALLY THE TYPE OF WOMAN WHO'D LOSE IT JUST 'CAUSE THE KING DIED?
HA!
...
NO.

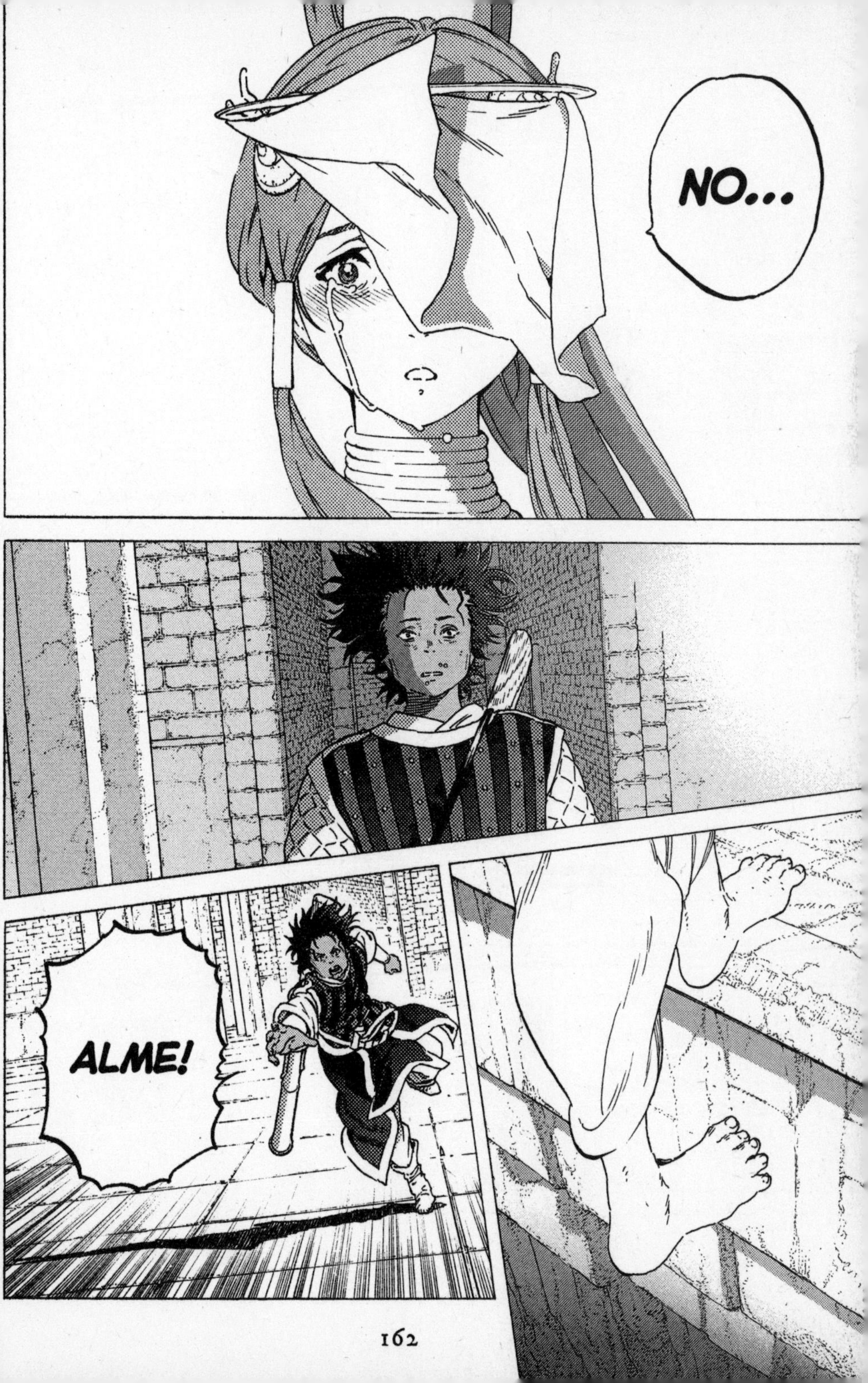
NO...
ALME!

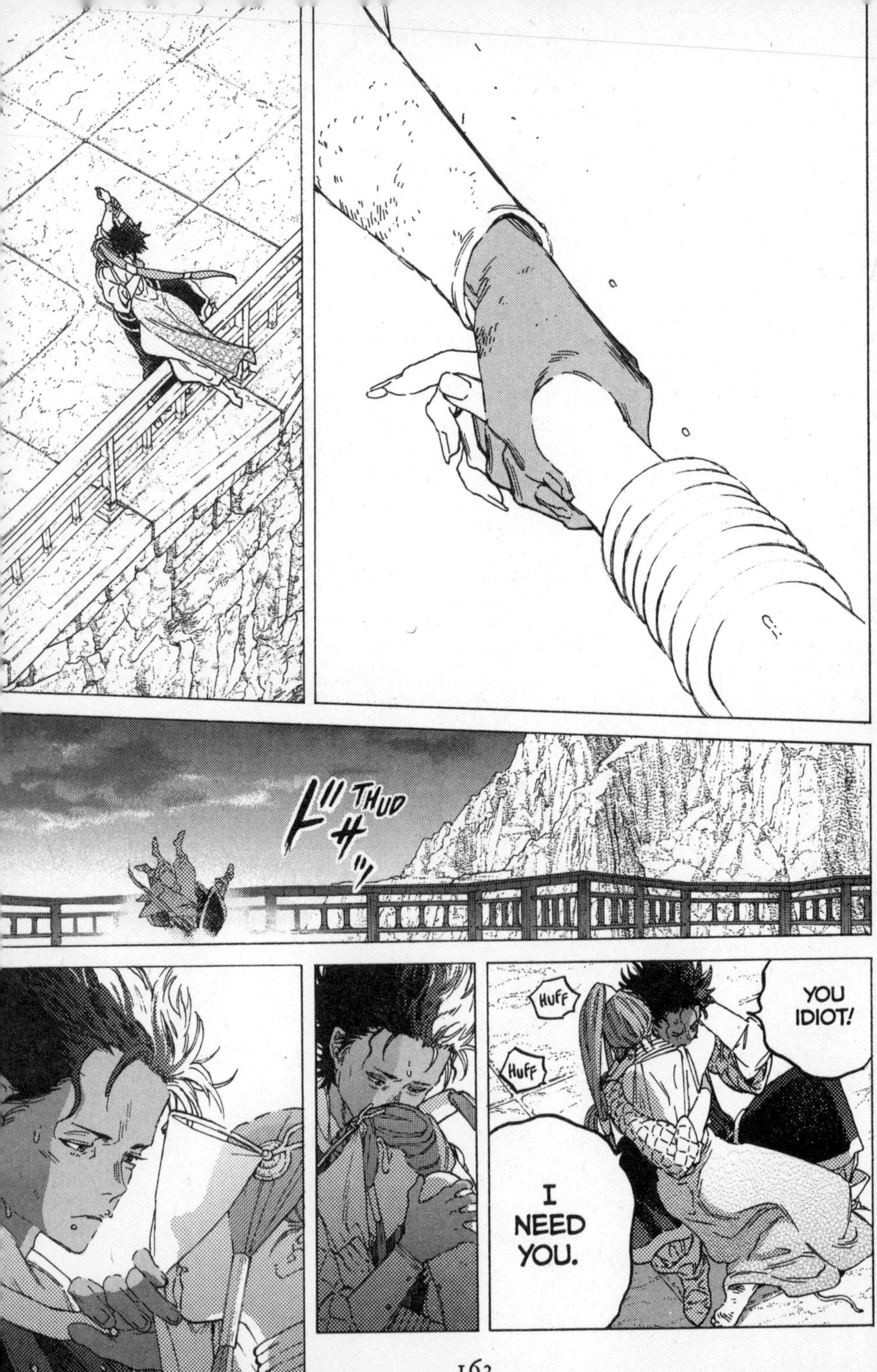
ドサッ
THUD
YOU IDIOT!
HUFF
HUFF
I NEED YOU.

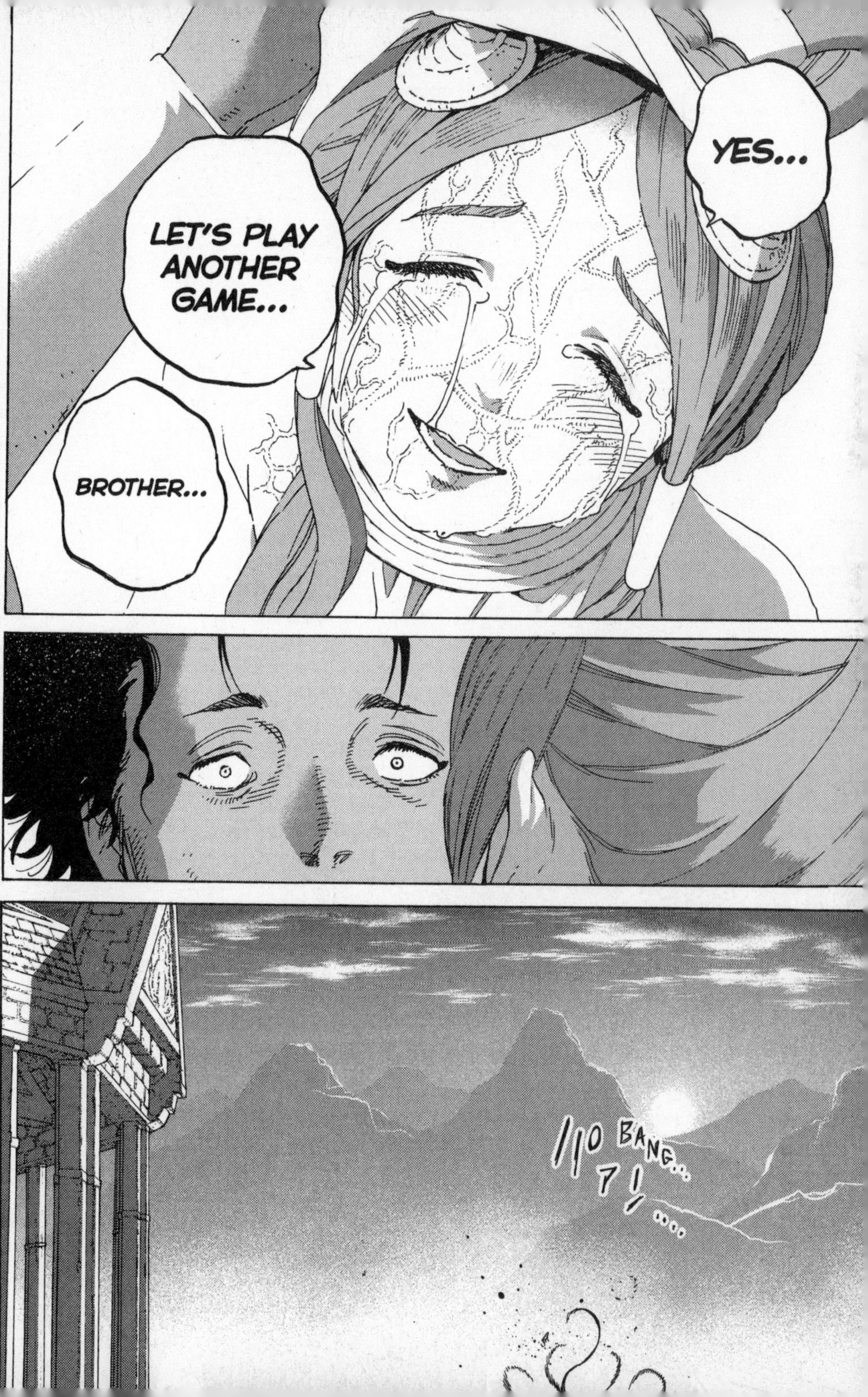
YES...
LET'S PLAY ANOTHER GAME...
BROTHER...
BANG...

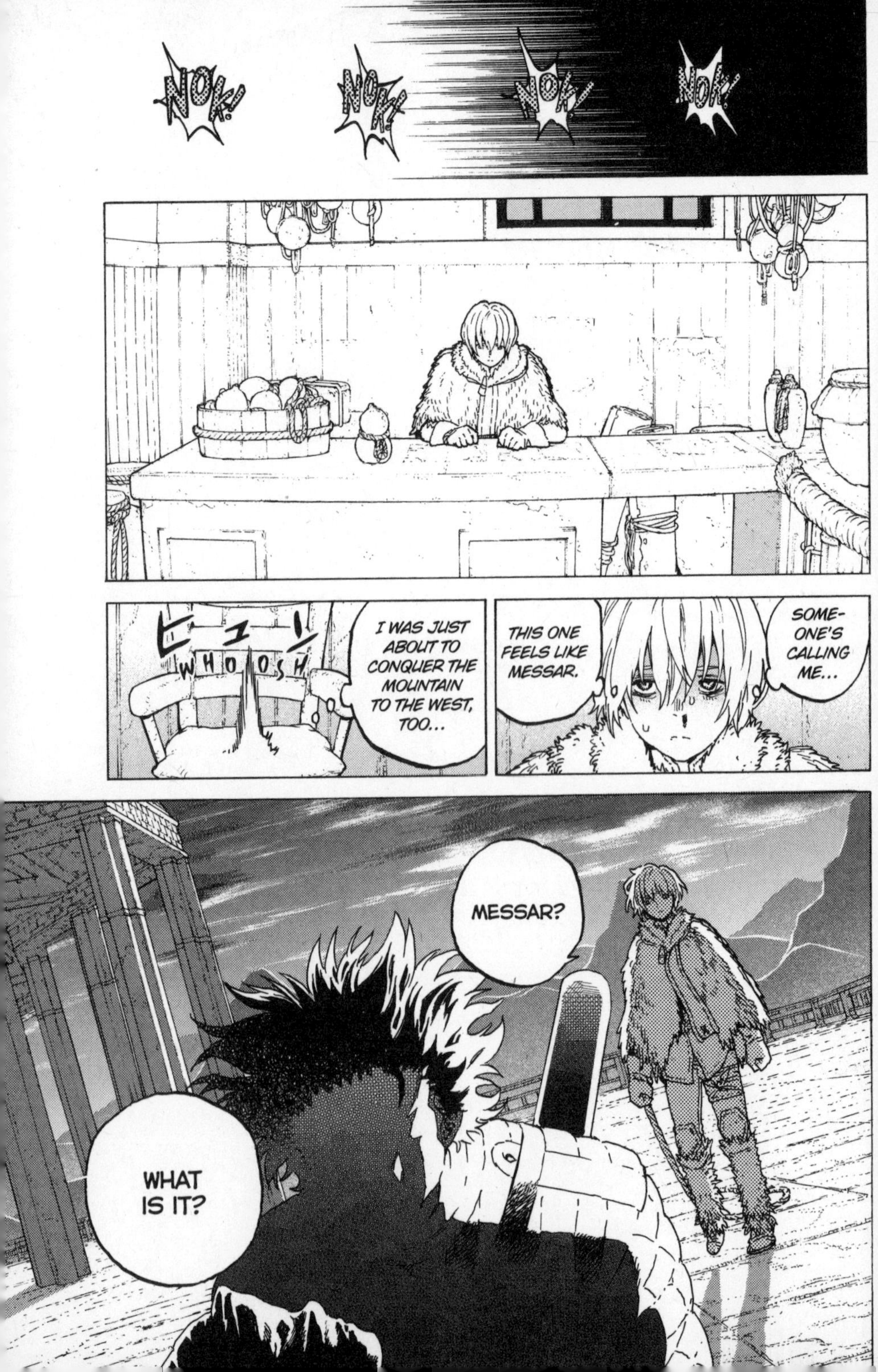
NOK!
NOK!
NOK!
NOK!
SOME-ONE'S CALLING ME...
THIS ONE FEELS LIKE MESSAR.
I WAS JUST ABOUT TO CONQUER THE MOUNTAIN TO THE WEST, TOO...
ヒュー
WHOOSH
MESSAR?
WHAT IS IT?

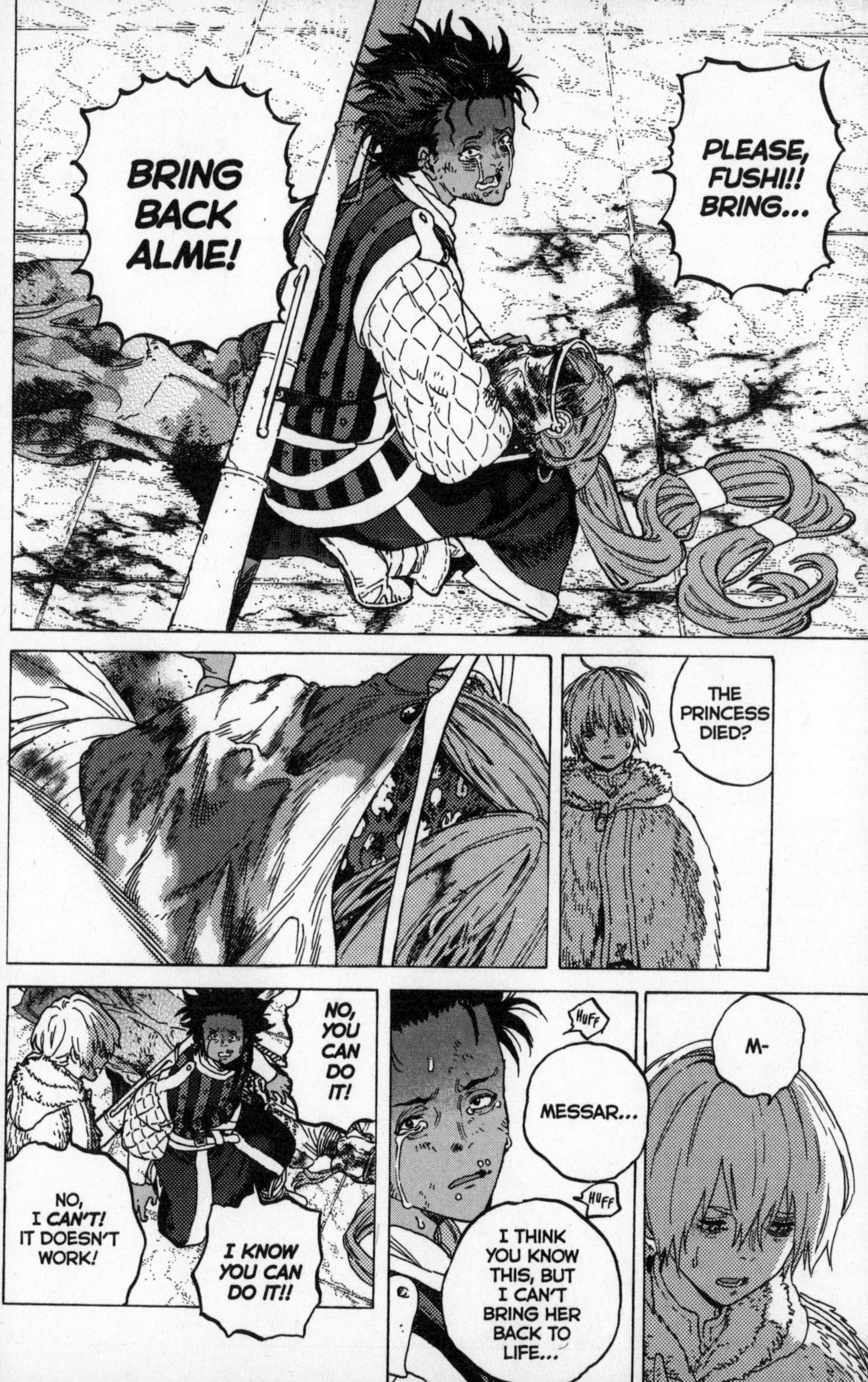
PLEASE, FUSHI!! BRING...
BRING BACK ALME!
THE PRINCESS DIED?
M-
HUFF
MESSAR...
HUFF
I THINK YOU KNOW THIS, BUT I CAN'T BRING HER BACK TO LIFE...
NO, YOU CAN DO IT!
NO, I CAN'T! IT DOESN'T WORK!
I KNOW YOU CAN DO IT!!

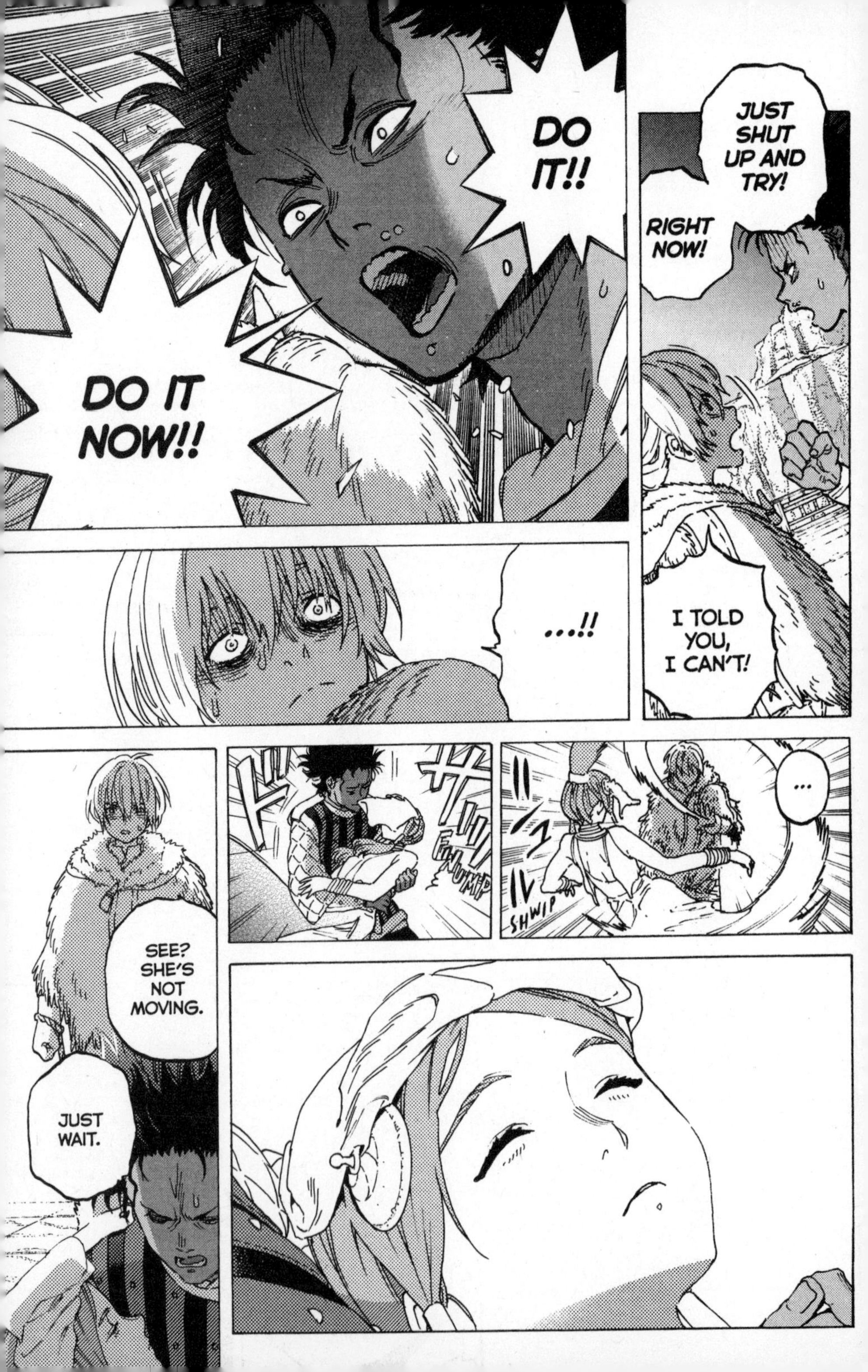
JUST SHUT UP AND TRY!
RIGHT NOW!
I TOLD YOU, I CAN'T!
DO IT!!
DO IT NOW!!
...!!
...
SHWIP
FWUMP
SEE? SHE'S NOT MOVING.
JUST WAIT.

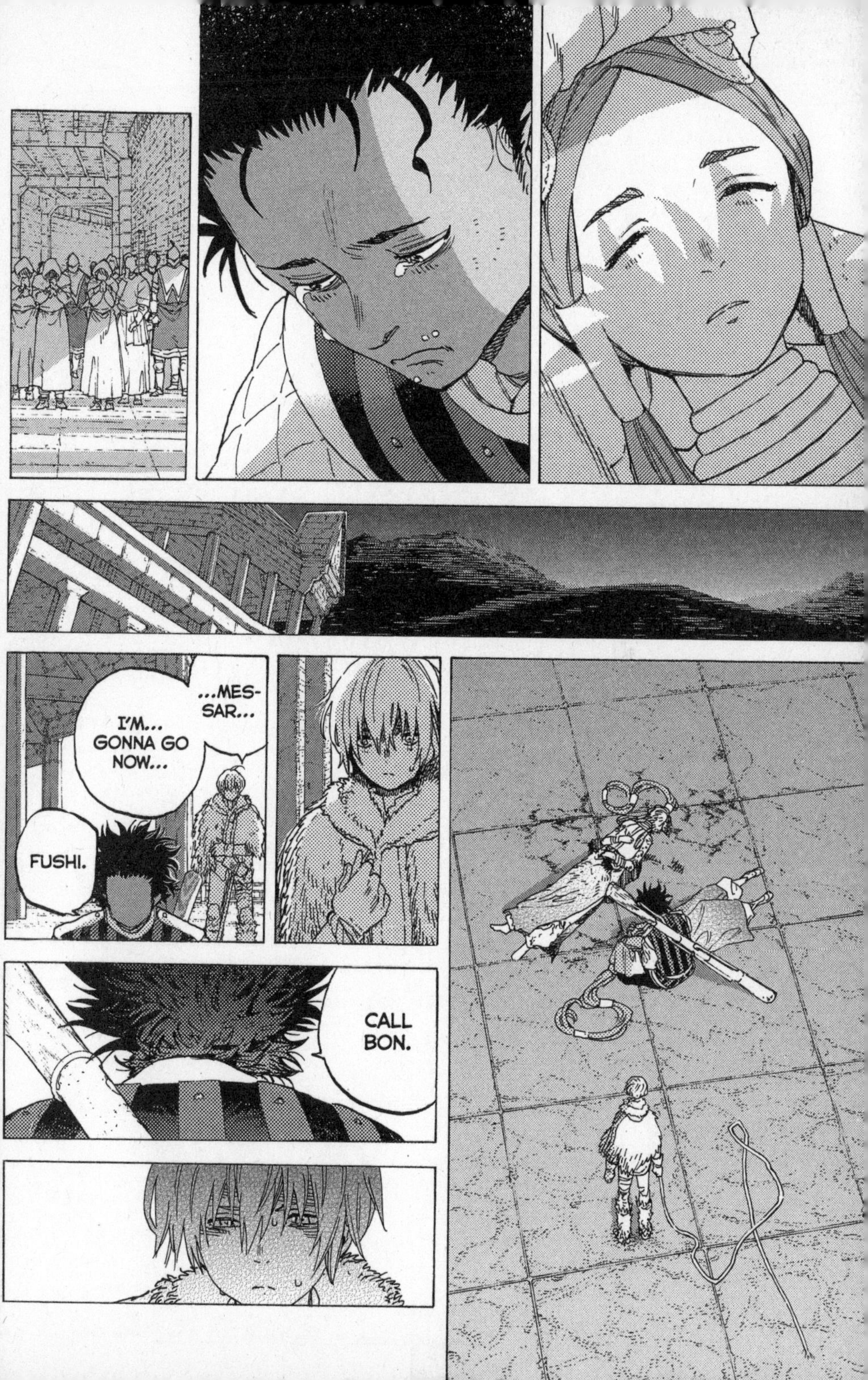
...MES-
SAR...
I'M...
GONNA GO
NOW...
FUSHI.
CALL
BON.

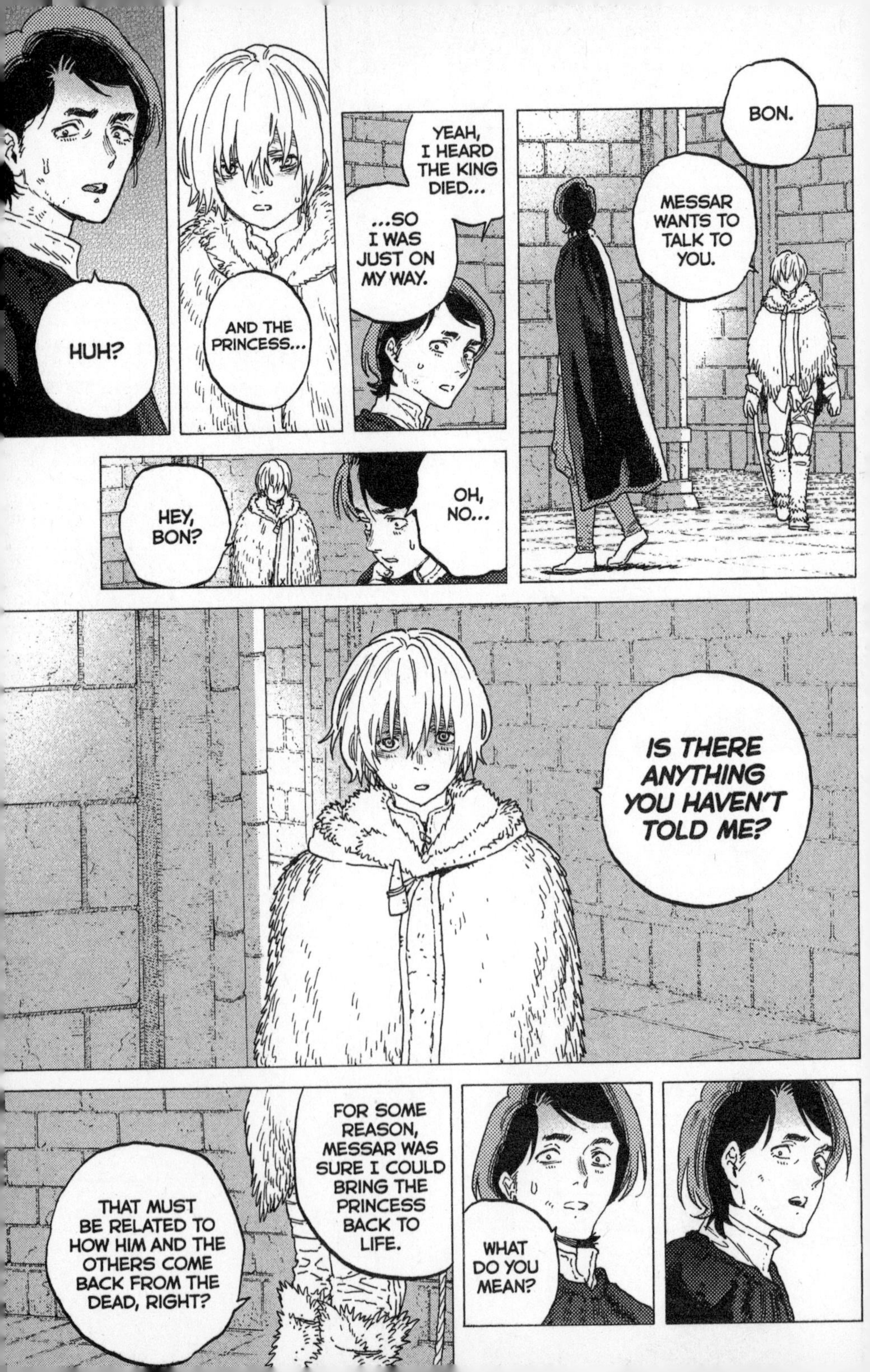
BON.
MESSAR WANTS TO TALK TO YOU.
YEAH, I HEARD THE KING DIED...
...SO I WAS JUST ON MY WAY.
AND THE PRINCESS...
HUH?
OH, NO...
HEY, BON?
IS THERE ANYTHING YOU HAVEN'T TOLD ME?
WHAT DO YOU MEAN?
FOR SOME REASON, MESSAR WAS SURE I COULD BRING THE PRINCESS BACK TO LIFE.
THAT MUST BE RELATED TO HOW HIM AND THE OTHERS COME BACK FROM THE DEAD, RIGHT?

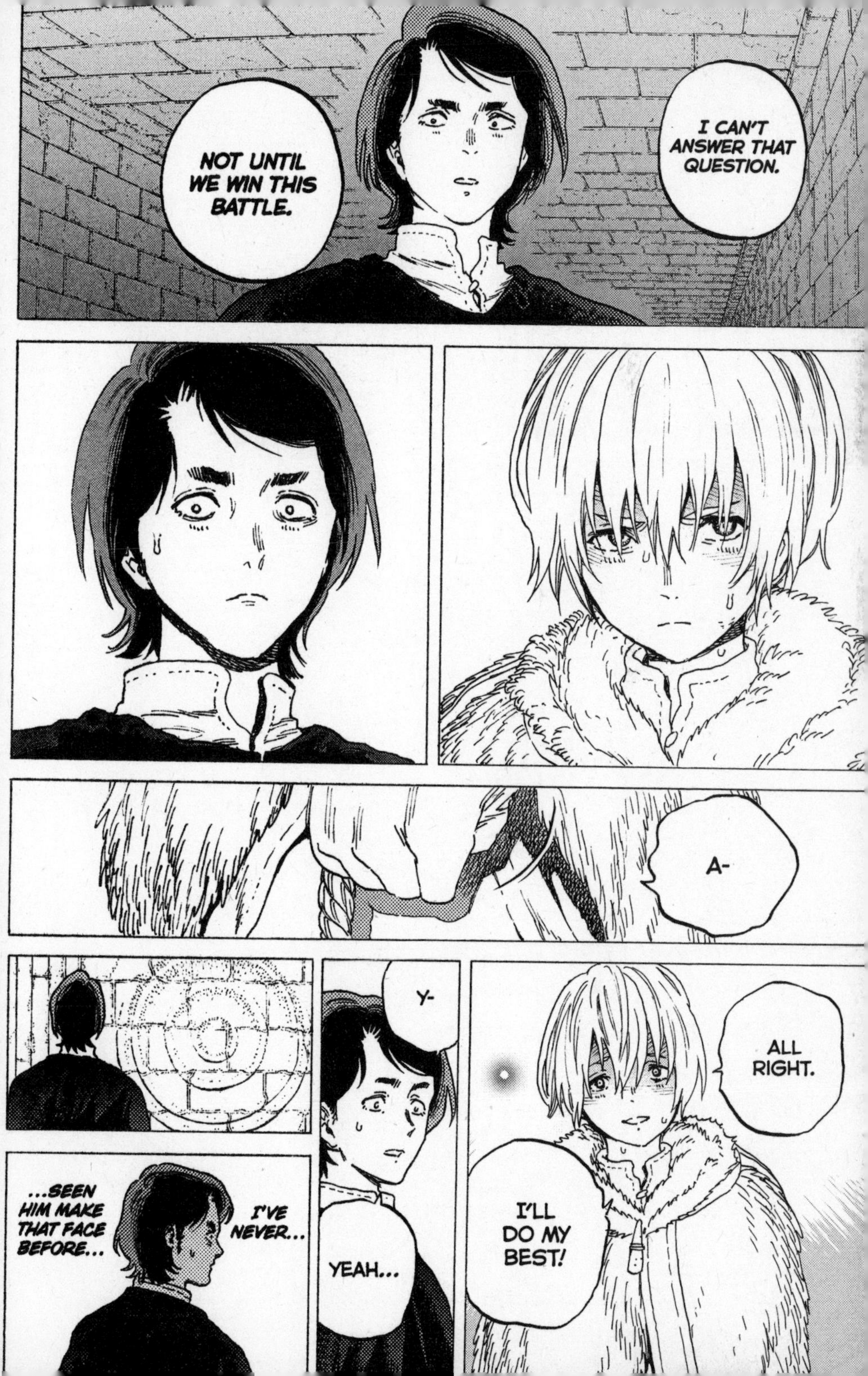
I CAN'T ANSWER THAT QUESTION.
NOT UNTIL WE WIN THIS BATTLE.
A-
ALL RIGHT.
I'LL DO MY BEST!
Y-
YEAH...
I'VE NEVER...
...SEEN HIM MAKE THAT FACE BEFORE...

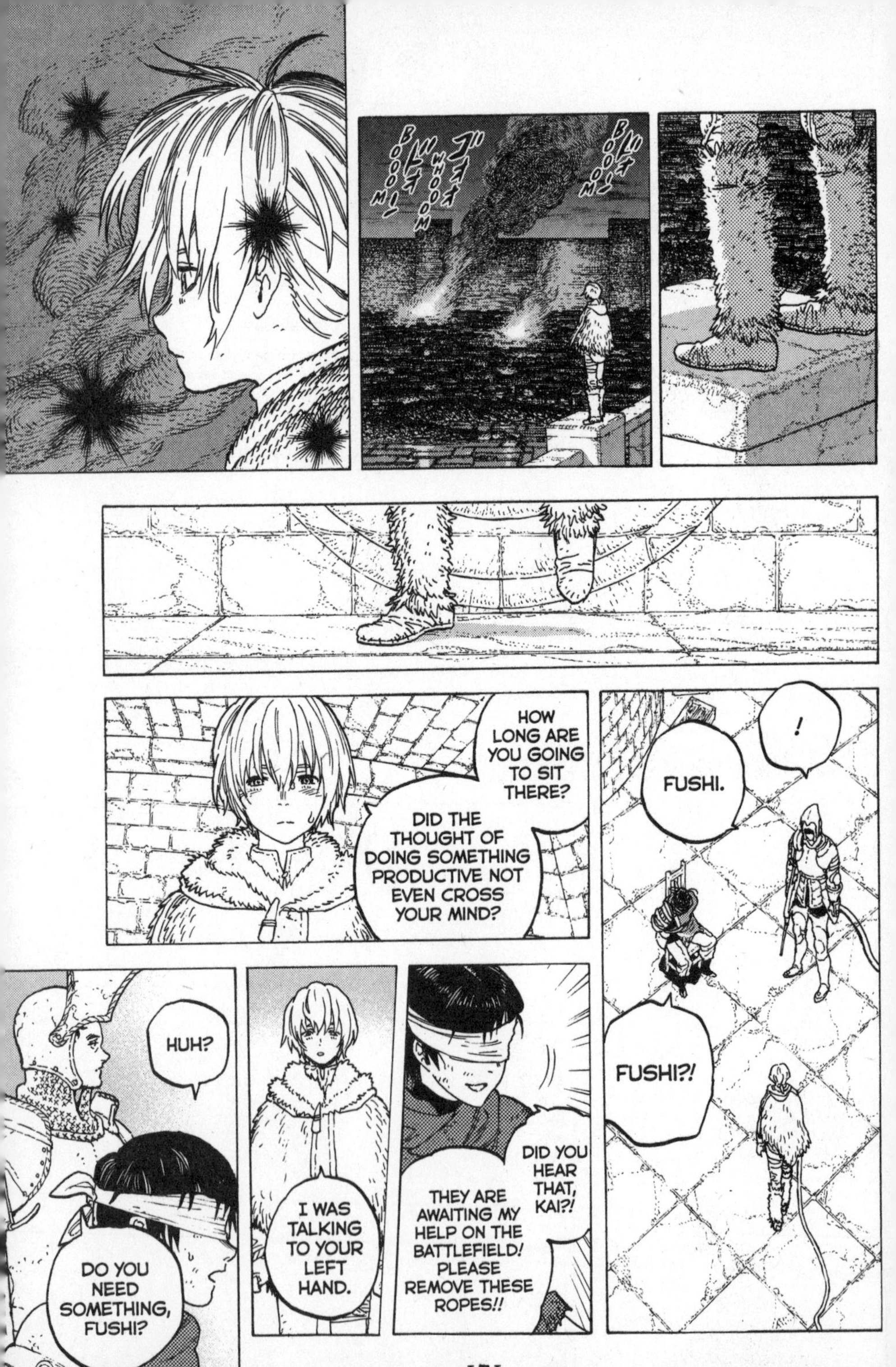
ドォン BOOOOM
ゴォオ WHOOOOM
ドォー BOOOOM
!
FUSHI.
FUSHI?!
HOW LONG ARE YOU GOING TO SIT THERE?
DID THE THOUGHT OF DOING SOMETHING PRODUCTIVE NOT EVEN CROSS YOUR MIND?
DID YOU HEAR THAT, KAI?!
THEY ARE AWAITING MY HELP ON THE BATTLEFIELD! PLEASE REMOVE THESE ROPES!!
I WAS TALKING TO YOUR LEFT HAND.
HUH?
DO YOU NEED SOMETHING, FUSHI?

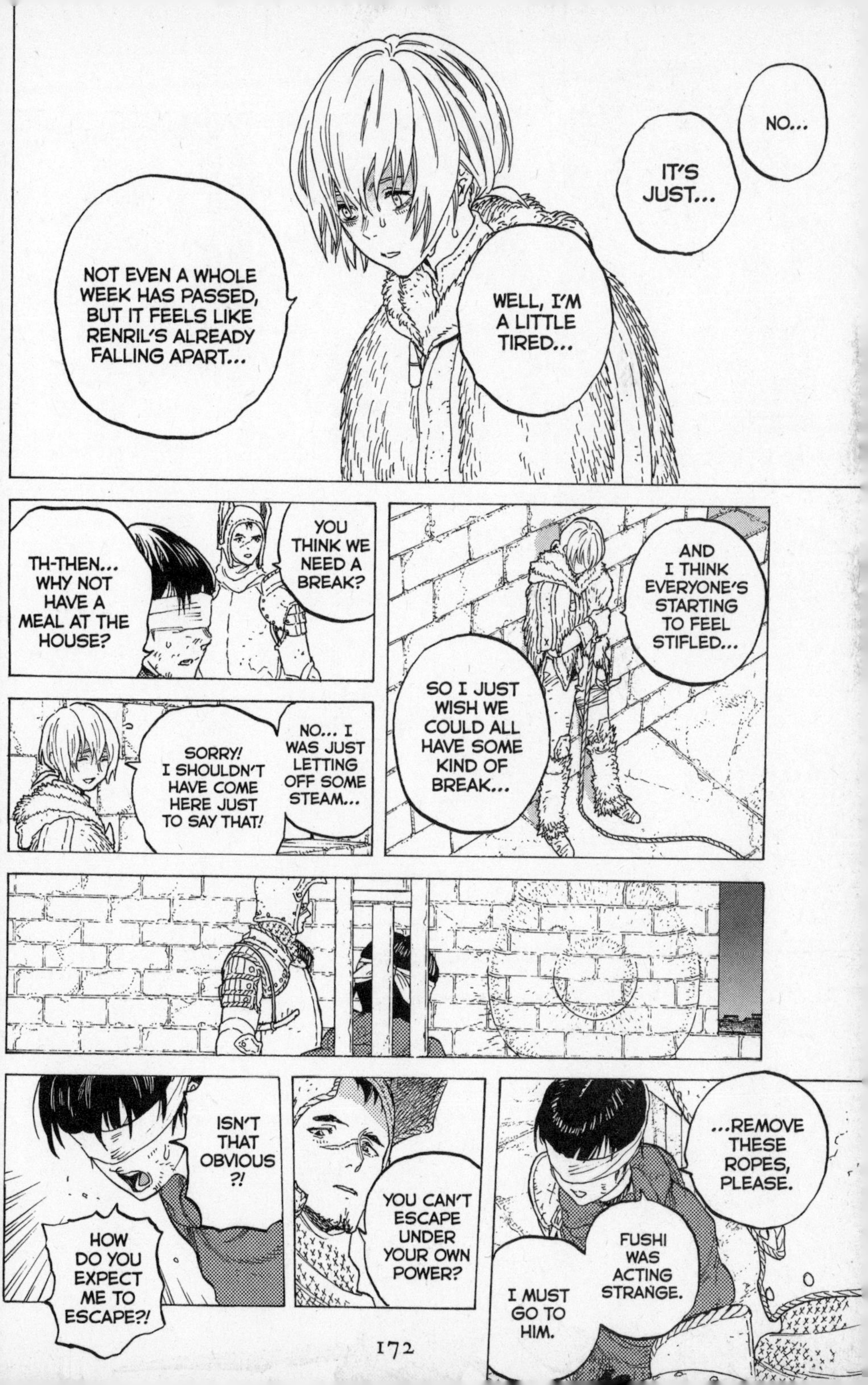
NO...
IT'S JUST...
WELL, I'M A LITTLE TIRED...
NOT EVEN A WHOLE WEEK HAS PASSED, BUT IT FEELS LIKE RENRIL'S ALREADY FALLING APART...
AND I THINK EVERYONE'S STARTING TO FEEL STIFLED...
SO I JUST WISH WE COULD ALL HAVE SOME KIND OF BREAK...
YOU THINK WE NEED A BREAK?
TH-THEN... WHY NOT HAVE A MEAL AT THE HOUSE?
NO... I WAS JUST LETTING OFF SOME STEAM...
SORRY! I SHOULDN'T HAVE COME HERE JUST TO SAY THAT!
...REMOVE THESE ROPES, PLEASE.
FUSHI WAS ACTING STRANGE.
I MUST GO TO HIM.
YOU CAN'T ESCAPE UNDER YOUR OWN POWER?
ISN'T THAT OBVIOUS?!
HOW DO YOU EXPECT ME TO ESCAPE?!

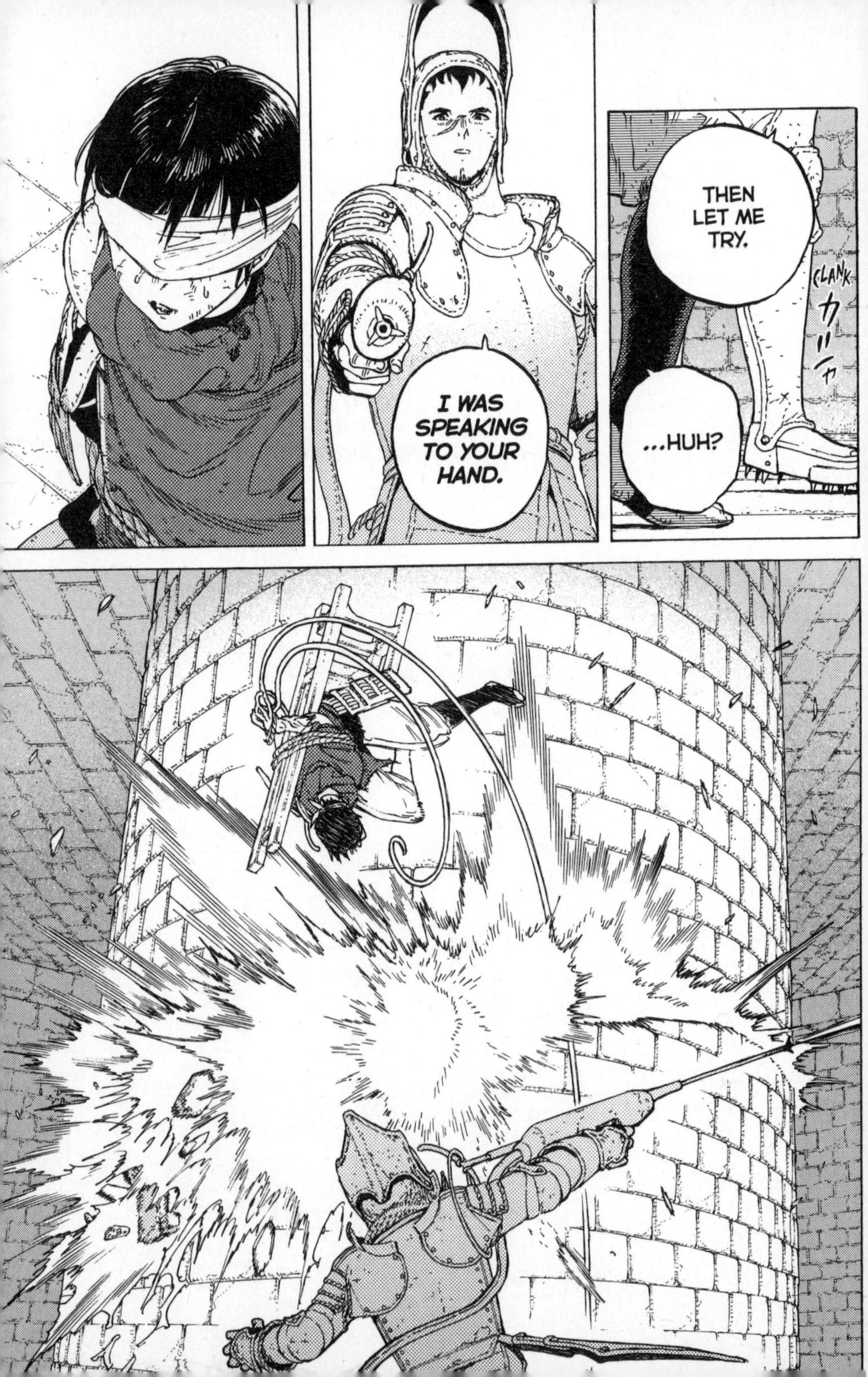
THEN LET ME TRY.
CLANK
カリャ
...HUH?
I WAS SPEAKING TO YOUR HAND.

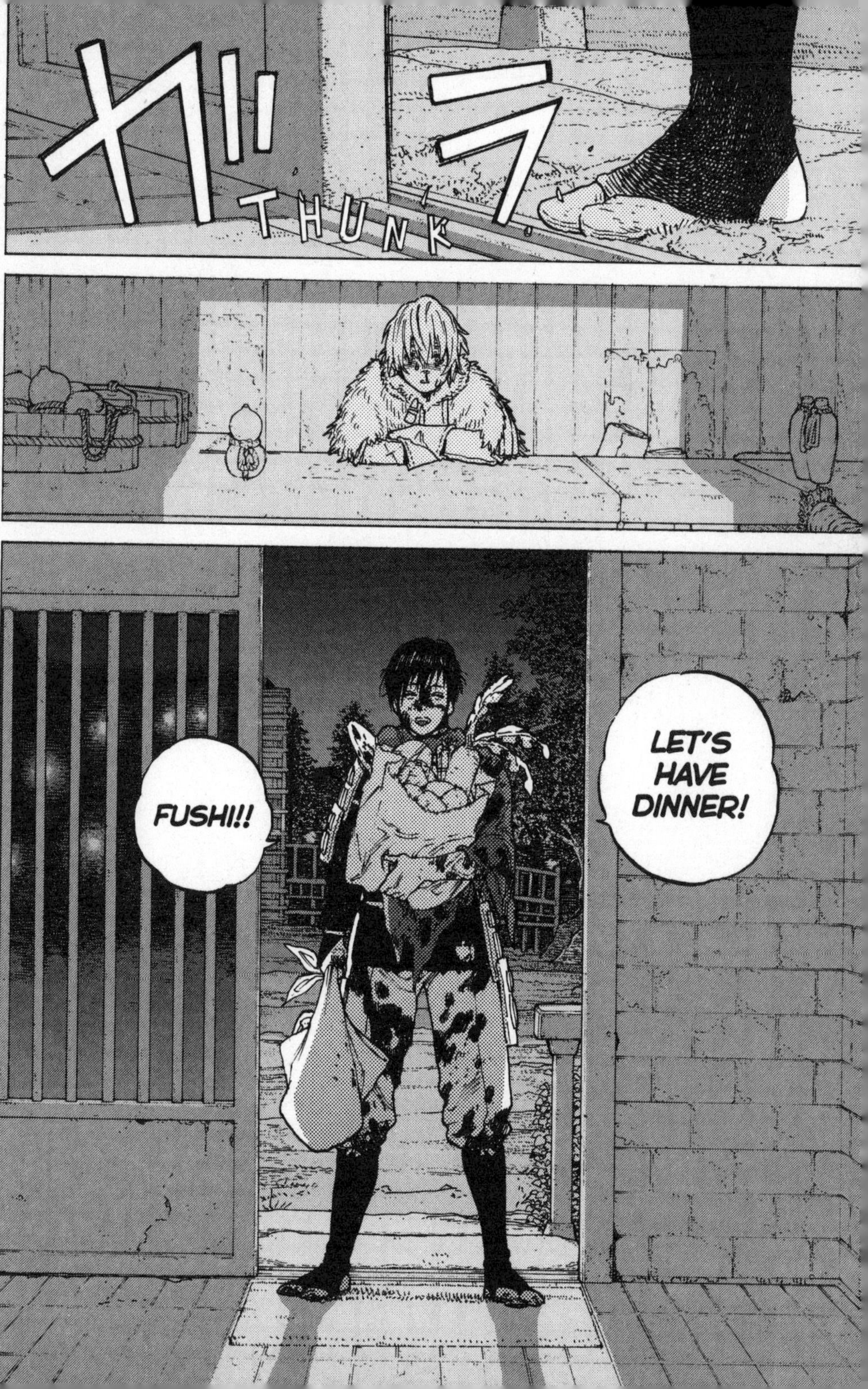
ガラ
THUNK
LET'S HAVE DINNER!
FUSHI!!

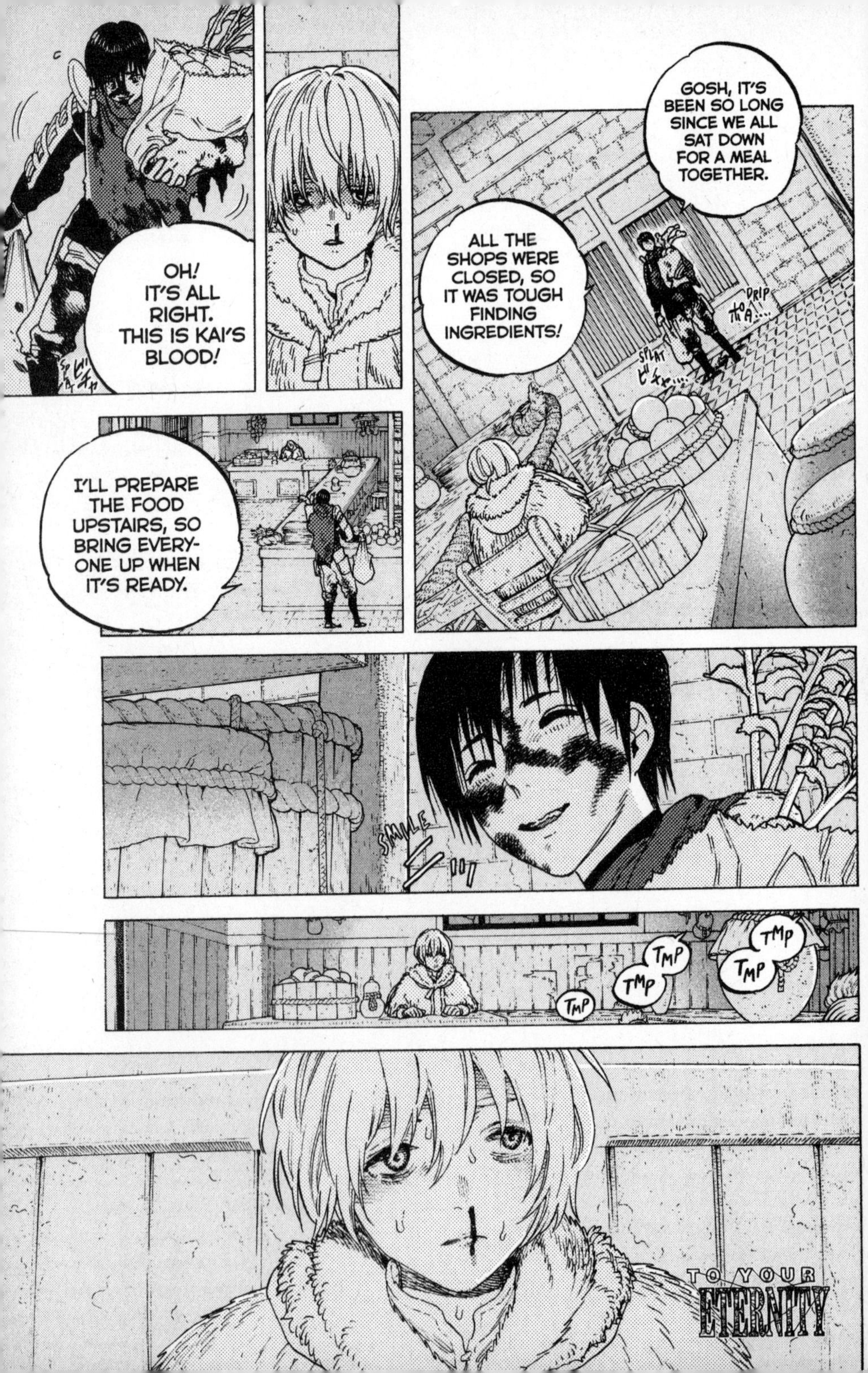
GOSH, IT'S BEEN SO LONG SINCE WE ALL SAT DOWN FOR A MEAL TOGETHER.
ALL THE SHOPS WERE CLOSED, SO IT WAS TOUGH FINDING INGREDIENTS!
DRIP
SPLAT
OH! IT'S ALL RIGHT. THIS IS KAI'S BLOOD!
SPLAT
I'LL PREPARE THE FOOD UPSTAIRS, SO BRING EVERY-ONE UP WHEN IT'S READY.
SMILE
TMP
TMP
TMP
TMP
TMP
TO YOUR ETERNITY

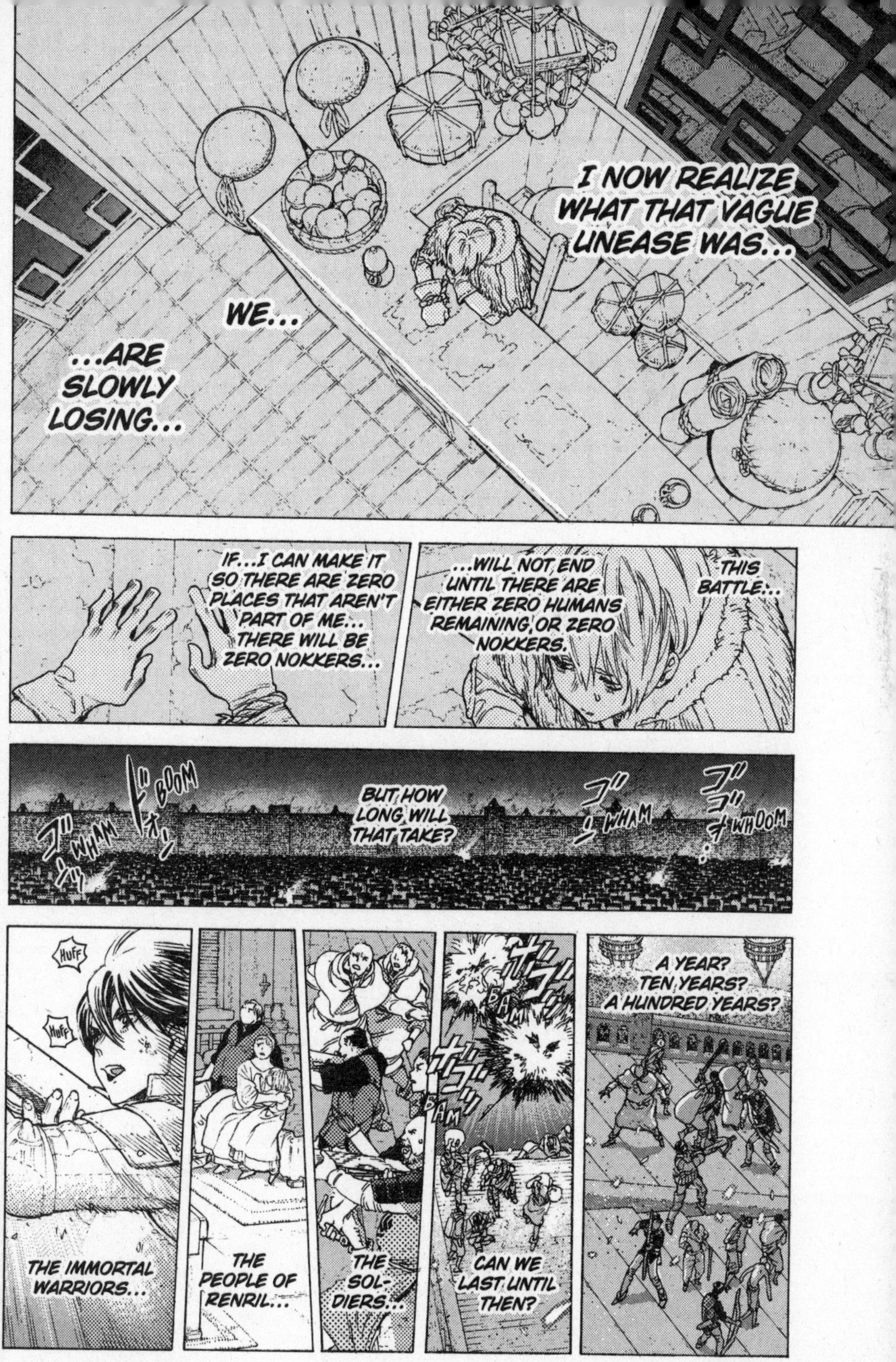
I NOW REALIZE WHAT THAT VAGUE UNEASE WAS...
WE...
...ARE SLOWLY LOSING...
THIS BATTLE...
...WILL NOT END UNTIL THERE ARE EITHER ZERO HUMANS REMAINING, OR ZERO NOKKERS.
IF...I CAN MAKE IT SO THERE ARE ZERO PLACES THAT AREN'T PART OF ME... THERE WILL BE ZERO NOKKERS...
WHOOM
WHAM
BUT HOW LONG WILL THAT TAKE?
BOOM
WHAM
A YEAR? TEN YEARS? A HUNDRED YEARS?
BAM
BAM
CAN WE LAST UNTIL THEN?
THE SOL-DIERS...
THE PEOPLE OF RENRIL...
HUFF
HUFF
THE IMMORTAL WARRIORS...

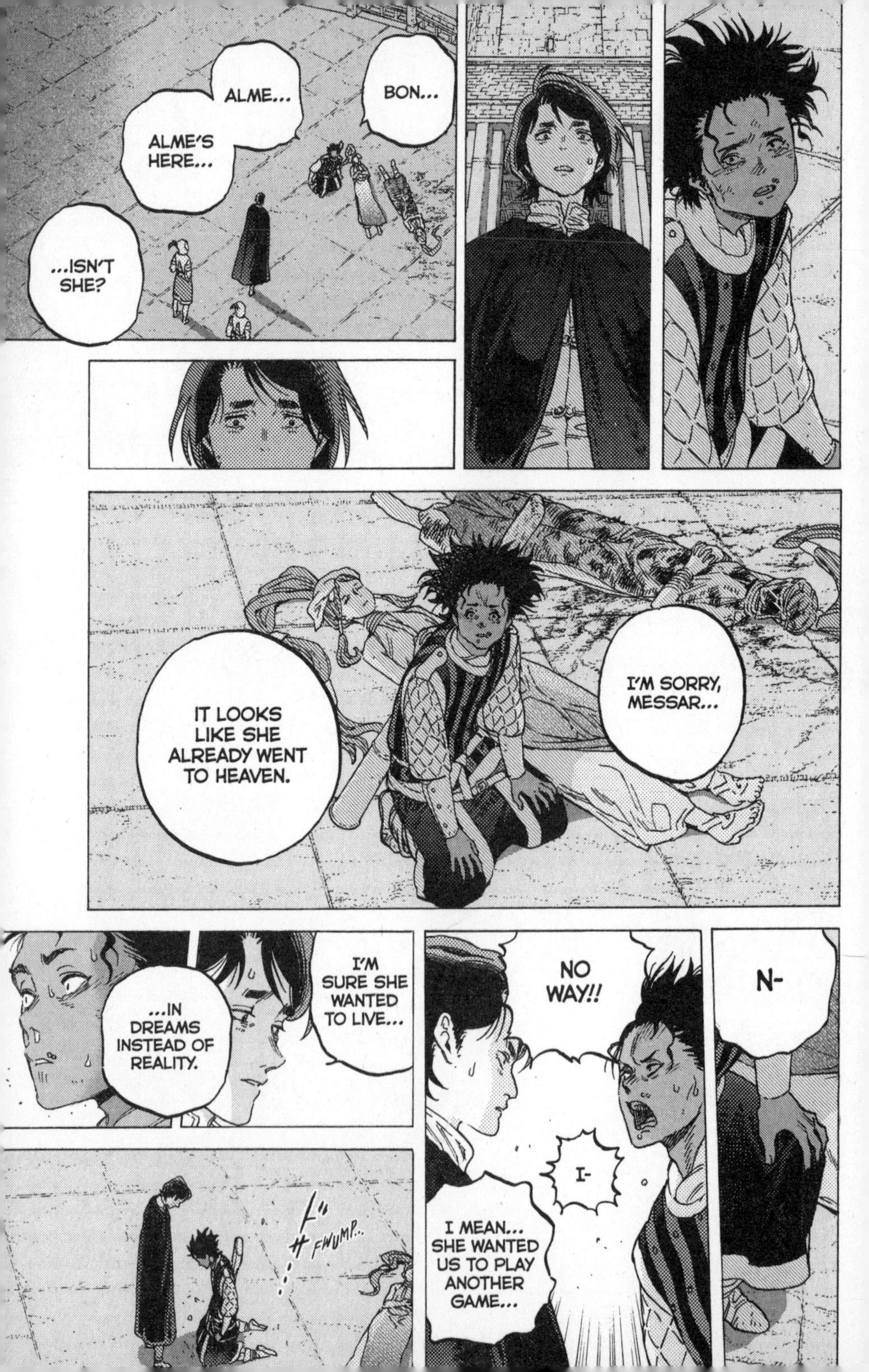
BON...
ALME...
ALME'S HERE...
...ISN'T SHE?
I'M SORRY, MESSAR...
IT LOOKS LIKE SHE ALREADY WENT TO HEAVEN.
N-
NO WAY!!
I-
I MEAN... SHE WANTED US TO PLAY ANOTHER GAME...
I'M SURE SHE WANTED TO LIVE...
...IN DREAMS INSTEAD OF REALITY.
FWUMP...

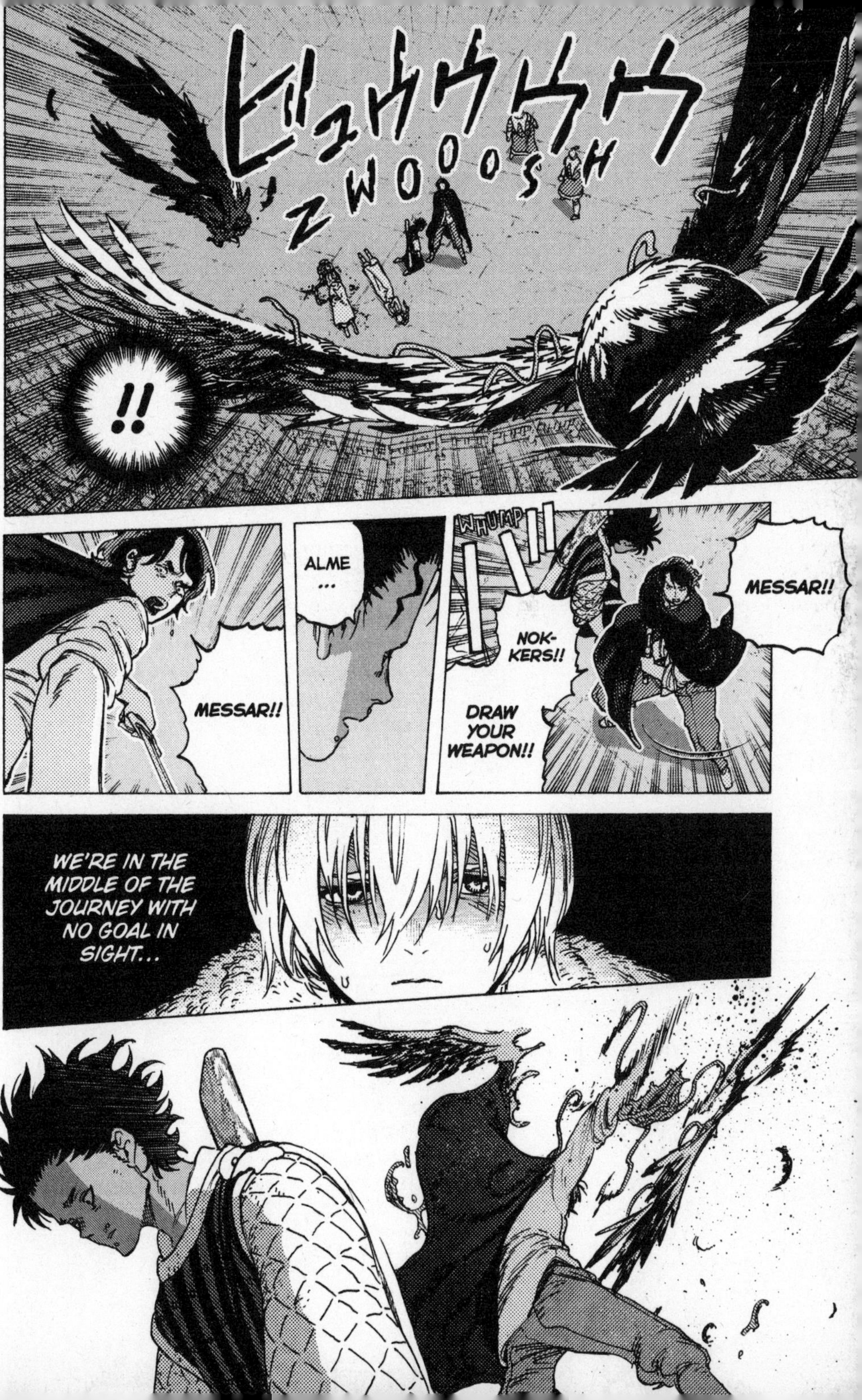
ビュゥウゥウ
ZWOOOSH
!!
MESSAR!!
WHUMP
NOK-KERS!!
DRAW YOUR WEAPON!!
ALME ...
MESSAR!!
WE'RE IN THE MIDDLE OF THE JOURNEY WITH NO GOAL IN SIGHT...

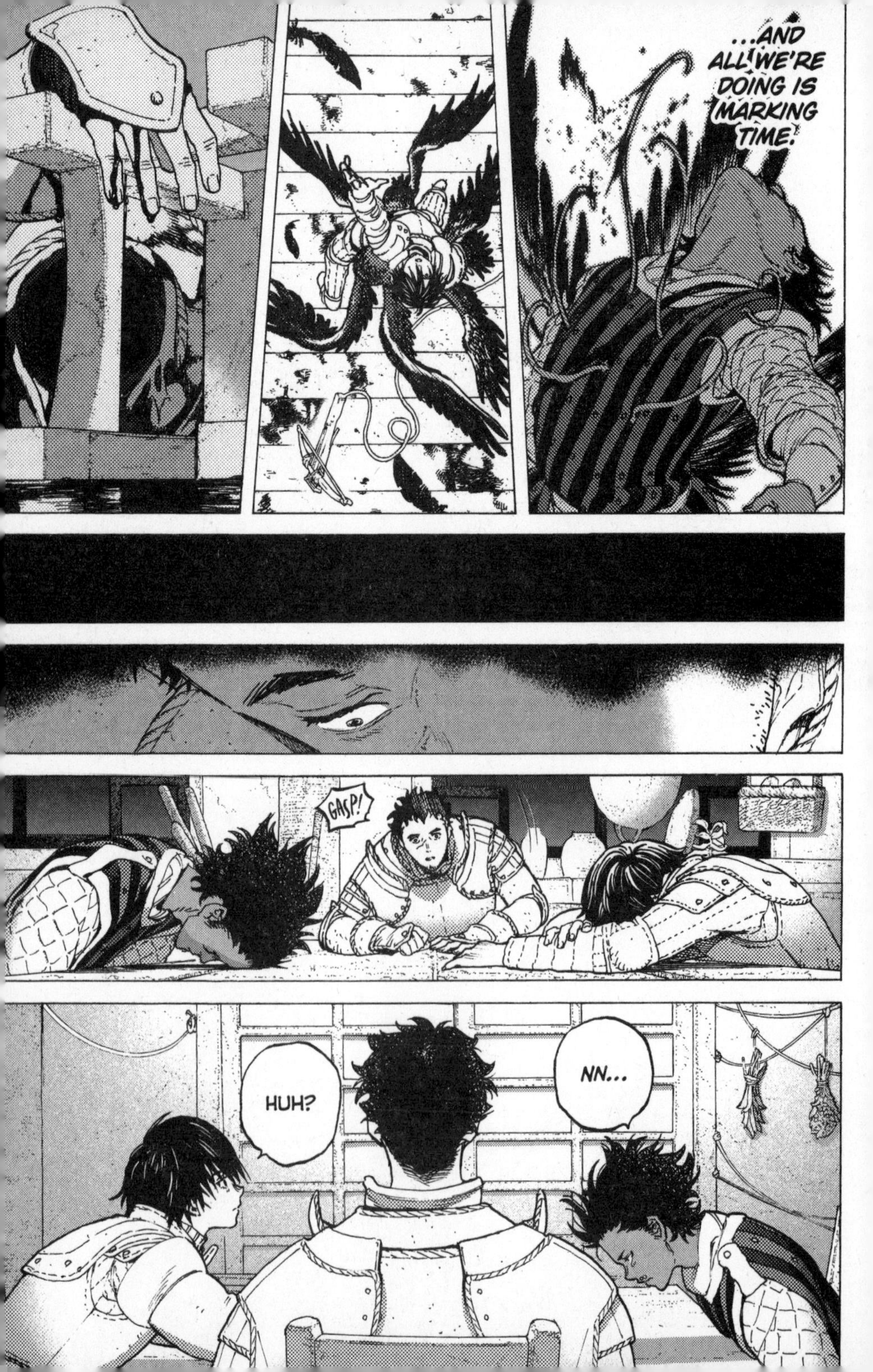
...AND ALL WE'RE DOING IS MARKING TIME.
GASP!
NN...
HUH?

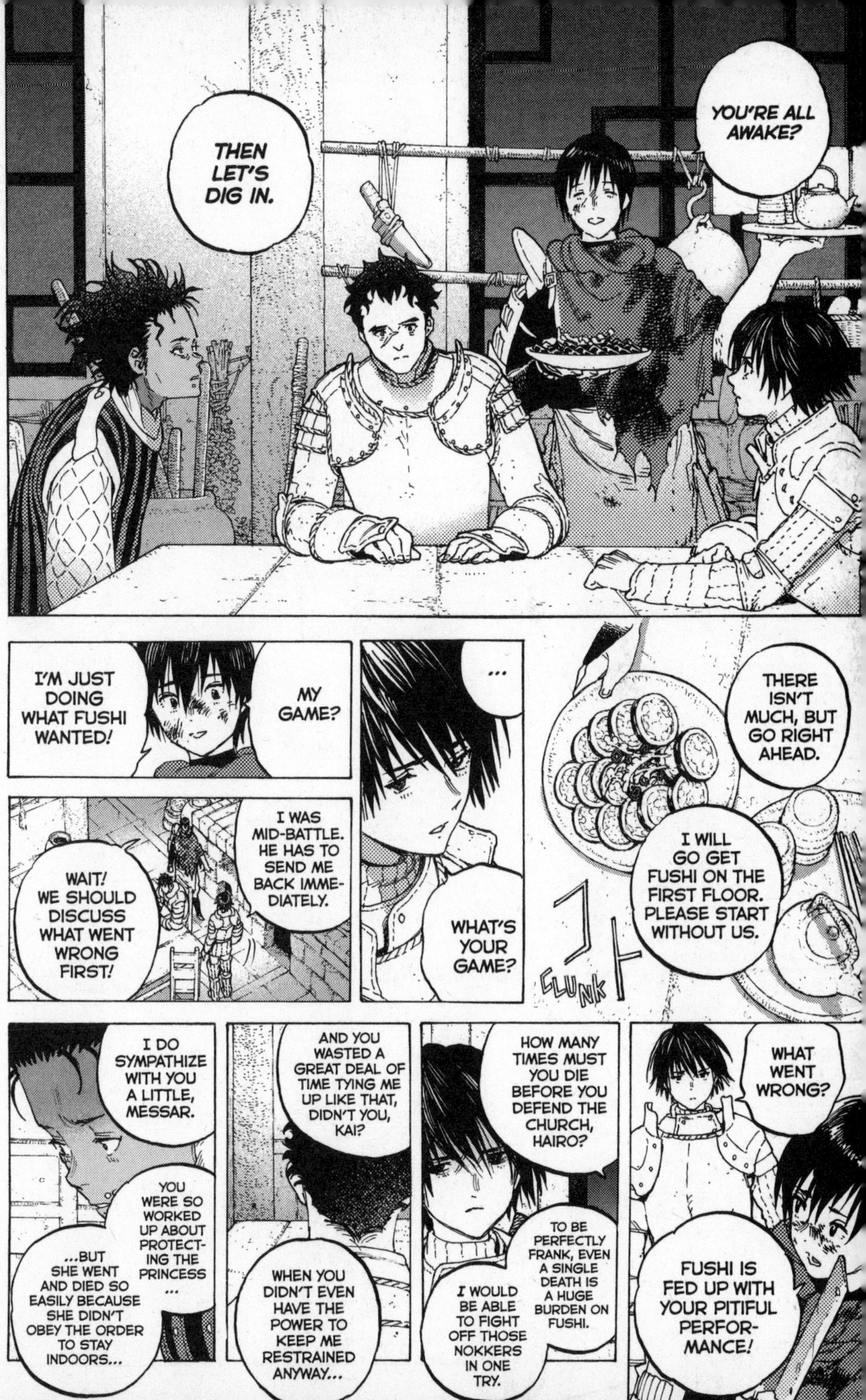
YOU'RE ALL AWAKE?
THEN LET'S DIG IN.
THERE ISN'T MUCH, BUT GO RIGHT AHEAD.
I WILL GO GET FUSHI ON THE FIRST FLOOR. PLEASE START WITHOUT US.
CLUNK
...
WHAT'S YOUR GAME?
MY GAME?
I'M JUST DOING WHAT FUSHI WANTED!
I WAS MID-BATTLE. HE HAS TO SEND ME BACK IMMEDIATELY.
WAIT! WE SHOULD DISCUSS WHAT WENT WRONG FIRST!
WHAT WENT WRONG?
FUSHI IS FED UP WITH YOUR PITIFUL PERFORMANCE!
HOW MANY TIMES MUST YOU DIE BEFORE YOU DEFEND THE CHURCH, HAIRO?
TO BE PERFECTLY FRANK, EVEN A SINGLE DEATH IS A HUGE BURDEN ON FUSHI.
I WOULD BE ABLE TO FIGHT OFF THOSE NOKKERS IN ONE TRY.
AND YOU WASTED A GREAT DEAL OF TIME TYING ME UP LIKE THAT, DIDN'T YOU, KAI?
WHEN YOU DIDN'T EVEN HAVE THE POWER TO KEEP ME RESTRAINED ANYWAY...
I DO SYMPATHIZE WITH YOU A LITTLE, MESSAR.
YOU WERE SO WORKED UP ABOUT PROTECTING THE PRINCESS...
...BUT SHE WENT AND DIED SO EASILY BECAUSE SHE DIDN'T OBEY THE ORDER TO STAY INDOORS...

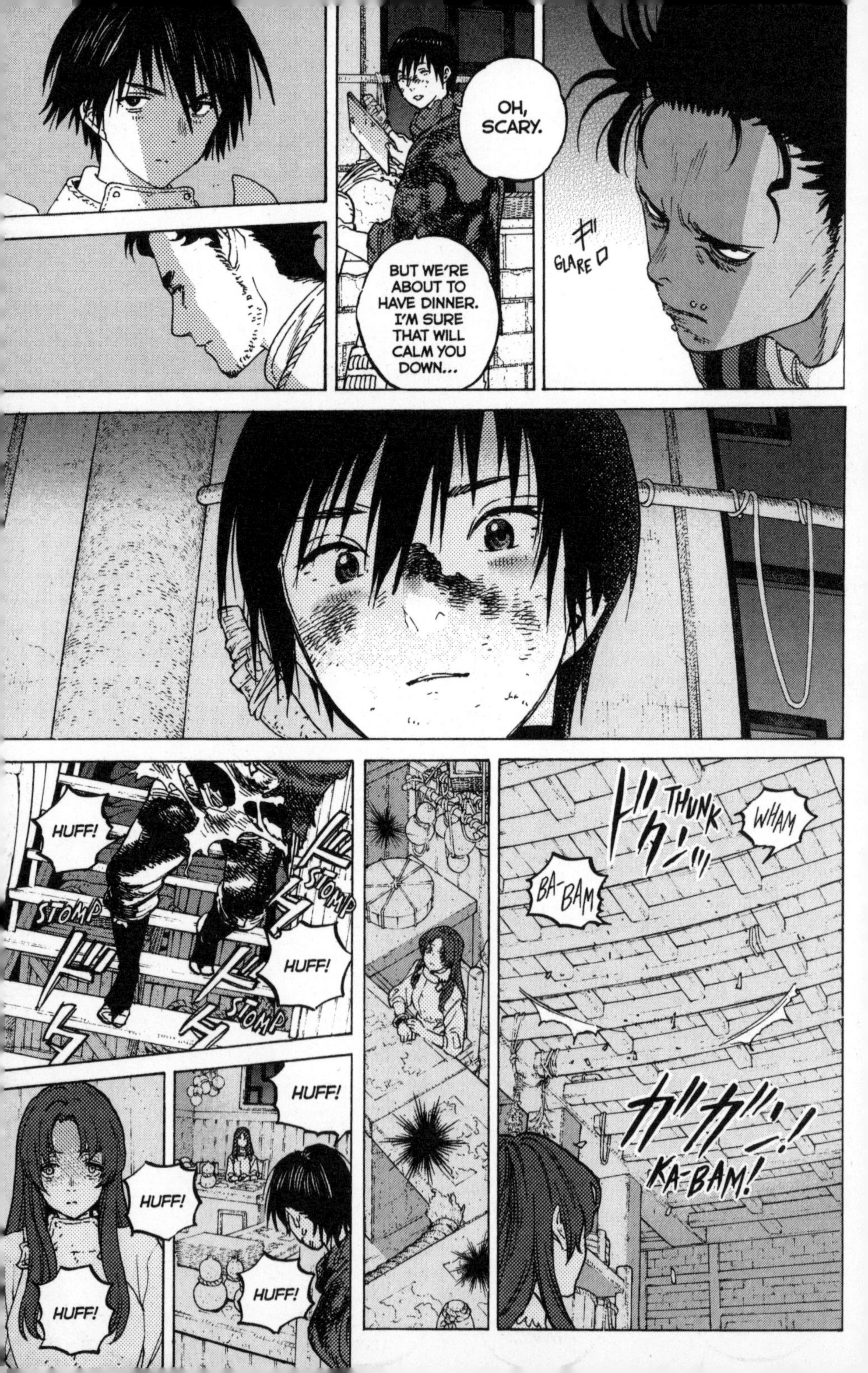
GLARE
OH, SCARY.
BUT WE'RE ABOUT TO HAVE DINNER. I'M SURE THAT WILL CALM YOU DOWN...
THUNK
WHAM
BA-BAM
KA-BAM!
HUFF!
STOMP
STOMP
HUFF!
STOMP
HUFF!
HUFF!
HUFF!
HUFF!

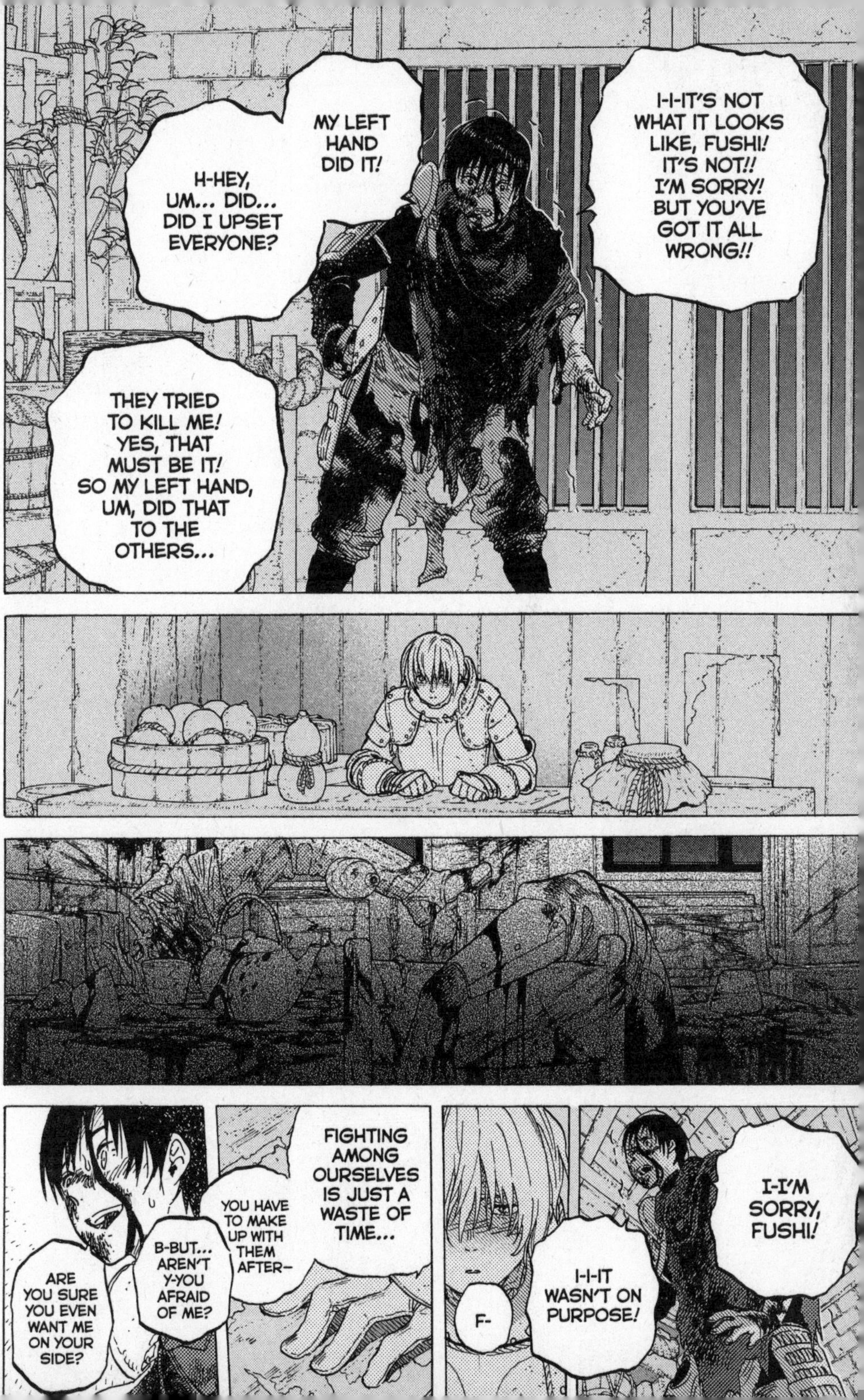
I-I-IT'S NOT WHAT IT LOOKS LIKE, FUSHI! IT'S NOT!! I'M SORRY! BUT YOU'VE GOT IT ALL WRONG!!
MY LEFT HAND DID IT!
H-HEY, UM... DID... DID I UPSET EVERYONE?
THEY TRIED TO KILL ME! YES, THAT MUST BE IT! SO MY LEFT HAND, UM, DID THAT TO THE OTHERS...
I-I'M SORRY, FUSHI!
I-I-IT WASN'T ON PURPOSE!
F-
FIGHTING AMONG OURSELVES IS JUST A WASTE OF TIME...
YOU HAVE TO MAKE UP WITH THEM AFTER–
B-BUT... AREN'T Y-YOU AFRAID OF ME?
ARE YOU SURE YOU EVEN WANT ME ON YOUR SIDE?

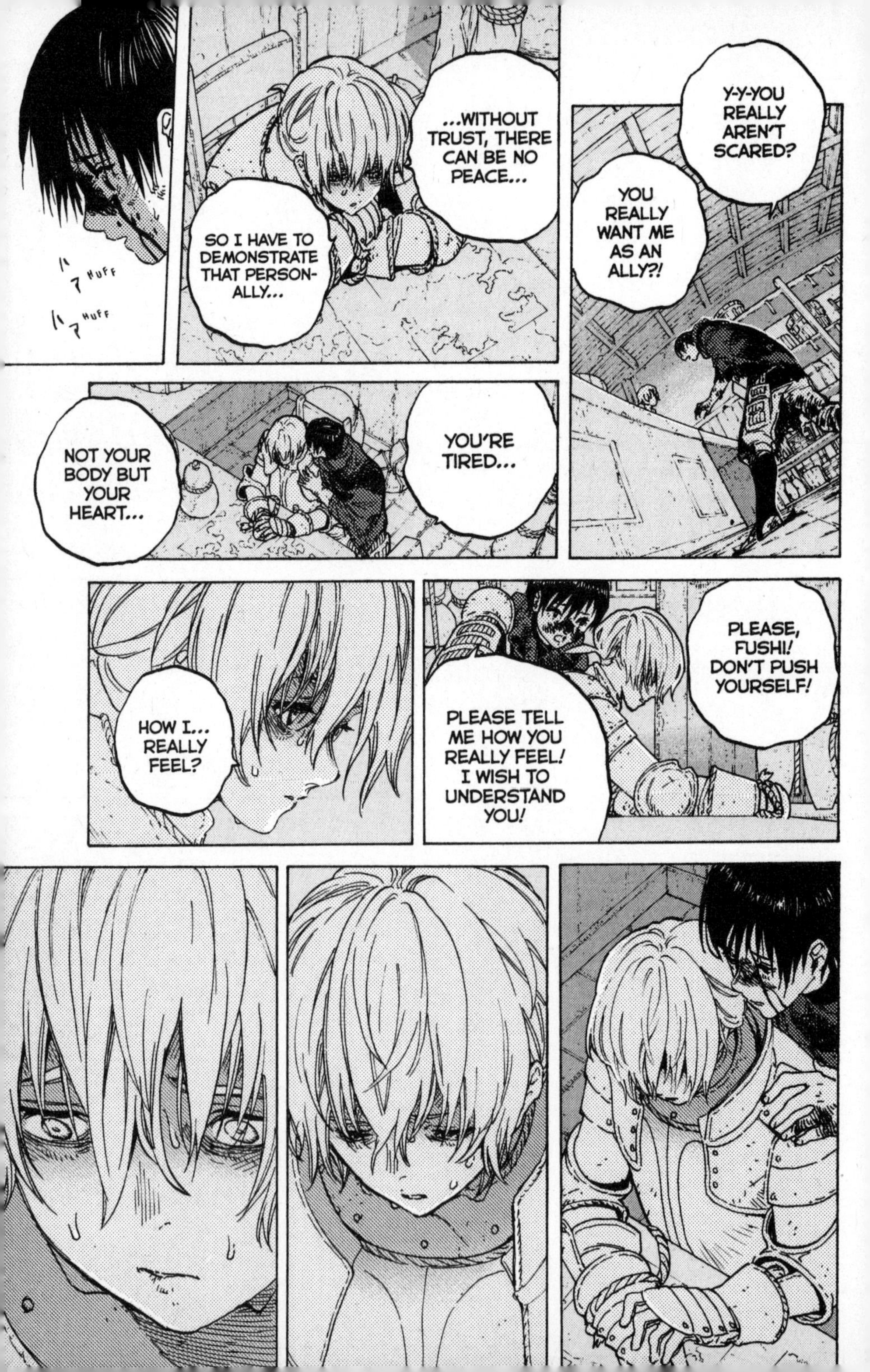

Y-Y-YOU REALLY AREN'T SCARED?
YOU REALLY WANT ME AS AN ALLY?!
...WITHOUT TRUST, THERE CAN BE NO PEACE...
SO I HAVE TO DEMONSTRATE THAT PERSON-ALLY...
ハァ HUFF
ハァ HUFF
YOU'RE TIRED...
NOT YOUR BODY BUT YOUR HEART...
PLEASE, FUSHI! DON'T PUSH YOURSELF!
PLEASE TELL ME HOW YOU REALLY FEEL! I WISH TO UNDERSTAND YOU!
HOW I... REALLY FEEL?

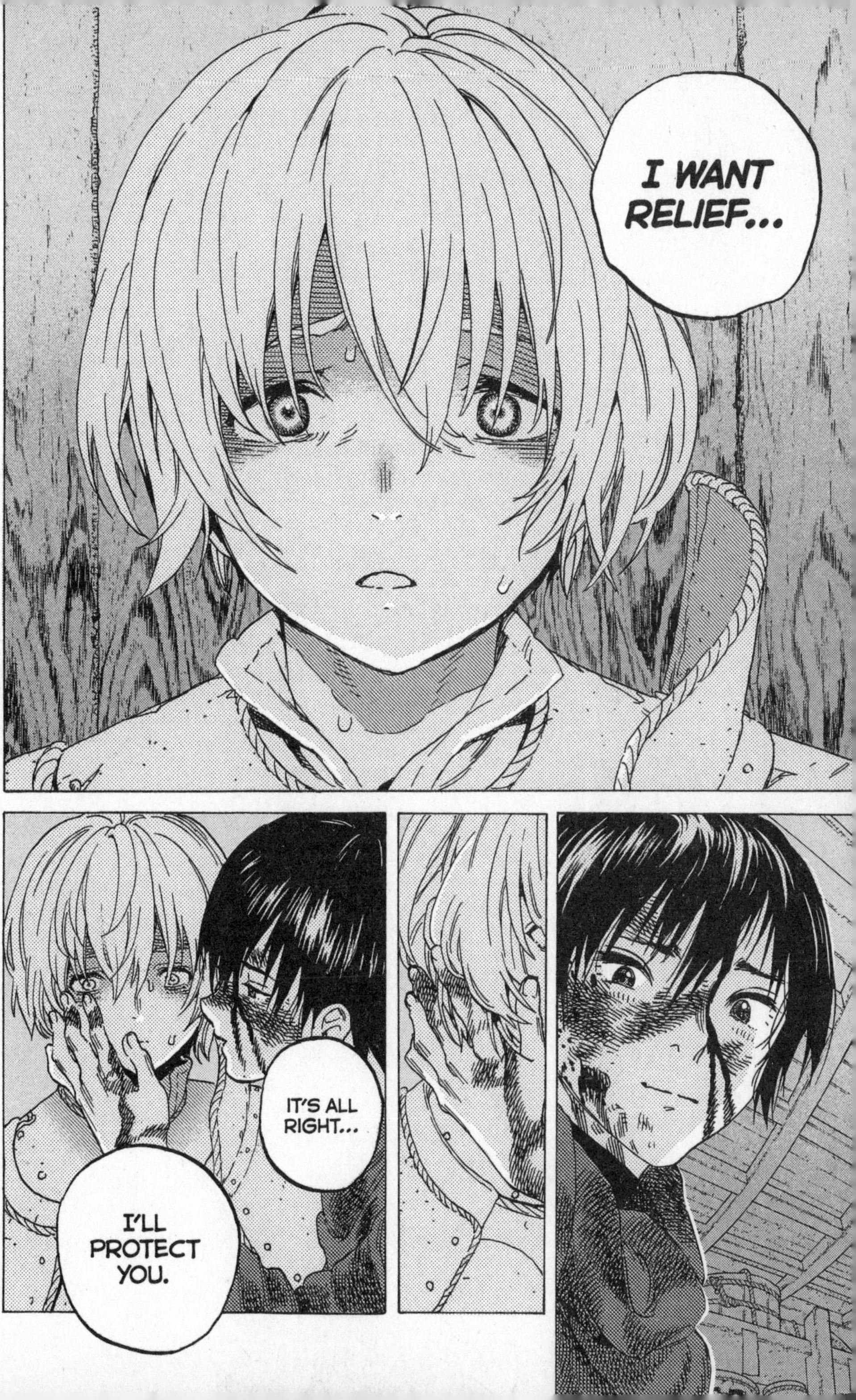
I WANT RELIEF...
IT'S ALL RIGHT...
I'LL PROTECT YOU.

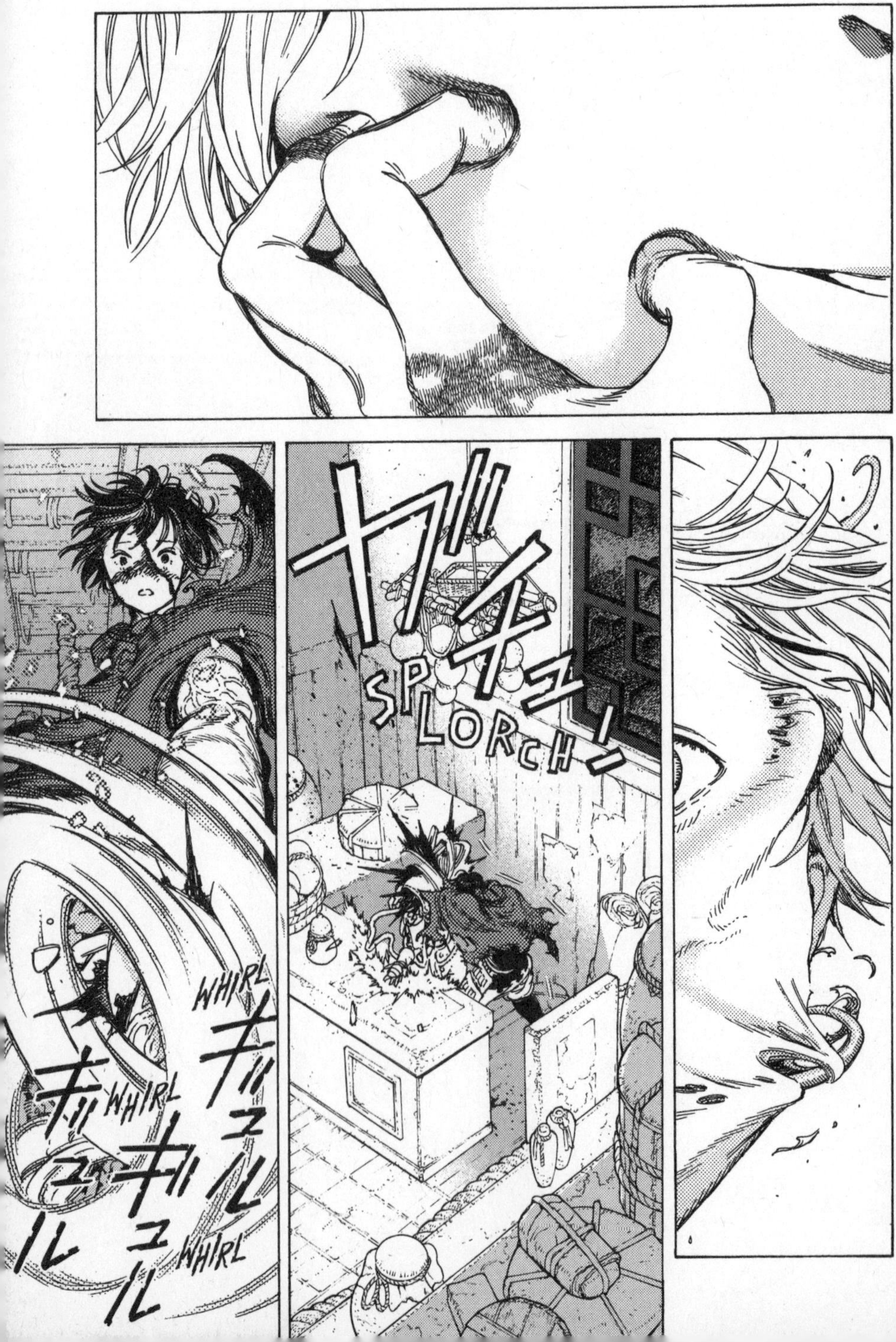
SPLORCH!!
WHIRL
WHIRL
WHIRL

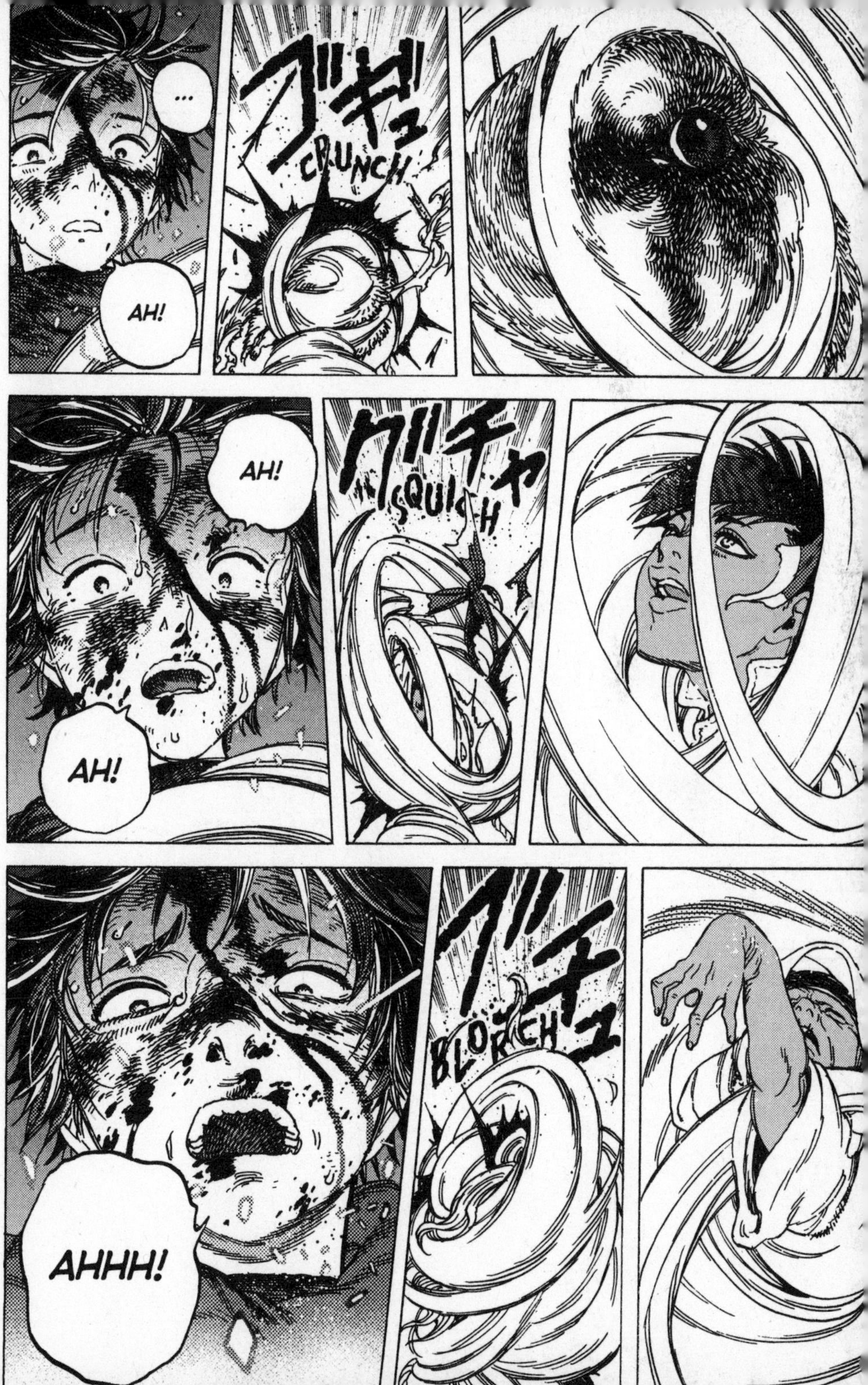
ゴギュ
CRUNCH
...
AH!
グチャ
SQUICH
AH!
AH!
グチュ
BLORCH
AHHH!

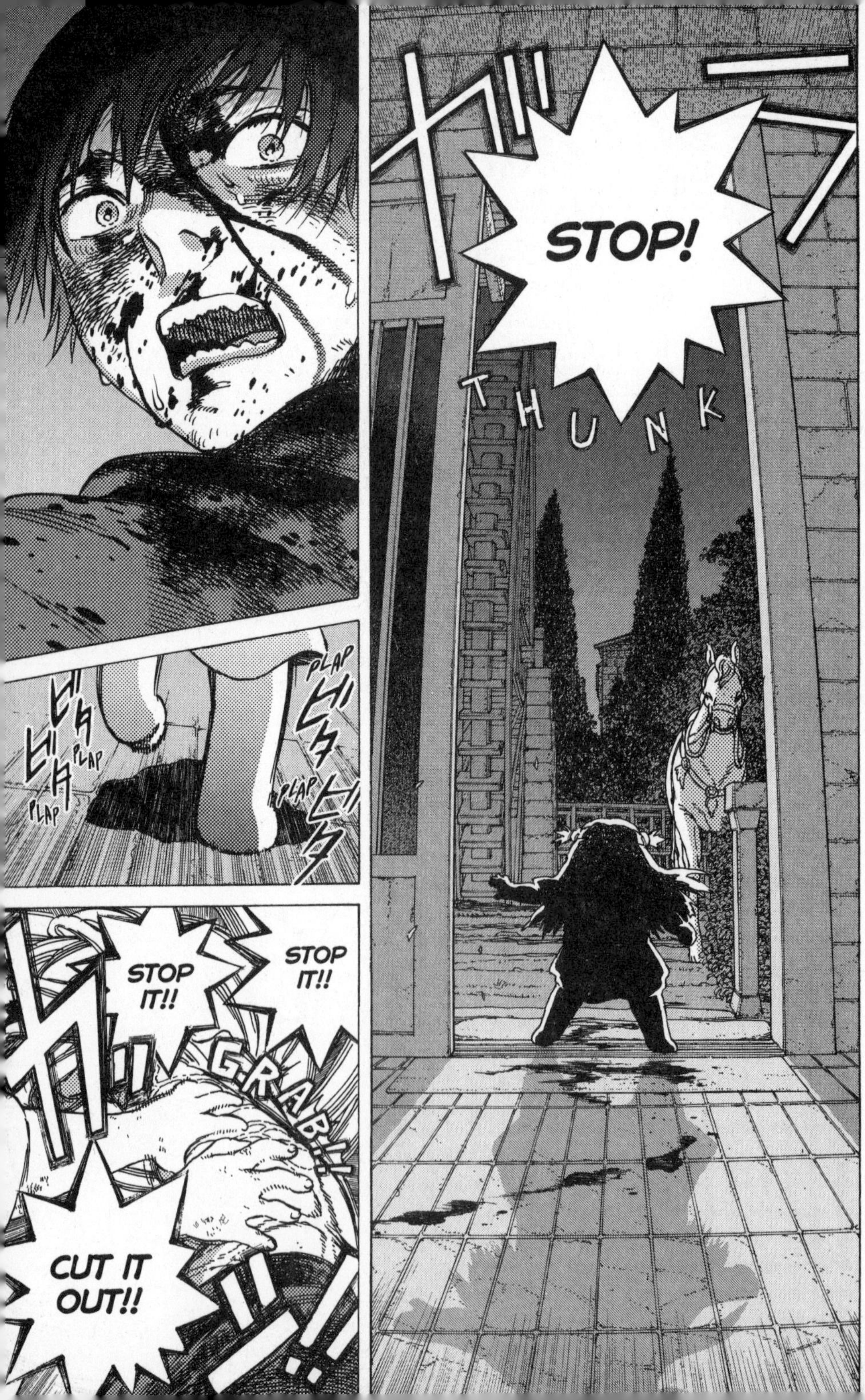
STOP!
THUNK
PLAP
PLAP
PLAP
PLAP
STOP IT!!
STOP IT!!
GRAB!!
CUT IT OUT!!

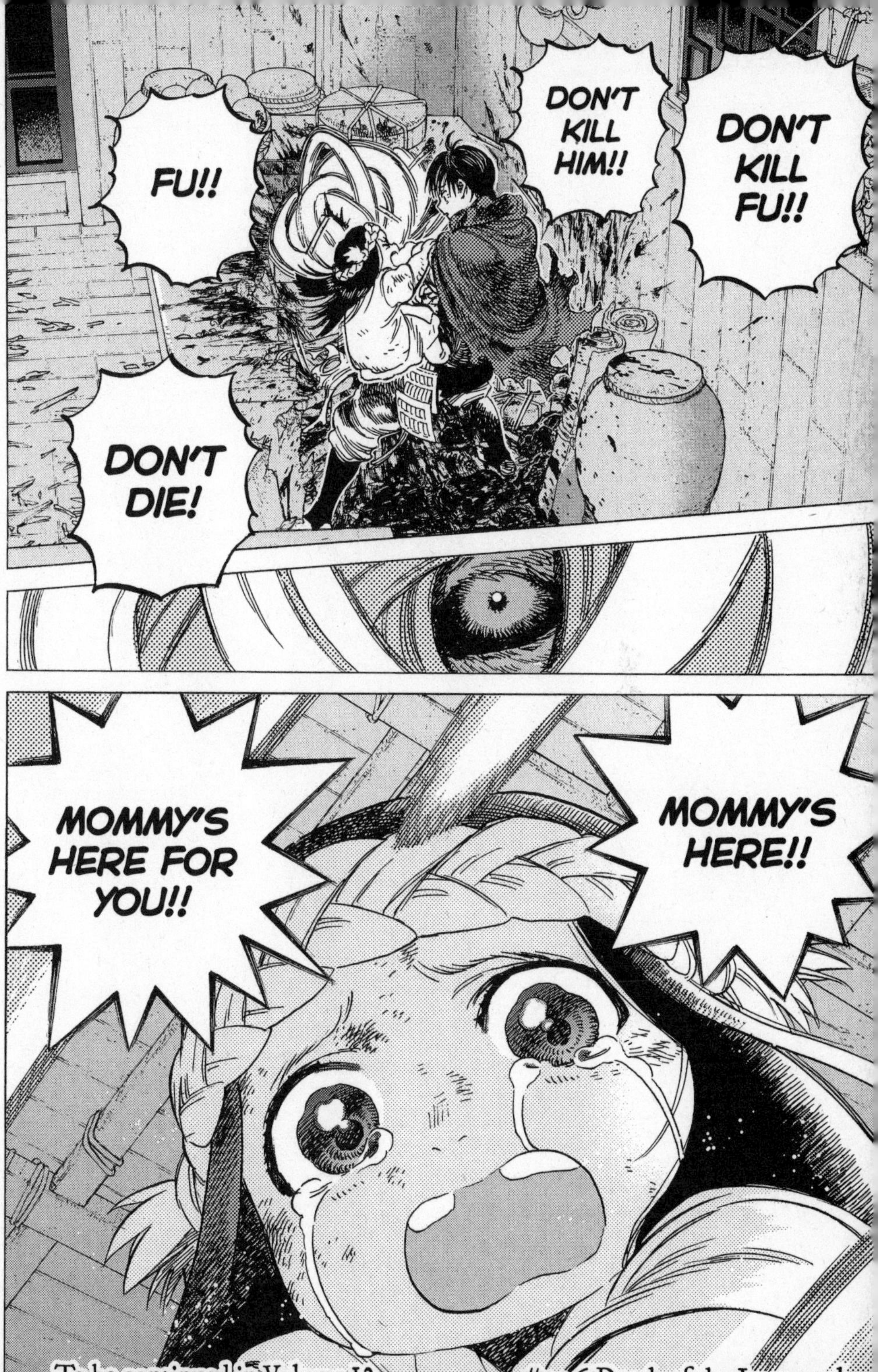
DON'T KILL FU!!
DON'T KILL HIM!!
FU!!
DON'T DIE!
MOMMY'S HERE!!
MOMMY'S HERE FOR YOU!!

To be continued in Volume 12

#106 Death of the Immortal

TO YOUR ETERNITY

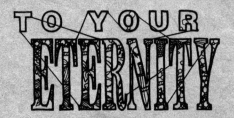